Contributions to Political Science

More information about this series at http://www.springer.com/series/11829

Christine Ante

The Europeanisation of Vocational Education and Training

Christine Ante
Hertie School of Governance
Berlin, Germany

Dissertation Hertie School of Governance, Berlin, Germany

ISSN 2198-7289   ISSN 2198-7297   (electronic)
Contributions to Political Science
ISBN 978-3-319-41569-7   ISBN 978-3-319-41570-3   (eBook)
DOI 10.1007/978-3-319-41570-3

Library of Congress Control Number: 2016946173

© Springer International Publishing Switzerland 2016
This work is subject to copyright. All rights are reserved by the Publisher, whether the whole or part of the material is concerned, specifically the rights of translation, reprinting, reuse of illustrations, recitation, broadcasting, reproduction on microfilms or in any other physical way, and transmission or information storage and retrieval, electronic adaptation, computer software, or by similar or dissimilar methodology now known or hereafter developed.
The use of general descriptive names, registered names, trademarks, service marks, etc. in this publication does not imply, even in the absence of a specific statement, that such names are exempt from the relevant protective laws and regulations and therefore free for general use.
The publisher, the authors and the editors are safe to assume that the advice and information in this book are believed to be true and accurate at the date of publication. Neither the publisher nor the authors or the editors give a warranty, express or implied, with respect to the material contained herein or for any errors or omissions that may have been made.

Printed on acid-free paper

This Springer imprint is published by Springer Nature
The registered company is Springer International Publishing AG Switzerland

Acknowledgements

This book is based on the dissertation I have defended at the Hertie School of Governance on October 1, 2015. I am thankful for all the support, encouragement and advice I have received during the time of writing the dissertation.

Firstly, I would like to thank my supervisor, Prof. Dr. Anke Hassel, who has supported me by providing academic guidance and encouragement throughout the entire research project. Her thoughtful advice helped me develop this project, ask relevant questions. I would like to express special thanks to Prof. Dr. Klaus Hurrelmann who has stepped in during a crossroad and helped successfully finalise the doctoral process.

My research project was funded by the Friedrich Ebert Foundation. During many discussions with the community of scholarship holders and during the foundation's events, I gained valuable insights for this work and beyond.

I would like to thank my interview partners for taking the time to share their perspectives on the Copenhagen process and its implementation in the member states. Without their commitment and openness, this book would not have been what it is today. During my field trip to the Netherlands, the Amsterdam Institute of Labour Studies has kindly hosted me and I am thankful for the hospitality and the engaging discussions.

Also the possibility to take part in different colloquia at the Berlin Graduate School for Transnational Studies helped me frame my research project. Moreover, I would like to thank Prof. Dr. Susanne Lütz and Prof. Dr. Marius Busemeyer for inviting me to their colloquia, where I received valuable comments on my project. The same stands for the research colloquium on education and labour markets of the Wissenschaftszentrum Berlin für Sozialforschung, the SASE 24th Annual Conference at the Massachusetts Institute of Technology and the "Europäischer Bildungsraum" conference at the University of Tübingen.

During many joint library hours and discussions on our dissertations, I could always turn to Alexander Kleibrink, Anna van Santen, Clara Weinhardt, Sven Rahner and Janine Romero Valenzuela for advice. Alexander Kleibrink, Anna van Santen, Clara Weinhardt, Diana Mirza-Grisco and Julia Thimm helped me improve my work through constructive feedback provided at different stages.

My friends did not only encourage me in times of doubt but have also kept me connected to other aspects of life. I am thankful for your friendship!

I am indebted to my family and especially to my parents and my brother for all their support throughout my years of studying and writing my dissertation. Thank you for always being there and for your love and encouragement.

Contents

1   **Introduction** 1
    1.1   The Political Economy of Skills and Europeanisation 5
        1.1.1   Varieties of Capitalism and Skills 5
        1.1.2   The Influence of Europe on National Systems 16
        1.1.3   The Europeanisation of Vocational Education
              and Training 23
    1.2   Research Framework and Methodology 25
    1.3   Structure 33

2   **The Copenhagen Process: A Political Economy Perspective** 35
    2.1   A Brief History of European Vocational Education and Training
        Policies 35
    2.2   The Copenhagen Process 41
    2.3   The Political Economy of the Copenhagen Process 55
    2.4   Conclusion 67

3   **The Impact of the Copenhagen Process on the German Training
    Regime** 69
    3.1   The German VET System 69
    3.2   Implementation of the Copenhagen Process in Germany 78
        3.2.1   Early Discussions on the European Qualifications
              Framework and the European Credit System
              for Vocational Education and Training 79
        3.2.2   Learning Outcomes 89
        3.2.3   The German Qualifications Framework (DQR) 92
        3.2.4   The European Credit System for Vocational Education
              and Training 101
        3.2.5   Validation of Non-formal and Informal Learning 107
        3.2.6   Quality Assurance 112
    3.3   Conclusions 116

4	**The Impact of the Copenhagen Process on the Dutch Training Regime**		123
	4.1	The Dutch Vocational Education and Training System	123
	4.2	Implementation of the Copenhagen Process in the Netherlands	134
		4.2.1 Learning Outcomes	134
		4.2.2 The Dutch National Qualifications Framework (NLQF)	137
		4.2.3 The European Credit System for Vocational Education and Training	147
		4.2.4 Validation of Non-formal and Informal Learning	152
		4.2.5 Quality Assurance	156
	4.3	Conclusions	160
5	**The Impact of the Copenhagen Process on the English Training Regime**		163
	5.1	The English Vocational Education and Training System	163
	5.2	Implementation of the Copenhagen Process in the United Kingdom	176
		5.2.1 Learning Outcomes	176
		5.2.2 Qualifications and Credit Frameworks	177
		5.2.3 The European Credit System for Vocational Education and Training	183
		5.2.4 Validation of Non-formal and Informal Learning	185
		5.2.5 Quality Assurance	186
	5.3	Conclusions	188
6	**Comparison and Conclusion**		193
	6.1	Comparison of the Impact of the Copenhagen Process on Germany, the Netherlands and the United Kingdom (England)	199
	6.2	Theoretical Implications	209
		6.2.1 Is Europe Liberalising National Institutions?	209
		6.2.2 Varieties of Capitalism and the Study of Europeanisation	217
		6.2.3 Further Contributions to the Political Economy Literature	219
		6.2.4 Implications for Further Research	221
	6.3	Implications for Policy Discussions	223

Appendix 231
Annex I: The European Qualifications Framework 231
Annex II: The European Quality Assurance Reference Framework 234
Annex III: Youth Unemployment Rates in European Countries 238

Bibliography 241

Abbreviations

A-Levels	General Certificate of Education at Advanced Level (England)
APL	Accreditation of Prior Learning
BA	German Federal Employment Agency/*Bundesagentur für Arbeit*
BBL	Dutch secondary vocational education programme/*beroepsbegeleidende leerweg*
BDA	Confederation of German Employers/*Bundesverband der Deutschen Arbeitgeberverbände*
BIBB	German Federal Institute of Vocational Education and Training/*Bundesinstitut für Berufsbildung*
BIS	Department for Business, Innovation and Skills (England)
BMBF	German Federal Ministry of Education and Research/*Bundesministerium für Bildung und Wissenschaft*
BOL	Dutch secondary vocational education programme/*beroepsopleidende leerweg*
BVP	Dutch practical work placements/*beroepspraktijkvorming*
CBI	Confederation of British Industry
Cedefop	European Centre for the Development of Vocational Training/Centre Européen pour le développement de la formation professionnelle
CINOP	Centre for Innovation in Education and Training/*Centrum voor innovatie van opleidingen*
CME	Coordinated market economy
DfE	Department for Education (England)
DIHK	German Association of Chambers of Industry and Commerce/*Deutscher Industrie- und Handelskammertag*
DQR	German National Qualifications Framework/*Deutscher Qualifikationsrahmen für lebenslanges Lernen*
DGB	German Confederation of Trade Unions/*Deutscher Gewerkschaftsbund*
ECTS	European Credit Transfer System

ECJ	European Court of Justice
ECVET	European Credit System for Vocational Education and Training
EQARF	European Quality Assurance Reference Framework
EQAVET	European Quality Assurance in Vocational Education and Training
EQF	European Qualifications Framework
ETF	European Training Foundation
EVC	Dutch accreditation of prior learning scheme/*Erkenning van Verworven Competenties*
EU	European Union
GSCE	General Certificate of Secondary Education (England)
HAVO	Dutch general secondary education/*hoger algemeen voortgezet onderwijs*
HBO	Dutch professional higher education/*hoger beroepsonderwijs*
ISCED	International Standard Classification of Education
KMK	Secretariat of the Standing Conference of the Ministers of Education and Cultural Affairs of the Länder in the Federal Republic of Germany/*Kultusministerkonferenz*
LEA	Local education authorities
LME	Liberal market economy
MBO	Secondary vocational education/*middelbaar beroepsonderwijs*
MOCW	Dutch Ministry of Education, Culture and Science/*Ministerie van Onderwijs, Cultuur en Wetenschappen*
NQF	National Qualifications Framework
NLQF	Dutch National Qualifications Framework/*Nederlands national kwalificatiekader*
NRTO	The Dutch Association of Private Education Providers/*Nederlandse Raad vor Training en Opleiding*
NVQs	National Vocational Qualifications (England)
O & O fondsen	Sectoral training funds/*Onderzoek en Ontwikkelingsfondsen*
OMC	Open method of coordination
OECD	Organisation for Economic Co-operation and Development
QCA	Qualifications and Curriculum Authority (England)
QCDA	Qualifications and Curriculum Development Authority (England)
QCF	Qualifications and Credit Framework
ROC	Dutch Regional Training Centre/*Regionaal Opleidingscentrum*
SBB	Dutch Foundation for Cooperation between Vocational Education, Training and the Labour Market/*Stichting Samenwerking Berofsonderwijs Bedrijfsleven*
SSC	Sector Skills Council
SME	Small and medium-sized enterprises
TUC	Trade Union Congress
UK	United Kingdom
VET	Vocational education and training

VMBO	Dutch pre-vocational secondary education/*voorbereidend middelbaar beroepsonderwijs*
VoC	Varieties of capitalism
VWO	Dutch pre-university education/*voorbereidend wetenschappelijk onderwijs*
WEB	Dutch Adult and Vocational Education Act/*Wet educatie beroepsvorming*
ZDH	Skilled Crafts Association/*Zentralverband des Deutschen Handwerks*

List of Figures

Fig. 2.1	Priorities for VET under the Copenhagen process	42
Fig. 4.1	Secondary education, VET and higher education in the Netherlands	124
Fig. 4.2	Development process of qualification files in the Netherlands	128
Fig. 5.1	Choices in 14–19 education and training in England	165
Fig. 6.1	Youth unemployment rates in selected countries in 2008, 2011, 2014	225

List of Tables

Table 1.1	Skills: General vs. specific: substantive vs. economic	11
Table 1.2	VET systems in Europe	30
Table 1.3	Core features of the three case studies	32
Table 4.1	Descriptor elements describing the Dutch qualification levels	140
Table 4.2	NLQF scheme	141
Table 5.1	Qualifications frameworks in England	179
Table 6.1	Overview on the implementation of instruments and principles on the national level	198

Chapter 1
Introduction

In recent times, the "lost generation" is discussed widely in public debates. The "lost generation" is the young generation in Southern Europe: In Spain and in Greece, close to half of all young people are unemployed. In Croatia, Italy, Cyprus and Portugal, it is more than 30 %.[1] With such difficulties in finding entry positions in the labour market, the young generation is faced with an insecure future. Without a job, it is difficult to be independent or to start a family. Both the personal and the economic independence suffer. Even more, unemployment in the beginning of a career is likely to hamper career perspectives also in the middle and long run, and hereby leads to difficulties in saving for retirement. In this generation, unemployment hits everybody: university graduates who are perceived to be overqualified—or those who left school early in order to take a well-paid job in booming industries such as the construction sector in Spain. No matter the individual reason: a generation is deprived of their hopes.

While this severe situation persists in Southern European countries since the beginning of the economic and financial crisis in 2009, in other European countries young people still have good chances of finding an entry position in the labour market. In countries such as Germany, Norway, Austria or the Netherlands, the youth unemployment rate is hardly higher in 2015 than it was in 2008. In Germany and Norway, it even decreased in this time period.[2] The recent economic and financial crisis has exacerbated the imbalances in European labour markets, and even more so for the young generation.

The "lost generation" and the imbalances across labour markets are pan-European problems. The European Union (EU) has the potential to address this issue of great urgency in order to attenuate the severity of current challenges. One policy option to address this issue on the European level is to support those

---

[1] Annual average unemployment rate for the age group below 25, 2015, Eurostat. See Annex III for detailed data on youth unemployment rates in European countries between 2005 and 2015.
[2] Annual average unemployment rate for the age group below 25, 2015, Eurostat. See Annex III.

countries financially that are especially affected and provide support regarding the design of national policies. Such an approach is taken with the Youth Employment Initiative which provides financial support (6.4 billion euros for the period 2014–2020) to regions with high youth unemployment quota and the Youth Guarantee, according to which all member states shall take measures so that each young person is offered quality training or a job within 4 months after completing school or after becoming unemployed. Within the framework of the Youth Guarantee, peer learning activities take place. For fighting youth unemployment, vocational education and training (VET)[3] policies are a key policy area. Second, another option is to take measures geared towards increasing the mobility across Europe. Since making qualifications comparable across Europe is as an important field of action for increasing mobility, VET policies are also at the heart of such strategies.

The importance of VET policies for increasing mobility across European countries and for improving national economies however is not only related to the recent economic and financial crisis, but has been addressed since the beginning of the European project. Coordination in the field of VET—including recognising qualifications and diplomas—had already been named an objective in the Treaty establishing a European Economic Community in 1957.

With its objective to make Europe "the most competitive and dynamic knowledge-based economy in the world" by 2010, the Lisbon strategy has turned the spotlight on the role of skills for the European economy (European Council 2000). Especially in advanced economies, a skilled labour force is a strong driver for innovation, productivity and growth. In this context, VET plays a vital role in qualifying school leavers, meeting companies' demands for a skilled labour force and securing the continuing adaptation and advancement of skills. As education is closely linked to the welfare state, VET regimes furthermore fulfil important social functions by enabling individuals to become active and responsible citizens as well as by fostering social cohesion and social mobility.

The launching of the Copenhagen process in 2002 marks a new phase of intensified European cooperation in VET. Main initiatives and principles developed within the realm of this process are the European Qualifications Framework (EQF), the European Credit System for VET (ECVET), the European Quality Assurance Reference Framework (EQARF), guidelines on the validation of non-formal and informal learning, and the focus on learning outcomes. It is a 'soft law' domain in which EU policies are not legally binding and no sanctions are available for non-compliance or non-achievement of commonly set objectives.

In the literature, the Copenhagen process has been criticised for focusing on economic needs in too narrow a fashion (Trampusch 2008; Dewe and Weber 2007; Ertl 2006). Against the background of a comparative political economy perspective

---

[3]This study defines Vocational Education and Training as those programmes providing initial training at the upper secondary level. Following Cedefop (2008: 19), VET can take place (a) within the school system or vocational schools, (b) in the form of apprenticeships or work-based learning, and (c) in special programmes.

on European coordination of VET policies, Trampusch (2008, 2009) argues that EU education and training policies are market-making policies. In her view, the Copenhagen process, and especially the two instruments ECVET and EQF, are market-making in nature (Trampusch 2008, 2009). This theoretical argument is paired with a discussion on the implications of European VET policies that took place in Germany, in which it has been widely argued that European cooperation in VET will lead to a liberalisation of national VET regimes. The debate has been summarised as follows: "Save the skilled workers—from their European grave diggers!" (Kremer 2007: 32).[4] Authors such as Dehnbostel et al. (2009), Hanf and Rein (2006a), Rauner (2006) and Werner and Rothe (2011a, b) all believe that European instruments, especially EQF and ECVET, will fundamentally transform VET in Germany. European VET policies can therefore be understood as a case for a larger debate taking place in the political economy literature. Scharpf (1999: 43–83, 2002, 2008a) and Leibfried (2005) argue that European integration focuses too intensively on 'negative' 'market-making' integration rather than balancing it with 'market-regulating' or 'market-correcting' 'positive' integration towards a European Social Model.

The Varieties of Capitalism (VoC) approach explicitly denies a convergence of national economies (Hall and Soskice 2001). On the contrary, Hall and Soskice argue that "nations often prosper, not by becoming more similar, but by building on their institutional differences" (ibid, 60). Firms derive comparative institutional advantages from the way the institutions of national economies are designed,[5] and, as rational actors, aim at keeping and strengthening given equilibria. Within the approach, VET regimes form an integral part of the national economy, which is bound to other institutions by institutional complementarities. On the basis of its micro-funded approach, VoC expects states to strengthen their respective comparative institutional advantage rather than to converge. From a VoC perspective, it is to be expected that the diverging nature of national institutions affects the take-up of European policies and instruments. National VET regimes are therefore expected to generate varying responses to a common impetus. From a VoC perspective, VET policies on the European level will not lead to a liberalisation of national VET regimes. This expectation should be even greater due to the non-binding nature of 'soft law' in the field of education and training policies, where no sanction options exist and the scope for action on the national level is even higher than in other policy areas. Therefore, in the light of the VoC literature and given the soft law nature of the Copenhagen process, the expectation that it will lead to a liberalisation

---

[4]Kremer is the former president of the Federal Institute for Vocational Education and Training, and with this statement he summarised the way the Copenhagen process was discussed in Germany. His own view as well as the debate in general will be analysed in Chap. 3.

[5]Institutions are defined as "a set of rules, formal or informal, that actors generally follow, whether for normative, cognitive, or material reasons, and organisations as durable entities with formally recognised members, whose rules also contribute to the institutions of the political economy" (Hall and Soskice 2001: 9).

of national VET systems is surprising. This puzzle is the starting point for this study.

By analysing the impact of European VET policies on member states, this study fills an empirical gap. Although "vocational training institutions occupy a central role in the contemporary literature on the political economies of the advanced democracies", as Culpepper and Thelen (2008: 22) point out, the impact of the enhanced European cooperation in VET so far has not been studied comprehensively. Do these initiatives really have an impact on member states' national institutions? If yes, in what direction?

The results of the empirical analysis add to the discussion on the nature of EU policies in general and regarding EU VET policies more specifically: Are the instruments and principles developed within the realm of the Copenhagen process market-making and liberalising? If so, can positive integration change institutional equilibria that are prevalent in the respective market economy? In addition, empirical analysis can help to address theoretical questions regarding the VoC approach: Can VoC serve as a framework to analytically address the direction of EU VET policies? Is the VoC typology of a coordinated market economies (CME) and a liberal market economies (LME) VET regime sufficient or does a third school-based CME VET regime exist?

In a nutshell, this book argues that the focus of the instruments and principles developed in the realm of the Copenhagen process are biased towards skill regimes prevalent in LMEs. As a consequence, CME VET regimes are challenged more by the Copenhagen process than LME skills systems. This argument is based on the distinction between CMEs, in which institutional support and high levels of coordination enable investment in specific assets, and LMEs, in which coordination is market-based and firms and other actors primarily invest in general skills. For the case of VET, the Commission advances market-making policies also in the areas of intergovernmental soft law via positive integration. In my case studies on Germany, the United Kingdom (England) and the Netherlands, I show that countries implement the initiatives and principles developed within the realm of the Copenhagen process in a way most conforming to their national skill systems. I find that changes on member state level are small-scale, and that member states use the scope for action associated with European soft law policies to implement them in the way most in conformity with existent institutions. This is even the case for ECVET in Germany, where European proceedings coincided with ongoing reform discussions, and the government and large firms tried to use EU policies as an opportunity for reform. At the same time, states have influenced the design of EU initiatives and principles in order to align them closer to their national institutions. The impetus on CME VET regime differs, and I argue that this difference is based on two distinctive typologies of CME training regimes: a more state-based type (the Netherlands) and a coordinated type (Germany). In sum, the impact of the Copenhagen process on member states is in line with what should be expected from the perspective of Varieties of Capitalism. According to the results of my study, the expectation that enhanced European cooperation in VET would lead to a liberalisation of national VET systems has not been met.

The chapter will proceed by reviewing the theoretical framework for this study. In a first step, I will lay out the main assumptions of the VoC approach and its perspective on skills and training. Here, I will also take into account further related contributions from the field of comparative political economy. The conceptualisation of change, the role of the state, and typologies is discussed from a VoC perspective and juxtaposed with the arguments of critics. In a second step, I will proceed to discuss contributions of the political economy literature on the impact of the EU on national systems. This perspective is then complemented by a short summary of the Europeanisation literature. Next, I will review existing literature on the Europeanisation of VET. On the basis of this literature review, I briefly lay out my research framework and my research methodology. The chapter ends with an outlook on the structure of this study.

1.1 The Political Economy of Skills and Europeanisation

1.1.1 *Varieties of Capitalism and Skills*

It is only recently that the field of education has received more attention from political scientists.[6] In the comparative political economy research strand—the focus of this book—scholars came to develop a strong interest in the importance and functions of skills within and across political economies. This interest largely developed as a consequence of the central role skills play within the seminal Varieties of Capitalism (VoC) approach. In the words of Thelen (2004: xi): "This literature has made it very clear that different skill formation regimes have important consequences for a variety of contemporary political economic outcomes."

Drawing on game theory and new institutionalism, the actor-centred VoC approach puts firms in the centre of analysis: "They are the key agents of adjustment in the face of technological change or international competition whose activities aggregate into overall levels of economic performance" (Hall and Soskice 2001: 6). As such, while building on an analytical tradition studying political economies on the macro level, its focus on firms enables the approach to offer micro-foundations to a theory that is concerned with the organisation of capitalist market economies (Hancké et al. 2007: 5). According to VoC, firms encounter coordination problems in different spheres of the economy, namely industrial relations, vocational training and education, corporate governance, inter-firm relations, and the workforce. Firms are supported when resolving coordination problems by institutions, organisations and culture. Institutions in one sphere of the economy are complementary to practices in other spheres.

---

[6]Jakobi et al. (2010) provide an overview on the study of education in political science. Busemeyer and Trampusch (2011a) review the policy field from the perspective of comparative political science.

In different political economies, the ways in which firms deal with these coordination problems vary systematically depending on the specific mode of coordination for which there is institutional support (Hall and Soskice 2001). Firms receive distinct institutional support which provides them with comparative institutional advantages so that they receive efficiency advantages for specific types of production. On the one hand, in LMEs the market is decisive for coordination. Interaction among firms is based on contracts. The functioning of the market is ensured by the rule of law and the government, for example when enacting antitrust laws. Banks receive information on firms mostly from sources that are publicly available, such as shareholder values, and not from insider information stemming from close interactions between firms and financial institutions. Unemployment protection is low, so that labour markets are fluid. Relationships between employer and employee primarily take the form of a market relationship, with the management having substantial power to 'hire and fire'. In such labour markets, general skills are of high importance since these can be applied in other firms, even in other branches (Hall and Soskice 2001: 27–33). Coordination and strategic interaction between firms and other actors on the other hand are central aspects of CMEs. Here, close networks between banks and firms enable financial institutions to base financing decisions on insider information. Employers' associations, often built around sectors, monitor firms. Associations and research institutes organise technology transfer—in contrast to LMEs, where technology transfer mostly takes place by employees changing jobs. Work Councils occupy much stronger positions than in CMEs, so that management has to cooperate with them. Labour markets are more rigid. These circumstances provide incentives for investing in industry-specific skills, which are often taught in VET (Hall and Soskice 2001).

Training in CMEs and LMEs

Within the VoC framework, a workforce skilled according to a firm's needs is an important aspect of its comparative advantage. Skills held by the workforce and demanded by firms are perceived as assets. It is a central aspect of the VoC framework that different types of capitalism produce different skill regimes. LMEs are characterised by low-skill and low-wage equilibria going hand-in-hand with deregulated labour markets as well as institutional set-ups in industrial relations and the capital market that discourage firms from making long-term investments in their employees' skills (Finegold and Soskice 1988; Hall and Soskice 2001; Streeck 1997). In contrast, CMEs rely upon high-skill and high-wage equilibria, which are advanced by higher levels of labour market regulation as well as long-term financial investments. In this environment, firms have high incentives to invest in their workforce (Hall and Soskice 2001; Finegold and Soskice 1988). In CMEs, institutions play a decisive role in overcoming collective action problems by assuring positive cost-benefit ratios to both employees and employers as well as by providing security to business that employees will not be poached extensively by other firms (Hall and Soskice 2001). Training is closely related to a specific production type which Streeck (1991) calls "diversity quality production". The skills available in CME allow firms to incrementally customise manufacturing production, as opposed to production styles that are based on Fordist mass production or continuous radical innovation (Culpepper 1999b: 44). In Germany, it is this system that enables medium sized companies to be world leaders in highly specialised products, and in general is the foundation for the competitive position of German products on the world market (ibid). Industrial relation systems in CMEs are characterised by strong unions and work councils, which is a driver for the approximation of wages of low-skilled and skilled workers—and provides incentives to firms to invest in training in order to raise the productivity of the low-skilled (Busemeyer 2009a, based on Streeck). In such systems, firms can hardly compete on the basis of wages and prices (Soskice 1994; Culpepper 1999b), which again is interrelated to the diversified quality production.

What are the characteristics of training regimes in coordinated market economies? Soskice (1993) argues that there is a certain set of socio-economic institutions which is necessary for a well-functioning system of company-based training. First, Soskice underlines the pivotal role of employer organisations because companies need advice from employer organisations' on how to set up training programmes. A deep knowledge of a firm's day to day business operations is necessary to provide such help, and firms are more willing to share this information with self-governed employer organisations than with government agencies. Employer organisations can also share best practices and thereby help to increase the quality of training. Second, companies need assurance that workers will not be poached by other firms once the training is completed. Wage determination systems are key here, and these again require a certain degree of coordination among firms. Third, several factors increase the bargaining power of employees, such as a skilled labour force, autonomous responsibility of the individual worker, company-specific skills of workers and marketable skills which allow them to find employment in other companies. Firms will therefore only invest in training if they know that employees will not exploit their bargaining power. This requires unions which are able to enter an (implicit) agreement and have enough power to ensure that the company implements its side of the understanding. A company will entrust a union with these powers only if employers themselves are collectively organised. Fourth, training is a long-term investment, and therefore it requires a long-term financial framework. Here, employer organisations are also useful in transmitting information on companies. Finally, Soskice points out that apprentices seek security of employment and higher earnings before they commit to training. Therefore, a certain quality of training is necessary, in addition to prospects of a good match between acquired skills and the labour market in case of job losses. In short, it is this combination of institutions that is characteristic for training in CMEs and that provides the foundation for the occupational, industry-specific medium-level skills in the first place.

In a recent volume, Busemeyer and Trampusch (2011b) discuss the Comparative Political Economy of what they call "collective skill formation systems". A core feature is that these are organised in a collective manner, which they define as follows: "first, firms are strongly involved in financing and administering workplace-based training; second, intermediary associations play an important role in the administration and reform of these systems; third, the systems provide portable, certified occupational skills; and fourth, training takes place not only in schools but also in companies, usually in the form of dual apprenticeship training" (ibid, 4). They add the state as an actor to the analysis of training in CMEs, and argue that a core feature of these systems is that both firms and the state are strongly committed to investing in VET (ibid, 14). Differences across training regimes can then be explained with the division of tasks between firms, associations, and the state (ibid, 11). Following this logic, Busemeyer and Trampusch analyse which factors determine firm and state involvement in VET. They see coordination among firms as being most decisive for their involvement. Similar to the above-described view of Soskice (1993), they acknowledge the role associations play to foster such coordination. Cleavages within the employers' camp can impact coordination. In line with Thelen (2004), they argue that historically the way the crafts sector and the industrial sector dealt with conflicts over training was decisive for the development of different training pathways. In collective skill formation systems, these conflicts are solved by intermediary organisations. Cleavages can, for example, occur between small and large firms, import- and export-oriented firms, or between sectors (Busemeyer and Trampusch 2011b: 23). In addition, there is a "logic of influence" (ibid, 22) which is shaped by the role of the state and political parties, cleavages within the trade union camp, and the balance of power between business and labour. The latter is important since trade unions demand general or industry-specific skills, whereas firms preferably invest in specific skills (ibid, 24). While in general the state can constitute a tipping point, it is especially important in state-centrist systems. With their volume, Busemeyer and Trampusch contribute to a better understanding of the functioning of CME VET systems.

All in all, comparative political economy scholars have been more concerned with the functioning of training systems in CMEs and its ability to overcome collective action problems than with training systems in LMEs. In LMEs, fluid labour markets and financial relationships focusing on public information on firms rather than on information stemming from informal networks, which makes long-term investment in skills more difficult (Hall and Soskice 2001). Firms are reluctant to participate in apprenticeship training since they fear that their graduates will be poached by other firms. Their competitors would thus be able to hire skilled workers without having to train them themselves. Workers face higher risks to lose jobs and changes of jobs are also more common, so that the acquisition of general skills is more important. General skills dominate in most educational strands from secondary education to higher education. Investments in high levels of general education facilitate the acquisition of specific skills. Firms do invest in training, which is usually highly specific. Consequently, as Hall and Soskice (2001: 30) point out, employees are well equipped for working in the service sector, while firms which need a workforce equipped with highly specialised skills might face recruitment difficulties.

Skill Types

Collective action problems—such as poaching—and returns on investments in *human capital* have already been addressed by Gary Becker (1964).[7] In order to invest in skills, certain risks have to be minimised: While employees face the risk that their skill investments might not be compensated for by wages after completing the training, employers' investments in their workforce's training might be redundant when employees are poached by other companies. In his influential work, Becker proposes a distinction between general and specific skills. On the one hand, "[g]eneral training is useful in many firms besides those providing it" (Becker 1964: 12). While employees are expected to gain higher wages on the labour market after investing in general skills, for firms there is no reason to invest in these: Since wages would rise likewise to the increase of the marginal product, companies could not capture any return. Specific training, on the other hand, is "[t]raining that increases productivity more in firms providing it" (ibid, 18). Labour turnover is a profound risk because the return on investment would be lost for both sides. Therefore, firms pay employees with firm-specific skills above-market wages—but still less than the marginal product. Hence, firms capture some of the return. Employees earn less than the marginal product but more than in other firms (ibid). Becker himself notes, however, that in practice it can be difficult to disentangle specific and general skills (ibid, 3). Firms have no incentive to invest in the general skills of their workforce, while both firms and the employer capture returns for specific skills training. Costs for obtaining specific skills are usually shared by firms and the employee, while the individual has to bear costs for obtaining general skills.

Becker's distinction between general and specific skills has been critically discussed and developed further by a number of scholars.[8] The idea of portable and non-portable skills was also followed up upon by VoC. Hall and Soskice (2001: 17) distinguish "specific" and "co-specific" assets on the one hand and "switchable assets" on the other.[9] Different kinds of skills can be linked back to the different types of capitalisms. In CMEs, institutional support and high levels of coordination enable investments in (co-)specific assets, while in the "fluid markets" of LMEs firms and other actors invest more heavily in general skills (ibid). Going beyond that dichotomy, Estevez-Abe et al. (2001) propose to distinguish three types of skills:

- Firm-specific skills are acquired in firms by on-the-job training and are characterised by low portability. Following Becker's distinction, firm-specific

---

[7]Becker (1964: 1) regards those investments as investments in human capital that "improve skills, knowledge, or health (...)".

[8]For an overview see Thelen (2004: 13–15).

[9]"Specific" and "co-specific assets" are defined as "assets that cannot readily be turned to another purpose and assets whose returns depend heavily on the active cooperation to others" (Hall and Soskice 2001: 17). "Switchable assets" are defined as "assets whose value can be realized if diverted to other purposes" (ibid).

skills are mainly useful in the training firm. According to Estevez-Abe et al., this allows firms to tailor the content of training to their needs. Another benefit for firms is that since skills cannot be used in other firms, specific skills do not provide employees with incentives to change jobs. For employees, the benefit of firm-specific skills is dependent on wages that capture some return of the training as well as high job security.

- Industry-specific skills are typical for apprenticeship training and can—depending on the design of curricula and the amount of internships or firm-based training—also be acquired in vocational schools. These types of skills are portable inside a specific industry where other employers recognise the acquired skills. Certification is a prerequisite for such portability.[10] As Thelen (2004: 18–19) points out, certification is a solution to decrease risks both employees and employers face when committing to training.[11] Estevez-Abe et al. point out that there are complementarities with social security institutions: employees have higher incentives to acquire industry-specific skills when unemployment benefits are designed in a way that allows unemployed to search for a job in their profession in order to make use of their skills.
- When social security systems do not provide these incentives, employees are better off investing in general skills. Estevez-Abe et al. follow the definition of Becker for general skills and point out that these are acquired mostly in tertiary education. In flexible labour markets, they argue, general skills are of special importance for employability since they can be used in different firms and professions.

In addition to providing a more fine-grid typology of skills, Estevez-Abe et al. therefore also connect social security systems and labour market regulations with different types of skills. They argue that rational employers will support social security and labour market regulation that is in line with their production strategy, so that in turn preferences on the design of welfare states can be explained with the degree of skill specificity prevalent in an economy. Busemeyer (2009a) adds that if the mobility on the labour market is lower, firms are more likely to invest in training. With more firms participating, able employees are creamed off the market,

---

[10] Busemeyer (2009a) argues that portability of skills is not only dependent on the specificity of skills. He argues that portability also relies on the degree of authoritative skill certification.

[11] Thelen's (2004: 17–19) argument goes as follows: In skill formation systems, apprentices share parts of the costs for training by accepting lower wages for a certain amount of time—even though towards the end of the training period they are already very well-educated and have a higher productivity than their wage. Therefore, skill formation systems need a "credible commitment" (Thelen 2004: 18) between employees and employers. Employees need to be sure that their skills pay off—whether in the form of long-term employment or by good opportunities to find adequate employment on the external labour market. Employers need to be sure that the apprentice stays long enough to capture some of the return at the end of the training. Skill certification provides a solution because it guarantees a certain quality of training (the percentage of apprentices that pass exams) and apprentices need to stay long enough to have their skills certified, which only then enables them to search for high-skilled jobs on the external labour market.

1.1 The Political Economy of Skills and Europeanisation

Table 1.1 Skills: General vs. specific: substantive vs. economic

		Economic definition	
		General = portable	Specific = not portable
	General = broad	Mathematics *Office cleaning*	Astrophysics *Car assembly (Japan)*
Substantive definition	Specific = narrow	Brain surgery *Central defence*	Byzantine history *Car assembly (U.S.)*

Note: High (academic, professional); Low (non-academic, occupational)
Source: Streeck (2011: 334). By permission of Oxford University Press (URL: www.oup.com).

which again increases the incentive for firms to get involved in training. Mobility on the labour market again is influenced by the portability of skills, which is shaped by VET regimes. Mobility is also reduced by more generous unemployment schemes which therefore constitute an incentive for firms to get involved in training (ibid).

Wolfgang Streeck (2011) closely examines the distinction between different kinds of skills and comes to the conclusion that a dichotomy of skills is oversimplified. He criticises that "the upshot is three allegedly congruent bipolar distinctions folded into one bipolar mega-distinction between two types of preference-producing work skills: *specific* skills of a *non-academic occupational* kind that are non-portable, specialized, and low, and *general* skills that are portable, broad, and high, as most typically embodied in *academic professional* skills" (332). His argument is that "general skills need not always be high, and high skills not always broad or portable; that specific skills are not necessarily low, and low skills not always immobile; and that occupational skills in some countries may be as high and broad as academic skills, and in others far from firm or even industry-specific" (ibid, 342). Instead, he concludes, with the underlying three characteristics which show two values each—portability (general/specific), breadth (broad/narrow), and level of skills (high/low)—there are eight possible combinations in total (see Table 1.1). Astrophysicists, as one of his examples, have high skills, and Japanese automobile workers non-academic skills, but both types of skills lack portability. Unskilled work on the other hand can be highly portable and broad. For the focus of this book, Streeck's more fine-grid typology of skills will be integrated into the three case studies.

Firms and Training

What role do firms play? In general, since firms derive comparative advantages from the institutional set-up of the political economy, they will seek to sustain the current form of coordination, whether through the market in LMEs or through strategic coordination in CMEs. In CMEs, firms both mould employer organisations and are bound to the self-regulation developed by the associations (Hassel 2007). In Germany, which is often seen as an example for a CME, all niches of the economy are subject to at least some degree of firm coordination (ibid). Here, firms support the given institutions that facilitate coordination (ibid). In case firms have doubts about the ability or willingness of the government to sustain the system, they are expected to prefer a shift towards a LME, since the flexibility in this model allows them to cope with the different economic situation (ibid). This does not imply that firms always support given institutions the way they are; they can still opt for alterations of existing institutions in order to bring these closer to their needs (ibid).

Employers do not necessarily speak with one voice. Culpepper (2007) argues that within the employers' camp, there are different preferences regarding skill provision: While large firms prefer more general and higher skills, small firms might not be able to bear additional costs. Small firms therefore prefer lower skill levels—regarding both specific and general skills.[12] As Culpepper (1999b: 49) specified in an earlier publication, large, industrial firms heavily invest in high quality training and often run specific training sites. Small craft firms on the other hand have lower skill demands and can integrate training in the production processes, so that they often break even (ibid). The skills provided by training in CMEs can be more general than small firms would actually need them to be (Culpepper 2003: 38). Skill needs of large and small firms also differ across CMEs (Culpepper 2003, 2007). Moreover, differences do not only prevail along the size of firms but also with respect to different industries. Different preferences can result from a number of factors, such as different product markets, labour markets, or capacities for coordination and resolving collective action problems (Hassel 2007). The way employers' associations are organised can also make a difference: if employers are organised along industry lines, associations often invest more resources in mediating conflicts among their members (ibid). Small employers in Germany—in contrast for example to small firms in the USA—do not have the capacity within associations to foster policy changes but can only block initiatives by producing cleavages. Especially since the mid-1990s, industry confederations and employers' associations in Germany have taken different positions on several important matters, such as social and labour market policies (ibid).

Why do individual firms get involved in training? Cost-benefit structures differ in LMEs and CMEs. In LMEs, firms rely on the external labour market for hiring employees who obtained general skills, whether these skills are low (usually after completing general secondary education) or high (usually after completing tertiary education). Training inside firms is highly specific and usually tends towards the short-term needs of firms. In CMEs, apprentices acquire not only specific, but also general and industry-specific, holistically-occupational skills. For political economy scholars it is an interesting question why firms train in CMEs and how they overcome collective action problems. For this system to work, individual firms still need cost-benefit calculations to be positive. In occupational labour markets, companies pay apprentices lower wages than the market wage, so that both parties

---

[12]Based on the cases of Austria and Switzerland, Culpepper (2007) argues that whether a country's skills system is more general or specific depends on which employer group dominates the employers' camp.

share training costs (Culpepper 1999a; Hinz 1999). During apprenticeships employers can screen the trainee's abilities before making a decision on long-term employment. The apprenticeship minimises search costs and provides a solid basis for deciding if a long-term employment relationship is worthwhile. This is more important in CMEs, where labour market regulation makes it more difficult to end employment contracts. In addition, cooperation between employers and employees is a prerequisite for such a skills system, and in turn advances further trust (Hinz 1999: 166). Ultimately, as Hartung and Leber (2004) show on the basis of a representative firm panel survey in Germany, a firm's decision to train depends on various factors: the general economic and labour market situation, the company's personnel structure and fluctuation, its involvement in collective bargaining, former experiences with training and its training tradition, size, sector, and subsidies, if any. The German Federal Institute for Vocational Education and Training (BIBB) continuously publishes analyses of a positive cost benefit ratio of apprenticeships in Germany (Beicht and Walden 2004; Pfeifer and Wenzelmann 2009; Schönfeld et al. 2010).

VoC and Its Critique: Change, the Role of the State, and Typologies

The VoC approach has been subject to substantial criticism regarding several aspects which are relevant for this book. In the following, I will summarise VoC's perspective on change, the role of the state and typologies, and juxtapose it with the arguments of its critics.

The VoC approach has often been criticised as being too static and having difficulties in dealing with institutional change (Crouch 2005; Culpepper 2003; Hay 2005; Howell 2003; Streeck and Thelen 2005; Streeck 2009). As Crouch (2005: 3) puts it: "actors seem to exist in an iron cage of institutions, which they cannot change." In Culpepper's view (2003), it is stability rather than change which is the strength of approaches that focus on equilibria. For example, Busemeyer and Trampusch (2011b) argue that they take a dynamic perspective on VET. In their view, VET systems "are vulnerable and, in part, even fragile institutional arrangements that need the continuous political support of relevant stakeholders" (ibid, 4). They emphasise the political nature of change and perceive skill formation systems as being always contested in terms of the distribution of power. Along different lines of conflict,[13] the development of skill formation is shaped during "critical junctures" when renegotiation of institutions might take place or not and future renegotiations are shaped (ibid, 8).

---

[13]Busemeyer and Trampusch (2011b: 5) distinguish four such lines of conflict: the way the provision of VET is divided between state, employers, and the individual; the way it is financed; the way firm autonomy and public oversight are organised; and the relationship between VET and other strands of the educational system.

In her study on the development of skill institutions, Thelen (2004) develops a historical-institutional perspective focussing on the dynamics leading to emergence, reproduction and alteration of institutions. In her influential work on the historical origins of cross-national differences of training regimes, she shows that skills regimes developed alongside and in inter-relation with other major political economy institutions, especially with employers' and crafts associations but also with unions and collective bargaining (ibid).[14] Streeck and Thelen (2005) argue that since changes in national capitalisms still occur, the VoC framework is not able to capture these incremental forms of institutional change. Based on a dynamic model of institutions in which continuous interaction between actors leads to continuous and incremental changes, Streeck and Thelen distinguish different, fine-grit forms of change: displacement, layering, drift, conversion, and exhaustion (ibid, 16). In a book on institutional change in the German political economy, Streeck (2009: 1) argues that "the institutions of a political economy (...) must be conceived not as a static *structure*, but as a dynamic *process*."[15]

However, it is controversial if these different ways to capture institutional change are indeed incompatible with VoC. According to the VoC approach, institutions change when institutional equilibria change. New developments can shift "the material situation, power and self-understandings of the actors" (Hall and Thelen 2005: 14). Moving towards a new equilibrium, however, is a costly and uncertain endeavour (Fioretos 2001: 220), so that economic agents have good reasons to stick to existing institutional structures by opting for adaptation and marginal institutional reform, and prefer re-creation of the comparative advantage over changes of the equilibrium (Fioretos 2001: 220; Hall and Soskice 2001: 62–66). In the end, in the view of Hall and Soskice 2003: 245), "although efficiency considerations of the sort our analysis identifies are relevant to institutional change, the latter is ultimately a political process driven by many factors and must be analysed as such." Hancké et al. (2007: 8) argue that "VoC has a strong, non-deterministic understanding of change, given its appreciation that the institutions that underpin coordination are subject to constant renegotiation." In their view, the difference between the two understandings is that VoC relies on rational calculation, whereas Streeck and Thelen stress the role of agency as well as open and power-driven outcomes. Hassel (2007: 273) argues that while Streeck and Thelen offer fine distinctions of change which help to understand patterns of transformation, in practice change processes often show a combination of various types: "In other words, it is not only, and maybe not necessarily, the finer

---

[14] In short, the early industrial period was decisive: During this time, "the *absence* of class conflict over skills was *necessary* for the survival of strong plant-based training, and the *presence* of such conflict was *sufficient* to undermine it" (Culpepper and Thelen 2008: 29). Furthermore, the state is a key actor as a facilitator of coordination and also plays a decisive role in shaping the coalitions that support the different skill regimes. The organisational form and the role of union are shown to be less decisive historically for the formation of cross-national differences among skill regimes (Thelen 2004; Culpepper and Thelen 2008).

[15] Italics as in original.

distinctions of forms of transformation that make us understand patterns of change but a better understanding of the driving forces" (ibid).

The critique that VoC is not adequately equipped to address institutional change has also been addressed by Hall and Thelen in a joint article (2009). They provide an elaborate understanding of change and stability congruent with VoC, seeking to show that "this perspective embodies a sophisticated understanding of institutional change that is eminently political and useful for analysing contemporary developments in the advanced political economies" (ibid, 9). VoC shares the functionalist assumption that support for an institution partly depends on the benefits received from the respective institution. Actors' calculations on their preferences are complex and include a range of different points of consideration. Actors are seen as being self-interested, so that VoC does not imply that an institution's effect on economic welfare influences the support of actors towards that institution. Yet, all this does not imply that institutions have been created ex ante to serve these benefits. Actors are seen as entrepreneurial, so that institutions are continuously subject to contestation since actors test the boundaries of the institutions in order to improve their positions: "Institutional equilibria change as developments shift the material situation, power and self-understandings of the actors" (ibid, 15). In the end, stability is largely if not completely determined by how well institutions serve the interests of relevant actors.

For discussing Europeanisation it is important to analyse what role governments play within the VoC framework. The approach has been criticised to offer "an extremely thin notion of politics and state action, in which governments, whose function is essentially to encourage coordination among economic actors, act largely at the behest of employers", as Howell (2003: 110) puts it. In the words of Schmidt (2011: 155): "One of the problems of the Varieties of Capitalism school is its scant attention to state action". VoC assumes that firms expect the state to act as a guardian of institutions of coordination (Hassel 2007; Wood 2001). This includes legislation as a framework for pursuing the production regime prevalent in the given political economy. Wood (2001: 248) argues that "a government's policy options are (...) fundamentally constrained, or biased, by the different organizational capacities of employers in CMEs and LMEs." Governments face additional pressures, such as for example pressures from the voting public or pressures resulting from their position on the political spectrum. While policies are mainly derived from firms' preferences, so he argues, the stability of institutions is also dependent on the ability and power of a government to steer reforms or reversals of institutions.

Hall and Thelen (2009) argue that firms can act as agents of adjustment or change, since changes in firms' strategy can, especially on the aggregated level, erode or strengthen institutions. In the medium and long run, institutions cannot prevail if they do not serve at least the interest of important groups of employers. It does not follow that other actors are unimportant. States react to developments such as the shifting of firms' strategies, and also to endogenous changes such as globalisation. Creating new institutions is hardly possible without the state. Hall and Thelen (2009: 16) argue that in fact "a good deal of the process of institutional adjustment in the developed economies can be understood as a *pas de deux* between firms and governments in which each responds to different pressures but has to cope with the moves made by the other side." Changes can moreover take place in subtle ways beneath formal institutions, via re-interpretation and defection. Reforms are seen as changes of institutions that are initiated or endorsed by the state. Here, coalition politics and capital usually play important roles in such reforms: "the kind of coalitional analysis that has been so important for explaining the origins of many institutions in coordinated market economies also provides the basis for a dynamic account of how shifting alignments of interests bring about the reconfiguration of institutions and forms of coordination in both liberal and coordinated market economies" (Hall and Thelen 2009: 26). Therefore, combining institutional analysis with coalitional analysis, including cross-class interactions, seems promising in their view. Herewith, institutional change can be steered by both exogenous and endogenous factors. In sum, Hall and Thelen show that VoC can combine an understanding of institutions which is at least partly based on equilibria with a perception of institutional change.

Another point of critique is the bipolar distinction between LMEs and CMEs. Especially, it is questioned whether the approach is able to capture the existing differences across CMEs. This is also the case for skills regimes, where notable differences can be observed across coordinated skill regimes (Anderson and Hassel 2013; Busemeyer 2009a: 386; Busemeyer and Trampusch 2011b; Ebner and Nikolai 2010: 619). Since this point is highly relevant for my case selection, I will discuss the question of VET typologies in more detail in Sect. 1.2.

1.1.2 *The Influence of Europe on National Systems*

In putting firms in the centre of analysis, the VoC approach does not seem to be a natural starting point for the analysis of Europeanisation. However, many political science studies on Europeanisation highlight the role of domestic politics and institutions in explaining different outcomes to the same European policies and procedures (Börzel 2005; Bulmer 2007: 48; Schmidt 2002; Trampusch 2008, 2009; see next subchapter), and, as Olsen puts it, "the actual ability of the European level to penetrate domestic institutions is not perfect, universal or constant" (Olsen 2002: 936). VoC provides a coherent institutional framework to undertake such research. Yet the research strands on European Integration or Europeanisation[16] on the one hand and Comparative Political Economy on the other hand developed distinct explanations, largely without profiting from insights from the other theory.

---

[16]Europeanisation is defined as the impact of the EU on polices, polity and politics of member states or neighbouring countries and accession states (Bulmer 2007: 47; Bulmer and Lequesne 2005: 11).

The Political Economy Literature

Höpner and Schäfer (2008a) develop an outline for a political economy perspective on European integration and point out the added value that such a perspective can provide. From a political economy perspective, actors differ in their capacities for placing and enforcing their interests in a multi-level governance system. European integration produces winners and losers, and can make actors better off or worse off. Existing research often does not question whether higher levels of integration constitute progress; critiques arguing in this direction are often believed to be anachronistic or nationalistic. Yet, national production and distribution regimes are diverse throughout the EU, so that research should question what degree of integration is preferable in the first place. Moreover, the modalities and direction of integration towards different ways of organising production and distribution should be addressed. If European integration is understood as a negotiation process which is largely consensual, these points are missed. In spite of a common understanding of the European Commission and the European Court of Justice (ECJ) as drivers of integration, researchers moreover often do not pay enough attention to the content of the decisions of these institutions. Instead, research often highlights the role of Commissioners as being bound by national governments or by the principle of consensus inside of the Commission. Such an understanding cannot take into account the emancipation of the Commission and the Court as political and strategic actors who influence the direction of European integration.

Höpner and Schäfer argue that European integration systematically focuses on liberalisation policies and hereby impacts national capitalisms. Supranational actors are well-equipped for creating market-making negative integration. Systematic research on the effects of negative and positive integration is lacking; research on Europeanisation often disregards questions of economic policy. At the same time, as the degree of European integration has proceeded, it contradicts some of the national production and distribution regimes. From a political economy perspective, the impact on member states differs because of the plurality of political economies, and is the more 'transformative' the more a political economy is 'coordinated' in a way that institutionally regulates the market and takes an active role in redistribution. While harmonisation of social standards might have been possible at earlier stages during European integration and was in fact (unsuccessfully) advanced by Guy Mollet during the negotiations of the Treaties of Rome (Scharpf 2002), in a union with 27 diverging welfare states and production regimes such an objective is extremely hard to realise. Hantrais (2007) points out that already the Treaty establishing the European Economic Community included a provision on the harmonisation of welfare states, implying a convergence of social policies. With more states joining the EU, the divergence of welfare states grew, leading to doubts on the feasibility and desirability of welfare state harmonisation, and the objective of harmonisation was no longer mentioned in the Treaties (ibid). Höpner and Schäfer (2008a) argue that European integration steers the competition between regimes. Although a race to the bottom is mostly denied in the literature, studies suggest that the Commission takes an active role in fostering competition in the field of taxes and public budgets which affects economic as well as labour market and social policies (ibid).

A final point Höpner and Schäfer (2008a) address is based on the work of Scharpf (1999, 2002, 2006, 2008a). Scharpf differentiates between 'negative integration' and 'positive integration'. Negative integration is defined as the abolishment of customs as well as of other restrictions and regulation on free trade or on free competition. Negative integration is market-making. Positive integration on the other hand refers to the establishment of economic policies and regulation on the level of a higher economic entity. Positive integration can be both market-making and market-correcting (Scharpf 2008a: 51). Scharpf argues that resulting from the advanced integration in the field of economic policies beginning with the internal market programme, the Single Act and the Maastricht Treaty, European integration developed to be asymmetrically biased towards negative integration and the promotion of market efficiencies (see also Schäfer 2006; Höpner and Schäfer 2008a; Leibfried 2005). Höpner and Schäfer argue that because the strength of European actors is 'negative integration', European integration systematically prioritises market-making policies and therefore constitutes one factor (among others) for a liberalisation of political economies within the EU. The European Monetary Union as well as the four freedoms and its juridical enforcement limit the possible scope of 'positive integration'. Therefore, while in some policy areas European integration is governed by negotiations, in others the European Commission, the European Central Bank and the ECJ govern in a hierarchical way, while in third policy areas both modes co-exist. Höpner and Schäfer point out that existing research often focuses on new forms of governance, such as the Open Method of Coordination (OMC), while hierarchical regulation such as the harmonisation as company taxation are not much investigated.

In the political economy literature, it is widely argued that legal constraints of European integration in the field of economic and monetary policies have limited the scope of action on the national level (e.g. Scharpf 2002; Höpner and Schäfer 2008a; Streeck 2013). As a consequence, there are economic incentives for competitive deregulation and tax cuts. In line with Scharpf, Streeck (2013) argues that the monetary union strengthens liberalising forces. In his perspective, the developments on the European level have created a multi-level governance system which is "serving to secure market conformity of previously sovereign nation states" (Streeck 2013: 164).[17]

A political economy perspective therefore also advances the view that there is a 'deficit of democracy' on both EU and member state level caused by EU integration, since the strength of 'negative integration' limits options for demand-side policies in a way which would otherwise not have majority support inside member

---

[17]Original: "(...) die der Sicherung der Marktkonformität vormals souveräner Nationalstaaten dient".

states. Options for policy change have become more limited on the national level without compensation on the European level.

In a similar vein, Höpner and Schäfer (2008b) argue that EU actors foster convergence towards LMEs, while CMEs oppose such attempts. Theories of European integration cannot fully explain these conflicts because they often do not analyse the direction of EU policies towards regulation or liberalisation. The ECJ and the Commission broaden their competences as "motors of liberalisation"—with the consequence that higher levels of European integration often lead to a strengthening of markets. Institutional differences across member states are seen as limiting the four freedoms and therefore are subject to political and juridical intervention. Höpner and Schäfer's claims are also brought forward by Streeck (2009: 196), who argues that the EU constitutes a "liberalization machine" that performs "international market-making by juridical decree".

So far, studying the influence of Europeanisation on national institutions against the background of the VoC approach is an endeavour only taken to a very limited degree. Menz (2003, 2005) bridges Europeanisation and VoC by focussing on the organisational power balance between social partners in re-regulating the single market in the case of service provisions. He finds that in this case employers' and employees' associations mediate national responses to Europeanisation. A combination of the organisational power and the access to government with the associations' preferences are decisive for the response, while the latter is derived from the respective type of capitalism. Therefore, Menz (2003: 549) argues that "national models of political economy can be said to respond differently to the common impetus of Europeanization given varying levels of power enjoyed by either organized labour or business."

Since Katzenstein (1978), the importance of domestic politics for the determination of foreign policies is widely acknowledged. It has been established empirically that voting in the Council of the EU does not take place with ad-hoc or non-stable coalitions—instead, voting decisions seem to follow a pattern of geographically divided groups of countries in North-South and West-East dimensions (see Naurin and Wallace 2008: 5–6).[18] Fioretos (2001), focusing on European integration rather than on Europeanisation, analyses the negotiations on the Maastricht Treaty against the background of VoC and argues that a country's preferences depend upon the expected implications of a certain policy or form of multilateralism for the country's market economy and comparative institutional advantage. For his two case studies—Germany and the UK—he shows that the countries' preferences are consistent with his argument: preferences do not only differ across market economies but are also in line with the internal logics of the respective market economy. Since transforming market economies is, as VoC suggests, a very costly process, economic actors prefer existing structures of shifts to another type of

---

[18]There are, however, methodological difficulties in analysing decision-making in the Council since negotiations take place behind closed doors and decision-making is largely consensual (Naurin and Wallace 2008).

market economy. While in international relations theory it is generally agreed that national preferences are key to explaining international negotiations, hardly any consensus exist on the question how national preferences in the realm of international relations and regarding the design of multilateral organisations come about. One argument prevalent in international relations theory is that a country's preferences depend on the distribution of power in the respective group of states. This argument is challenged by Fioretos' analysis, since he finds that the two countries' preferences differ according to the set-up of their national economies in spite of similar political movements in power. Preferences on European policies remained constant in spite of changes of governments in the national realm.

As a final point, the non-binding forms of governance—such as in the field of VET policies—have been addressed by Schäfer (2005). He argues that the EU adopts modes of governance which previously had been used by the OECD and the International Monetary Fund. The reason can be found in lacking consensus and compromise among member states on substantial questions of economic policies as well as regarding production and distribution regimes. As a way out, the EU turns towards coordination on the basis of soft law and monitoring. This method is attractive especially in case there is no consensus and governments are reluctant to transfer competences or actors block each other. Most often, the decision on the degree of bindingness does not follow from functionality or content-based decision-making, but rather from political reasoning. Exceptions exist: the Maastricht Treaty constitutes a rare moment in which consensus on ideas and a coalition of actors that combined power and assertiveness came together. With greater heterogeneity among member states, finding consensus on policies becomes more difficult.

The Europeanisation Literature

After Maastricht, more and more scholars became interested in the impact of the EU on member states (Börzel 2005: 47). Although, as Olsen (2002) remarks, the term 'Europeanisation' has been used somewhat blurrily, and can hardly be considered an elaborated theory (Knodt and Corcaci 2012). Europeanisation is a phenomenon (Bulmer 2007: 47; Bulmer and Lequesne 2005: 22; Olsen 2002: 944) and perceived as a process (Knodt and Corcaci 2012).

In theorising the effect of this phenomenon, scholars of Europeanisation have identified several, sometimes slightly differing, mechanisms with which member states respond to pressures from the EU as well as mechanisms of change on the national level. Reviewing the existing research, Börzel (2005) identifies five mechanisms by which change takes place on the domestic level: 'institutional compliance', 'changing domestic opportunity structures', 'policy framing', 'judicial review', and 'regulatory competition'. Radaelli (2003: 37f) and Börzel (2005) distinguish between different degrees of change: retrenchment (Europeanisation leads to an increased misfit), inertia (no change), absorption (superficial or small scale adaptation) and transformation (fundamental change of policies, politics and/or polity).

While these different approaches recognise that impact varies across member states and policy areas, most studies agree that there has to be a 'misfit' (Börzel 2005)[19] between the European and the domestic level. This "goodness to fit" (Risse et al. 2001) between the two levels is decisive for the extent of adaption pressures (Börzel 2005: 50). Only if there are differences between the European and the domestic level, will countries feel the necessity of change. Misfit can refer both to policies or institutions (ibid). While Europeanisation research argues that the higher the misfit, the higher the pressure on member states to adapt (ibid; Risse et al. 2001; Bulmer 2007: 51), research on compliances comes to the conclusion that such a claim is only weakly supported empirically (Falkner et al. 2007).[20] The latter findings, however, do not question misfit as a necessary condition for change. Yet, research on compliance with EU directives is contested, and other studies come to different conclusions.[21]

In Europeanisation research, this necessary condition is then complemented by "mediating factors" (Börzel 2005: 52). This can be seen as a mediation process, in which a European impetus is accommodated on the national level. Scholars of rational institutionalism in Europeanisation research argue that the European level can function as an external constraint on national actors, and can alter or limit their opportunity structures (ibid). In this context, five mediating factors have been identified: political and organisational cultures, learning, differential empowerment of actors, veto points, and facilitating formal institutions (Risse et al. 2001).[22] These factors comprise theoretical approaches of both rationalism and constructivism. Furthermore, Knill (2001) argues that for the impact of Europeanisation, changes in the strategic position of domestic actors are decisive factors in shaping policy outcomes.

While Europeanisation was initially developed as a 'top-down' analysis (Börzel 2005: 46), consensus has been established that also states can influence European policies, institutions and processes in a bottom-up process (Börzel 2005: 62). Especially in areas of 'soft law', Europeanisation is described as a process of reciprocal and dynamic nature, with numerous interactions taking place (Büchs 2007; Trampusch 2008; Wallace 2000; Zeitlin 2005, 2009). The reciprocal

---

[19]The notion of 'fit' has been conceptualised as 'misfit' by Börzel (2005), as 'mismatch' by Héritier (1996), and as 'goodness to fit' (Risse et al. 2001).

[20]Falkner et al. (2007) also find robust support for the hypothesis of institutional decision-making constraints, according to which factors such as federalism, veto players, and the effective number of parties influence compliance with EU directives. Effects hold for the 'goodness-to-fit' and 'institutional decision-making' hypotheses. The two hypotheses 'interministerial co-ordination' and 'culture' (referring to conflict resolution, democracy, common norms, and rule of law) also show robust effects, but have less explanatory power due to a small N (ibid).

[21]Angelova et al. (2012) provide a research synthesis on compliance.

[22]Moreover, socialisation approaches identified two further mediating factors: norm entrepreneurs and cooperative informal institutions. The strand of literature dealing with institutional adaptation has identified coercion, imitation and normative pressure, competitive selection, and framing as mediating factors (Börzel 2005).

relationship between the EU and its member states can be explained by conceptualising it as a two-level game (Putnam 1988).[23] Member states can moreover try to 'up-load' policies to the EU level in order to reduce 'misfit' and thus costs for adaptation, prevent losses in competitive advantages and address policy issues which cannot be dealt with on the national level alone (Börzel 2005: 63).

After the Lisbon Council in 2000 and the introduction of the OMC, a strand of literature emerged that deals with new questions and research agendas brought up by the OMC and the increased importance of 'soft law' policy areas on the EU level (Bulmer and Lequesne 2005: 14; Menz 2003). Zeitlin (2005, 2009) and Büchs (2007) provide overviews of existing research. One disputed question is if 'soft law' can have any influence on national policy making at all.[24] Another question of interest is the impetus of EU governance on member states.[25] Scholars studying the effects of the OMC differentiate several mechanisms of Europeanisation. Reviewing the existing literature, Zeitlin (2005) distinguishes five "mechanisms of influence": 'external pressure', 'financial support', 'socialisation and discursive diffusion', 'mutual learning', and 'creative appropriation by domestic actors'.[26] The last mechanism is named 'leverage effect' by Erhel et al. (2005) and 'selective amplifier' by Visser (2005); all refer to the strategic use of issues and concepts discussed on the European level as a window of opportunity for policy reform or shifting powers in the national arena. Empirically, the 'leverage effect' and 'uploading' are the two best-established strategies (De la Porte and Pochet 2002; Zeitlin 2005).

Scholars of Europeanisation often highlight the importance of domestic politics for the way EU policies are adapted and used. Many studies of Europeanisation have drawn on various strands of institutionalism as well as on comparative political economy—less so, however, on the Varieties of Capitalism approach. Trampusch (2009) bridges Europeanisation literature with the literature on the

---

[23]Börzel (2005: 62) conceptualises the two-level game as follows: Actors on the national level pressure the government to push for policies fitting the own interest. Member states on the other hand pursue policies following domestic pressures and interests on the European level. Büchs (2008) adjusts Putnam's (1988) two-level game to the legally non-binding OMC and argues that governments—and non-governmental actors—can use the EU level selectively by applying "invited dutifulness". According to this strategy, they pressure for policies at the European level that then serve as a reason or legitimisation for reforms on the domestic level.

[24]See Chalmers and Lodge (2003) for a pessimistic and Trubek and Trubek (2005) for an optimistic view.

[25]Börzel confirms the usefulness of the 'goodness to fit' approach for soft law policy areas, arguing that EU integration "may equally challenge domestic institutions, policies, and processes inducing processes" (Börzel 2005: 51). In contrast, other scholars (Bulmer 2007: 52–53; Menz 2005: 6) render the 'misfit' approach not 'appropriate' for use in soft law areas. Furthermore, critics state that the misfit approach underestimates the multi-faceted nature of EU policy-making (for an overview see Bulmer 2007: 52–53).

[26]Büchs (2008) furthermore identifies 'mimicking' as a way the OMC can have an impact on member states.

political economy of skills and bases her analysis on a dynamic perspective on the process of Europeanisation and the role of institutions.

More recently, the interest in Europeanisation research has decreased. Blavoukos and Oikonomou (2012) show empirically that fewer publications have been published on the topic. Now, diffusion theories gain more attention, albeit neither a theory of policy diffusion nor a common terminology have been developed so far (Heinze 2013). Börzel and Risse (2011) regard Europeanisation as a special instance of diffusion of policies and institutions.[27] For diffusion processes different mechanisms have been defined,[28] which are largely compatible to the Europeanisation literature.

In conclusion, the Europeanisation literature is a natural starting point for any political scientist seeking to analyse the impact of European processes and initiatives on member states. Since the Europeanisation literature understands Europeanisation as a phenomenon and highlights the role of national mediating factors for the way it affects the national sphere, a promising way is to combine it with a sound and theoretically-underpinned analysis of national institutions.

1.1.3 The Europeanisation of Vocational Education and Training

Similar to the argument that European integration focuses too intensively on 'negative' 'market-making' integration rather than balancing it with 'market-regulating' or 'market-correcting' 'positive' integration towards a European Social Model (Scharpf 1999: 43–83, Scharpf 2002; cf. Leibfried 2005), authors such as Dewe and Weber (2007), Ertl (2006) or Trampusch (2008) criticise that EU education and training policies too narrowly focus on economic needs. If liberalisation of VET and adult lifelong learning systems could be observed across countries, it could imply a convergence of systems in the long run. Since given equilibria provide comparative institutional advantages, VoC explicitly denies a convergence of political economies (Hall and Soskice 2001). Therefore, as specified above, member states are expected to strengthen their respective comparative institutional advantage rather than to converge.

---

[27]They define diffusion as "a process through which ideas, normative standards, or—in our case—policies and institutions spread across time and space" (Börzel and Risse 2011: 5).

[28]Börzel and Risse (2011) distinguish between direct influence mechanisms, in which policies or institutions are diffused by active promotion from an agent to a receiving actor, and indirect influence mechanisms. Here, actors search for 'best practice' solutions to a given problem. Heinze (2013) distinguishes learning, socialisation, externalities and common response. While the first two mechanisms broadly follow known concepts, the externalities approach refers to a policy transfer that is based on most competitive policies or countries. According to the common response mechanism, countries independently choose similar policies when facing similar challenges.

Few publications address the Europeanisation of VET from a political science perspective. A comprehensive study that analyses the implementation of all major principles of the Copenhagen process in a comparative manner does not exist in this field. Several publications exist with an educational science background (see for example Ertl 2002, 2006; Dewe and Weber 2007; Grollmann et al. 2006) as well as reports published by the European institutions or Cedefop. Scholars of comparative and international education have also addressed the internationalisation of education and training systems. Mostly, the focus of these works lies on better understanding and improving national education systems by learning from comparison with other countries (Powell and Solga 2008: 5).

In the field of political science, an exception is the work of Trampusch (2008, 2009) and Powell and Trampusch (2011). Trampusch (2009) studies the Europeanisation of the Austrian and German training systems. She argues that EU education and VET policies are "market-making policies" (Trampusch 2008) and underlines that the objectives of EU VET policies are closely related to the common market. In her view, the market-making nature is also embodied in the Copenhagen process and its specific instruments, especially with regard to ECVET and EQF. She argues that an important rationale of qualifications frameworks is modularisation, which she understands as dividing a VET course into certifiable units. In her view, modularisation is a core element of the EQF (ibid). Modularisation facilitates referencing national qualifications to European semantics (ibid). Similarly, Powell and Trampusch (2011: 286) state that the EQF and similar National Qualifications Framework (NQFs) "break integrated occupations down into their component skill modules". Moreover, they argue that the principle of learning outcomes is at odds with the vocational principle (Powell and Trampusch 2011). Permeability also poses a challenge to collective skill formation systems since it increases the competition between VET and higher education (ibid). In sum, Trampusch (2008, 2009) and Powell and Trampusch (2011) argue that the Copenhagen process seriously challenges CME VET systems.

While I share the view that modularisation might facilitate dealing with the EQF—and even more in dealing with ECVET—, in Chap. 2 I argue that the way both instruments are designed, modularisation is neither a major principle nor mandatory.

In her two case studies on the most similar cases Austria and Germany, Trampusch (2009) finds that these show different dynamics of Europeanisation. In Germany, Europeanisation is the result of proactive reform. A conflict arose when the government and large firms took the initiative to use the EQF as a lever to foster the flexibilisation of VET systems. Employers' organisations are dominated by large firms, but small and artisanal firms have fewer advantages arising out of liberalisation and therefore also opposed flexibilisation if taken too far.[29] Trade

---

[29] See Chap. 3 for the German case, in which Trampusch's argument and my empirical observations are discussed in more detail. Thelen and Busemeyer (2008) come to similar conclusions on the actors' constellation.

unions opposed the development and simultaneously lost influence in the policymaking process. In Austria, a "change by default" took place which occurred without conflicts (Trampusch 2009). Regarding both countries, Trampusch as well as Busemeyer and Thelen (2011) point out that European developments fed into a debate on modularisation which was already taking place in the national arena. In line with Busemeyer (2009b) and Busemeyer and Thelen (2011), she therefore perceives European VET policies as a tool used by national actors for enacting reforms—or even for overcoming reform backlogs.

In a joint book chapter on the impact of Europeanisation on several collective skill systems, Powell and Trampusch (2011) take up the conclusion that national actors use European VET policies as a reform lever. By combining Europeanisation literature with an informed perspective on domestic politics and institutions, they argue that responses to a common European impetus differ across CMEs.[30] The main conclusion is that in one group of countries, conflicts over Europeanisation occurred because several actors used EU policies as a lever—which other actors opposed. In another group of countries, consensus on Europeanisation has facilitated the adaptation of European policies and advanced reform discussions that were previously ongoing at the national level. While Germany and Switzerland constitute examples for the first type of response, Austria, Denmark and the Netherlands are examples for the second.

1.2 Research Framework and Methodology

This book studies the following questions: *Have instruments and principles developed in the realm of the Copenhagen process led to a change of national vocational education and training institutions? And is the impact in line with what should be expected according to a VoC perspective?*

In order to answer these questions, I firstly specify different degrees of change that can occur when the Copenhagen process is implemented on the national level. Hereby I build upon the typology of change developed by Hall (1993), and on Trampusch's (2010a) study on the Europeanisation of VET. Hall distinguishes first, second and third order changes. First and second order changes are instances of "'normal policymaking', namely of a process that adjusts policy without challenging the overall terms of a given policy paradigm" (Hall 1993: 279). Policy patterns usually bear "broad continuities" which are left unaffected by first and second order changes (ibid). While first order changes are usually characterised by incrementalism and decision processes that follow usual routines, second order changes show

---

[30]In a similar vein and against the background of the VoC framework, Graf (2009) argues that the internationalisation of universities impacts British and German universities differently—and that the mode of coordination of the respective higher education system is the reason for such diverging outputs to a common input.

some strategic action and are often accompanied by the introduction of new policy instruments (ibid, 280). In both cases, the underlying hierarchy of policy objectives is kept. A third order change on the other hand is characterised by "radical changes in the overarching terms of policy discourse associated with a 'paradigm shift'" (ibid, 279). As such, it constitutes a periodic discontinuity (ibid). First and second order changes can occur without necessarily being followed by a third order change. Another distinction between various degrees of change is made by Trampusch, who studies the Europeanisation of VET and hereby differentiates between "self-preserving change" through small steps which correspond to the path of the VET system, and "transformative change" which "is more profound and brings new institutional arrangements into the training system and/or leads to new practices inside existing institutions" (Trampusch 2010a: 188).

In this book, I distinguish three types of change:

1. *No change*. Instances where member states already had the respective instruments and principles in place before the Copenhagen process or instances where the instruments and principles developed within the realm of the Copenhagen process have not been implemented (so far). In this category, I also include first order changes (Hall 1993) or self-preserving change (Trampusch 2010a) to instruments and principles that already had been in place on member state level prior to the Copenhagen process;
2. *Small-scale change*. Instances of small-scale change for which the decisive factor is that the direction of change is in line with the given institutional set-up. This degree of change includes second order changes (Hall 1993) and self-preserving change (Trampusch 2010a); and
3. *Transformative change*. Instances where at least one of the core features of national VET institutions change. Such a fundamental change would constitute a "third order change" (Hall 1993) or a "transformative change" (Trampusch 2010a).

In order to identify the different categories of change, I need to define which factors are decisive for the institutional set-up of national VET systems. Without doing so, I would not be able to distinguish if a change is in line with the given institutional set-up (small-scale change) or if it constitutes a fundamental change. From the political economy literature, it is possible to derive core features of national VET institutions. In this study, these core features serve as a standard to measure the degree of change: If I observe in my case studies that one or more of the core features of a national VET system change, I will argue that a transformative change occurs. From the political economy literature, the following core features of national VET regimes and their possible values can be derived:

- the form of governance (firm coordination/market/state);
- main place of learning (firms/schools);
- the type of skills (industry/general/specific);
- the skills level (high/intermediate/low);
- the level of standardisation of contents and qualifications (high/medium/low);

- certification and portability of skills (high/medium/low); and
- the status of VET within the educational system (high/medium/low).

What are my expectations regarding the degree and direction of change on the national level?

Hypothesis: The impact of the instruments and principles of the Copenhagen process on member states' VET institutions will be in line with the path of national vocational education and training institutions.

The expectation is that the impact of the "instruments and principles of the Copenhagen process" (independent variable) on "member states' VET institutions" (dependent variable) differs according to the mode of coordination prevalent in national VET systems. If change occurs on the national level, I expect the degree of change to be a first or second order change (Hall 1993)—but not a "transformative change" (Trampusch 2010a) or a "third order change" (Hall 1993).

In a CME, a first order change in line with the path of vocational education would for example be the establishment of a new training ordinance for an apprenticeship that was developed following established ways of decision-making. The introduction of a new policy instrument designed to increase or preserve the involvement of firms in training would constitute an example for a second order change. A third order change or fundamental change would for example be the abolishment of compulsory attendance of vocational schools during apprenticeships. In LMEs, a first order change in line with the path of national VET institutions would for instance be the annual adjustments to the financing of VET schemes that were carried out against the background of prior experiences and according to routine procedures of decision-making. A second order change would be the introduction of a support scheme for firms to offer training at their production sites. An example for a third order change would be a new regulation to standardise apprenticeships regarding their duration and industry-specific occupational skills. While these are general examples for CMEs and LMEs, it will be possible to specify pathways for small-scale or second order changes as well as for fundamental change or third order change in more detail for each case on the basis of their core institutional features (see Table 1.3).

Discussing change on the member state level, it is necessary to return to critiques of VoC which argue that the framework cannot account for institutional change. As outlined above, from the perspective of the VoC literature, existing equilibria provide firms with comparative institutional advantages on which the macro-foundations of the economy are based. Hall and Thelen (2009) provide an elaborated understanding of change and stability that is congruent with VoC. They argue that institutions depend on the support they receive—which is in turn dependent on the benefits they provide to entrepreneurial rational actors (ibid). In the view of Hall and Thelen, in order to analyse potential institutional change, institutional analysis should be combined with coalitional analysis, including cross-class interactions. Change can be triggered by both exogenous and endogenous factors (ibid). For this to work, it is firstly important that preferences of the major actors on the national level are taken into account. Secondly, the objective is to give a dynamic account of the question of whether—and if yes how—reconfiguration takes place in national VET institutions. Thirdly, this study aims at distinguishing change stemming from endogenous factors, from EU initiatives, and from further exogenous factors other than the EU.

Methodology

This book carries out in-depth case studies to explain patterns, similarities and variation of the impact the enhanced European Cooperation in VET have on member states. A small-N research design is chosen because of my focus on causal relations as well as the complexity and detail of causal mechanisms in studying Europeanisation (George and Bennett 2005: 19–20). Measuring the effects of Europeanisation is a challenging task: A clear distinction between changes caused by the EU and changes that would have occurred also without the presence of the EU is necessary but difficult to undertake (Anderson 2003; Bulmer and Lequesne 2005: 14–15; Haverland 2006: 135, Haverland 2007: 63). Haverland discusses methodological issues related to the study the impact of the EU on member states—as this work does—and points out that process tracing is a methodologically "adequate strategy" to deal with the methodological challenges (Haverland 2007: 66; cf. Haverland 2006; Anderson 2003: 50).

Process tracing "(...) attempts to trace the links between possible causes and observed outcomes" (George and Bennett 2005: 6). Resources are examined in order "to see whether the causal process a theory hypothesises or implies in a case is in fact evident in the sequence and values of the intervening variables in that case" (ibid). Process tracing can take different forms (see George and Bennett 2005: 210–213). In this study, it refers to a theoretically informed analysis that traces change on national level and tests variables. Process tracing is especially useful for this research project because it is a powerful tool in establishing causal relationships in complex processes while avoiding spuriousness (Mahoney 2004: 89; George and Bennett 2005: 205–216). For discovering causal chains and causal mechanisms, process tracing is very well suited (George and Bennett 2005: 207). With the help of process tracing it is possible to take into account reciprocal and dynamic processes which are characteristic for Europeanisation (see Sect. 1.2).

Even if the best-suited methodological approach for a specific research question is chosen with care, there are always limitations to the research design chosen, and it is the task of the researcher to evaluate these in a transparent manner. Regarding process tracing, problems with internal validity prevail: Other (independent) variables can cause similar results and unfold their impact at the same time (Haverland 2006: 137; cf. Anderson 2003). Developments such as globalisation and Europeanisation can moreover enfold their effects at the same time, and even influence and shape each other (Anderson 2003: 48–49). It is therefore necessary to distinguish if the EU in fact was the cause for changes at member state level. While carefully conducted process tracing cannot serve as a guarantee to tackle these challenges, George and Bennett (2005) remark that the strength of this method lies in being able to account for different pathways that might have led to the given outcome.

Another problem is that compliance with EU initiatives might differ systematically. Yet, Falkner et al. (2007) study the implementation of six labour law directives in the EU-15 and find evidence for three "Worlds of Compliance".[31] Different factors within these types of compliance can explain modes of treating transposition. Interesting for this work is that the United Kingdom, the Netherlands and Germany all belong to type, namely the "World of Domestic Politics". Therefore, although compliance research mostly deals with directives and not soft law, the three cases of this book do not systematically differ in their way of implementing European policies.

Case Selection

Different VET regimes exist across Europe. In the literature, many efforts have been made to cluster VET regimes according to different typologies. Most of these typologies are qualitative in nature and based on country cases. According to the VoC framework, the theoretical background of my study, different types of capitalism produce different skill regimes. In this chapter I already laid out that according to VoC, two countries in Europe are often mentioned as meeting the prototypes of an LME—namely the United Kingdom—and of a CME—namely Germany. In the literature, the dichotomy between CME and LMEs is, however, subject to criticism, also when it comes to VET regimes (Anderson and Hassel 2013; Busemeyer 2009a: 386; Busemeyer and Trampusch 2011b; Ebner and Nikolai 2010: 619). Already in the original VoC volume, a more differentiated typology has been developed by Estevez-Abe et al. (2001). Building on this typology, Hancké and Rhodes (2005) associate different Western European countries with the VET types developed by Estevez-Abe et al. (2001). On the basis of these two publications, it is possible to map different European VET regimes (see Table 1.2).

While Hancké and Rhodes associate the VET systems of Southern European countries with LME skills regimes, Molina and Rhodes (2007) argue that market economies in Southern Europe are "mixed market economies". Eastern European VET regimes are not included in these typologies. National economies in Eastern Europe as well as their VET regimes are highly diverse (Martinaitis 2010).

Building on Busemeyer (2009a: 376), Busemeyer and Trampusch (2011b) develop a typology for which they consider two dimensions important: the degree of firm involvement and the degree of public commitment (or state involvement). The latter includes state subsidies, certification and standardisation policies, the creation of occupational profiles, and the position of VET as an alternative to university education (ibid, 11–12). With these two dimensions, they identify four training regimes:

1. *Statist skill formation, or state-run training;* characterised by high public commitment and low involvement of firms; the authors name Sweden and France as examples;

---

[31]They reviewed their clustering after the EU enlargement and added a fourth type (Falkner and Treib 2008).

2. *Collective skill formation systems;* characterised by high cooperation between firms, associations and the state, high public commitment and high firm involvement; an example is Germany;
3. *Liberal skill formation systems with on-the-job-training;* characterised by low public commitment and low firm involvement; an example is the United Kingdom;
4. *Segmentalist skill formation systems based on self-regulation;* characterised by low public commitment and high firm involvement; Japan is named as an example.

Anderson and Hassel (2013) propose to add the role of the state—and especially the role of vocational schools—as a decisive factor for explaining variation across CMEs. Building on a political economy rationale, they name Germany and the Netherlands as examples for two different types. These two countries share many similarities: there is a division between general and vocational education, training at the workplace is important (even though to higher degrees in Germany than in the Netherlands), and social partners have key functions in administrating the system as well as in certifying skills. Both rely on firm-specific and industry-specific skills. Yet, there still is important variation between the two countries. Especially, as they point out, in the Netherlands school-based training is more important and has a better reputation. This has important consequences: first, the Dutch system relies more heavily on the provision of general skills. The importance of general skills has further increased in the Netherlands since the 1960s. Second, the Dutch training regime is less vulnerable to economic cycles. Third, the state has a more active role.

Table 1.2 VET systems in Europe

VET type	Countries[*]
Firm, industry, or occupational Industry-specific skills are combined with high unemployment protection. The high employment protection also provides incentives for firm-specific training.	Germany, Austria
Industry or occupational Industry-specific skills are combined with high levels of unemployment protection. Often, small firms predominate in the economy so that high levels of employment protection are more difficult to enact. As a consequence, workers are reluctant to contribute to investments in firm-specific skills.	The Netherlands, Belgium, Denmark, Finland
Firm or occupational While wage protection for the employed is high, unemployment protection is low. This combination offers incentives to invest in firm-specific skills.	Italy, France, Finland
Occupational or general With low employment and low unemployment protection, this system provides incentives to invest in general skills.	Ireland, United Kingdom, Spain, Portugal, Greece

Sources: Estevez-Abe et al. (2001); country clustering according to Hancké and Rhodes (2005)
[*]Norway and Sweden are in the middle ground between two types of VET regimes. Sweden is characterised by very high employment protection but at the same time by lower unemployment protection. Norway is above average regarding both unemployment and employment protection but without achieving high scores on both dimensions according to Estevez-Abe et al. (2001)

This shows in higher financial involvement as well as in active efforts to link social partners to VET institutions. Knowledge Centres have key functions in skill certification and in matching VET to the need of business (see Chap. 4 for more detail). Moreover, the degree of institutional innovation is much higher in the Netherlands, especially when compared to the predominating institutional stability in Germany (ibid). Therefore, the Netherlands constitutes an example for a distinct skill regime which is characterised by the high importance of school-based VET as a main distinguishing feature from dual apprenticeship systems.

Although they propose different ways to conceptualise variety across CMEs, Anderson and Hassel (2013) and Busemeyer and Trampusch (2011b) both name school-based occupational skill systems as a third skill regime. Both contributions state that in the Netherlands, VET is largely school-based. This is also in line with Van Lieshout (2007), who argues that the Dutch skills systems in many aspects constitute "some sort of middle ground" between the US and Germany (ibid, 261). I therefore argue that the Dutch VET system constitutes an example for an own distinct type of VET regime.

The following three countries are selected as case studies: the United Kingdom (England),[32] Germany and the Netherlands. These countries are chosen to be representative for a LME, a CME, and for a third type of school-based training which is positioned between LMEs and CMEs. Germany, the United Kingdom and the Netherlands constitute "most different cases" (Przeworski and Teune 1970: 31–39) of national VET systems in Europe. The idea is that explanatory power is given to a causal relationship if it holds across most different cases, in this study across most different European VET regimes. As specified above, my research design is based on a common independent variable: the principles and instruments developed within the realm of the Copenhagen process. This study seeks to analyse effects on three most different cases with national VET institutions on the dependent variable. The central question is: Is there a common logic regarding the impact of EU VET policies on member states which holds across these three most different cases? To be more specific: Does change, if it occurs at all, impact the core features of national VET systems or is it in line with national VET systems—and does such a conclusion hold across the most different VET systems?

Above I have identified three degrees of change that can occur as a result of the European impetus analysed in this study. As the third type of change, a third order or transformative change, I identified cases where at least one of the core features of institutions change. After specifying my case selection, it is now possible to define the core features of national VET systems for each case (see Table 1.3). If any of these core features changes, the change will be characterised as a fundamental change.

---

[32]For a case study on the UK (instead of England) four distinct case studies would have been necessary. In the UK, in a range of policy fields power has been devolved to three devolved governments: Scotland, Wales and Northern Ireland. De jure, the UK is a unitary state, since devolved powers are ultimately in the hands of the central government, which has the power to alter or abolish legislation concerning devolution. England does not have a devolved parliament and is governed by the government of the UK and legislated by the House of Commons.2008).

Table 1.3 Core features of the three case studies

	Germany	The Netherlands	The United Kingdom (England)
Governance	High involvement of employers' organisations; institutionalised co-operation of state and social partners	Strong role of the state; institutionalised co-operation of state and social partners	Market-based structure; little involvement of social partners
Main place of learning	"Dual training" mode: mainly firms and partly schools	Mainly schools and partly firms	Mainly firms
Skill type and skill level	Mix of broad and industry-specific skills at an intermediate level	Industry-specific skills with a higher share of general skills, at intermediate level	Firm-specific, narrow and low skills
Standardisation	High level of standardisation of qualifications and content	Medium level of standardisation of training content due to school autonomy and diversified qualifications	Low level of standardisation of qualifications, content, and assessments
Portability of qualifications	High	High	Low
Status of VET	High	Medium to high	Low

Empirical Data Sources

This study is based on two empirical sources. First, 51 semi-structured interviews have been conducted with major actors in the field of VET. The objective has been to gather empirical data for the process analysis and thus to discover and gain insights into the recent history regarding the way, scope and policy direction of mutual influence between the EU and its member states. Interview partners included stakeholders and representatives from employers and other private sector organisations (PRIV); trade unions (UN); and state bureaucracies, the European Commission and other public institutions (PUBL). I assured the interview partners that their names would be treated with confidentiality. Interviews were conducted in English, German and Spanish and took place in Germany, the Netherlands, the United Kingdom (UK) and in Belgium. Six interviews were conducted as phone interviews. While in the Netherlands the language did not pose a barrier due to the high language proficiency of my interview partners, I still chose to increase validity and reliability for the case study on the Netherlands by carrying out more interviews in the Netherlands (20) than in Germany (12) or England (9). On the EU level, 10 interviews were carried out. In all the semi-structured interviews, an interview guideline was used that addressed the way the different instruments and principles of the Copenhagen process were implemented in the country.

I secondly undertook a desk research of documents on actors' preferences, on VET systems, on the impact of the European instruments and principles on member states, and on the European instruments and principles themselves. Documents included primary documents, official EU documents, position papers, publications of actors' representatives, and other articles in scientific studies as well as the analysis of the Copenhagen process. The results of my desk research are cited throughout this work in conjunction with the interviews.

The time horizon in which process tracing is conducted is limited to the developments after the Copenhagen declaration in 2002. With the Copenhagen process, the level of European coordination of VET policies intensified tremendously. It can therefore be seen as a turning point for cooperation in education and training, and thus makes impacts on member states more likely. Within the Copenhagen process itself, 2010 was originally set as a time frame for a first evaluation of the achievements of the process. I conducted my interviews (see below for more detail on interviews) in the following time frame:

- for the Dutch case between September and December 2011;
- in Brussels between October and December 2011;
- for the German case between December 2011 and April 2012; and
- for the English case between April and June 2012.

Processes taking place following this observation time frame have only been included in exceptional cases.

1.3 Structure

The structure of this book is as follows: Chap. 2 analyses the Copenhagen process against my theoretical framework. I analyse if the Copenhagen process is geared towards a certain set-up of national institutions (LMEs or CMEs) and how the EU VET instruments and principles potentially affect these different VET regimes. By doing so, I develop a political economy perspective on EU VET policies. Chapters 3–5 deal with the three case studies: Germany (Chap. 3), the Netherlands (Chap. 4), and the UK (England) (Chap. 5). The final chapter compares the cases, discusses theoretical implications and outlines implications for policy discussions.

Chapter 2
The Copenhagen Process: A Political Economy Perspective

In this chapter, I will develop a political economy perspective on the Copenhagen process. In order to understand the origins of the Copenhagen process, I will begin with providing a short overview on the main initiatives of European cooperation in the field of VET. I will then turn to analysing the instruments and principles and the governance of the Copenhagen process. In a final step, I will analyse the Copenhagen process against the background of VoC. In this final section, I will show that it is biased towards LME VET regimes, and therefore has a potentially more far-reaching impact on CMEs than LMEs. It seems that countries with school-based VET systems are, however, less impacted than countries relying mainly on dual apprenticeships. There is scope left to the member states regarding the concrete implementation of the different instruments and principles, so that the degree of the impact can be influenced by member states.

2.1 A Brief History of European Vocational Education and Training Policies

In order to understand the Copenhagen process, it is important to understand how it came about. Rather than giving a detailed and comprehensive overview on the development of the European dimension of VET policies, this chapter aims at providing a brief overview on the topic by distinguishing four different strategies for policy-making on the European level: harmonisation, equivalencies, recognition, and intergovernmental coordination. There were times in which several of these strategies were pursued simultaneously. Several processes and strategies also continued in parallel to the Copenhagen process.

A European dimension of education and training was already established with the creation of the European Coal and Steel Community (ECSC) in 1953 and the European Economic Community (EEC) in 1957. In these early days of European cooperation, the focus has been on those aspects of VET that are related to the freedom of movement and to competition (Hantrais 2007: 47). The EEC Treaty included objectives such as the coordination of activities in the field of VET (art. 41), recognition of qualifications and diplomas (art. 57), cooperation in technical and further education (art. 57) as well as the support of exchange programmes in education and employment (art. 50) (Powell and Trampusch 2011). Article 128 called for the establishment of "general principles for the implementation of a common policy of occupational training capable of contributing to the harmonious development both of national economies and of the Common Market". The Council of the European Economic Communities (1963) formulated these general principles which remained on an abstract level and focused on economic needs, such as adapting the skills of the workforce to changes in the economy and production technologies. Several activities were launched later, including facilitating employability and re-training with the help of the ESF.

Four Strategies: Harmonisation, Cooperation, Equivalencies, Recognition
A first strategy that can be identified is harmonisation. The general principles on VET laid down by the Council in 1963 clearly stated that "the common vocational training policy must, in particular, be so framed as to enable levels of training to be harmonised progressively" (ibid, eighth principle). However, after the principles were passed, progress was slow (Milner 1998). Countries' preferences diverged: It was especially France that promoted the harmonisation of social policies because it feared that competitive disadvantages might result from its high social charges on employment (Hantrais 2007: 28–29). This objective was opposed by other countries, such as the United Kingdom and Germany (ibid). In the negotiations, the UK regarded social policy regulation as a threat to competitiveness. Germany argued that competitiveness is not only determined by labour costs but rather by a balance between labour costs and other factors such as taxes, labour productivity or labour relations—and this balance might be disrupted by Europeanising social policies (ibid). Southern European countries feared the costs of increasing social standards and Sweden a decrease of their social policy regulations (ibid). Because of these diverging preferences, agreement on harmonisation of social and education policies could not be found.

Still, efforts to expand the European dimension on VET continued. The Council of Ministers intensified cooperation in the 1970s and established a first VET action programme in 1971 (Powell and Trampusch 2011: 288). The Directorate General for Research, Science and Education was founded. The 1973 Janne Report called for a common European policy on education on the basis of closely linking education policies to economic policies (ibid). In 1975, the European Centre for the Development of Vocational Training (Cedefop) was founded. In 1981, the Eurydice education information network and its data bank on education and training followed. Disagreements on the degree of harmonisation continued and member states opposed several initiatives on harmonisation stemming from the European level (Jakobi 2009: 89).

2.1 A Brief History of European Vocational Education and Training Policies

The focus of European VET policies—such as social policies in general—shifted from harmonisation to cooperation and subsidiarity (Hantrais 2007: 54). Upon the initiative of Jacques Delors, the Single European Act in 1986 for the first time acknowledged divergences in social policy regulation on the member state level and opted for "coherence" instead of harmonisation (Hantrais 2007: 29–30). The document, however, also underlined the importance of social and economic cohesion and herewith of a European dimension of education (ibid, 5–7). In 1989 the European Commission (1989: 4) underlined this focus on cooperation: "Blanket harmonisation or standardization of the educational systems is entirely undesirable; it is not the Commission's objective in this field." Instead, the objectives of policies in education and training were seen to enhance cooperation, information and contact as well as policy learning. In the words of the European Commission (1991: 10): "Whilst the Community will need to allow for significant differences between Member States in the ways of acquiring qualifications and the various ways of validating competences acquired in the labour market, it will also need to encourage European-level cooperation to ensure progress in defining the problems and the methods for tackling them". This approach can be described as a "forward-looking conception of subsidiarity, based not only on normative distinctions between areas of competence but rather on interaction between Community and national policies" (European Commission 1991: §48). Three principles are decisive: The co-ordination of policies on the basis of general principles and action programmes (§46); the convergence of initiatives on the basis of a framework of common objectives laid out by Council (ibid); and transnational cooperation. In sum, while the approach of cooperation and subsidiarity leaves ample scope for action to the member states, it also foresees a certain degree of convergence of activities and objectives.

An important European cooperation activity—which does not impact national systems directly—is the exchange of young people, teachers, apprentices and students. Programmes were launched on the basis of the 1976 Education Action Programme (Council of the European Communities 1976) and put in practice at a time when the Community gained momentum by actions such as the Single European Act (European Commission 1993a). Different programmes exist that are targeted towards different groups and each has specific motivations. For the field of VET, LEONARDO DA VINCI is the most important programme, aiming at placing 150,000 VET students between 2005 and 2013.

From the mid-1980s onwards, partly in parallel to the above described shift from harmonisation to cooperation, a new strategy gained in importance: establishing "equivalencies" by comparing individual occupations. In a first sectoral approach, the Council decided on lists of equivalent qualifications in 1974. A decision of the Council of the European Communities (1985a) then defined practical job descriptions and identified corresponding qualifications in other member states. The decision moreover laid down a specific procedure: upon proposals of member states, employers or worker organisations, the Commission prepares mutually agreed-upon job descriptions and then matches them to nationally recognised training qualifications (ibid, article 3). However, this procedure is complex, and equivalencies established in the process were not accepted widely (Hanf 2012). From the perspective of an interview partner at the European level, the problem was that efforts to establish comparisons did not take into account institutional and structural differences (interview EU_PUBL-4). In the end, the procedure was stopped in 1992 (ibid).

A strategy that proved to be longer-lasting was the strategy of recognition. The process culminated in the Recognition Directive (European Parliament and Council 2005). The importance of recognising qualifications for implementing the freedom of movement had been acknowledged very early, and already in 1963 the Council laid the foundation for recognition policies (Council of the European Economic Communities 1963: eight principle). In spite of these early activities, the European Commission (1989: 7) perceives the recognition of qualifications as a "field where for years it had proved difficult to make progress". In order to fully and formally recognise occupations across countries, a legal framework on the European level was established on a sectoral basis, covering a variety of branches.[1] These recognition directives aimed at recognising pathways of learning and certificates (Powell and Trampusch 2011). In some branches and occupations, as for example health professions, practices proved too complex for such a sectoral approach. For these cases, directives were issued to coordinate training and to provide recognition of diplomas and qualifications (Hantrais 2007: 55).[2] Once the occupation or industry was covered, professionals were allowed to establish themselves in any other member state when fulfilling the other member state's requirements. In some cases, adaptation periods or aptitude tests were required (ibid, 56). The Council adopted two directives on the recognition of professional education and training that did not deal with specific occupations: The 1989 directive covered higher education diplomas and diplomas of training of at least 3 years (Council of the European Communities 1989) and the 1992 directive extended this approach to other post-secondary qualifications and training courses (Council of the European Communities 1992). The 1989 directive was considered "a very important step forward" (European Commission 1991: §54). The two directives were complemented by Directive 2005/36/EC, which consolidated sectoral directives and general system directives (Hantrais 2007: 56). The objective was to facilitate the provision of regulated services that depend on acquiring appropriate competencies and qualifications (ibid). The general recognition system provides recognition depending on the migrant's level of qualifications—which has to be at the same level or one level below the level of qualifications that is required by the host country.

In spite of this progress on recognition, the approach boasts several problems. Establishing recognition on the European level is a complex and time-consuming process: For example, it took 18 years to install a framework for architects and

---

[1]For an overview, see Annex A of the Council Directive 92/51/EEC (Council of the European Communities 1992).
[2]See for example Council of the European Communities (1977, 1980, 1985b).

16 years for pharmacists (Gordon 1999: 204; see also European Commission 1989). Because of the distinctiveness of national VET systems, complex methodological and legal issues are involved (Powell and Trampusch 2011). Moreover, concrete decisions on recognition were subject to criticism. For example, training in firms was classified below school-based VET—which led to sincere criticism from Germany (ibid). Most importantly, in practice recognition affected firms' recruitment strategies only to a very limited degree. In conclusion, efficiency and effectiveness are enduring problems in establishing recognition procedures across member states.

With the influential "Memorandum on Vocational Training in the European Community in the 1990s", the European Commission (1991) consolidated European VET policies towards a "Europe of training" (ibid, 94). Based on a broad discussion on Community and member state level, the purpose of the memorandum was to steer debate on the topic. In a way, the memorandum foresaw the governance mode of intergovernmental cooperation: "Community action on training has two strands: setting common objectives to be pursued by Member States and identifying objectives and actions to be pursued by the Community to support and complement national policies" (ibid, 5). Harmonisation is explicitly excluded.

Intergovernmental Coordination: The Open Method of Coordination (OMC)
The balance between the four strategies—harmonisation, cooperation, equivalencies, and recognition—changed substantially with the Treaty of Maastricht in 1992. In the view of Powell and Trampusch (2011), Maastricht constitutes a "watershed event" for EU VET policies. The Treaty banned harmonisation and prioritised subsidiarity. The powers of the European Union were strengthened by introducing the co-decision procedure of article 251 TEU for education policies and by strengthening the OMC.

Using the OMC as a governance tool in the areas of social, employment and education policies stems from the diverging nature of national welfare systems as well as diverging national preferences on the level of social protection (Hantrais 2007). The OMC is characterised by four elements (Schäfer 2006): first, the Council issues guidelines and a timeline for their implementation. Best practices and mutual learning shall, second, be based on quantitative and qualitative indicators which facilitate comparisons. Third, national governments implement the European guidelines on the basis of action plans. As a final step, mutual assessment and monitoring of national reform programmes take place with the help of reports drawn by the Commission. These reports also aim at supporting the advancement of the guidelines. The Commission proposes new guidelines, which are adopted by the Council after hearings by the European Parliament, the Economic and Social Committee and the Committee of the Regions. Moreover, the Council can issue concrete recommendations to individual member states with a qualified majority (Ostheim and Zohlnhöfer 2004: 378). While the OMCs are soft law procedures, meaning that sanctions do not exist, the rationale of the method is still to put pressure on member states, and to advance national developments by sharing best practices, increasing transparency and comparability across countries.

Such new forms of coordination on the European level also included questions related to VET. The importance of education and training policies on the European level was strengthened by understanding them as a central component of employment policies. Commission papers such as the white paper on "growth, competitiveness and employment" linked employment issues to broader economic strategy and emphasised the need of a pro-active education and training policy (European Commission 1993b). As a follow-up to the provisions of the Treaty of Amsterdam which required member states to work together on a coordinated employment strategy (article 125), in 1997 the Luxembourg European Council launched the European Employment Strategy (also called "Luxembourg process"). The working procedure developed into a slightly modified form of an OMC (Ostheim and Zohlnhöfer 2004: 377). Questions of employability, lifelong learning, transitions from school to work and youth unemployment constituted central aspects (European Commission 2001a: 24; Ostheim and Zohlnhöfer 2004: 380; Hantrais 2007: 53).

Against the background of the different strategies that I have previously distinguished, the principle of cooperation was strengthened over time and is conducted in a more coordinated form with the Treaty of Maastricht and the subsequently introduced OMC. While the strategy of advancing recognition was still advanced in parallel by the Directorate-General for Internal Market and Services, the strategy of equivalencies was no longer pursued and harmonisation was banned by the Maastricht Treaty. After Maastricht, the Commission continued to play an active role—not for working towards harmonisation but as a steering actor for soft law.

Lisbon and Beyond

With the launching of the Lisbon strategy in 2000, a "transformation" (Powell and Trampusch 2011: 284) took place. The Lisbon strategy aims at making Europe the "most competitive and dynamic knowledge-based economy in the world capable of sustainable economic growth with more and better jobs and greater social cohesion" (European Council 2000). Education and training became central policy fields to reach this objective: "Vocational education and training have a vital role to play in reaching the Lisbon goals, in terms of providing people with the competences and qualifications, which respond to the rapidly evolving needs of the modern labour market. The diversity and specificity of vocational education and training systems and provisions in Europe present particular challenges in relation to transparency, quality and recognition of competences and qualifications. In particular, levels of mobility (...) remain low in relation to those in higher education" (Council of the European Union and European Commission 2004: 5). Concrete targets were identified, among others increasing human resource investments, which reduced the number of young people who attained only lower-secondary education and do not take part in further education or training by half, and identified a common European format for the curricula vitae. The Lisbon Council highly influenced the development of European VET policies: "From Lisbon onwards, Community education and training policy has gained a dynamic hitherto unknown. (...). For the first time, substantial political cooperation is taking place at European level in these areas, and there is an effort to integrate all initiatives into coherent education and training policies at European and national levels" (European Commission 2004: 5).

Following Lisbon, the heads of state asked the ministers of education to develop an ambitious programme for the modernisation of the education systems with a focus on common priorities and with respect to the diversity of national systems. The work programme "Education and Training 2010" was developed that included objectives for education and training policies as well as procedures for assessing achievements in the framework of the OMC (Council of the European Union 2002b). Objectives were to improve the quality and effectiveness of education and training, facilitating access to education and training systems, and opening up systems to the wider world. The work programme established instruments and tools such as benchmarking on the basis of indicators, best practice, monitoring, evaluation, peer review, exchange of experiences and mutual learning. A standing group on indicators and benchmarks as well as working groups were established (European Commission 2006b: 7). With the work programme, for the first time a common framework for European cooperation was created which was based on the idea to improve national education and training systems with the support of EU principles and instruments as well as with exchanges among countries (Van der Sanden et al. 2012).

In addition to the detailed draft programme, education ministers and the Commission set five goals (European Commission 2002: 4): (1) Making education and training in Europe a worldwide reference for quality and relevance of its educational institutions; (2) Making systems compatible and therefore allow citizens to move between them; (3) Effectively validating qualifications, knowledge and skills throughout the Union; (4) Providing citizens of all ages access to learning; and (5) Being open to cooperation with other regions in the world and becoming the most-favoured destination for students, scholars and researchers. While efforts on the programme continued in parallel to the Copenhagen process, the ambitious programme could not completely fulfil its objectives (see for example Van der Sanden et al. 2012: 77). In 2009, the "Education and Training 2020" strategy was launched as a follow-up. Its four strategic objectives are: (1) Improving the quality and efficiency of education and training; (2) Making lifelong learning a reality; (3) Promoting equity, social cohesion and active citizenship; and (4) Enhancing creativity and innovation, including entrepreneurship, at all levels of education and training.

2.2 The Copenhagen Process

The process of enhanced cooperation in VET launched in November 2002 with the Copenhagen Declaration marks a new phase of European cooperation in VET. 33 countries—EU member states, candidate countries and the European Economic Area/European Free Trade Association countries—as well as the European

2002: Copenhagen declaration
- Strengthen the European dimension
- Improve transparency, information and guidance systems
- Recognise competences and qualifications
- Promote quality assurance

2004: Maastricht communiqué
- Put Copenhagen tools into practice
- Improve public/private investments
- Address the needs of groups at risk
- Develop progression and individualized paths
- Strengthen planning and partnerships; identify skill needs
- Develop learning methods and environments
- Expand teachers' and trainers' competences
- Improve VET statistics

2006: Helsinki communiqué
- Improve image, status, attractiveness of VET; good governance
- Develop further, test and inplement common tools by 2010
- More systematic mutual learning; more and better VET statistics
- Take all stakeholders on board

2008: Bordeaux communiqué
- Implemented tools and mechanisms
- Raise quality and attractiveness

Fig. 2.1 Priorities for VET under the Copenhagen process. *Source*: Cedefop (2010a: 19)

Commission take part in the process. With Copenhagen, a set of priorities for European cooperation in VET is defined (see Fig. 2.1). Most importantly, the Copenhagen process aims at increasing mobility, transparency, and quality of VET across Europe (interview EU_PUBL-4). The declaration stresses that cooperation is voluntary in nature (Council of the European Union 2002a): The instruments, guidelines and principles are 'soft law', meaning they are not legally binding and no sanctions are available for non-compliance or non-achievement of objectives.

The "Maastricht Communiqué on the Future Priorities of Enhanced European Cooperation in Vocational Education and Training (VET)" reviewed the Copenhagen Declaration in 2004. Countries agreed to work not only on European objectives, but also on national priorities. At Maastricht, priorities were fine-tuned, the main framework for 2004–2010 was developed, and the Communiqué gave a mandate to develop the ECVET and the EQF. The 2006 Helsinki communiqué consolidated the process. A deadline was set to implement instruments and principles by 2010. The importance of the instruments and principles was reaffirmed with the Bordeaux communiqué in 2008, together with a first assessment of the effects of the economic crisis on VET. The 2010 Bruges Communiqué aligned the Copenhagen process closer with the general working programme on Education and Training 2020, which in turn is closely attached to the Europe 2020 strategy.

Much of the work on the process has been accomplished in different working groups on the European level. During the course of the process, working groups have been established for EQF, ECVET, EQARF (see below for details on the different instruments), and for the validation of non-formal and informal learning. Members of these working groups include national governments, social partners, higher education representatives and education providers. Peer learning activities and sharing best practices are fostered within the working groups.

Instruments and Principles
In this section, I will look in more detail at the instruments and principles which were developed within the Copenhagen process. Although each of the instruments and principles has its own objective and purpose, they are related to each other, and hence "need to be integrated and implemented coherently" (Cedefop 2010a: 26).

Learning Outcomes
The focus on learning outcomes is a central and important aspect of the Copenhagen process. As an interview partner (EU_PUBL-4) reports, Cedefop already worked on the concept at the end of the 1990s. The idea to focus on learning outcomes also resulted from experiences with the strategy of comparing qualifications based on learning input—a strategy which ultimately failed and was stopped in 1992 (see Sect. 2.1). The concept became increasingly important after 2000 and with the Commission's Communication on lifelong learning (European Commission 2001b). Learning outcomes are closely related to—or even a necessary prerequisite of—qualifications frameworks, credit systems and the validation of non-formal and informal learning. Cedefop (2010a: 26) defines learning outcomes as "statements of what an individual learner knows, is able to do and understand following completion of a learning process." The concept of learning outcomes focuses on the demand side—instead of 'learning inputs' such as the type of institution or the length of an educational programme. Some countries—such as Germany and the Netherlands—refer to learning outcomes as "competences"

(ibid). On the European level, a Learning Outcomes Group has been established that fosters discussions and peer learning.

The possible impact of a shift towards learning outcomes should not be underestimated: Implementing the principle "(...) significantly changes the way objectives are formulated, standards are set and curricula are described and thus influences teaching and learning directly" (Bjornavold and Coles 2007: 205). A shift to learning outcomes moreover has consequences on assessments, teaching methods and learning conditions (Cedefop 2010a). The importance of the principle is underlined by the EQF, which strongly relies on learning outcomes. Yet, the introduction of learning outcomes leaves ample scope for action on member state level. It is still discussed if learning outcomes should be related to tasks only or furthermore include social and personal skills (ibid). An aspect which is perceived differently even within countries or institutions is the question of whether learning outcomes can be understood as "overarching goals of VET" or as "results of a study programme or teaching unit" (ibid, 27; Baethge et al. 2008). Becker and Spöttl (2006: 119) believe that in spite of the efforts undertaken by Cedefop, a common understanding of terms such as "qualification", "skills", or "competence" is still lacking. This also leaves more scope for action regarding the implementation of European concepts on the national level.

The implementation and use of learning outcomes differs across EU member states. While some countries—such as the UK—had already focused on learning outcomes prior to the Copenhagen process, others—such as the Netherlands—increasingly use outcome approaches, and again other countries were starting to implement first changes in the direction of outcome-based systems in 2010 (Cedefop 2010a: 27). A Cedefop study of nine countries shows that all of these—including my country cases—either already adopted or are adopting reforms of VET curricula towards the use of learning outcomes (ibid, 26). Introducing learning outcomes is, however, a gradual and complex process (ibid, 27).

European Qualifications Framework (EQF)

Already in 1985, shortly after it was set up, Cedefop developed a five-grid qualifications framework that made training levels for VET, tertiary education and employment comparable without providing formal recognition (Coles 2006: 8; Gordon 1999: 204–205). New Zealand was the first country to introduce a NQF in 1990, and soon other countries followed (Jakobi 2009: 112). International organisations such as the International Labour Organisation (since 2000) and the OECD (since 2001) took up the idea of qualifications frameworks and promoted their use (ibid, 8f). On the European level, the agreement to adopt the EQF was reached in 2004 with the Maastricht declaration. Between 2004 and 2005, an expert working group developed the first draft of the instrument. After a discussion on the European level and a revised draft prepared by a technical working group, a public consultation was launched in 2005. After incorporating the results, a revised version of the EQF was drafted in mid-2006. It was only in 2008 that the European Parliament and the Council adopted a recommendation on the EQF. It called upon all member states to take actions to relate their qualifications to the EQF by

2010. By 2012, all certificates and diplomas are expected to include a clear reference to the respective EQF level. The EQF is fully compatible with the Framework of Qualifications of the European Higher Education Area.³ It covers both vocational and general education and comprises eight reference levels (see Annex I). Initially, the EQF had been developed together with ECVET (see below), and the instruments were separated only later on (DGB 2005). As the EQF comprises all strands of education and not only VET, it is no longer governed within the Copenhagen process (interviews EU_PUBL-1, EU_PUBL-5).

The introduction of qualifications frameworks across Europe has a twofold objective. First, the EQF serves as a meta-framework for NQFs and hereby aims at making national qualifications systems more comparable. Cedefop (2010a: 9–10) defines NQFS as follows: "National qualifications frameworks (NQFs) describe what learners should know, understand and be able to do based on a given qualification as well as how learners can move from one qualification to another within a system." Second, NQFs can unfold change on the national level. Cedefop (2010a: 27) names nine potential objectives for the introduction of NQFs, of which all apply (additionally or solely) to the national realm. NQFs aim at improving the transparency of qualifications, they can moreover facilitate strategic planning, contribute to linking education to labour markets, and serve a basis for wage bargaining (Coles 2006). In the literature, there seems to be a common understanding that the introduction of qualifications frameworks brings about a new understanding of education—or at least has the potential to do so (Bjornavold and Coles 2007: 204; Coles 2006; Gehmlich 2009; Jakobi 2009; Kleibrink 2011). The impact on national education systems can be profound. In the words of Coles (2006: 3): "(...) NQFs can have a deep penetration into the workings of the qualification system. Reform for a wide range of purposes becomes possible as a result of this penetration, for example improving the identification of skills/qualification needs, changing the influence of stakeholders, raising standards, improving quality, improving participation in learning, improving efficiency and changing practice in education and training delivery." Peter Grootings from the European Training Foundation (ETF) concludes: "Frameworks are potentially a powerful lever for vocational education and training reform within countries (...)" (foreword Grootings to Coles 2006). The impact of qualifications frameworks on national systems has been intended as a means to bring about such changes: "The EQF also has an aim to support and promote change in national systems of qualifications" (Coles 2006: 25); it shall serve as a reform lever on the national level (Bjornavold and Coles 2007: 204). This goal is based on the Lisbon agenda which aimed at enhancing access to lifelong learning by improving permeability as well as advancing the quality of education systems. While this objective to steer national reforms

---

³The Framework of Qualifications of the European Higher Education Area was developed as part of the Bologna process. It was adopted in 2005 during a meeting of the ministers responsible for higher education from all countries taking part in the process. It encompasses three levels: Bachelor, Master, and Doctor. These correspond to EQF levels six, seven and eight, but in contrast to EQF levels, they systematically build on each other.

has been made clear from the beginning, as an interview partner at the European level argues (interview EU-2), it certainly is less visible and potentially more controversial.

Yet, this is not to say that member states have to subscribe to all objectives the introduction of NQFs *can* have. In spite of the objective of the EQF to serve as a reform lever, it is up to the member states to make use of the instrument for such purpose: "National qualifications frameworks then become reform instruments. These are, and one certainly has to add that too, (...) in the hands of the member states (interview DE_PUBL-2)."[4]

After political agreement had been reached to develop the EQF, member states quickly began to conceptualise NQFs. Cedefop (2010a: 20) concludes that the development of NQFs constitutes "perhaps the clearest evidence of influence" of the Copenhagen process on member states. An interview partner from the Commission (EU_PUBL-1) states: "We (...) hoped that there would be an impact on the national level. To some extend (...) it is going beyond our expectations". In fact, all countries were in the process of developing NQFs or had done so already (Cedefop 2010b). Those countries in which NQFs had existed prior to the agreement to establish an EQF—such as the UK, Ireland and France—had advanced most regarding the practical implementation in 2010. In contrast, several countries apparently did not share some or all of the objectives (Cedefop 2010a: 27) and other countries seemed to be reluctant to link their NQFs to the EQF (ibid, 28). An interview partner from the European Commission points out that the EQF has not led to change, but rather facilitated change that was needed (interview EU_PUBL-1).

On the EU level, the EQF advisory group was formed in order to support the implementation of the framework and foster coherence and transparency of the referencing process. The group comprises representatives from member states, social partners, civil society organisations, VET organisations, associations representing institutions that award qualifications, the European Commission and Cedefop (interview EU_PUBL-1). In a first step, group members have agreed on criteria for the referencing of qualifications. Subsequently, countries report on their progress and present referencing reports. Member states then receive comments and questions and are asked to take these into account for the final version of national reports. In addition, the group discusses a broad variety of topics such as the validation of non-formal and informal learning or the recognition directive (interview DE_PRIV-1). Peer learning activities take place on a regular basis. Another instrument for exchange of information and best practice are expert workshops in which member states' representatives discuss experiences regarding the development of NQFs and the referencing process. In general, as the German Ministry of Education and Research (*Bundesministerium für Bildung und Forschung,* BMBF) concludes, the Commission closely monitors the implementation process (BMBF 2012b: 3).

---

[4]Original: "Die nationalen Qualifikationsrahmen werden dann die Reforminstrumente. Die sind, und das muss man allerdings dann auch sagen, die sind in der Hand der Mitgliedsstaaten."

2.2 The Copenhagen Process

In general and independent from European developments, NQFs can take many possible forms and vary in important dimensions. A review from the English Qualifications and Curriculum Authority (QCA) for the ETF shows that while some NQFs focus on vocational education and on improving linkages to the labour market, other NQFs include all sectors of education (Coles 2006: 3).[5] Yet, although the design of NQFs is characterised by a great variety in principle, within the Copenhagen process the choices of member states are more limited. First, this is because EU policies focus on an outcome-oriented approach and highlight the validation of non-formal and informal skills. It should be expected that NQFs are in line with these commonly agreed goals. Second, NQFs have to be related to the EQFs and are therefore at least partially dependent on the choices that have been made when designing the EQF. From a juridical perspective, although member states are free to decide *if* they wish to adopt a NQF, there are limits as to *how* they implement an NQF once they decide to do so (Herdegen 2009). The implementation process aims at establishing overall coherence (BMBF 2012b: 3), which implies a certain degree of common principles regarding the implementation of NQFs. Since the EQF aims at making qualifications comparable across Europe, the idea of a "effet utile" implies that member states are required to construct NQFs in a way that every EQF level has an equivalent level in respective NQFs (ibid). While the European Commission can consult member states on NQFs, no power to govern the process or the NQFs derives from the recommendation (ibid). Third, Drexel (2005: 42) argues that since the Commission has provided rather detailed descriptions for the EQF levels, the scope of action left to the member states is in fact even more limited. The Commission had added two non-binding annexes to the EQF—officially with the objective to support countries when linking their VET systems to the EQF. One of the two documents, however, includes not only more detailed information on occupational tasks related to specific EQF levels, but also concrete information on input factors. It specifies characteristics of educational tracks for each EQF level—including the location of learning and bodies to control and regulate educational tracks (ibid, 43). According to Drexel, these documents therefore put pressure on convergence towards the VET systems, after which the EQF has been modelled.

In practice, only limited divergence from EQF concepts can be observed among NQFs. Most countries have chosen to introduce NQFs with eight levels similar to the EQF, although NQFs exist that have 12 levels (Scotland), 10 levels (Iceland and Ireland) or seven levels (Poland) (Cedefop 2010a: 28). Because countries can decide on the balance between different kinds of skills, national descriptors differ considerably (ibid). For example, the German NQF comprises four descriptors for each level, which have been introduced in order to capture the holistic approach to

---

[5]In general, NQFs can encompass all qualifications or only certain educational pathways or sectors; can be designed by a central agency or developed gradually by all stakeholders; can be based upon a voluntary or legal basis; and can focus on learning inputs or on learning outcomes. NQFs usually have levels, whether these are explicitly defined or assumed implicitly. National actors choose which educational programmes (input factors) are related to which levels.

occupations in Germany (*Berufsprinzip*) more adequately. Austria separates higher education and VET by using distinct descriptors for academic and for VET qualifications (ibid). The French NQF then again does not comprise general education (BMBF 2012b).

The design of the EQF has been subjected to critique. The German Academic Association enacted a resolution which summarises several points of critique which have also been brought forward elsewhere (Deutscher Hochschulverband 2010). First it criticises that eight levels provide for a rough grid only, and therefore its use in practice is contested (see also interview NL_PUBL-2). On the contrary, interview partners from German companies confirmed the usability of the EQF when it comes to providing first information on an applicant's qualifications (interviews DE_PRIV-2, DE_PRIV-4). A second point of critique is that education contributes to the personal development, and the focus of qualifications should therefore not be limited to key skills. Third, the three categories—knowledge, skills and competences—are believed to lack a precise and commonly agreed definition. The German trade unions argued that descriptors are too complex, which limits their usability in practice (DGB 2005); Hanf (2012) points out that descriptors are defined in a very abstract manner and doubts that a common language exists that can establish a transnational validity for the different categories underlying such a framework. A Dutch interview partner argues that although it has been a goal of the EQF to foster labour mobility, such effects are unlikely in practice (interview NL_MIXED-5). Specificity will rather be fostered by the "European Typology of Skills, Competences, Occupations" in which a detailed map of qualifications, their learning processes and the labour market requirements will be established (ibid). Finally, as an interview partner in the Netherlands remarks, qualifications such as bachelor degrees that are related to the same EQF level differ regarding their de facto level (interview NL_MIXED-2). The value of qualifications is perceived and ranked differently across states (interview NL_MIXED-1). In the end, the success of the EQF will also depend on the coherence of the referencing across countries; countries have made use of the scope left to them in different manners (interview NL_MIXED-8). Yet, an interview partner from the Commission (interview EU_PUBL-1) argues that the countries' referencing is discussed in the advisory group in order to achieve a coherent referencing across countries. While qualifications on the same level might not be exactly the same, the interview partner is confident that differences will be small. Another interview partner (EU_PUBL-4) also highlighted the importance of the peer process, which could balance national interests on the European level and provide for trust. Of course, there are no sanction mechanisms since the EQF is soft law, albeit incoherent referencing might undermine the EQF (ibid).

European Credit System for VET (ECVET)

Member states agreed to "investigate" options for establishing a credit system for with the Copenhagen declaration (Council of the European Union 2002a). In 2003, a working group discussed proposals for the introduction of such a system. At that time, the instrument was understood as a means to transfer elements of the

European Credit Transfer System (ECTS)—the credit point system in higher education—to VET (Fahle and Thiele 2003: 12). However, there was substantial disagreement on the design of the instrument. The working group had prepared a document for a consultation process that aimed at introducing a comprehensive credit point system which would combine vocational and general education only in the medium run (Drexel 2005: 30). The Commission replaced this proposal with a paper which had the objective to introduce an encompassing credit point system—comprising vocational and general education including higher education—already in the short run (ibid). Member states did not agree (interviews DE_PUBL-1, DE_PRIV-3; Drexel 2005). An interview partner from the European level reports that social partners in particular preferred separate systems (interview EU_PUBL-4). As a consequence, several studies that were commissioned by the Commission in 2005 dealt with the introduction of credit points only in the field of VET (Le Mouillour and Gelibert 2007). A public consultation took place between October 2006 and March 2007 which dealt with an ECVET system solely encompassing VET (European Commission 2006a).

In addition to the question which educational strands a credit point system should encompass, another point of conflict was the way learning outcomes should be transferred between countries. The Commission initially planned a much more fluent system, which would allow an individual—in presentations the Commission used the example of a "Mr. X"—to complete modules in different countries and have them recognised as a full qualification in any member state (interview DE_PUBL-1). In practice, this would have meant that "Mr. X" could take one vocational class as a module in country A, another module in country B, another in country C, and have all of these recognised in country D. Such a system, however, was opposed by several member states, including Germany (ibid).

A recommendation on the establishment of ECVET was issued only in 2009 (European Parliament and Council 2009b). The instrument focuses on VET and does not include transfers of credits to general or higher education; member states are merely asked to build up expertise in order to increase the complementarity and compatibility with ECTS. The recommendation asks member states to take measures so that ECVET can be used from 2012 onwards. The objective of ECVET is to enable transferring, recognising and accumulating learning outcomes across the EU (ibid). Where appropriate, this shall include non-formal and informal learning. The way ECVET works is to describe a qualification in terms of a unit of learning outcomes and associate it with points. Competent institutions and partners decide on the way units are designed and can be accumulated for a given qualification on the basis of national or regional rules (ibid). Units are then assessed in one setting/member state and can be transferred to another, where they are validated and recognised. Units can be credited to the qualification the learner aims to achieve. The competent institutions and partners involved in the process decide on the assessment, validation and accumulation of the unit. Credit points are defined in order to show the weighting of the respective learning outcomes as a part of the whole qualification. As a rough guideline, 1 year of full-time learning in formal VET is seen to be equivalent to 60 ECVET points. ECVET points have a meaning only in relation to the qualification in question, unless regulation on member state level allows further applications. Partnerships are supposed to be established in order to facilitate credit transfer and to provide a general framework of cooperation and networking. Thus, Memoria of Understanding contribute to establishing mutual trust between the institutions. They set the conditions for the partnership and facilitate credit transfer by accepting each other's assessment, validation and recognition. Individuals receive learning agreements and personal transcripts during the course of their mobility experience. In sum, the process of transferring credits is fully in the hands of competent partners, so that national legislation on the accumulation of units and the recognition of learning outcomes is fully respected. The recommendation clearly states that citizens are not entitled to automatic recognition.

The take-up of ECVET on national level was mixed regarding the commitment and the focus of governments (Cedefop 2010a: 32–33). On the one hand, the number of ECVET projects rises continuously with 130 projects already existing in 2012 (BMBF 2012a: 73). The Commission often refers to the Finnish and the German case as best practices. The Finnish Finecvet (2005–2011) focuses on fostering European mobility (ibid, 33). The German DECVET initiative (2008–2012) aims at improving options for moving between different parts of the VET system on the national level. The Commission did not initially intend to steer such permeability reforms on the national level with ECVET, but took up this idea as a good example so that the second generation of ECVET projects increasingly focus on permeability within member states (interviews DE_PRIV-2, DE_PRIV-3, DE_PUBL-8). An interview partner from an employers' organisation stressed, however, that it is surprising that member states accept these measures since this area falls within their responsibility (interview DE_PRIV-2). In Germany, in spite of this project, doubts prevail regarding the cost-benefit relationship of ECVET, as an interview partner from the federal public administration remarks (interview DE_PUBL-2). Other countries still hesitate to implement ECVET, mostly because of the complexity of the instrument. Norway, for example, argues that ECVET lacks relevance and questions the compatibility with the Norwegian VET system (Cedefop 2010a: 33). Switzerland, a country with a dual VET system, does not intend to implement ECVET because it is considered too difficult to establish a system comprising both the dual system and general education. Moreover, Swiss employers fear ECVET could undermine the occupational principle (*Berufsprinzip*) (Bieber 2010).[6] To sum up, the take-up of ECVET differs remarkably across countries, and there has been a considerable disagreement regarding the instrument.

Critics have pointed out that because of the close connection between EQF and ECVET—the EQF can serve as a basis for transferring qualifications or elements of a qualification of the same level—implementing the EQF prior to implementing

---

[6]Both Switzerland and Norway are not members of the EU, although Norway is a member of the Copenhagen process and Switzerland has implemented EU education policies in other cases (see Bieber 2010), so that EU membership might make a difference regarding the take-up of ECVET.

ECVET would have been advisable (interview NL_PUBL-4). Short-term success should not be expected: An interview partner reports that a chair of an off-the-record meeting on the European level, a Commission official, remarked that the implementation of ECVET "will take a generation" (ibid). Another point of discussion is that ECVET is orientated towards input criteria rather than towards learning outcomes (interview NL_PUBL-2; Brockmann et al. 2010). An interview partner from the European level argues that this is an "ideological position" and that it should be possible to find a compromise that combines both learning outcomes and—at least to some extent—the workload (interview EU_PUBL-4). On the European and national level, interview partners agreed that the objectives of ECVET are not clear enough and that this is an important reason for the slow take-up (interviews EU_PUBL-4, NL_MIXED-3). A Dutch public official believes that the Commission has been too ambitious regarding ECVET (interview NL_PUBL-4). An interview partner in Brussels (interview EU_PRIV-2) has observed "power plays": The Commission fostered launching the instrument, while member states show only a small commitment. An interview partner from Cedefop concludes that ECVET "has been a very complicated thing" (interview EU_PUBL-4).

Quality Assurance: The European Quality Assurance Reference Framework (EQARF)

For the successful implementation of both EQF and ECVET, it is important that certain quality criteria are met across all countries and VET programmes. The Copenhagen declaration as well as subsequent declarations underlined the importance of quality in VET; the Barcelona Council in 2002 established the objective to make European education and training systems "a world quality reference by 2010" (European Council 2002: 43). Already in 2001, the European forum on quality in VET was established. A working group on quality in VET was assigned the task to develop a common quality framework on the basis of national best practices (Küßner 2009). In 2004, the Council endorsed the Common Quality Assurance Framework as a systematic approach to quality assurance and invited member states to voluntarily promote the framework together with relevant stakeholders (Council of the European Union 2004a). This quality assurance framework was characterised by a high degree of detail and complexity. A German public administration official reports that the framework had 200 indicators, and it was commonly agreed that the instrument was hard to handle (interview DE_PUBL-6). In October 2005, the European Network for Quality Assurance in VET (ENQA-VET) was established with the purpose to facilitate cooperation between countries and implement the framework. The exchange on the European level made clear that in spite of the heterogeneity of VET systems across Europe, states face similar challenges when it comes to the development of quality criteria and measurement instruments, so that European cooperation can support member states in this field (Küßner 2009).

In June 2009, a recommendation on EQARF was adopted (European Parliament and Council 2009a). The recommendation invites member states to devise a national quality assurance approach until April 2011, establish a Quality Assurance National Reference Point for VET, participate in a network which is chaired by the Commission, and undertake a review of the implementation every 4 years. EQARF builds on the Common Quality Assurance Framework but focuses on concrete procedures and criteria which are easier to operationalise, which makes the instrument less complex and detailed (Küßner 2009). With EQARF being based on a recommendation of the European Parliament and the Council, the standing of quality assurance increased. EQARF is geared towards improving transparency and consistency of VET policies in and between member states. It introduces a monitoring process which shall encompass VET systems, providers and the awarding of qualifications (ibid). At the heart of the quality process is a cycle of planning, implementation, assessment, and review. The continuous analysis of VET systems is foreseen to be carried out both qualitatively and quantitatively (ibid). The latter is carried out with the help of ten indicators, which serve as a "toolbox" from which countries can choose those indicators most relevant for the advancement of their own system (see Annex II). The character of a toolbox instead of benchmarks was chosen since employers (interviews DE_PRIV-2, DE_PRIV-3) and several member states (interview DE_PUBL-6) opposed compulsory benchmarks in this field. European Parliament and Council (2009a: 3) underline that the use of the framework is voluntary, and implementation can easily be in line with national practices: "The Framework does not prescribe a particular quality assurance system or approach".

The European Quality Assurance in Vocational Education and Training (EQAVET) was founded as a network bringing together member states, social partners and the Commission with the objective to facilitate collaboration and implementation of quality assurance on the basis of EQARF. Two working groups on quality assurance exist on the European level: One is working on guidelines, one on indicators (interview NL_PUBL-1). Members of the working groups include national administrations, social partners, and VET providers. The European Commission and Cedefop are also present at the meetings. Interview partners for this work have reported that the network is very active (interviews NL_PUBL-1, DE_PRIV-3).

Assessments of the impact of EU quality assurance differ. On the one hand, German employers argue that the instrument opens up de facto steering competences on the European level in spite of its voluntary nature (KWB 2010: 2). This is because annexes to the recommendation provide detailed proposals for the implementation in member states as well as establish encompassing reporting requirements. As a consequence, "in reality, full implementation by the Member States would result in an EU competence for steering and monitoring education policy which goes well beyond the competences described in articles 149 and 150 TEC" (KWB 2010: 2). On the other hand, an interview partner from the German public administration reports that the search for consensus among member states has made the EU concept very broad (interview DE_PUBL-1). Ultimately, the design of the instrument leaves the effectiveness of quality policies in the hands of member states. An interview partner from the public administration in Germany points out that the impact of EQARF could be high if it was indeed implemented as a quality circle on the macro level—however, member states and stakeholders are reluctant to do so, especially because of the potentially far-reaching consequences (interview partner DE_PUBL-2).

Implementing EQAVET is seen as a complex and long-term endeavour. Some countries use the quality model on which EQAVET is based, others are discussing to use the indicators in the national realm (such as Germany, the UK/Northern Ireland and Scotland), and again others have already aligned their indicators (including the Netherlands and the UK/England and Wales) (Cedefop 2010a: 30). Countries in which quality mechanisms for VET had been in place for many years (including Germany and the UK) have a tendency towards applying more encompassing approaches (ibid). In general, Cedefop notices a shift towards increasingly measuring quality with output standards and targets rather than focussing on input criteria and processes, as well as linking financing to results (ibid). Although improving the quality of VET systems is a complex task involving many different institutions, most countries have developed strategies or regulations for improving quality assurance in VET as well as for encouraging a culture of quality (ibid). Since national VET systems and quality assurance systems are heterogeneous, there still is scope for action for initiatives on the European level, as an interview partner from the Dutch public administration believes (interview NL_PUBL-1). In sum, the Commission believes that implementation differs across countries, and implementing EQARF is not the first priority for some member states (interview with a Commission official, EU_PUBL-2). The method of peer learning is believed to be efficient, as assessments of the Commission suggest (ibid) and as a Dutch public official states in an interview for this work (interview NL_PUBL-1).

Validation of Non-formal and Informal Learning

From 1985 onwards, Cedefop developed detailed comparisons for the skilled worker level. Just as early, the issues of non-formal and informal training as well as competence-based qualifications came up in this context (Gordon 1999: 205). Beginning with the Commission's memorandum on lifelong learning (European Commission 2000), the validation of non-formal and informal learning was discussed more intensively both on the European level and in national debates (Frank et al. 2003). Since validation mechanisms across member states were shown to be very heterogeneous, European principles on identifying and validating non-formal and informal learning (Council of the European Union 2004b) were adopted in 2004. The objective was to create common points of reference. In 2009, more detailed guidelines on the validation of non-formal and informal learning were issued (Cedefop 2009). Searching for a consensus among member states made the EU concept very broad, as an interview partner from the German public administration reports (interview DE_PUBL-1). In 2012, a Council recommendation was issued that asked member states to have validation arrangements in place by 2018.[7]

The guidelines issued in 2004 and 2009 entail both the European as well as the national perspective. The individual is seen at the centre of the process. Organisational structures, process structures, methods, and practitioners are also addressed. Fundamental principles of validation are established: Validation procedures should take place voluntarily, respect the privacy of the individual, guarantee equal access and fair treatment, involve stakeholders, comprise mechanisms for guidance and counselling, be based on quality assurance mechanisms, and assure professional competences for validation practitioners.

Validation of non-formal and informal learning is closely related to learning outcomes and qualifications frameworks. Since it enables workers to demonstrate their skills and competences no matter where they have been obtained, it is perceived to improve the individual's learning and employment prospects in finding jobs that adequately reflect their skills as well as in the progression to further education. Thereby, the validation of non-formal and informal qualifications increases the significance of learning at work. By providing an alternative route of learning, validation procedures increase the flexibility of education institutions and education systems (Cedefop 2010a: 31). Groups with special needs, such as migrants or early school leavers, might especially benefit from the introduction of validation mechanisms.

According to Cedefop, about half of the countries have made validation of non-formal and informal learning a priority. Several countries use the European guidelines as a reference point. For many countries, the introduction of validation mechanisms seems to be linked to introducing NQFs and implementing the shift towards learning outcomes. This is because qualifications frameworks make non-formal and informal learning more visible and integrate validation into an overall approach. Moreover, also quality assurance mechanisms facilitate the introduction of validation mechanisms, since they provide credibility regarding the value of the acquired qualifications (Cedefop 2010a: 31–32). Highly developed validation systems, on the other hand, were in place in only four member states in 2010 (European Commission 2012). Seven further countries have systems that are either only being developed or that cover only parts of the system or sectors (ibid).

Europass

Europass was established in 2004 (European Parliament and Council 2004) based on the call of the Copenhagen declaration to integrate the European CV, diploma supplements and the Common European Framework of Reference for Languages into one single framework. The objective of Europass is to support geographical and job mobility by making qualifications better understood across Europe (Cedefop 2010a: 34). It addresses the individual. Some countries have set up Europass centres to help promote and disseminate Europass (ibid). In conclusion,

---

[7]This recommendation was issued after the observation period of this work and hence is not part of my analysis.

while Europass is a valuable instrument to foster the "readability" of qualifications across Europe, it focuses on the individual and therefore will not impact member states' institutions.

2.3 The Political Economy of the Copenhagen Process

This chapter will analyse the Copenhagen process against the background of VoC. I will proceed in two steps. First, I argue that in general—meaning beyond the Copenhagen process—EU VET policies are biased towards both general skills and market-making policies. Here, I will take a broader view, including the historical development of European VET policies and European education policies and programmes. In a second step, I will analyse in what ways instruments and guidelines developed in the realm of the Copenhagen process might have an impact on CMEs and LMEs. I will show that also the specific instruments and principles have a—potentially—more far-reaching impact on CMEs than LMEs.

EU VET Policies Focus on General Skills and Market-Making Policies
The reason why the EU became involved in education and training policies already in 1957 was the importance of education policies for the completion of the internal market. Education and training policies were relevant insofar as they might constrain the four freedoms (Hantrais 2007: 47). Member states opposed any further regulation in this policy field (Jakobi 2009: 89). The importance of human resources for economic growth was the reason behind putting education at the centre of the Lisbon strategy. Herewith, the Commission's concept of education and lifelong learning consequently frames education against the background of human resources and leaves the responsibility for learning and skills in the hands of the individual, rather than of the state (Kleibrink 2011: 76).

EU VET policies focus on general skills, as becomes obvious in several ways. First, the involvement of the EU in education and training policies is closely intertwined with the internal market, freedom of movement and growth. Therefore, mobility and employability have been important aspects of EU VET policies from the beginning. Such a focus has specific consequences on the kind of skills the EU tries to advance: for mobility and employability, general skills are more advantageous than specific skills. It is in the nature of these concepts that they relate much better to general skills, which can be used in any other company or industry. Specific skills can be used only in the company where they have been obtained. Industry-specific skills are of use in the respective industry—however, VoC assumes that skills are very much interrelated with complementary institutions that are largely country-specific so that they can, arguably, only partially be transferred to the same industry in other countries.

Second, in line with this theoretical argument, several official documents show a strong focus on promoting general skills. The following two documents can serve as examples:

- In its white paper on education and training (European Commission 1995), the European Commission sketches out challenges to the way economies and societies work—the transformation towards an information society, internationalisation of trade, and impacts of science and technology—and concludes that two responses to these challenges are needed. First, it is necessary to give each person access to a broad knowledge base, which is not only important for initial learning, but also the foundation for retraining workers (ibid, 10). Second, every person should have the abilities to take part in economic life and employment. Herewith, the skills "most favourable to employment" are "broad and transferable" (ibid, 13) and consist of a body of both fundamental and technical knowledge;
- One target of the 2000 Lisbon Council was to identify new basic skills. These skills shall be compiled within a European framework and shall include skills in IT, foreign languages, technological culture, entrepreneurship, and social skills. In the influential Memorandum on Lifelong Learning, the Commission explains that action in this field becomes necessary because "economic and social change are modifying and upgrading the profile of basic skills that everyone should have as a minimum entitlement" (European Commission 2000: 10). Although these basic skills are primarily taught within primary and secondary compulsory education, the Commission relates the changing requirements towards basic skills to VET: "General, vocational and social skills hence increasingly overlap in content and function" (European Commission 2001b: 22).

Third, a focus on general skills can also be seen in the EU's measures and initiatives. In all mobility programmes such as Leonardo, language skills and intercultural competencies are promoted. The reason for EU initiatives supporting language learning is threefold: these skills have high labour market relevance in a globalised economy, they are necessary components for the completion of the internal market and they can promote European citizenry. Language skills and intercultural competencies, however, are general skills. The same is true for ICT skills, which are promoted by the EU in various ways.

Fourth, the EU hardly promotes the acquisition of specific skills. Since skills are the more specific the more firms are involved in the formation of skills (Busemeyer 2009a: 382), the EU could promote the acquisition of specific skills by promoting the engagement of firms or by fostering training on the firm level. In the past, references to fostering apprenticeships could be found in several documents, such as in the 1995 White Paper on Education and Training (European Commission 1995), and it was one of the objectives of the Leonardo da Vinci mobility programme (Baron 2007). However, from 2007–2013, superordinate targets of the lifelong learning programme and of Leonardo da Vinci no longer included the advancement of apprenticeships (Baron 2007).[8] Moreover, substantially fewer apprentices than university students make use of mobility programmes. In sum,

---

[8]Together with Comenius, Erasmus, Gruntvig and the Jean Monnet programme, the Leonardo da Vinci programme was integrated into the Lifelong Learning Programme during this period.

fostering specific skills to considerably smaller degree than general skills makes EU education policies biased towards general skills.

Fifth, EU policies prioritise tertiary education. The Education & Training 2020 strategy aims at increasing the share of 30–34 year olds with tertiary education attainment to at least 40 %. This benchmark is based on the 1997 International Standard Classification of Education (ISCED) which includes, for example, German advanced occupational *Meister* professionals (master craftsman or technician) qualifications.[9] The Council argues that a high share of university graduates is necessary to meet the needs of the labour market and of research (Baron 2007). Within the Bologna process, efforts are being made to increase the share of university graduates (ibid). However, this can lead to a competition between higher education and VET, as well as to creaming off if secondary education graduates who would formerly have started VET now attend higher education programmes.[10]

The Impact of the Copenhagen Process: How It Potentially Challenges CMEs and LMEs

In line with the argument that EU VET policies are biased towards general skills and market-based provision of VET, this section shows that the instruments and guidelines developed within the realm of the Copenhagen process challenge CMEs much more than they challenge LMEs. As a consequence, I argue, they are biased towards LMEs.

Looking at the documents and declarations published as part of the Copenhagen process, there is some evidence that it is geared towards flexibilisation and liberalisation of VET. For example, the recent Bruges Communiqué emphasised the idea to make VET more flexible (European Ministers for Vocational Education and Training et al. 2010). In this Communiqué, the Education Council, social partners and the Commission jointly set priorities for European cooperation in VET from 2011 to 2020. The term "flexible pathways" is mentioned several times. It is also mentioned in the agreement on short-term deliverables for 2011–2014 as a means for raising the participation of low-skilled (ibid, 16).

When assessing the potential impact of the Copenhagen process on CMEs and LMEs, it is however necessary to not only refer to abstract statements but to analyse the instruments and principles more closely. Yet, it is important to keep in mind two aspects which greatly influence the impact the Copenhagen process will have on member states. First, there is reasonable scope left to the member states regarding the implementation of the different instruments and guidelines. This scope can make a substantial difference regarding how far core factors of coordinated skills regime are challenged. However, this scope is also limited by decisions taken on the European level, such as numerous proposals for implementation. The instruments

---

[9]According to data from Eurostat, the EU average was 22.4 % in 2000 and rose to 33.5 % in 2010. For the country cases of this work, the figures are as follows: Germany, 25.7 % (2000), 29.8 % (2010); the Netherlands, 26.5 % (2000), 41.4 % (2010); the UK, 29 % (2000), 43 % (2010).

[10]For a detailed discussion on the relationship between higher education and VET see for example Powell and Solga (2008) and Graf (2013).

and guidelines developed are, second, soft law and non-binding. Even though the Europeanisation literature ascribes a certain amount of peer pressure to the functioning of the OMC, states can choose to not or only partially implement all or single instruments.

In the literature, assessments of potential effects of ECVET and EQF on national VET systems differ greatly. This is partly due to different understandings of the nature of EU VET policies. Many authors do not distinguish between the two instruments but perceive it as one coherent system. While I argue above that member states do have a considerable degree of scope regarding the implementation of the Copenhagen process, authors often do not address this aspect.

In Germany, a controversial debate on the impact of the Copenhagen process took place. Especially, it was vividly discussed if European VET policies would affect the occupation-based nature and holistic approach to occupations *(Berufsprinzip)*. In a similar vein, Swiss employers stated that ECVET challenges the *Berufsprinzip* (Trampusch 2010a: 187). Many authors have argued that EU VET policies have the potential to put an end to dual VET systems such as the German one (Drexel 2005; Rauner 2006: 37). Authors such as Drexel (2005), Hanf and Rein (2006a), Rauner (2006), and Werner and Rothe (2011a: 3) all believe that EQF and ECVET require a very encompassing degree of modularisation that will fundamentally transform the German apprenticeship system. Drexel (2005) takes a very critical stand on EU VET policies and regards EQF and ECVET as a distinct system which is incompatible with the German system. Moreover, she argues that the implementation of EU instruments would require broad changes of both curricula and didactics. In Drexel's opinion, the implementation of EQF and ECVET would imply abolishing the occupational principle *(Berufsprinzip)* as well as the capability to perform an occupation autonomously *(berufliche Handlungsfähigkeit)*.[11] These critical assessments are fed by a study edited by the BMBF, in which Gehmlich (2009: 5) develops a proposal for introducing a NQF which largely abolishes standardised educational pathways and degrees.

If the Copenhagen process would lead to such a liberalisation of national VET systems, what would be the consequences? Finegold (1999) discusses the advantages and disadvantages a change towards a "competence-based system", as he calls it, would have for Germany. On the one hand, such a shift would lift "performance over standards" and foster innovation among providers. Moreover, access to the status of skilled workers might be facilitated and broadened, to the advantage especially of older workers (ibid) and the (numerous) outsiders. On the other hand, such a transformation would have severe disadvantages: "The most powerful objection to a competency-based system is that it risks reducing the quality and breadth of the nationally recognized apprenticeship qualifications, by encouraging

---

[11]Moreover, Drexel (2005) argues that the full implementation of EU policies would demand a liberalisation of initial VET, the privatisation or closing down of public VET schools, and stopping public financing for the VET system (81–82). She does, however, not give detailed reasons why all this necessarily follows from EU VET policies.

2.3 The Political Economy of the Copenhagen Process

individuals and their firms to focus just on the specific competencies which are tested, with insufficient attention to the underlying knowledge, general skills, and work socialization process needed to prepare individuals who are flexible enough to adapt to the changing economy" (ibid, 416). Therefore, with deconstructing skill profiles, employers and apprentices might stop investing in the acquisition of broader and transferable skills. The *Berufsprinzip* on the contrary is based on the idea that an occupation constitutes more than the sum of single units (Drexel 2005) and that the individual is able to act and reflect autonomously. As a consequence, the fine balance of incentives for both employers and apprentices to take part in training will change. Following VoC, a shift towards a liberal market VET system would, moreover, have consequences on complementary institutions,[12] especially because of the high importance of VET for the "diversified quality production" (Streeck 1991).

The possible consequences of a shift towards a liberalised VET system in the direction of a liberal skill regime would be far-reaching. Yet, can the Copenhagen process unfold such an impact? In the following, I will examine the possible impact of the instruments and principles more closely.

As a first point, modularisation in fact corresponds to the logic of making qualifications comparable across Europe. The higher the modularisation of VET systems, the better transparency across VET systems can be achieved (see for example Rauner 2006: 41). Already in the 1990s, the Council looked at the modularised English National Vocational Qualifications (NVQs) as a role model for mutual recognition of VET qualifications across Europe (Baron 2007: 75). This is because single competences can be compared and transferred more easily than whole VET qualifications: VET qualifications that take years to accomplish always comprise a certain bundle of competences, and it is unlikely that a VET qualification in another country is made up of the exact same combination of competences or learning outcomes.

While modularisation therefore *facilitates* the implementation of EQF and ECVET, is it a *necessary* precondition of the Copenhagen process? And will it put an end to CME VET regimes?

Different assessments exist in the comparative political economy literature. Powell and Trampusch (2011) argue that the initiatives foster modularisation as well as the permeability between the different strands of education. In their perspective, learning outcomes is opposed to the principle of vocational education and to the normative and political foundations of CME skills systems. Permeability might lead to increasing competition between VET and tertiary education—and VET actors fear that such a competition would be disadvantageous for them. Moreover, "modularization demands the dividing up into component parts of

---

[12]For example on wage bargaining: "From a union perspective, common standards prevent a differentiation of occupational profiles that would increase conflict between workers over wage levels, which would in turn interfere with the smooth functioning of the collective wage bargaining system" (Thelen and Busemeyer 2008: 14).

what is considered comprehensive vocational capability (...)—upon which the strength and uniqueness of collective skill formation systems are founded" (ibid, 286).

A different assessment is provided by Thelen and Busemeyer (2008: 17) who argue that modularisation threatens the *Berufsprinzip* only if it is implemented in a way that deconstructs skill profiles. If modularisation solely refers to the way skills are acquired, in their view it is compatible with the *Berufsprinzip*. Kremer (2007: 38) agrees with this perspective. He argues that while modularisation is a necessary component of the EQF, and ECVET then can make these units assessable, still units could also be examined as a whole and within nationally regulated full qualifications.

The latter point of view is underlined by the Austrian case. As Trampusch (2009) reports, in Austria discussions on modularisation had started prior to the Copenhagen process and in 2006 the system was modularised. It is recommended—explicitly not in a mandatory way—that apprenticeships are divided into a basic module, main modules, and special modules. Trampusch reports that this reform is widely perceived to take place within the system and without implying a shift towards a LME VET regime. The Austrian VET system comprises a vital dual apprenticeship system with a strong VET track combining a full VET qualification with a University entrance qualification. While it therefore can be considered as a dual system with influences of school-based training, the Austrian VET regime meets the criteria for a CME VET system (Busemeyer and Trampusch 2011b). Ergo, if modularisation can be implemented in Austria in a way that is in line with its existing VET system, EU initiatives cannot be incompatible with CME VET systems per se.

When it comes to ECVET, it is important to distinguish between the way the Commission had originally envisioned the instrument and the way it was put in practice by the 2009 recommendation. It has already been outlined above that the Commission originally planned to introduce a system in which each individual ("Mr. X") would have been able to conduct modules—in informal, non-formal or formal learning—in any member state or different member states, and have them recognised as a full qualification in any member state (interview DE_PUBL-1). Mike Coles, who had been involved in several reports which laid the ground work for the EQF, has written a report for the ETF on the ways qualifications frameworks can be designed and used (Coles 2006). Analysing the relationship between qualifications frameworks and credit systems, he brings forward the idea to relate credit to learning requirements in other qualifications. Individual units are assessed and accumulated, so that they serve as building blocks towards a specific qualification. They can also be transferred to another setting and serve as building blocks towards a different qualification (ibid). For example, transferred to the German context, a unit on oenology for restaurant specialists (*Restaurantfachleute*) may be given credit in similar apprenticeships, for example hotel specialists (*Hotelfachleute*). A challenge is that learning units would have to be related to distinct qualifications levels. A unit on the diagnosis of motor defects, for example, might be more complex for *KFZ-Mechatroniker* (3.5-year-apprenticeship for car mechanics) than for *KFZ-Servicetechniker* (2-year-apprenticeship for car mechanics). Coles argues that in order to fulfil this function, credit frameworks have to provide "a universal measure of the *volume of learning* for a unit" (ibid, 21; italics as in original). Usually, this volume of learning is measured as the time it takes to learn the respective competence (ibid). It is worthwhile to look at Coles' argument in such detail since the way he presents credit systems certainly implies a high degree of modularisation. However, the 2009 recommendation on ECVET reduces the instrument to focus on mutual exchange in which national systems are left unaffected. This way, ECVET increases options for individuals to move between systems, but does not focus on reforming national VET systems (interview EU_PUBL-4). It seems that there is a difference in the policy concepts as they are envisioned by the Commission and as they are acceptable to member states which is underlined by the different preferences regarding the instrument that have been pointed out above (see Sect. 2.2). In sum, the way the instrument has been envisioned on the European level, it is not hard to foresee problems for CMEs regarding almost all their core features. However, the way the actual ECVET recommendation is designed, there is ample scope for action regarding the way instruments are implemented—and therefore it largely depends on the national implementation in how far the *Berufsprinzip* is affected or if and what modularisation is carried out.

At the same time, the origin of one of the most important and the most widespread instruments of the Copenhagen process, the EQF, is heavily based on the concept of qualifications frameworks already existing in LMEs such as the UK. Experts from the English QCA[13] have published extensively with European experts on qualifications frameworks and the EQF (Bjornavold and Coles 2007; Coles 2006, 2007). In fact, the design of the EQF shares many similarities with the English qualifications framework. Moreover, the logic of NQFs corresponds much more to LMEs than to CMEs: Qualifications frameworks in the UK were developed as a response to problems resulting from low standardisation (Kohlrausch 2009). They are a means to providing orientation and fostering comparability of qualifications. As such, qualifications frameworks serve as a currency in a market in which qualifications, providers, regulation as well as the design and tasks of public bodies change continuously. In CMEs on the other hand, VET is much more standardised regarding qualifications, contents, and providers. Therefore, qualifications frameworks are, arguably, less needed in CMEs than in LMEs in the first place.

As pointed out above, the EQF has a twofold objective. First, it aims at providing a basis for comparing qualifications across the EU and second of steering reforms on the national level. As Powell and Trampusch (2011: 294) point out, qualifications frameworks cannot be seen as mere technical instruments but also have social and political functions. As an instrument stemming from the logics of LME

---

[13]The QCA was an English non-departmental public body; its tasks were to advise the government on qualifications, curriculum and assessment as well as to regulate quality and standards of qualifications.

qualifications systems and with the purpose of steering national reforms, qualifications frameworks are clearly biased towards reforms in the direction of a LME skills regime. While this is a rather abstract argument, it can be underpinned by practical examples. On lower levels of the EQF, corresponding NQFs might manifest or formalise qualifications that are below the threshold of what is formally considered a full VET qualification in CME VET regimes. Qualifications on this level might not be able to comprise a holistic approach to VET. For the individual, qualifications below such a threshold are often related to instable employment prospectives. Consequences on wages and wage bargaining might follow. As pointed out previously, strong wage bargaining in CMEs leads to an approximation of wages of low-skilled and skilled workers, so that firms have incentives to better align the productivity of low-skilled to their wages by investing in their training (Busemeyer 2009a, based on Streeck). Moreover, the underlying concept of learning outcomes is criticised to not fully reflect a holistic understanding of VET qualifications, which also includes an individual's development of the personality (Dehnbostel et al. 2009) or the ability to reflect and act autonomously (interview DE_UN-1). The BIBB argues that descriptors overemphasise cognitive competences, which advances learning in VET schools (Baron 2007). Related to this, furthermore, an interview partner from a trade union (interview DE_UN-1) argues that descriptors on higher levels of the EQF are biased towards university qualifications. This would make the referencing of vocational qualifications to higher EQF levels more difficult than for general a education, which might undermine the status of VET. In sum, introducing NQFs has the potential to challenge two core features of CME VET regimes, namely the standardisation and the status of VET.

While the EQF and ECVET are potentially most far-reaching regarding possible impacts on national systems, the other instruments of the Copenhagen process are also biased towards LME VET systems. The validation of non-formal and informal learning as well as the shift towards learning outcomes imply that it does not matter where a qualification has been obtained. This challenges the dual system, which exactly relies on the balance between training in companies and vocational schools. It is this balance of places of learning and their specific learning methods which enables the mix between specific and general training. Traditional input-based certificates include aspects such as learning contents, educational objectives and didactics of a certain educational programme (Drexel 2005: 34). In the words of Deissinger et al. (2011: 398): "The idea of a flexible, individual and ongoing acquisition of competences which should be independent from 'input factors' corresponds with open learning arrangements that are no longer linked to specific courses, curricula, training times or examinations." These would all become much less relevant. An interview partner from Cedefop (EU_PUBL-4) points out that the concept of learning outcomes, however, can be implemented in various ways and taking into account national contexts and traditions, including a way of implementation that focuses on comprehensive qualifications. If combined with the way the

2.3 The Political Economy of the Copenhagen Process

Commission originally envisioned ECVET ("Mr. X"), this challenge would have been multiplied: According to this concept, units that were acquired via any type of learning in any country would form part of qualification in any other country. In the end, the validation of non-formal and informal learning as well as a shift towards learning outcomes at least provide a window of opportunity for a reform that challenge the *Berufsprinzip*.

The validation of non-formal and informal learning has the potential to challenge another core aspect of CME VET systems: the standardisation of contents and the certification of skills. Especially regarding industry-specific skills, certification is important for portability (Busemeyer 2009a; Estevez-Abe et al. 2001). Standardisation moreover decreases the risks employers and apprentices face when getting involved in apprenticeships (Thelen 2004: 18–19). Thelen and Busemeyer (2008: 8–9) point out that in "collectivist skill regimes", certification and the definition of skills largely rely on coordination between social partners. Standardisation of training content and certification play such important roles because once occupations are obtained, they are recognised by all firms across the whole country. In CMEs, the way validation procedures are implemented defines the impact of the procedures on the national VET systems. For example, in Germany options for external participants to take part in the VET examinations carried out by the Chambers (*Externenprüfung*) were facilitated in 2005. Here, the validation of non-formal and informal learning refers to whole occupations only, so that the skill profile itself is not affected. However, it has to be noted that hurdles for individual learners to get competences and skills recognised are lower if units of certification are smaller. Installing validation procedures that build on smaller units on the other hand bears the risk of creating an ' la carte system' next to the original VET system. Employers might not train apprentices for full qualifications, but instead only for a few units and have these validated subsequently. This would not only change the balance between general and specific skills but might furthermore crowd out the formal system. As a final point, in several CMEs, certification practices involve social partners: examination committees are tripartite, and firms send their trainers to take part in the examination procedures. This mechanism might collide with validation mechanisms. Werner and Rothe (2011b: 60) argue that the German examination system will have difficulties in certifying small units since it will be too costly for firms, especially for small firms, to let their trainers participate in examination procedures too often. Therefore, Drexel (2005) argues that the implementation of the Copenhagen process leads to a certification market. Kremer (2007: 42) disagrees with this expectation: He underlines that the impact will depend on the concrete details of the implementation and that a "commercialisation" of certification procedures will not necessarily follow (ibid).

Quality assurance mechanisms in CMEs are challenged more than in LMEs. In CMEs, quality assurance is strongly based on corporatist self-supervision, national regulation of contents, and on certification. In Germany, on the local level, semi-public Chambers of Industry and Commerce (*Industrie- und Handelskammern*) monitor the content and quality of VET. Thus, they ensure the comparability of qualifications across the country (Thelen and Busemeyer 2008: 9). Examination committees are tripartite. Basic standards exist for training premises, and trainers in companies are monitored on the local level. Trade unions and employee representation in companies moreover can monitor how VET is carried out in firms. Apprentices have a set of rights based on labour legislation (Drexel 2005). Drexel (2005: 92) assumes that all these quality mechanisms would fall away with the introduction of the Copenhagen process and give place to a very heterogenic set of regulation. Since EQARF only proposes a planning cycle and a toolbox of indicators, this seems unlikely. Similar to the proceedings of Common Quality Assurance Framework, which in the end turned out too complex to steer substantial changes, the EQARF does not address a replacement of CME quality assurance. Yet, quality mechanisms developed on the EU level are more in conformity with quality assurance mechanisms of LMEs.

Another important aspect is that the more firms are involved as providers of VET, which is usually the case in apprenticeship systems, the more challenging the introduction of quality mechanisms might be. According to an interview partner, the Commission had school-based VET in mind when drafting quality assurance mechanisms (interview DE_PUBL-6). In school-based VET, the introduction of comprehensive quality mechanisms is easier (ibid). As a consequence, states with dual VET systems opposed comprehensive regulation on quality assurance (ibid). EQARF is supposed to be applied not only at the level of national VET policies, but also aims at monitoring training providers and the awarding of qualifications. Quality assurance mechanisms, however, might increase training costs for firms, and therefore change the fine balance of costs and benefits of training. Because of their cost-consciousness (Culpepper 2007), this holds especially for small and medium-sized enterprises (SMEs). SMEs have fewer resources to develop complex quality insurance measures (ENQA-VET 2008: 15). This is also why social partners understand EQARF "as a basic instrument to assist countries in developing their VET systems towards greater effectiveness" and emphasise that it should be in line with the national situation and meet the demands of SMEs. They stress that "national stakeholders should decide on how the implementation of a quality approach is made at provider-level" (ibid, 16).[14] While trade unions accept all ten EQARF indicators, employers point out that the most important indicators are the placement rate of graduates and utilisation of acquired skills at the workplace. Employers make their support of EQARF dependent on understanding indicators as a toolbox from which countries can freely choose (ibid). In sum, in general it should

---

[14]The cited paper is the outcome of a conference held in Berlin in October 2008. Social partner organisations from 15 countries took part: Austria, Cyprus, Czech Republic, Denmark, Finland, Germany, Ireland, Italy, Lithuania, Luxembourg, Malta, Norway, Poland, Slovenia, and Sweden.

2.3 The Political Economy of the Copenhagen Process   65

be possible to discuss the topic of quality of VET at provider level in all VET systems, including apprenticeship questions. It seems the way EQARF addresses quality at provider level potentially challenges firms as training providers, which is a topic prevalent in dual VET systems more than in LMEs or school-based VET systems.

Politics of Reform and Actors' Positions[15]
Social partners play an important role in the design of instruments: they take part in debates, working groups, and discussions. Four social partner organisations—the umbrella organisations of trade unions, employers, SMEs, and public employers—take part in Director General meetings (interview EU_PUBL-5). European employers' associations welcome the Copenhagen process and its initiatives (interviews EU_PRIV-1, EU_PRIV-4). Employers support ECVET and believe it is a "good instrument", as an employee of an umbrella organisation interviewed for this work reports (interview EU_PRIV-1). The EQF is seen as a "really a big step" for cooperation on EU level, which is necessary for competing on a global level (interview EU_PRIV-4). Yet, European employers' organisations criticise that there is a gap between Bologna and Copenhagen, and VET at the tertiary level is believed to be a weak spot (ibid). On the other hand, the EQF might also put pressure on universities to link their programmes to labour markets because of the competition with higher vocational degrees (interview EU_PRIV-1). In the view of business, a comprehensive credit points system is missing. For developing ECVET further, a bottom-up approach as well as further experiences are necessary (ibid). Employers' organisations fully support units, but only to a certain degree in order "to not dilute the content" (interview EU_PRIV-1). The interview partner favours an approach which makes some parts of a VET qualification compulsory, and leaves flexibility to add additional elements: "We want to keep a sensible balance on everything. And this should not be a 100 per cent flexibilisation, but it should not be 100 per cent of the German system" (ibid). Employers support quality assurance mechanisms but oppose any standardisation (ibid). Intermediary organisations can support SMEs with resources for covering implementation costs (ibid). There is a consensus between employers and trade unions in the field of education and training in general, also regarding objectives such as mobility and mutual recognition (interview EU_PRIV-4). Trade unions also welcome enhanced European cooperation on VET as well as the instruments and principles of the Copenhagen process (interview EU_UN-1). ECVET is seen as a good result; the interview partner emphasises especially its use for European integration as a result of mutual

---

[15]While the focus of my empirical analysis is on the three country case studies, conducting interviews with European actors has been necessary for this study in order to profoundly analyse the instruments and principles developed in the realm of the Copenhagen process. This section should be understood as providing first insights rather than a similar thorough process tracing and empirical analysis as in the country cases.

exchange. Negative effects can be hindered with the right implementation of the instrument. The validation of non-formal and informal learning is seen as a chance for those 80 million European workers without formal qualifications but with work experience (ibid).

The Commission sees itself as being "quite important" in the field of VET and to be "the institution that takes most initiative" (interview EU_PUBL-5). The Commission is "a little bit surprised" that the large majority of member states treats EQF and ECVET as separate instruments (interview EU_PUBL-1). A Commission official expects that in the long run, around 2020, EQF will have stronger links to credits: "A European credit and qualifications system might not be inconceivable. (…) I expect that this should be the way to go, linking up qualifications frameworks and credit systems" (ibid). This is closely related to a call for the introduction of 'flexible à la carte' concepts (European Commission 2010: 4): VET systems should be "more flexible and modularised and should offer individualised learning pathways" (ibid, 8). As an interview partner from the European Parliament remarks, the Commission either does not believe that à la carte systems pose problems, or aims at leaving room for interpretation (interview EU_PUBL-3). It is clear that the Commission understands flexible pathways as an advantage for individuals changing pathways or careers, getting access to VET, upgrading skills, combining learning with having a family or with working, or making learning possible for individuals with disabilities. In general, with flexible pathways, individuals can move more easily (interview EU_PUBL-5). In line with this, flexibility is understood as flexibility "first of all of the systems, so that they don't close doors (…). Also, flexibility is to let people learn at a time and a place which best suits them" (ibid). This also includes fostering modularisation. As another interview partner from the Commission (interview EU_PUBL-1) states:

> It is a fact that people nowadays need to refresh their skills more often than they used to (…). So I think going towards a more modular approach will be just about necessary. This does require a credit-based approach. (…) There is more and more talk on flexible pathways in learning and in occupations because this is (…) an objective need. And certainly one tool to (…) react to this objective need will be modular systems, and then credit systems become the only way to make the link between the content and the formal recognition of the content. So this will be the necessary way to go.

The interview partner therefore clearly supports a combination of credit points, modularisation and flexible pathways. By portraying such policies as an "objective need", instruments and principles are framed as technical instruments. As I showed above, this is not the case if instruments and principles are analysed against the background of a political economy perspective.

A sequence from an interview with another Commission official provides interesting insights, albeit the interview partner clearly states that it is a personal opinion and not an official EU position:

Interviewer	"In Germany, many people fear that the European processes will (...) lead towards (...) a modularisation of the VET system.
Interview partner	Would that be a (...) bad thing?
Interviewer	Well, would you say it's one of the intentions of the European Commission?
Interview partner	No, no I'm not saying that, no. But I really can't understand the argument, that's why would modularisation be a bad thing? Because I myself come from a system which is highly modularised, and I can't (...) see why it shouldn't be. This is my personal opinion. It opens so many possibilities, you can combine what you have learned, and then you find (...) your way in the labour market. (...)
Interviewer	Of course it is also the question how you understand modularisation, because it can refer to two different things. It can refer to (...) on the one hand (...) to different units within a VET course, but it would aim at a (...) full qualification, or on the other hand, secondly, modularisation could be a really flexible à la carte system.
Interview partner	Yes.
Interviewer	Of course that is two different things.
Interview partner	Yes. And I find both things quite good, but I (...) haven't really followed the German discussion on that so I don't want to take any position on that. (...) We know that in Europe there are systems which are almost, or to a very great extent, à la carte systems, and they cater very very well the special needs of different persons."

2.4 Conclusion

In this chapter, I argue that the instruments and principles developed within the realm of the Copenhagen process are biased towards general skills and liberalisation—and hence towards LME VET systems. Partially, instruments and principles are based on existing practices in LMEs. Another important finding is that the European Commission had envisioned the instruments to be even more challenging to CMEs. As regard to ECVET, I found that the Commission aimed at designing the instrument in a more far-reaching way: individuals ("Mr. X") would have had the opportunity to acquire modules in any member state and have these recognised as a full qualification in any (other) member state. In the end, European actors did not find the necessary support on the member state level for these proposals. In my interviews with the European Commission and my document analysis, I found that the European Commission still at least sees many advantages in flexible pathways, a combined qualifications and credit system, and an à la carte system.

Numerous authors, especially in Germany, argue that EQF and ECVET require a modularisation of the system. This opens the door for and might be combined with de-standardisation of training contents and assessments. As a consequence, such institutional changes might lead to a dilution of CME VET systems, since employers might stop investing in broader industry-specific skills but pick and choose only those firm-specific skills they have an immediate need for. I conclude that modularisation *facilitates* the implementation of EU VET policies. Making qualifications more transparent and transferring them across Europe is easier with smaller units than with complex qualifications. I argue that an impact on the VET systems' core institutions is a possible outcome of the Copenhagen process in spite of the nature of the instruments as "soft law". Within the group of CME countries, there seems to be a difference in how far countries are challenged by instruments and principles endorsed by the Copenhagen process, with the question in how far VET provision is school-based being one decisive factor for this difference.

Yet, another important conclusion is that different assessments exist in the literature regarding the question if modularisation is a *necessary* precondition for the implementation of the instruments and principles developed within the realm of the Copenhagen process, especially since ample scope is left to member states regarding different options for implementation.

Chapter 3
The Impact of the Copenhagen Process on the German Training Regime

This chapter presents the case study on Germany. The first subsection will provide an overview on the German VET system under consideration of current changes and challenges and derive core features of the German collective skill formation system. The second subsection will firstly present the early discussion on EU policies and then secondly lay out the implementation process for each instrument. In each subsection, I will link my analysis both to actors' positions and the core features of the system. The conclusion will summarise my findings and then discuss them against the background of the core features of the system and the existing literature.

3.1 The German VET System[1]

Dual VET is often considered to be a show-piece, "a flagship of the German education system and a major pillar of the economic strength of Germany" (BMBF 2010: 9).[2] Today, this seems true more than ever, since many countries turn to the German dual system to understand the comparatively low youth unemployment rate. Moreover, the system is widely believed to be an important pillar among those institutions that support the German "diversified quality production" (Streeck 1991), which also has been called the "high skill, high wage, high value-added ('high everything') economy" (Thelen 2004: 6). The training regime stands out as the reason for the large percentage of the workforce with skills on the intermediary level. Political economy scholars developed an interest in the system, since it is able to solve collective action problems that usually trouble private-sector

---

[1]Section 3.1 is partially based on Ante (2008) and Ante (2009).
[2]Original: "Die duale Berufsausbildung ist ein Flaggschiff des deutschen Bildungssystems und eine tragende Säule der ökonomischen Stärke Deutschlands."

training regimes (Busemeyer and Thelen 2011; Culpepper 1999a, b; Finegold and Soskice 1988; Hall and Soskice 2001; Soskice 1994; Thelen 2004). The central point is that firms in Germany invest in skills that are potentially useful to other firms, including their competitors.

The German apprenticeship system has a long tradition dating back to the crafts in the Middle Ages. Certifications of skills, standardisation, and broad and comprehensive training contents were decisive for the development of the German VET system (Busemeyer and Thelen 2011).[3] The dual system is an occupation-driven system that combines on-the-job training in firms with training spent at part-time vocational schools. Schools cover both general education—such as history or languages—and subjects related to the occupation. This "dual" combination of learning locations was established in order to combine learning with working and structured knowledge with occupational proficiency. The underlying idea is the "vocational principle" (*Berufsprinzip*) according to which a worker has a holistic understanding of the occupation and is able to perform his tasks autonomously. Therefore, the dual system produces "broader skills than required by immediate product or labor market pressures" and an "excess pool of 'flexible', polyvalent workers and skills" (Streeck 1991: 53). The distinct mix of skills is the outcome of specific training at firms and broad and general skills acquired at schools. Companies can fit training to their needs but also have to follow regulation on training content. The balance of skills is slightly biased towards specific skills (Anderson and Hassel 2013). Still, skills are transferable to other employers in the sense that they are industry-specific (Estevez-Abe et al. 2001, see Sect. 1.1). They are non-academic/occupational, broad and portable in the sense of Streeck's (2011) framework.

Apprentices enter the system after secondary education from the age of 16 onwards, although the average age of entrance rose to approximately 20 years (BIBB 2012a). Around a fifth of the new apprentices possess a university entrance qualification. Apprentices apply to companies for apprenticeships. Subsequently, a close-by school is allocated. The apprentice spends 1 or, at the most, 2 days per week at school. Firms decide on the number of apprenticeship places they offer. After a testing phase of 3 months, it is legally difficult for the employer to terminate apprenticeships prior to its full completion. Yet, 23 % of all contracts are terminated early, with differing numbers across sectors and regions (BIBB 2012a, data for 2010). As a precondition for the participation in the exams, the apprentice has to keep minutes on the training. Independent Committees of local Chambers of Industry and Commerce—and respectively the Chambers of the craft sector—organise examinations for all recognised vocational qualifications. Examinations are carried out by a tripartite committee of employers, employees and VET school teachers.

---

[3]See Thelen (2004) for an analysis of the German system from a historical institutionalism perspective.

3.1 The German VET System

The German VET system is characterised by strong collective elements and high levels of coordination. Chambers organise examinations, monitor whether companies fulfil the required regulations, and appoint consultants who supervise training in firms. Regulation exists for the suitability of training premises and of trainers in firms as well as the appropriateness of the ratio between apprentices and skilled staff. Sanction mechanisms—such as taking away the training license—can be imposed on companies. Chambers provide support to stakeholders and pass on information to and between firms, which is important for coordination among firms and hence for overcoming strategic defection (Culpepper 1999b). Social partners are involved in VET Committees, which exist on regional level, in each *Land*,[4] and on the federal level via the advisory "main committee" of the BIBB. Furthermore, social partners negotiate the apprentices' salaries in collective bargaining. Apprentices' wages are usually low, often below a living wage, and depend on the respective occupation. On the firm level, work councils have statutorily embedded rights to monitor the firm's apprenticeship programmes and participate in decision-making on VET.

Together with social partners, the state sets the framework for VET. The content of training is regulated by standardised training ordinances (*Ausbildungsordnungen*), which are enacted by the Federal Ministry of Economics and Technology after having been developed in close co-operation with social partners in a standardised procedure. Here, employers ensure that skills match the needs of firms, while trade unions lobby for skills to be broad and general rather than firm-specific and narrow (Culpepper 2003). This procedure leads to training contents being highly standardised. Taken together with the certification of skills after final examinations, standardisation leads to a high acceptance of apprenticeships skills by other employers. Therefore, there is a vital external occupational labour market (Soskice 1994). Apprenticeship graduates are able to find employment in other companies with adequate remuneration. Firms on the other hand are also able to recruit skilled labour on the external labour market.

For an apprenticeship system, firm involvement is crucial. Training apprentices is a major recruiting strategy for companies (BMBF 2007; Walden 2006). About a quarter of the German companies train; there are differences depending on company size, economic sector and region. The motivation to train differs across firms (Anderson and Hassel 2013; Busemeyer and Thelen 2011; Culpepper and Thelen 2008; Soskice 1994). In this literature, it is argued that on the one hand, especially in manufacturing, large and medium-sized companies train in order to fill their internal labour markets. Large companies often run separate training facilities and are motivated to get involved in training because they can train high-skilled employees according to their production needs. Training is often more intensive and costly than regulation would require. At the same time, they use

---

[4]Germany is a federal republic. *Länder* (singular: *Land*) are partly sovereign constituent states of the federal republic. The 16 *Länder* have jurisdiction in some important policy areas, such as in education, culture and media policies.

apprenticeships as a prolonged test period. Large firms might also fear an image loss if they do not participate in training, and they can use training as a political tool in their relationships with state and unions. On the other hand, in the craft sector training usually takes place on the job and training is often less sophisticated in the usage of technology. During busy times, apprentices can be used as cheap labour, while additionally required instruction can take place during slack periods. The ratio of apprentices that continue working at the training company after completing training is much lower. Albeit motivations for getting involved in training differ, the benefits outweigh costs.[5]

Firms are therefore highly involved in the financing of VET, but the state also invests. Most importantly, the state runs VET schools. *Länder* are responsible for VET schools' curricula and employ teachers, while local authorities are in charge of schools regarding materials and maintenance. The federal state funds the BIBB, which provides research and advises policy makers. The Federal Employment Agency (*Bundesagentur für Arbeit*, BA) and *Länder* finance vocational preparation schemes (see below). Furthermore, apprentices contribute to financing by accepting lower wages during the training period. Data from Dustmann and Schoenberg (2008: 91) suggest that while apprentices even bear more than 70 % of training costs, both firms and apprentices still gain returns from participating in training (ibid). The costs of training are therefore shared between firms, the state, and apprentices. In the understanding of the political economy literature, sharing costs for training is a "balancing act" (Anderson and Hassel 2013: 175).

VET in Germany: Only Standardised Apprenticeships in the Dual System?

While the apprenticeship system is the most important strand in German VET and the majority of school leavers has a preference for starting an apprenticeship after graduation (BMBF 2007: 59–65), there are two further pathways in German VET. First, full-time school-based VET can lead to full vocational qualifications. This form of VET is most important in the social and health sector, for media and IT occupations, and for science-related assistance and laboratory occupations (*Assistentenberufe*). School-based training is usually regulated by *Länder* governments; for some professions, especially in the health sector, federal frameworks exist. Phases of training in firms or internships are always integrated into curricula. While vocational schools in the above-mentioned occupations are widely acknowledged, school-based VET can also be offered as an alternative to the apprenticeship

---

[5]The positive cost-benefit calculation has been underpinned by continuous research by the BIBB (for example Schönfeld et al. 2010). It is found that important incentives for firms to get involved in training are reducing costs for the recruitment of personnel and a better performance of employees who have been trained in the own company. Moreover, offering apprenticeships improves the image of the company. 90 % of all companies are satisfied with the cost-benefit of training (ibid).

system. In these cases, a clear hierarchy developed according to which vocational schools only constitute the second-best option compared to an apprenticeship.[6]

Second, there are a number of different programmes bundled in the so-called "transition system" (*"Übergangssystem"*). They aim at helping school leavers who are not yet ready enough to start an apprenticeship (*"ausbildungsreif"*) to enter the dual system. Programmes include the various vocational preparation schemes offered by the BA. Moreover, there are two school-based programmes which last 1 year, namely *Schulisches Vorbereitungsjahr* and *Berufsgrundbildungsjahr*, the latter higher-ranking since it can be credited to an apprenticeship. *Berufsfachschulen*, a specific type of vocational school, are usually considered to be a part of the transition system although they do not offer certificated vocational education but general school-leaving qualifications on different educational levels. Among other programmes, they include vocational baccalaureate diplomas (*Fachhochschulreife*). These do not only prepare for VET, but also enable graduates to enter universities of applied sciences and therefore differ slightly in their aim and target group. In conclusion, it is apparent that the programmes of the "transition system" differ considerably regarding the level of training. They are not connected with each other. Only few can be credited towards an apprenticeship, and in practice it depends on the firm if it is possible to do so. With increasing numbers of participants, the "transition system" has been heavily criticised, as will be outlined below. Qualification modules (*Qualifizierungsbausteine*) have been introduced for specific target groups in vocational preparation schemes, which are "only loosely related to the content of occupational profiles" (Thelen and Busemeyer 2008: 18).

Within the dual system, differentiations have developed at both ends. The federal government had already called for more differentiation in apprenticeships since the late 1980s (Busemeyer and Thelen 2011). First, at the lower end, shortened apprenticeships of 2 years were established in 2003. The idea behind this reform was to increase the number of apprenticeships and create opportunities for school leavers who might not be able to complete a full, "regular", apprenticeship. At the same time, studies had identified firm needs for qualifications that are below full apprenticeships and tailored specifically to the needs of the firm (Busemeyer 2012). Currently, there are 40 shortened apprenticeship occupations which make up for almost one tenth of all apprenticeships (BMBF 2012a: 20). Trade unions oppose the introduction of 2-year-programmes.[7] School leavers with lower academic records would need better support and more time, not less, to finish an apprenticeship. Moreover, trade unions believe that shortened apprenticeships are lacking quality and permeability. Indeed, a BIBB study shows that only 28 % of graduates

---

[6]For a more detailed discussion on the role of schools in German VET see Anderson and Hassel (2013), Baethge et al. (2007), Feller (1999), Franz and Soskice (1995), Walden (2006).

[7]Instead, they favour "training by stages" (*Stufenausbildung*), in which the next stage of an apprenticeship can only be entered after the prior stage has been completed successfully. The difference is that it does not depend on the firm if apprentices can continue with their training.

from 2-year apprenticeships continue training in order to then graduate from standard apprenticeships of 3 or 3½ years (Uhly et al. 2011). Second, on the higher end of VET, "dual study" programmes (*duales Studium*) have become increasingly popular with around 50,000 students in 2009 (Purz 2011). There are different types of programmes, but all combine training in companies with studies at a tertiary level mostly leading to bachelor's degrees. The programmes are more demanding than apprenticeships regarding their pace and level. For companies, dual study programmes are a means to increase the number of highly qualified employees, to recruit them for working in their company and for training tertiary students in firm-specific skills (ibid). To conclude, new programmes at both ends of the dual system apparently filled a need for more differentiation.

In addition, another 5.3 % of all apprenticeships have been financed by the state in 2011 (BIBB 2012a: 18). Here, training is offered either by external providers in close co-operation with local enterprises (*betriebsnah*) or as non-company training (*außerbetrieblich*). The share of 2-year programmes is high. Although evaluations show that apprentices who were trained in close co-operation with local enterprises attain comparable results as graduates from dual apprenticeship programmes (Berger and Walden 2002), in practice stigmata exist. This is because firms cream off the best school leavers. After unification, extra-company training was heavily used in Eastern Germany, since the market could not provide sufficient numbers of dual apprenticeships. Since the relationship between supply and demand of apprenticeships is improving, funding for extra-company training has been reduced.

While most continued training is market-led, several options for upgrade training (*Aufstiegsfortbildung*) exist for which contents are regulated. Candidates take final examinations that are vastly portable. Examples are *Meister* qualifications,[8] technicians, and business administration specialists. For participants in these programmes, financial support for the costs of preparatory courses and final examinations is available as well as contributions for their living expenses during exam preparation periods.

Changes and Challenges

During the last two decades, the relative number of participants in the different VET tracks changed substantially. While the percentage of school leavers that enter the dual system decreased, the number of participants in the "transition system" rose tremendously. One reason has been a mismatch between supply and demand of apprenticeships at the beginning of the 2000s. There had been a substantial shift on the demand side due to demographic trends without a similar increase on the supply side due to an economic downturn and an unfavourable situation on the general labour market. After 2006, the supply-demand-relationship began to improve again. Yet, the relationship between the different pathways has changed permanently: Participation rates increased slightly in school-based VET and, more rapidly, in higher education. With the number of school leavers decreasing and more school

---

[8] Also called master craftsman; certifies comprehensive and advanced occupational competence as well as knowledge of business administration.

graduates entering higher education, recruiting apprentices becomes more difficult. In spite of these developments, a substantial numbers of "outsiders" is still not able to enter the dual system.

The problems at the transition stage from schools to apprenticeships are likely to have structural reasons. The number of school leavers who do not find an apprenticeship is still considerable even today, when firms are complaining about the lack of applicants—and the number of outsiders is much higher than official statistics suggest at first glance: approximately 1.4 million young persons between the ages of 20 and 29 are non-skilled (BIBB 2009: 215). Success rates of the various pre-apprenticeship programmes differ, and it is often criticised that in practice not enough participants actually move on to apprenticeships in the dual system. One reason for these problems is a mismatch between the skills that school leavers inherit and those skills firms are looking for. On the one hand, training ordinances became more and more demanding over time. This upskilling was jointly promoted by employers' organisations, trade unions and the government (Streeck 2011) and was undertaken in order to meet market developments and keep track of technological advancement (Culpepper and Thelen 2008). On the other hand, demand for training on lower levels grew with the expansion of education, immigration and the political objective to diminish unskilled labour (Anderson and Hassel 2013). Firms could not fully respond to these requests, especially not with the decreasing size of the artisan sector, which traditionally takes in academically weak students (ibid). Elementary and secondary schools cannot keep up with the trend of upskilling, either.[9]

The mismatch between supply and demand which culminated around 2006 leads to another question: Why have firms not, as they previously did in times when demand for apprenticeships exceeded supply, offered more places? During the mismatch between supply and demand created by demographic changes and the effect of the oil crisis occurred in the late 1970s, firms increased the number of apprenticeships (Baethge et al. 2007: 24; Busemeyer and Thelen 2011). While in particular large firms would tune down their programmes, small firms would offer more places and benefit from cheap labour. As a last resort, employers' organisations would pressure their members to provide more places (ibid). The literature presents several reasons why firms did not pursue the same strategies in the last decade: firstly, companies' scope of action is believed to be more limited in the light

---

[9]The question of whether more and more school leavers do not have the necessary qualifications for starting an apprenticeship ("*Ausbildungsreife*") is contested. On the one hand, surveys among firms (i.e. DIHK 2010) find that firms more often cannot fill all places since they have fewer applicants and believe that those who do apply often lack (social and formal) qualifications. On the other hand, a BIBB study shows that the number of applications also depends on the way firms design the transition process and on the attractiveness of the firm (Gericke et al. 2009). The authors, moreover, criticise that firms' expectations regarding competences and soft skills are too high. An interview partner from the federal administration suggests that it is easier for firms to claim there are problems outside of the dual system than to invest in the quality of training (interview DE_PUBL-2).

of global competition and global financial markets. Cost-consciousness increased, the governance and management of companies changed, rationalisation took hold and production processes were altered (Baethge et al. 2007: 35; Crouch et al. 1999; Hillmert 2002). Company structures changed (Baethge et al. 2007; Euler 1998). Therefore, companies might couple the number of apprenticeships closer to their own future skill needs while paying less attention to political lobbying. Secondly, the power of employers' organisations to mobilise their members declined and it is more difficult for them to influence firms' training decisions or even exercise control (Streeck 2011). Finally, while the artisan sector in the past pushed for more apprenticeship places when demand exceeded supply, the sector has declined in size (Anderson and Hassel 2013).

Analysts of the German VET system have observed that training strategies have changed. In the last decades, the number of firms that offer apprenticeships decreased. Smaller firms are more likely to refrain from training than bigger firms, as they are more vulnerable to the rising costs involved (Culpepper and Thelen 2008). Streeck (2011) points at specialisation, competitive pressures and turnover among SMEs, which all increased over time. At the same time, employers' organisations are less able to control their members, and therefore are less able to provide mutual assurance that the majority of firms take part in training (Streeck 2011). Moreover, another worrisome trend is looming: due to demographic trends, the number of school leavers is going to decrease. Against the background of experiences in Eastern Germany, where demographic change took place earlier, this is likely to lead to a divided labour market in which skilled workers have a high market value and at the same time unemployment or unstable and low-paid employment prevails for unskilled workers (Ante 2010). The crafts sector and regions with fewer school leavers—such as Eastern Germany—will have to increase efforts to find apprentices (Troltsch et al. 2012). In these regions and sectors, firms might increasingly back out of the apprenticeship system. There might be a tipping point after which incentives to participate in VET continuously decrease because poaching increases (Culpepper 1999b).

Different assessments exist in the literature regarding the question of whether the rise of the service sector poses structural problems to the dual system. Although manufacturing is still comparatively strong in Germany and will remain an important source of jobs, the service sector has grown in importance. This poses a threefold challenge to the dual system: first, newly emerging companies in the service sector do not have a VET tradition and therefore are less likely to train. Secondly, there are signs that companies in the service sector have different recruitment strategies and tend to hire either unskilled workers or university graduates (Thelen 2004). Finally, several authors argue that the skills needed in the service sector are different from those needed in manufacturing, namely broader and more systematic (Aff 2005; Anderson and Hassel 2013; Baethge et al. 2007; Gonon 2004). Culpepper and Thelen (2008: 35) put it this way: "Many elements of the service sector depend less on the broad technological training that is a requisite for diversified quality production." In the end, the industrial origin of the apprenticeship system might hinder its take-up in the service sector (Baethge et al. 2007;

Thelen 2007). Even more, it might slow down the growth of the service sector as such (Baethge et al. 2007) and impede adjustment to de-industrialisation (Anderson and Hassel 2013).

The comparative political economy literature so far has not paid attention to the arguments put forward by authors of the BIBB regarding the suitability of the dual system for services. On the basis of empirical analysis, they show that the share of apprentices as a percentage of the total employment differs only slightly in secondary and tertiary sectors (Uhly and Troltsch 2009; Walden 2009). Instead, the growing relative importance of the tertiary sector for employment is coupled to the distribution of apprenticeships (Uhly and Troltsch 2009: 20). The share of apprentices in these occupations is lower than the share of employees in these occupations. It is, however, important to distinguish between primary and secondary service-orientated occupations[10]: While in primary service-related occupations the share of apprentices is gaining on the respective share of employees, in secondary service-related occupations it has been about 15 % lower in 2006 (ibid). In the latter group, the qualifications level of employees is higher than the average. Over time, a decrease of low-skilled employees can be observed, while the importance of apprenticeships has been traditionally low but did not further decrease (Uhly and Troltsch 2009: 26f; Walden 2009). In sum, while apprenticeships are a substantial part of firms' recruiting strategies in the service sector, the importance of intermediate skills is indeed lower in the knowledge-intensive secondary service occupations.

As a final point, Busemeyer and Thelen (2011) argue that the German VET system drifts away from collective skill formation towards segmentalism. This is advantageous especially for large training companies, since training is increasingly orientated towards internal labour markets. Segmentalisation stems from trends such as the shifts from manufacturing to services or intensified competition in globalised markets which put pressure on labour markets and on wage policy. As a result, preferences of firms become more heterogeneous. Moreover, both the trend of decentralisation in bargaining and a rise in low-wage jobs lead to a higher wage differentiation. This affects VET because incentives to train are reduced and pressures for more differentiation in jobs increase. Busemeyer and Thelen argue that incremental adjustments have been made to accommodate these new needs. There is increasing skill differentiation and demands for modularisation and decentralised examinations. With rising wage differentiation, firms more and more realign payment structures to match the skill content of jobs. They align both quantity and content of training more specifically to concrete needs (ibid). The 2005 Vocational Training Act allowed for the inclusion of additional competences as an optional variant in order to meet demands arisen from changes in technology

---

[10]Primary service-orientated occupations include occupations such as trade, office management and general services such as cleaning, catering, storing, and transportation. Employment in secondary service-orientated occupations includes knowledge-intensive activities such as research, development, organisation, management, coaching, consulting, teaching and publishing (Uhly and Troltsch 2009).

or from distinct needs in certain regions or industries (Thelen 2007). Firms still have to fulfil national standards, but have more options to customise training within broad profiles. While large firms lobby for more decentralisation of wage bargaining and flexibility in training with a stronger focus on internal labour markets, small firms increasingly opt out of both (ibid). Busemeyer and Thelen (ibid, 70) conclude: "The result is a relaxation of the external supports for Germany's collectives system of training and a noticeable shift toward a more segmentalist training system."

Core Features of the German Training Regime

So far, this section has laid out constitutive features of the German collective skill provision regime as well as changes and challenges to the system. The following four aspects are defined as constitutive for the German training regime: the high involvement of employers' organisations in the organisation and financing of training and an institutionalised cooperation between state and social partners; the "dual training" mode which provides a distinct skill mix of broad and industry-specific skills on an intermediate level; highly standardised certification and training content leading to a high portability; and the high status of VET as a viable educational path after secondary education.[11] The following section will trace the implementation of the Copenhagen process in Germany and analyse in how far central pillars of the German VET systems have potentially and actually been affected by them.

3.2 Implementation of the Copenhagen Process in Germany

Discussions on the European level about the Copenhagen process and its instruments soon made their way to Germany and ignited a fierce discussion on the potential impact of EU policies on German VET. Before the recommendations on EQF and ECVET—the most influential instruments in this debate—were issued in 2008 and 2009 respectively, the discussion was mostly based on assumptions about the design of EU instruments, unpublished reports of those experts taking part in discussions on the European level and, later on, on the documents of the consultation processes. Since this debate does not focus on the implementation of the instruments but took place beforehand, Sect. 3.2.1 covers the early discussion on the impact of the Copenhagen process. It is followed by subsections on the implementation of the concrete instruments. The observation period for the German case lasted until the summer of 2012 and interviews were carried out between November 2011 and April 2012. Only in a few exceptions were posterior events included.

---

[11]This definition largely follows Trampusch (2010b: 551). While Trampusch defines three constitutive elements of the German VET system, here the status of VET as a viable alternative to tertiary education is added as a fourth element.

3.2.1 Early Discussions on the European Qualifications Framework and the European Credit System for Vocational Education and Training

From about 2005 onwards, a vivid and controversial debate on EU VET policies and their impact on the apprenticeship system took place in Germany. Discussions took place mostly in expert circles, but at several points in time—which will be mentioned throughout this chapter—the issue was present in mainstream media. The federal parliament discussed EU VET policies several times (Deutscher Bundestag 2006, 2007, 2008, 2009, 2010a, 2011, 2012).

It is important to note that the discussion on EU initiatives started when the system's malfunctioning was discussed; thus, it was intertwined with aspects that had already been debated in the national realm. The mismatch between supply and demand of apprenticeships had reached a peak around 2005. This steered discussions on the future of the system. At the same time, the lacking permeability towards higher education and continuing VET had already been criticised for many years. Frank and Hensge summarise the European influence on the reform discussions as follows: "The European efforts to create a European education area increase the pressure to foster transparency, comparability and permeability and hereby ensuring the connectivity with European standards on qualifications (Frank and Hensge 2007: 41)."[12] In a similar vein, Hanf and Rein (2007: 8) point out that discussions on the German Qualifications Framework (*Deutscher Qualifikationsrahmen für lebenslanges Lernen*, DQR) took up different aspects and problems that had already been discussed at the national level.

The debate on the European policy initiatives has been very controversial. The issue of modularisation, which had already been discussed in the 1990s on the national level (Busemeyer 2012), was intertwined with EU VET policies. Authors such as Dehnbostel et al. (2009), Hanf and Rein (2006a), Rauner (2006), and Werner and Rothe (2011a: 3) all believe that EQR and ECVET require a very encompassing degree of modularisation that will fundamentally transform German VET. Mucke (2004), another BIBB expert, underlines the expectation that ECVET would have vast effects. According to her assessment, the instrument would not only be used for transferring and accumulating credit points for learning outcomes that are accomplished abroad, but also for those acquired within Germany. A joint credit system for all different educational sectors is perceived to be crucial for mobility across different economic sectors, for permeability between VET and universities and for mobility across European countries. Mucke points out that she has an "optimistic" view on the future implementation of ECVET (Mucke

---

[12]Original: "Die deutsche Berufsbildung muss auch international anschluss- und wettbewerbsfähig werden. Die europäischen Bestrebungen zur Schaffung eines europäischen Bildungsraumes erhöhen den Druck, mehr Transparenz, Gleichwertigkeit und Durchlässigkeit zu fördern und auf diesem Wege die Anschlussfähigkeit mit europäischen Qualifikationsstandards sicherzustellen."

2004: 12), which also indicates the positive attitude of the BIBB towards VET reform. In a similar vein, Hanf and Rein (2006a), working on the EQF/DQR at the BIBB, believe that the introduction of a national qualifications framework would require substantial changes. They emphasise that qualifications would need to be tailored closer to firms' needs and enable a "pin-pointed personnel recruitment and development". Individuals would then have "easier access to qualifications" and benefit from a "shorter duration of education and training". Although the vocational principle and the combination of practical and theoretical learning should not be abolished, Hanf and Rein's understanding of what is necessary to implement a qualifications framework still implies a shift towards a more market-based system. In sum, several authors from the BIBB argued that EU VET policies would foster changes in the direction of more market-based institutions and expected fundamental changes as a consequence of the implementation of EQF and ECVET.

Not only authors from the BIBB, but also other experts expected fundamental transformations. Rauner (2006: 52) argues that ECVET implies an "a la carte" system, in which apprentices and firms can freely choose which units to pick. In an article in the weekly newspaper *DIE ZEIT*, Rauner (2005) claims that by following the EU lead on qualifications frameworks, actors in German education policy would "(...) accept the risk of sacrificing a highlight of German business culture for an inferior European solution."[13] If modularisation is understood as such an "à la carte" concept in which firms can "pick and choose" from modules instead of relying on standardised occupational profiles, this would indeed imply a profound transformation of the German VET system (Busemeyer and Thelen 2011). Apprentices would learn to perform tasks that are useful to the firm only. Drexel (2005) takes a very critical stand on EU VET policies and sees EQF and ECVET as a distinct system which is not compatible with the dual system. In her view, the full implementation of EU policies would lead to modularisation, the abolishment of the *Berufsprinzip* and the capability to perform an occupation autonomously (*berufliche Handlungsfähigkeit*), broad changes in curricula and didactics, a liberalisation of initial VET, the privatisation or closing down of public VET schools, and stopping public funding of VET. She understands validation of informal learning as a substitute for currently existing educational pathways and learning outcomes as focussing on economic aspects only. In her view, two routes for the development of the system are possible: replacing the German dual VET system with EU instruments or the co-existence of both systems. However, Drexel's expertise is criticised as lacking substantial evidence for her claims on the impact of EU instruments (interview DE_PUBL-2). While Drexel might be among the most critical authors on EU VET policies and predicts more fundamental effects on the national system than other authors, yet in sum several authors shared the view that the Copenhagen process requires encompassing changes of the dual system towards modularisation and privatisation.

---

[13]Original: "(...) das Risiko in Kauf nehmen, einen der Glanzpunkte deutscher Unternehmenskultur einer schlechteren europäischen Lösung zu opfern."

Other contributions to the debate argued that although EQF and ECVET would require vast changes, instruments and principles could be implemented in a way that is in line with the German VET system. Kremer (2007) argues that the EQF implies the ability to combine different qualifications, and for this they have to be divided into smaller units. ECVET can make these assessable. Still, units could also be examined as a whole, within nationally regulated full qualifications (ibid). This understanding is in line with the portability and certification of skills. Thelen and Busemeyer (2008; cf. Baethge et al. 2007) also point out that modularisation would be consistent with the existing system if it refers to skill acquisition.

Reform Proposals and Initiatives

At that time, several initiatives and reform proposals were discussed that aimed at flexibilising VET. The idea was to increase incentives for firms to get involved in training and for offering more apprenticeships. In spring 2006, the Federal Minister of Education and Research at that time, Annette Schavan, initiated an "innovation circle on VET" (*Innovationskreis Berufliche Bildung*). The government argued that reforms are necessary because of European proceedings; the innovation circle was initiated to develop reform proposals (interview DE_PUBL-1). Members included representatives from *Länder* administrations, social partners, the BIBB, the BA, VET schools, firms, and researchers. Thelen and Busemeyer (2008: 18) argue that members were chosen for "attenuating the voting and opinion power of potentially 'obstructionist' parties."

The circle commissioned an expertise (Euler and Severing 2006) that was influential for the debate on modularisation, so that it is worthwhile to look at it in detail. Euler and Severing propose to divide apprenticeships into smaller modules—called "building blocks" (*Ausbildungsbausteine*). They argue that building blocks can improve transitions between schools and apprenticeships as well as provide options for amplifying competences, in addition to and on top of apprenticeships. Building blocks are defined as standardised entities that together make up a holistic and occupation-orientated apprenticeship. Apprenticeship contracts would still cover whole apprenticeships and final examinations would not be abolished. Vocational preparation schemes could be credited towards apprenticeships or extra-company training. This should, so the authors argue, contribute to easing the problems on the apprenticeship market. The expertise lays out two different variants for reform. The first includes an intermediate examination after the first year as well as a final examination, whereas in the second model each building block could be followed by an examination which then would be credited towards the final examination. In the latter variant, building blocks could be assessed directly at the place of learning. The authors believe that modularisation would help increase the fit to Europe (ibid). In sum, while both variants leave the skill profile unaffected, the more encompassing second variant challenges the portability of skills, since parts of the examinations could be shifted to the training firm.

In 2007, the innovation circle presented its final recommendations (Innovationskreis Berufliche Bildung 2007). One of the ten so-called guidelines deals with the introduction of "building blocks": A pilot project was initiated in order to test the introduction of such "building blocks" in 25 regions in Germany. Moreover, social partners were asked to test a new structure for apprenticeships which is geared towards a common core qualification for occupation groups and subsequent specialisation. Although this does not imply full-scale modularisation, Thelen and Busemeyer (2008: 18) argue that "now occupational profiles themselves are broken down into modules." The new concept also foresees that modules can be acquired in different places of learning, and firms can choose to offer only elements of VET (ibid). The guidelines moreover call for fostering permeability between VET and higher education—including opportunities for easier admission to tertiary education after completing an apprenticeship and for crediting VET to higher education programmes.

The idea of building blocks was also taken up within the "qualification initiative" (*Qualifizierungsinitiative*) in 2008. Within this framework, federal and *Länder* governments agreed on a number of activities to foster lifelong learning. The BMBF initiated the "JOBSTARTER CONNECT" programme, which develops and tests building blocks for training. It is based on the idea to improve transitions from school to apprenticeships. Those building blocks are already used in vocational preparation schemes (interview DE_PUBL-1). Until January 2013, 40 regional projects took part in a qualification designed on the basis of building blocks. An evaluation concludes that they improve the quality of training in transition programmes, publicly financed school-based VET and second-chance qualifications (BMBF 2013). Given the small number of participants and its focus on vulnerable groups, this programme is unlikely to affect core features of the VET system as a whole.

Politics of Reform and Actors' Positions

Before the EQF recommendation was issued, German employers' organisations presented their own proposal for a qualifications framework in March 2005 which could be implemented both on the European and on the national level (KWB 2005). It is based on an initiative of the Crafts Association (*Zentralverband des Deutschen Handwerks*, ZDH) (Esser et al. 2005; see also Brunner et al. 2005; Hanf and Rein 2006b). It comprises six levels and encompasses VET and higher education. While the higher four levels share many similarities with the later EQF/DQR proposals, all qualifications below tertiary qualifications and comparable continuing VET are grouped on two levels only: all apprenticeships on level two and all vocational preparation schemes on level 1 (ibid). Descriptors are designed to reflect the concept of occupational competence. The framework is based on modularisation. At this point, employers generally believed that this would be necessary for implementing EQF and ECVET: in their view, otherwise it would hardly be possible to compare and credit whole VET qualifications across Europe (KWB 2005). In sum, employers propose a framework in which descriptors are adapted to the national context, in which both the skill profile and portability of skills would be unaffected and which would not provide incentives for differentiations and de-standardisation of apprenticeships.

After the Commission presented its EQF draft and initiated the EQF consultation process, employers prepared a joint statement in which they take a positive stand on the development of the EQF in general. In their perspective, the EQF should focus on occupational proficiency and a holistic understanding of qualifications, as well as on learning outcomes. The way EQF descriptors are designed is seen critically: in the employers' view, the differentiation between levels is not always clear-cut and the distinction between the three descriptors is artificial. Furthermore, descriptors should be complemented by a credit system (ibid) and the comparability between ECVET and ECTS should be ensured (KWB 2005). The recognition of prior learning should not take place automatically, but should be dependent on the agreement of VET providers—firms (ibid, interviews DE_PRIV-2, DE_PUBL-2, DE_UN-1). The reason is that firms would otherwise have to adapt training plans, which takes a lot of effort and is costly (interview DE_UN-1) and which may make firms hesitate to hire graduates from vocational preparatory schemes (interview DE_PRIV-2).

Employers are divided on the issue of modularisation. The Confederation of German employers (*Bundesverband der Deutschen Arbeitgeberverbände*, BDA) supports modularisation and flexibilisation of training while keeping the comprehensive and holistic orientation of apprenticeships. In a proposal for VET reform (BDA 2007), the confederation underlines that qualifications should fit the needs of firms. In times of continuous change, skills have to be updated constantly, and skill needs increasingly differ across firms. The BDA aims at strengthening dual VET by increasing flexibility, differentiation, permeability and transparency. Sectors should undertake reforms according to their own needs on the basis of several reform options:

- Apprenticeships could be divided into building blocks within occupational profiles;
- Groups of related occupations could be created for training;
- Apprenticeships could be divided into a first block of 2 years with training for competences in related occupations and a second optional block with specialised training for a specific occupation ("2 plus x").

The BDA believes that firms themselves or awarding bodies could carry out examinations, especially if sectors choose to modularise apprenticeships—since such a task would then be too time-consuming for Chambers' examination committees.[14] Intermediary examinations would then be credited towards a final

---

[14]In general, large firms increasingly challenge the nature of final examinations. This is because they send more employees to examination committees than SMEs, which is costly. Moreover, they believe that examination contents diverge too much from real work processes—if firms would hold exams they could ensure that contents matches work processes (Busemeyer and Thelen 2011). Several projects have tested different options for such firm-based examinations, including variants

examination, which could consist of a single task in which the apprentice shows her ability to act in a holistic-occupational way (ibid). Although the BDA is the employers' umbrella organisation representing all employers (interview DE_PRIV-3), it is "skewed towards the interests of large industrial firms" (Busemeyer and Thelen 2011: 87). In fact, large firms benefit the most from a segmentalist turn in VET, since they have a higher demand for more specialised skills and the necessary facilities and resources to offer specialised apprenticeships (Busemeyer and Trampusch 2011b; Thelen and Busemeyer 2008; interview DE_PRIV-1). The BDA does not support an 'à la carte' system and argues that modules should not be too small (interview DE_PRIV-3). In sum, the BDA proposal on VET reform is far-reaching and challenges the standardisation, certification and portability of skills and would require changes in the qualification structure. In their view, the EQF initiative strengthens their reform position (Trampusch 2008).

The Association of Chambers of Industry and Commerce (*Deutscher Industrie- und Handelskammertag, DIHK*) does see a need for reform of the VET system, but is not in favour of a full modularisation. The DIHK developed their own reform proposal called "dual with choice" ("*Dual mit Wahl*"), according to which dual apprenticeships would be divided into two phases (DIHK 2007). The first phase lasts 1 or 2 years and comprises core competences for a sector or for groups of occupations. In the final year, apprentices can subsequently choose between different standardised modules which they need for the respective occupation and which "accommodate the firm-specific requirements and possibilities" (ibid, 3). Apprentices with strong achievements can choose to take additional modules. Since the modules are standardised, the proposal allows for specialisation without high costs (ibid). The DIHK membership is over-proportionally made up of SMEs (interview DE_PRIV-1), so that these preferences are not surprising: Unless they have a need for very specialised skills, SMEs rely on occupational labour markets and therefore do not support a more flexible system (Busemeyer and Trampusch 2011b; Thelen and Busemeyer 2008). Even if some smaller firms might have a demand for specialised profiles, they do not have the facilities and capacities to offer specialised apprenticeship programmes (ibid). Chambers oppose a full modularisation of apprenticeships (DE_PUBL-3). In their view, companies and society need "skilled employees that are holistically educated"[15] in the sense of vocational proficiency (interview DE_PRIV-1). The idea to integrate training for related occupations in the first phase is meant to counteract disproportionate "upskilling" (see Sect. 4.1), which creates higher costs, especially for small firms. Examinations shall take place after each of the two phases (DIHK 2007). Obviously, Chambers have self-interest in defending final examinations (Busemeyer and Thelen 2011). In sum,

---

in which one trainer from another firm joins the examination in order to increase objectivity (interview DE_PRIV-3). Still, the comparability of qualifications would decrease, which proponents of such a reform acknowledge. Yet, they point to high gains from increasing flexibility (Busemeyer and Thelen 2011).

[15] Original: "ganzheitlich gebildete Fachkraft."

Chambers aim at increasing flexibility and specialisation while at the same time keeping the holistic skills profile. It allows large companies to develop their own modules, while SMEs have fewer capacities to do so (ibid).

The ZDH also opposes modularisation. Craft firms usually demand broader skills (Busemeyer and Trampusch 2011b). Moreover modularisation would decrease their options to integrate training into production processes as it would reduce the flexibility of firms regarding the point of time at which certain content is discussed or practiced (interview DE_PRIV-2). In the view of the ZDH, units or modules would make the system less flexible (ibid), and this could hinder firms—especially SMEs—from getting involved in training. The ZDH also argues that a comprehensive design of initial VET is more successful in meeting the demands of the labour market. Modules should be created for specific groups only. Furthermore, if modularisation implies examinations for each unit, costs for small firms would increase under the given system. In case they were introduced, a publicly funded examination system should be established as a second-best option (ibid). Furthermore, the ZDH is sceptical about shortening the duration of apprenticeships. As outlined above, their business case on training is based on the full contribution of apprentices to the production in their third year of training while they are still paid lower apprentice wages (Busemeyer and Thelen 2011).

Trade unions support the idea of a European education area, but at the same time they are sceptical regarding the consequences of EU instruments and their implementation on the national level. From a union's perspective, a European Education Area provides advantages to the individual when it improves options for learning and working in other European countries (DGB 2005). Improving horizontal and vertical permeability have been on the trade union's agenda for a long time. At the same time, many members criticise the economic orientation of the European project (Kuda and Strauß 2006). More specifically, unions fear increasing differentiation of qualifications and wages, a narrower set of skills as well as decreasing social equality. This is highly important since broad apprenticeship profiles improve the employability of their members and the transferability of skills (Thelen and Busemeyer 2008). Unitary skill profiles—with standardised duration of training and standardised qualifications—hinder differentiation of occupational profiles which lead to conflicts over wage levels between workers which would affect collective bargaining (ibid). Unions oppose both 2-year apprenticeships and modularisation. From their perspective, the latter could enable firms to pay for training only as long as it fulfils their immediate needs, and not for encompassing apprenticeships (Busemeyer and Thelen 2011). In sum, similar to the crafts sector, unions oppose changes to the core institution of the VET regime.

Unions prepared contributions to the consultation processes on EQF and ECVET. In their opinion, the Commission's EQF proposal does not meet important objectives: encompassing and easy access to education and VET; responsibility of the society for education; improving workers' rights; and increasing broad vocational qualifications and occupational proficiency (DGB 2005). Similar principles should hold for ECVET (DGB 2007). The Commission's objectives regarding the EQF are seen as too ambitious, with the risk that the benefits of the instrument are too small compared to the efforts put into implementation on the national level. Still, the trade unions believe that the EQF has the potential to increase the transparency and comparability of qualifications. Trade unions argue that the EQF should be revised and based on fewer levels and with the clear objective to rule out de-standardisation of contents and learning methods (ibid). Regarding ECVET, unions argued that it should not lead to an accumulation of units based on the certification of single units and fragmented qualifications, since this would undermine the vocational principle (DGB 2005). Kuda and Strauß (2006) argue that research on the potential impact of the instrument is lacking.

The government aimed at steering a reform of the system towards modularisation and flexibilisation of VET. This is obvious, since the innovation circle and the qualification initiative have both been initiated by the government. On the one hand, the objective is to improve transitions from school to VET and among different VET paths. On the other hand, initiatives shall support firms on which the government depend for the provision of VET. With the innovation circle, modularisation and Europeanisation were actively intertwined while reform proposals stemmed from the national debate (Trampusch 2008, interviews DE_PUBL-1, DE_UN-1). The argument that the government sees European policies as a window of opportunity for increasing flexibility within the national VET system is underlined by the statement by BMBF and the Secretariat of the Standing Conference of the Ministers of Education and Cultural Affairs of the Länder in the Federal Republic of Germany (*Kultusministerkonferenz*, KMK) in the consultation process on ECVET (BMBF and KMK 2007): "The most important potential benefit of the planned ECVET system is seen in *increasing the flexibility of the VET system* in the medium run besides increasing cross-border mobility" (BMBF and KMK 2007: 7; my italics)[16] ECVET is seen as a reform lever for modularisation (BMBF and KMK 2007: 4). The government argues that ECVET should be implemented in accordance with the dual VET system; the occupational principle and the final examination should be kept, and modules should not be divided into too small sections. The government believed to have support for a reform: "A beneficial factor is the circumstance that almost all decision-makers are interested in an advancement of the VET system in order to make it more flexible and more effective."[17]

It is interesting to observe that while the innovation circle has been in favour of modularisation, a joint statement of social partners and *Länder* is more cautious on the subject (BIBB Hauptausschuss 2007). They support the BMBF pilot initiative on building blocks in principle but underline that building blocks should be subordinated to dual VET and that the initiative should not undermine apprenticeships. It should therefore be limited to times of mismatch between supply and

---

[16]Original: "Als wichtigster potenzieller Nutzen des geplanten ECVET-Systems wird neben der Verbesserung der grenzübergreifenden Mobilität mittelfristig die gesteigerte Flexibilisierung des Berufsbildungssystems gesehen."

[17]Original: "Begünstigender Faktor ist der Umstand, dass fast alle Entscheidungsträger an einer Weiterentwicklung des Berufsbildungssystems interessiert sind, um es flexibler und effektiver zu machen."

demand of apprenticeships (ibid). Since this statement has been issued by the social partners and *Länder*, it seems that it is especially the federal government that steers reform towards modularisation. Regarding their principal policy goals, they also have support from the *Länder* level; an interview partner from a *Länder* administration stresses that the labour market is lacking a category between full apprenticeships and non-skilled workers—and that these can only be defined with the help of modularisation (interview DE_PUBL-4).

Although the federal government has supported modularisation and increasing flexibility, it opposed the introduction of an 'à la carte' system (interviews DE_PUBL-1, DE_PUBL-2). According to my interview partners from the federal administration, all stakeholders support the vocational principle and final examinations. Modularisation and flexibility should always be based on full qualifications (interview DE_PUBL-1). Units should not be too small. An interview partner from the federal administration highlighted that modularisation or building blocks will not automatically lead to dissolution of the occupational profile (DE_PUBL-1).

Moreover, the government actively contributed to preventing two initiatives that could have undermined the dual VET system. First, the European Commission aimed at introducing an automatic recognition of qualifications. According to this initiative, for example, a metal worker would be a metal worker—no matter where she acquired her qualification. The government did not support this proposal, arguing that both training regimes and the quality of VET are too heterogeneous for this to work (ibid). Second, the government did not support an automatic accumulation of learning outcomes. The interview partner highlights:

> "There is a famous 'Mr X' in all of the Commission's presentations who cruises through five different countries, and collects something here and something there and something there, and then approaches any recognition body in any member state, and gets recognised that he has virtually completed a whole VET course. In spite of the fact that he has never passed through anything successively (...), holistically. And we have fought this massively so that by now it is largely unmentioned in papers (...)" (interview DE_PUBL-1).[18]

An interview partner from the European level (interview EU_PUBL-3) underlines that the German government intervened on the European level because it believed that European proceedings could undermine the German VET system.

---

[18]Original: "Da gibt es einen berühmten ‚Mr. X' in allen Präsentationen von der Kommission, der einfach rumfährt, durch fünf verschiedene Länder, und sammelt da mal ein bisschen was und da mal ein bisschen was und da mal ein bisschen was, und dann kommt er zu irgendeiner Anerkennungsstelle in irgendeinem Mitgliedsstaate, und bekommt dann da anerkannt, dass er quasi eine komplette Ausbildung hat. Obwohl er nie etwas sukzessive durchlaufen hat, ganzheitlich durchlaufen hat. Und da haben wir uns massiv gegen gewährt, sodass das in den Papieren eigentlich inzwischen weitgehend raus ist (...)."

Brief Evaluation

Before the Commission issued details on the design of the instruments, a vivid debate on the impact of the Copenhagen process started. While at the early stage of the discussion there was hardly any doubt that EU instruments would require modularisation, impact assessments differed. Some voices argued that the fundamental pillars of VET could be kept. Others argued that an 'à la carte' system would emerge with far-reaching consequences for all constitutive elements of the dual system. It is important to keep in mind that EU initiatives were introduced in times when inherent problems of the system piled up, and that they affected issues already discussed against the background of increasing segmentalism of the VET regime. The discussion of EU instruments has been linked to national reform discussions via the question of modularisation. The way modularisation was proposed by the innovation circle does not intend a full-scale modularisation of VET, but would allow firms to offer only individual modules which could lead to a more segmental or market-based provision of VET. Modules would be independent of the place of learning, which challenges the dual nature of training.

Actors' positions diverge. The government aimed at reforming VET by introducing modularisation and increasing the flexibility of the system. It actively fostered change, firstly by launching the so-called innovation circle which developed reform proposals and secondly by subsequently introducing pilot projects on modularisation. Since the federal government cannot pursue such reforms alone, pilot projects are an attractive option, although their impact can hardly be predicted. However, the government opposed the Commission's activities to introduce automatic recognition of qualifications and automatic accumulation of learning outcomes across countries. Trade unions oppose modularisation and anything that would challenge the fundamental pillars of dual VET. They aim at hindering any further differentiation of apprenticeships, the introduction of an 'à la carte' system and an understanding of education based only on economic considerations. Employers made a joint proposal for an integrated EQF-ECVET system that would require modularisation but which is in line with the fundamental pillars of the system and based on descriptors that aim at reflecting the specific balance of skills in dual apprenticeships. Employers are divided on the issue of modularisation. The BDA made a reform proposal that would increase flexibility and challenges the balance of skills, certification and portability. In the view of the BDA, sectors could optionally introduce modularisation and reduce the duration of training. Firms could then decide to carry out examinations for single building blocks or hire awarding bodies to do so; final examinations would be reduced to one task that tests the holistic-occupational competence of the apprentice. The DIHK proposes to bundle training in related occupations in the first 2 years of an apprenticeship, and then offer a choice of modules for more specialised training in the third year. This adjustment would make skills broader and more firm-specific at the same time, while being largely in line with the fundamental pillars of dual VET. The ZDH opposes modularisation, since it would reduce the flexibility of firms to integrate training into their business routine. In their view, modules should be limited to specific target groups; because of the cost-benefit relation for apprenticeships the duration of training should not be reduced.

After discussing the early debate on a possible impact of European cooperation in VET before the instruments were actually launched, I will now discuss the impact of each instrument.

3.2.2 Learning Outcomes

The idea to solely define qualifications in terms of learning outcomes is alien to the German understanding of VET. Recently, however, European proceedings have steered a debate on learning outcomes in Germany (BMBF 2012c). In the view of the government, introducing national qualifications frameworks often leads to a "paradigm change" in the way regulations on the content and structure of qualifications (*Ordnungsmittel*) are formulated (ibid).

Learning outcomes are understood as "competences" (*Kompetenz*). While the German term is per se more encompassing than the English terms "competence" or "competencies",[19] in the context of training it is understood as the ability to autonomously solve occupation-related tasks in a holistic manner (Frank 2012b; see also BMBF and KMK 2009: 5). The German DQR defines competence as "the ability and willingness of the individual to use knowledge and skills as well as personal, social and methodological skills and to act thought-out as well as individually and socially responsible. In this sense, competence is understood as encompassing occupational competence."[20] In conclusion, the German understanding of competence inherits a certain derivation from the European concept of learning outcomes and is thus adjusted to the national sphere.

In how far are learning outcomes already implemented? Examinations already focus on assessing occupational proficiency (Born 2012) and curricula in VET schools are mostly orientated towards competences (interview DE_PUBL-6). In 1996, cultural ministers of the Länder introduced outline curricula that focused on occupational competence (*Handlungskompetenz*) (Dilger and Sloane 2012). A new version was issued in 2011, which includes a reference to the German qualifications framework (ibid) and herewith to the underlying principle of learning outcomes.

---

[19]The German word *Kompetenz* is neither exactly similar to the English word *competence* nor to *learning outcomes*. It is more encompassing and less focused on a concrete practical situation (Dehnbostel et al. 2009). "Skills" and "competencies" are even more related to work processes (ibid).

[20]Original: "Kompetenz bezeichnet im DQR die Fähigkeit und Bereitschaft des Einzelnen, Kenntnisse und Fertigkeiten sowie persönliche, soziale und methodische Fähigkeiten sowie persönliche, soziale und methodische Fähigkeiten zu nutzen und sich durchdacht sowie individuell und sozial verantwortlich zu verhalten. Kompetenz wird in diesem Sinne als umfassende Handlungskompetenz verstanden."

The picture is even more diverse when it comes to training ordinances. Studies show that it varies in how far ordinances are oriented towards competences already (Frank 2012b; Hanf and Rein 2007; Rauner and Grollmann 2006). Since the 1980s, occupational profiles—starting with electro- and metal-related occupations—were re-designed with a focus on occupational proficiency (ibid) and in an occupation-related manner (Born 2012). Current reforms of VET curricula follow this idea (ibid). Therefore, occupations that have been modernised recently are more likely to be orientated towards competences. Due to the consensus-driven process, reforms can be time-consuming and have not been undertaken for all professions. Consequently, observers such as Hanf and Rein (2007) believe that VET in Germany is still mainly input-orientated and in 2007 the "innovation circle on VET" recommended that training ordinances should be realigned towards competences more consequently (Innovationskreis Berufliche Bildung 2007). An expert group that was commissioned with linking qualifications to the DQR during its testing phase in four areas stated that this task was difficult to carry out exactly because qualifications are not sufficiently formulated in terms of learning outcomes. In sum, examinations as well as curricula of VET schools are largely orientated towards competences. For training ordinances, such a shift was initiated for several occupations decades ago and is recently fostered by the innovation circle on VET, but reform procedures are time-consuming so that many—or even the majority—of VET qualifications are still based on input-orientated ordinances.

There seems to be a broad consensus on competence orientation (Hanf and Rein 2006a). In January 2012, the major stakeholders of the German education system agreed to formulate all qualifications in a competence-orientated manner in the future (BMBF 2012c). Frank (2012a), working on the subject at the BIBB, proposes that a reform towards "competence-orientated" regulations of content and structure of qualifications should take place according to existing procedures. Both VET school curricula and training ordinances should be combined into one common training qualification. Moreover, standards for modernised qualifications should be based on the four dimensions of competence used by the DQR matrix (ibid). Frank concludes that it will be a challenge to create common standards on the basis of the DQR matrix and to implement them in practice, also because a joint decision by all stakeholders is necessary (Frank 2012b). The BIBB has led two projects in which curricula for training in companies and in schools were formulated in an outcome-orientated manner for 16 occupations in total (BIBB 2012d). In sum, while a formulation of VET qualifications is both possible and generally supported, such a change will take time if it is carried out according to the existing procedures.

Politics of Reform and Actors' Positions

In the view of an interview partner from the federal public administration, learning outcomes are "not an absolute priority" in Germany (interview DE_PUBL-2). Since occupational competence is already a major focus of VET in Germany, the need to introduce reforms is seen comparatively lower than in other countries (ibid). Yet at the same time, the focus on outcomes on the European level is seen to be an advantage for dual VET since it can enhance its status. Once all qualifications on all educational strands are outcome-orientated, it will be possible to see how far dual VET qualifications differ from similar professions in other countries where they are acquired at tertiary level (interview DE_PUBL-1).

Interview partners from employers' organisations argue that because of the competence-orientated reforms of training ordinances, the learning outcomes approach has already been implemented "relatively well" in those occupations (interview DE_PRIV-2). They have a positive attitude towards extending these reforms to further occupations (ibid).

Trade unions have criticised the idea to completely focus on learning outcomes instead of combining it with input-criteria (DGB 2007, 2011). With a focus on learning outcomes, questions such as contents, didactics, and places of learning do not matter—trade unions therefore argue that focussing on learning outcomes increases the arbitrariness of learning methods and contents (DGB 2008). In the end, the quality of learning outcomes depends on the way prior learning processes have been designed; therefore they should be complemented by improving the quality of VET (DGB 2007). The European concept is seen to focus solely on employability without taking societal responsibility and emancipatory questions into account, which might lead to a market-based understanding of education (DGB 2008). If learning outcomes are designed in a narrow manner, this would counteract the vocational principle with its idea of a broad and holistic occupational qualification. These are, however, in the interest of workers and trade unions. If competences neither focus on the vocational principle nor on the development of the personality, "a rupture with the grown structures of VET in Germany (...) would be inevitable" (DGB 2007: 4).[21] An alternative to focussing on learning outcomes would be to describe competences in terms of requirements derived from specific work contexts (ibid).

Brief Evaluation

While the idea to define qualifications solely in terms of learning outcomes is new to Germany, the concept is translated into the national realm as a focus on "competences". This concept is slightly broader than its European equivalent, which reflects the balance of skills prevalent in German VET. The concept of competence orientation gained momentum already in the 1980s and 1990s, so that reforms of training ordinances and curricula towards a focus on competences were ongoing. With ordinance reforms being consensus-led and often time-consuming, German VET is still seen to be mostly input-orientated. Implementing a full competence-orientation of VET is doable without severe problems, but faces

---

[21]Original: "Gelingt dies nicht, ist ein Bruch mit den gewachsenen Strukturen der beruflichen Bildung in Deutschland (...) vorprogrammiert."

challenges regarding the duality of training ordinances and school curricula and the fit to the DQR matrix. New commitments have been made to speed up these reforms, and these were influenced by the Copenhagen process.

The government perceives the already existing orientation towards competences as an advantage in improving the position of the German VET system in international arenas—arguing that it strenghtens the status of VET in relation to higher education. Employers are in favour of extending the competence-orientation of training ordinances and argue that with ongoing reforms of ordinances, the shift towards learning outcomes is already on its way. In contrast, trade unions criticise that with a shift towards learning outcomes, learning methods and contents become arbitrary; moreover, there is the risk that learning outcomes refer to a narrower set of qualifications. This would mean that a focus on learning outcomes could counteract a core feature of the German VET system, namely the balance between general and specific skills. However, given that the implementation is focused on a shift towards competences along the lines of recently modernised training ordinances in which the balance of skills was not affected, changes to the pillars of the training regime are highly unlikely to occur. Therefore, there are no signs that the actual implementation of learning outcomes in Germany will challenge the vocational principle or core features of the VET regime.

3.2.3 The German Qualifications Framework (DQR)

In line with and as a response to European proceedings, BMBF and KMK agreed to develop a national qualifications framework, the DQR, as early as October 2006 (BMBF and KMK 2012). A co-ordination group between both administrations was set up. It steered the process on the DQR and initiated a DQR working group (*Arbeitskreis Deutscher Qualifikationsrahmen*). In the latter working group, a vast variety of stakeholders is represented: social partners, actors from higher education and further education, VET stakeholders, education experts and researchers. The DQR working group could draw on preparatory work and proposals already undertaken by a smaller working group from the BIBB main committee (interview DE_PUBL-4).[22] The main difference here is that in the latter, members comprise only the federal and *Länder* administrations, social partners and the Conference of University Presidents (*Hochschulrektorenkonferenz*) (ibid). Cooperation in all of these working groups is based on consensus. The BMBF contracted the organisational work on the DQR to a consortium of consultancies and a university institute (Deutscher Bundestag 2008). The bureau was established in December

---

[22]Sometimes the latter working group is referred to as the "editorial group". While in the other two working groups several stakeholders send a number of representatives—for example, the working group on the DQR has 31 members—, this group has only five members and therefore has been able to reach compromise more easily. Compromises as well as lines of conflict were then presented to the larger working group on DQR.

2007 and supports the ministry with organisational and administrative tasks as well as with preliminary thematic work related to the development of the DQR.

After a long discussion, German stakeholders agreed on the design of the DQR in 2009. Similar to the EQF, it comprises eight levels which are described in terms of learning outcomes. While the EQF is based on the descriptors "knowledge", "skills" and "competence" for each level, the DQR distinguishes between "professional competences" (*Fachkompetenz*) and "personal competences" (*Personale Kompetenz*). The first descriptor is further subdivided into "knowledge" (*Wissen*) and "skills" (*Fertigkeiten*), and the latter into "social competences" (*Sozialkompetenz*) and "self-competence" (*Selbstkompetenz*). This design was introduced in order to better accommodate the vocational principle (*Berufsprinzip*). The descriptor "knowledge" was included in the matrix on the demand of schools and the higher education sector (interview DE_PRIV-3). It is considered a major achievement for the field of VET that all eight levels are accessible for both vocational and general qualifications. The descriptor "knowledge" is sub-divided on levels 5–8 in order to reflect the different kinds of knowledge in academics and VET. Universities originally had preferred an "upsilon-structure" for these levels, while VET stakeholders preferred a differentiation with an "or" (Deutscher Bundestag 2010a). After a long discussion (interview DE_PUBL-1), the latter variant was introduced. While Frank (2012b) argues that DQR descriptors still do not completely reflect the encompassing understanding of competence developed in pedagogics, interview partners widely highlighted that the adjustment of descriptors to national particularities is an important achievement of the DQR process. A first draft with eight levels was presented in February 2009. Since the process was consensus-led, all stakeholders generally approved the draft.

While the process on designing the DWR was still ongoing, a study edited by the BMBF argued that in order to implement the EU instruments in a coherent and encompassing way, standardised educational pathways and degrees would have to be largely abolished (Gehmlich 2009). As one of three researchers, Gehmlich is a member of the working group on the DQR. His proposal is based on an add-on or learning pathways "menu" system, according to which units of learning outcomes lead to qualifications, and qualifications lead to DQR levels. Crediting units across educational sectors is possible in this system; final examinations would not be necessary. He argues that if curricula are designed in the right way, fragmentation does not necessarily follow from such a reform. Moreover, he questions the tripartite procedure of establishing training ordinances and argues that they are too complicated against the background of qualifications frameworks. In sum, Gehmlich provides the most radical reform proposal for the implementation of a national qualifications framework in Germany. His proposal would make the system more flexible in a market-based fashion, establish a new governance structure and would decrease the portability of skills. It is surprising that this expertise, edited by the BMBF, was published as late as 2009.

In a testing phase, referencing processes for the DQR were carried out for qualifications out of four occupational and thematic fields—IT, trade, health and metal/electronics—from May 2009 onwards. Expert working groups were set up for each field, each group included representatives from all major stakeholders. They concluded that referencing of qualifications to the DQR poses several difficulties. While most qualifications are not yet formulated in terms of outcomes, they have to be linked to an outcome-based matrix. In many cases, a deviance of one level is possible since a matrix with eight levels provides a rather rough grid only. For example, the expert group for metal and electronics occupations proposed to reference vocational preparation qualifications either to level 1 or to 2, depending on the specific way the programmes are designed. Moreover, the group could not establish a consensus regarding the referencing of 2-year-apprenticeships: While experts had different opinions regarding the referencing for one of the analysed 2-year apprenticeships (which was considered to be whether on level 3 or 4), another was believed to largely fulfil criteria for level 4. A majority in the end voted for linking all 2-year apprenticeships to level 3. Furthermore, it was agreed to link all 3-year-apprenticeships to level 4, although several of the analysed apprenticeships also fulfil important aspects of level 5. Similar results—regarding variances within one DQR level and input-based referencing of qualifications to the DQR—can be found in all working groups and for all DQR levels. Considerable differences between the various qualifications which are grouped on the same level remain, and the horizontal and vertical relationship between qualifications is not clear-cut. Still, the working groups agreed that in principle, it is possible to link existing qualifications to the DQR.

Working groups on the DQR agreed on a second draft in March 2011. The categories and levels of the first draft remained. Qualifications on one level are seen as having equal value, not as being homogenous.[23] It is explicitly stated that the DQR does not change admission rules. In a similar vein, it is highlighted that levels are not related to collective agreements or public sector pay scales—an aspect that was reinforced by a statement of the BIBB main committee (2011a). The DQR does not imply any new rights and duties (ibid).

A consensus was found for most qualifications regarding their referencing to the DQR. Vocational preparation schemes are grouped on level 1 and 2. Several qualifications of continuing education—namely *Meister, Fachwirt*, and graduates of *Fachschulen*—are grouped on level 6 (BMBF and KMK 2012). In line with European decisions on the relationship between EQF and the Qualifications Framework of the European Higher Education Area, Bachelor, Master and PhD are linked to level 6, 7, and 8 respectively. It is widely recognised that it is an important—or even "a quite revolutionary" (interview DE_PRIV-2)—step to link both *Meister* and *Techniker* to the same level as a bachelor's degree. Before this consensus was achieved, many VET stakeholders had been worried that the higher education sector would try to reserve the three highest DQR levels to academic qualifications (interviews DE_PRIV-2; DE_PRIV-3), since this had previously been the informal position of the universities (interview DE_PUBL-4).

A conflict arose on the question of on what level the general qualifications issued by secondary schools (*Abitur*) for university entrance should be grouped. The conflict was taken up by mainstream media (see for example Ata 2011; Banse

---

[23]"*gleichwertig*" instead of "*gleichartig*". This is often highlighted.

2012; Böhm 2012; Kühne 2012; Vitzthum 2012; Völpel 2012). Within the debate, qualifications on one level of the DQR were associated with being of the same value; hence, the relationship between general and vocational education was at the centre of the conflict. The KMK proposed to group the qualification on level 5 together with higher-ranking apprenticeships, while the majority of apprenticeships would be referenced to level 4, and (optionally) 2-year apprenticeships to level 3 (interviews DE_PUBL-3, DE_PUBL-4, DE_PUBL-5). The KMK argued that this proposal is based on several expert workshops and expert opinions and based on learning outcomes (interview DE_PUBL-5). Moreover, linking all apprenticeships to level 4 would mean to undervalue them. On the other hand, the general qualification for university entrance should not be linked to a lower level than apprenticeships (ibid). However, it has never been defined clearly which apprenticeships the KMK would understand as higher-ranking (Esser 2012). Although critics argued that other countries have linked university entrance qualifications to level 4, school teachers claimed that the German one comprises more subjects and languages and in contrast to other countries, usually no additional admission tests are carried out by universities (Lehmann 2012). This position of the KMK is believed to largely reflect teachers' opinions (interview DE_PRIV-2).

As a response, the standing conference of the Ministers of Economics of the Länder in the Federal Republic of Germany (*Wirtschaftsministerkonferenz der Länder*)—a body not often present in public discussions and opening a conflict within *Länder* governments (interview DE_PUBL-4)—issued a counter-statement in August 2011 (Esser 2012). They conclude that general university entrance qualifications and apprenticeships should be linked to the same level. Moreover, it was argued that a considerable share of apprentices has a general university entrance qualification. For this group, taking up an apprenticeship might then be perceived as a downward move, and employers feared that they would be reluctant to enter into an apprenticeship (Ata 2011). In addition, university entrance qualifications are not of direct relevance on the labour market and therefore should not be grouped higher than those qualifications which actually have a direct value on the labour market (interview DE_PRIV-2). The federal parliament dealt with the issue and in an unusual consensus, all fractions agreed that apprenticeships and general school leaving qualifications should be linked to the same DQR level (Deutscher Bundestag 2012). The main board of the BIBB (2011a) pointed out that the level of the general university entrance qualification should be comparable to similar qualifications in other countries. At the same time, German VET should not be "undervalued" in international comparisons. Therefore, general university entrance qualifications should not be linked to a higher level than dual apprenticeships and should be referenced to level 4 (ibid). Moreover, it was argued that regarding personal and social competences, apprenticeship graduates have at least the same competence level as school graduates (see for example DGB 2010, interview DE_PRIV-1). Social partners did not agree to reference several VET professions to level 5, since they oppose increasing differentiation in VET (interview DE_PUBL-3). Trade unions and the craft sector even threatened to exit the DQR working group if the general university entrance qualifications would be referenced higher than apprenticeships. The KMK discussed the issue again but kept its opinion (KMK 2011). In sum, the KMK was isolated but because of its nature as a veto player could not be overruled.

In spite of the disagreements described above, all actors agreed that a solution should be found in order to be able to implement the DQR. In November 2011, the social democratic fraction of the federal parliament proposed to abstain from referencing general school qualifications to the DQR if no consensus could be reached on this topic (Deutscher Bundestag 2011). This proposal was backed by employers who believed that EQF and DQR provide an added value by relating qualifications to the labour market—while general education does not prepare directly for the labour market but for VET or university education (interviews DE_PRIV-1, PRIV-3). The idea was taken up by Federal Minister of Education and Research Schavan (interview DE_PRIV-3) and agreed upon in a high-level meeting on January 31, 2012 between BMBF, KMK, national and federal economic ministries, social partners and the BIBB. Participants decided to link secondary education qualifications to the DQR only by 2017 (BMBF and KMK 2012). It was also agreed that apprenticeships will be linked to level 4, and 2-year-apprenticeships to level 3. Options for referencing both apprenticeships and secondary school leaving certificates to higher DQR levels will be investigated and developments on the European level and in other countries will be monitored.

The DQR bureau has been appointed as the national coordination point for the EQF. The national referencing report was presented in the EQF advisory group in December 2012. The DQR was put into effect in May 2013, on the basis of a joint decision by the KMK, BMBF, KMK, and the Federal Ministry for Economic Affairs and Technology (*Bundesministerium für Wirtschaft und Technologie*).

Open Questions and Further Implementation

The referencing process still has several shortcomings. First, referencing activities are criticised as blurry on the first two levels: Vocational preparation schemes are spread over levels 1 and 2, while differences between them are not very clear-cut. Moreover, important qualifications of the "transition system", such as the programmes of the Federal Labour Agency, are not yet included in the referencing processes (Deutscher Bundestag 2010a).

Second, representatives of several occupations claim that their qualifications are not represented adequately within the DQR. For example, it is claimed that several health professions are linked to level 4 but in other countries they are taught on the tertiary level (see for example Deutscher Bundesverband für Logopädie 2012; interview DE_PRIV-3). The argument is underlined by the testing phase: Expert groups argued that several apprenticeships fulfil criteria for level 5, and originally linked the qualification for physiotherapy to level 5. While for employers it is most important that qualifications meet the demand of the labour market—which should be reflected in DQR levels—(interview DE_PRIV-1), trade unions believe that individual VET qualifications could be linked to level 5 if their profiles are sufficiently complex (interview DE_UN-1). However, if any apprenticeships or school-based VET is linked to level 5, this will steer discussions on the referencing of general university entrance qualifications in 2017 as well as Furthermore, it would increase the differentiation within the system. In the long run, such developments might also lead to upskilling (interview DE_PUBL-4).

Another open question is, third, the relationship between the outcome-based understanding of the DQR and the process of linking formal qualifications to the DQR. Referencing took place primarily based on inputs. So far, referencing has taken place on the basis of inputs. Interview partners from the public administration argued that in the long run it will be revised for each qualification individually (interviews DE_PUBL-1, DE_PUBL-4) and might be adjusted (interview DE_PUBL-4). In the end, this might lead to upskilling (interviews DE_PUBL-1, DE_PRIV-1). For employers, this is critical since in their view qualifications should primarily reflect the needs of firms (interview DE_PRIV-1) and not predominantly focus on fitting DQR descriptors.

Fourth, it is questionable if DQR and EQF improve the international standing of the dual VET system. In Germany, it is commonly believed that previous efforts aimed at increasing the transparency of qualifications—such as the OECD's ISCED and the EU directive on the recognition of professional qualifications—undervalued the German dual system (see for example Deutscher Bundestag 2006). Although for VET stakeholders it can be seen as a success that the EQF links *Meister* qualifications to the same level as bachelor's degrees, most VET qualifications are referenced to the lower DQR levels 3 and 4 (Busemeyer 2012). Moreover, while in Germany qualifications such as nurses are part of the dual system, in other countries they are taught at universities—although competences of those qualifications might differ, it is questionable if these differences can account for two levels on the scale of the qualifications frameworks. Several observers moreover believe that other countries have referenced their qualifications to higher levels than Germany (interviews DE_PUBL-5, DE_PRIV-3). In sum, the standing of VET has improved compared to prior methods for international comparisons, but is still ambivalent.

Fifth, interview partners from employers' organisations stress that it is not yet clear if the DQR will have consequences on wage levels in the future (interview DE_PRIV-2) or, at the most, provide a first orientation (interview DE_PRIV-1), others believe that an impact on pay scale classifications is likely in the long run (interviews DE_PUBL-1, DE_PUBL-2, DE_PUBL-3), although this was clearly excluded. Within the DQR matrix, several key words can be found which are also used in collective agreements (interview DE_UN-1). Moreover, the DQR might steer developments regarding the establishment of continuing education programmes on level 5, a level which is currently not substantiated to a sufficient degree; here, consequences on collective agreements are likely (interview DE_UN-1).

A final point is the question of permeability. From the beginning, the DQR was supposed to stimulate permeability between the different educational pathways against the background of lifelong learning (Innovationskreis Berufliche Bildung

2007; BIBB 2011a: 2). It is questionable if the DQR currently fulfils such claims. This is because recognition and crediting of prior learning outcomes as well as admission rules are explicitly not regulated by the DQR. For example, *Meister* qualifications are referenced to level 6, but a *Meister* cannot automatically enrol for a master's degree which is linked to level 7. This has, however, never been the objective of the DQR process: at most, the DQR can be understood as ground work for permeability, since it combines all areas of education in one framework and establishes a ranking of qualifications on the basis of levels.

Still, interview partners have widely highlighted the importance of the DQR as the first mutually accepted framework that encompasses the different pathways of the education system. The process of developing the DQR improved the mutual understanding and relationships among actors of the different strands of the educational system. Discussions on equal footing with the other educational strands were a new development (interview DE_UN-1) and were enabled by the lead VET departments took in the DQR process within the federal administration (interview DE_PUBL-1). The process therefore might be a first step for overcoming the historically strong separation between education and VET which is often referred to as "education schism" (Baethge 2006).

In relation to the DQR, VET stakeholders have hoped that the permeability between VET and higher education would improve. Improving permeability between VET and higher education is both an advantage and a disadvantage for employers: On the one hand, the attractiveness of VET for high achieving school graduates might increase; on the other hand, they might not remain with the firms to fill skilled workers positions.[24] In Germany, there are several shortcomings regarding the permeability at this transition stage. First, although education ministers of the *Länder* have facilitated taking up tertiary studies without possessing a general university entrance qualifications, every *Land* implements the non-binding resolution (KMK 2009) in a different way and often with detailed regulations. Therefore, for the individual it is still not easy to find out how to proceed to tertiary education (Nickel and Duong 2012). Second, German universities offer few flexible programmes, such as distance learning or extra-occupational and part-time programmes (Autorengruppe Bildungsberichterstattung 2008). Third, universities can already credit prior learning to tertiary study programmes, even up to 50 % of a programme (Freitag 2012)—yet, they often do not make use of this (Autorengruppe Bildungsberichterstattung 2008). Finally, in Germany there is no qualification that combines a general university entrance qualification with an apprenticeship. Such a qualification exists in Austria (*Berufsmatura*) and has existed in the former German Democratic Republic. The DQR did not change any of these issues, although in the long run it might contribute to steering reforms.

---

[24]In all other dual systems and collective skill regimes, the permeability between VET and higher education is higher than in Germany. Improving permeability therefore does not affect collective skill regime institutions per se.

Politics of Reform and Actors' Positions

In Chap. 2 it is highlighted that the EQF has a two-tier objective: It aims at improving mobility across Europe and at steering reforms on the national level. In a speech at a symposium on the DQR, the Federal Minister of Education and Research confirmed this twofold objective for the DQR (Schavan 2010). The government stated that "with the EQF approach, we can and want to strengthen the vocational principle Europe-wide, *make it more flexible* and connect it to lifelong learning" (Deutscher Bundestag 2006: part I; my italics).[25] However, in the view of a government official at the *Länder* level, the implementation process of the DQR is a bureaucratic exercise rather than a process of change (DE_PUBL-5).

Employers' associations have continuously highlighted that the DQR should be orientated towards the needs of the labour market and of firms (KWB 2008a). In order to achieve this, descriptors should be clearly defined and easy to use (ibid)—a quest that in their opinion has largely been fulfilled (KWB 2010). In the view of employers, the DQR can improve the permeability between VET and tertiary education, since it improves options for learners to show what competences they have already acquired. Employers demand that all apprenticeship graduates should be able to take up studies on the tertiary level, and that in turn, competences of university drop-outs should be recognised in VET (ibid). The DQR can support this objective by showing pathways and points of transition. Moreover, it can help firms to quickly evaluate the competences of an applicant. The DIHK points out that with the DQR, firms might change recruiting behaviour by becoming more open towards applicants with a VET qualification (Deutscher Bundestag 2010a).

Employers had different opinions regarding referencing apprenticeships to several DQR levels, which would advance a diversification of apprenticeships. Employers of four branches—IT and media, metal, machine building, and high tech industries—issued a joint statement in which they propose to link apprenticeships to three different levels (BITKOM et al. 2007). While not only these four branches but also the BDA supported grouping apprenticeships to several levels of the DQR, the DIHK did not support such an initiative (interviews DE_PRIV-3, DE_UN-1). These diverging opinions among employers are largely in conformity with the positions outlined in Sect. 3.2.1 regarding the flexibilisation and modularisation of the VET system.

Trade unions argued that the DQR should be an instrument to increase the permeability within the education system, especially regarding transitions from VET to tertiary education. They stressed that both a public debate and more research on the impact of qualifications frameworks is necessary (Kuda and Strauß 2006; DGB 2008). Trade unions contributed actively to adjusting the descriptors to

---

[25]Original: "Mit dem EQR-Ansatz können und wollen wir das Berufsprinzip europaweit stärken, flexibilisieren und mit dem Lebenslangen Lernen vernetzen." The motion was passed with support of the conservative and social democratic government fractions as well as of the liberal and green parties.

the dual VET system and have continuously stressed that these should reflect the vocational principle as well as self-competence and participation (interview DE_UN-1). However, unions fear negative consequences for the vocational principle because qualifications below the level of skilled workers are linked to lower levels of the qualifications framework. In the long run, qualifications on this level could focus on narrow and low learning outcomes (DGB 2005). In their view, linking VET qualifications to different levels on the DQR advances differentiation of VET—instead one level for apprenticeships would have been sufficient (interview DE_PRIV-3). This is why they originally had proposed a qualifications framework which is based on a five-level structure (DGB 2008). In the view of the DGB, hopes that the EQF will foster the international standing of German dual VET have not been fulfilled (ibid).

Brief Evaluation

As a response to European proceedings, the process to develop a DQR was initiated in 2006. After a testing phase in 2009 and 2010, the DQR working group agreed on the framework in 2011. While the eight-level-structure resembles the EQF, descriptors were adjusted to reflect the distinct balance between broad and specific skills of the German VET system. The DQR does not have an impact on collective agreements, public sector pay scales or admission rules. While the latter limits its impact on fostering permeability, the DQR is the first framework that comprises all educational pathways, and it is an important achievement that the implementation process improved the mutual understanding among actors from different education subsystems. The most important formal VET qualifications were quickly linked to the DQR: Vocational preparation schemes are referenced to level 1 and 2, 2-year apprenticeships to level 3, standard apprenticeships to level 4, and upgrade training—such as *Meister*—to level 6 together with bachelor's degrees. A conflict arose on the referencing of the general qualification for university entrance; the KMK had argued that it should be referenced to level 5 together with high-ranking apprenticeships but was isolated with this position. As a compromise, stakeholders agreed to postpone referencing all secondary school qualifications until 2017. In the end, the DQR improves the standing of VET in Germany since all levels will be open for both general and VET qualifications and upgrade training is on the same level as bachelor's degrees. The latter aspect can also be seen as improving the status of dual VET in comparison to other international education frameworks. However, both national and international effects are also ambivalent and should not be overestimated. The differentiation between 2-year and regular apprenticeships is manifested by the DQR. Open questions regarding the future referencing process, the referencing of qualifications on the first two levels and of high-ranking apprenticeships remain, as well as on a potential impact on the design of training ordinances.

The federal government understands the DQR as an instrument for increasing permeability and flexibility in the national realm and for improving mobility across

Europe. It is questionable if such objectives have been fulfilled in practice. Länder governments perceive the DQR as a technical exercise rather than a political instrument. Employers are largely satisfied with the DQR and descriptors. In their view, the DQR helps firms to carry out first assessments of applicants' qualifications and might change recruiting behaviour to the advantage of VET graduates. They demand further improvements regarding permeability between VET and tertiary education. With the support of the BDA, employers from IT, metal, machine building and high tech sectors had demanded to reference apprenticeships to three levels. Crafts and Chambers oppose such differentiation. Trade unions originally proposed a five-level-structure with all apprenticeships on the lowest level. Hence, they oppose any further differentiation of apprenticeships and are concerned that the DQR might strengthen the standing of qualifications below the level of skilled workers.

3.2.4 The European Credit System for Vocational Education and Training

The implementation of ECVET is still at its beginning in Germany. The government, as one of few governments in Europe, has launched an initiative on ECVET, which is called DECVET.[26] The focus is on permeability within Germany rather than on facilitating the movement of workers across Europe. 10 pilot projects ran from 2007 to 2012 with the objective to develop models for crediting competences to qualifications so that learning outcomes and competences can be measured, transferred and credited. In order to do so, qualifications are structured into assessable learning outcomes. By improving transitions, the attractiveness of VET shall be increased while waiting times, redundant training and dead-ends shall be avoided. DECVET includes transitions from vocational preparation schemes to VET, between occupations of the dual system, between school-based full-time VET and dual apprenticeships, and from initial to continuing VET. In June 2012, the results of the pilot projects were presented at a conference. Three different procedures for the recognition of competences seem to be successful:

- Procedures for shortening an apprenticeship by recognising competences that have been acquired beforehand;
- Procedures that allow for the inclusion of additional advanced training content on the basis of saving time by recognition of prior competences;
- Procedures that flexibilise preparation of and admission to examinations, especially regarding transitions between initial and continuing VET (BMBF 2012a).

---

[26]The full title of the programme is DECVET—Development of a Credit Point System for VET (Original: *DECVET-Entwicklung eines Leistungspunktesystems in der beruflichen Bildung*).

The project is therefore closely connected to the validation of non-formal and informal learning, as it also develops procedures for assessing competences. The importance of the project is strengthened by the involvement of VET stakeholders (interview DE_PUBL-1). Employers, however, also criticise the project, since they believe that it is extremely difficult to transfer modules from school-based VET or extra-company VET to apprenticeships (interview DE_PRIV-2). Firms might be reluctant to do so for two reasons: firstly, there is insecurity on contents and level of prior learning, and secondly—especially for the crafts sector—cost-benefit relations of training might be affected. While the government plans to keep the creditation of prior learning in the hands of providers on a voluntary basis, it seems unlikely that firms would subscribe to the procedures on a large scale.

The results of the project shall be combined with results from other initiatives on increasing permeability and in the medium run be discussed with VET stakeholders (BMBF 2014). It is therefore unlikely that the project affects core pillars of the German VET system for several reasons. First, the initiative was a pilot project and has not been mainstreamed into the VET system. Results shall only be discussed with VET stakeholders in the medium run. Second, while the procedures developed within the project address moving from different VET sectors to others, the government stresses that the project is about permeability and does not affect the focus of qualifications to be holistic and based on the occupational principle. A 'pick and choose' form of modularisation is not intended. Third, firms can be expected to be unenthusiastic about crediting prior learning to apprenticeships.

That being said, if DECVET is mainstreamed, challenges to the core features of the VET system might still occur. Critical points against the background of the core features of the German VET system are the accreditation of prior training to final examinations, flexibilisation of examinations which may then lack portability, and large-scale accreditation of training to dual VET programmes that makes up a substantial part of the training and that has been acquired in only one location of learning, leading to a changing balance of skills. Up to now, far-reaching changes in these directions seem unlikely.

In addition to DECVET, the "National Agency Education for Europe at the BIBB" (*Nationale Agentur Bildung für Europa beim Bundesinstitut für Berufsbildung*) is active in the implementation of ECVET. The agency funds innovation and mobility projects related to ECVET as a national priority within the Leonardo da Vinci programme (BIBB 2011b).[27] A national coordination point for ECVET was established at the agency in 2010 with the aim to support national actors and to provide information on transnational mobility. A group of ECVET

---

[27] An interesting example is "MOVET" ("Modules in Europe—Recognition at Home. On the way to ECVET"). Between 2008 and 2010, modules and recognition procedures were developed for the transnational training of mechatronics in Germany, Denmark and Finland. Apprentices from these countries can participate in training and examinations in partner countries. The partner institutions have developed memoranda of understanding as well as procedures for assessing competences. The transcript of record is issued after theoretical and practical examinations as well as a technical discussion between trainer and apprentice have been successfully completed (BIBB 2011b).

experts—coordinated by the ECVET coordination point with EU funding—help promote the instrument in Germany. Guidelines on using ECVET have also been created (BIBB 2012d).

Already before, several regulations and initiatives on international mobility had existed. With the reform of the Vocational Training Act (*Berufsbildungsgesetz*, BBiG) in 2005, options to integrate mobility experiences in apprenticeships were amplified: A maximum of one fourth of the training duration can take place abroad (§2 BBiG). The "innovation circle on VET" also placed an emphasis on increasing mobility during VET. In practice, the number of funded mobility experiences has been increasing but is still low: currently about 4 % of initial VET students go abroad during training (BIBB 2012d). Only about a fifth of these experiences abroad are longer than 6 weeks (BIBB 2012c). In comparison to other EU countries, this is however not unusual.

There have been hardly any mobility experiences with the instruments up to now. Hence, ECVET so far has not contributed to increasing the number of mobility experiences (Küßner 2012). Education providers believe that the instrument is too complicated. Moreover, "up to now, the eponymous element of 'credit points' turns out to be rather a hurdle" (ibid, 2).[28] Herewith, it is important to note that the English term "credit system" has been translated with "*Leistungspunktesystem*" in German, which in turn could be translated to "credit *point* system" in English. An interview partner from the federal administration concludes that credit points are "an artificial currency—which currently it is no currency because there is no exchange"[29] (Interview DE_PUBL-2). Küßner, who works at the national coordination point, proposes that ECVET tools should be substantiated and education providers should be supported with using ECVET. This includes the support of regional or sectoral communities of practice, developing minimum standards and qualifying education personnel (Küßner 2012). Common formats, common definitions of concepts and terms, and understandable descriptions of learning outcomes should be established (BIBB 2012d). Furthermore, using ECVET would be easier if curricula were formulated in a competence-orientated way (see Sect. 4.2.2) (Küßner 2012, interview DE_PUBL-2). Küßner concludes that ECVET is a useful instrument for steering mobility but that it is still in its initial phase of implementation. In her view and against the background that the implementation of the credit system for higher education (ECTS) took 10 years, she believes that ECVET still is on the right track (ibid).

---

[28]Original: "Auch erweist sich das namensgebende Element der ‚Leistungspunkte' bislang eher als Hürde."

[29]Original: "Das ist eine künstliche Währung—die momentan keine Währung ist, weil es keinen Tausch gibt."

Politics of Reform and Actors' Positions

According to the national coordination point of ECVET, there is disagreement on the implementation of ECVET (Küßner 2012). The BIBB concludes that the idea of awarding qualifications on the basis of accumulated credit points, which is associated with ECVET, is not common practice in German VET and "is disapproved by the predominant share of actors since it appears to be incompatible with the vocational principle and a holistic occupational proficiency as the objective of VET (BIBB 2012c)."[30] The fact that the credit point system in higher education, ECTS, is increasingly criticised—only 43 % of credits obtained abroad get recognised, so that many actors and experts belief that the instrument does not fulfil its objectives—further burdens discussions on implementing such a system for VET (interview DE_PUBL-3).

The government supports modularisation and flexibilisation of training with numerous activities (see Sect. 4.2.1), and proactively uses ECVET to steer reforms in this direction. This becomes obvious in the way DECVET is designed: it focuses on the national level and on modularisation. Interestingly, as an interview partner from an employers' organisation reports, "it was said from the beginning: These ten projects are not related to ECVET. That was said on the national level, and then in Brussels it was said: 'This is the implementation of ECVET'" (interview DE_PRIV-3).[31] Hereby, the government created confusion (interview DE_PRIV-2). The Commission took up the idea of applying ECVET to domestic matters only after noticing the German approach to ECVET (ibid). An interview partner from an employer organisation stressed that while he prefers a bottom-up and flexible implementation of ECVET, this is "not enough" for the BMBF (interview DE_PRIV-2).

However, Schavan (the Federal Minister of Education and Research at that time) highlights that the implementation of the instrument will be in accordance with the German VET system (BWP 2007: 6). She underlines that the government supports final examinations, which "cannot—contrary to some concerns—be substituted with an accumulation of partial qualifications that have been acquired throughout Europe" (ibid).[32] In her perspective, ECVET is a means to recognition of pre-apprenticeship qualifications and informal learning in the medium run (ibid). This underlines that in the medium run an effect on the national system is indeed intended. The way DECVET is designed it focuses on addressing deficiencies of the

---

[30]Original: "(...) vom weit überwiegenden Teil der Akteure abgelehnt wird, weil sie nicht mit dem Berufskonzept und einer umfassenden beruflichen Handlungskompetenz als Ausbildungsziel vereinbar scheint."

[31]Original: "von Anfang an immer gesagt wurde: Diese zehn Projekte haben nichts mit ECVET zu tun. Das wurde auf nationaler Ebene gesagt, und in Brüssel wurde dann gesagt: Das ist die Umsetzung von ECVET."

[32]Original: "In der beruflichen Ausbildung heißt das, dass an der Abschlussprüfung festgehalten wird und diese—entgegen manchen Befürchtungen—nicht durch eine Kumulation von in Europa erworbenen Teilqualifikationen ersetzt werden kann."

German system. While that might also facilitate mobility—it is easier to organise mobility around existing units—modularisation is neither a prerequisite of EU instruments nor the only way to deal with inherent problems of the German VET system. The push for modularisation therefore can be seen as a political choice.

For the government, ECVET also has an international component. An interview partner from the federal administration stressed that in the long run, ECVET tools such as memoranda of understanding will serve as a standard for mobility experiences (interview DE_PUBL-2). The government can foster this development by linking funds of lifelong learning programmes to ECVET (ibid). For Schavan, the voluntary nature of the ECVET process, the subsidiarity to national arrangements and the bottom-up principle are important features of the instrument (BWP 2007: 6).

Employers argue that by describing qualifications in terms of outcomes, ECVET provides an added value for mobility (KWB 2012; BMBF 2012a: 78). While tools for the description, evaluation and recognition of learning outcomes should be tested further, these procedures should not substitute formal examinations. Employers believe that the introduction of credit points has not been as successful as initially envisaged. In their view, credit points would only be beneficial if they were related to a reference framework in which they would have a value. This is not the case in many member states. Moreover, since ECVET is not linked to ECTS, in their opinion the approach itself is questionable. Already during the consultation process on ECVET, employers had argued that while they support the objectives of fostering transparency, mobility and the transfer of VET qualifications, they doubt if ECVET can contribute to meeting these goals (KWB 2007). They believe that ECVET is too abstract and lacks details for practical procedures, so that it does not provide enough added value. Since ECVET is not a fully-fledged system, it should rather be implemented in a bottom-up approach and unfold its advantages in the medium or long run (KWB 2007, 2012).

In the trade union's perspective, ECVET is primarily concerned with mutual trust and is a means to make qualifications and vocational proficiency visible that have been acquired abroad (interview DE_UN-1). This however, is not always clear in the German debate, which also stems from the translation with credit *points* (ibid). Therefore, trade unions argue that if points are associated to competences without any additional qualitative criteria, learning efforts will shift to only focus on creditable learning outcomes (DGB 2007). If the idea to describe interchangeable units should lead to the modularisation of apprenticeships in their structure, trade unions would strongly oppose such developments since this might counteract the vocational principle. They are concerned that if competent bodies define units and—as in their view implicitly prevalent in the EU proposal—certification of single units takes place, a fragmentation of qualifications might occur (DGB 2007: 5). Furthermore, trade unions argue that ECVET does not consider major aspects of the trade unions' objectives for European VET policies (see Sect. 3.2.1).

Brief Evaluation

Two measures for implementing ECVET have been taken so far. First, a national coordination point for ECVET has been established and measures have been taken to facilitate and fund mobility experiences. These measures focus on a bottom-up implementation of ECVET. They are mostly means for fostering mobility during VET, which is still low. Here, ECVET is likely to serve as a standard for mobility experiences in the medium run. Second, the BMBF tried to foster permeability, flexibility and modularisation in Germany via the DECVET initiative, which aims at improving transitions within VET and across educational strands by measuring, transferring and crediting competences. The active role of the government in using ECVET in the national arena becomes obvious when taking into account that this way of implementing ECVET had not been intended by the Commission originally but was taken up on the EU level later on. However, during European negotiations, Germany opposed the idea that an automatic accumulation of partial qualifications across Europe could lead to full VET qualifications. Thus, the government actively opposed policies that would have affected the core features of the German VET system. Employers believe that the instrument is too abstract and incomprehensive; it should be implemented bottom-up and should not substitute for final examinations. While employers' preferences differ regarding modularisation (see Sect. 4.2.1), they do not support automatic recognition of prior competences that lead to shortening the duration of apprenticeships. Trade unions support an understanding of the instrument that fosters transnational mobility by setting standards. They are critical towards developments that could lead to a sole focus on creditable learning outcomes, modularisation or certification of single units.

While the first approach to ECVET as a bottom-up initiative is unlikely to influence fundamental pillars of VET, DECVET runs very close to affect core features of the German VET system. One aspect is the question of the dual training mode: if learning taking place in vocational preparation schemes or solely in schools can be accredited towards apprenticeships, this changes the balance between general and specific skills in the direction of general skills. If accreditation was made obligatory for firms, which it is not, their involvement in VET might decrease. The portability of skills will depend on the trustworthiness of the training carried out in forms other than dual learning. Another aspect is the flexibilisation of examinations, albeit procedures established within the pilot projects focus especially on transitions from initial to continuing VET. This being said, the DECVET project focuses on permeability on the basis of holistically occupational full VET courses. Modularisation is not understood as a 'pick and choose' concept for firms. Even more, firms can be expected to be unenthusiastic about crediting prior learning to apprenticeships due to cost-benefit relations and the insecurity that will always remain on content and depth of prior learning. DECVET has been carried out in the form of pilot projects, and the transfer of its results will only be discussed with other VET stakeholders in the medium run. Therefore, in sum,

DECVET does not affect core pillars of the German VET system. Its impact in the medium run remains to be seen.

3.2.5 Validation of Non-formal and Informal Learning

Procedures for validation of non-formal and informal learning are traditionally weakly developed in Germany. The education system is highly formalised, so that qualifications obtained outside of the formal system have less significance (interview DE_PRIV-1). A notable exception is the option to take part in the chambers' apprenticeship examinations as an external candidate (*Externenprüfung*) in accordance with §45 of the Vocational Training Act. Preparatory courses—often organised as extra-occupational courses—are offered for this exam. Candidates are required to either have work experience of a period at least one and a half times as long as the duration of the respective apprenticeship or must prove that they have acquired occupational proficiency in another way. 28,000 external candidates successfully completed examinations in 2009 (BMBF 2011). Another less-often mentioned exception is the option of upgrade training according to the Vocational Training Act (*Aufstiegsfortbildung*) (see Sect. 4.1): Here, validation of non-formal and informal learning is already possible and final examinations can be taken without participation in preparatory classes (Arbeitsgruppen zur Einbeziehung nicht-formal und informell erworbener Kompetenzen in den DQR 2011, interview DE_PRIV-1). Moreover, at the firm level, agreements on tariffs and competence development of the labour force sometimes include non-formal and informal competences.

There are discussions about increasing options for validation. Several programmes and initiatives with this objective had already been established before the Copenhagen process was launched (see Frank et al. 2003). For example, the federal government's lifelong learning programme had highlighted that procedures on measurement and assessment of individual competences should be developed (ibid), and recognition of informal learning was made a cornerstone in the 2004 lifelong learning strategy (BLK 2004). While this early discussion was partially steered by the EU, for example by the memorandum on lifelong learning (Frank et al. 2003), the topic became more present with the development of the DQR. The DQR should comprise all formal, non-formal and informal learning outcomes. However, in the testing phase as well as in the referencing process, only formal qualifications have been linked to the DQR. The DQR working group held its first meeting on validation in June 2010. In this meeting, different positions on validation were expressed (AK DQR 2012). Expert opinions pointed out different paths forward (Gutschow and Seidel 2010). First, validation could be implemented within the existing system in a selective way and on the basis of existing procedures in each educational pathway. In this scenario, validation would be linked to existing qualifications only. Second, a separate and systematic procedure for validation could be established. It would address existing qualifications as well as additional certificates. Third, a coherent competence-based system would be established for all qualifications. Existing qualifications would have to be formulated in competence-based terms and be opened up for the inclusion of informal and non-formal learning (ibid).

Two expert working groups were established in June 2011 with the objective to propose validation procedures. On the basis of expert hearings and several meetings, they published a joint recommendation in November 2011 (Arbeitsgruppen zur Einbeziehung nicht-formal und informell erworbener Kompetenzen in den DQR 2011). Based on a broad understanding of non-formal and informal learning,[33] they recommend that all forms of non-formal and informal learning should be made visible within the DQR. In their view, validation procedures comprise four steps: identification of competences, ascertainment, assessment, and certification. Information centres and competent bodies should be installed that have a monitoring function and solve conflicts. In the area of non-formal learning, education providers that fulfil certain quality criteria would propose to reference their educational programmes to a certain DQR level and competent bodies would carry out subsequent accreditation procedures. Established certificates of non-formal education, such as the Diploma in English Language Teaching to Adults (DELTA) could be linked to the DQR directly. In the area of informal learning, competent bodies would oversee the validation of individual competences. Quality standards and standards for the analysis of competences should be developed. One working group recommends that competent bodies should be independent and include social partners. As a final point, one working group recommended that when non-formal and informal qualifications do not fulfil all criteria of a NQR level, they should be linked to the DQR as elements of a full qualification (*"Qualifikationsteile"*). The recommendation stresses that this should not lead neither to any contradictions with the vocational principle nor to modularisation. In sum, these recommendations are very far-reaching and might challenge the standardisation of qualifications, since a bundle of qualifications or small-sized competences is put on equal footing with full VET qualifications.

The DQR working group discussed the recommendation in September 2012 and agreed with their main propositions (AK DQR 2012). It was proposed to install another expert group with the task to link 15 non-formal qualifications to the DQR by way of an example. After the Commission had issued a proposal for a new recommendation on validation of non-formal and informal learning (European Commission 2012), the BMBF announced launching another working group (AK DQR 2012). The DQR working group discussed the results of the latter ministry's working group with respect to possible consequences for the DQR.

---

[33]It is seen as continuing education (*Weiterbildung*) for both young persons and adults that can take place in associations, in educational institutions, during volunteer work, at the workplace, during mobility experiences, or in any other experience in which competences have been acquired.

In November 2011, the "Act for improving the assessment and recognition of vocational education and training qualifications acquired abroad"[34] improved and broadened procedures and criteria for the recognition of immigrants' qualifications. The Act establishes a right for the individual to have her qualifications assessed both regarding content and duration of training as well as regarding professional experience. About 10 million euros are invested in establishing new procedures (interview DE_PUBL-1). The initiative focuses only on full qualifications and does not introduce procedures for having partial qualifications recognised towards full qualifications. Procedures are primarily based on input-criteria. While the law coincided with the development of the DQR, the two processes were not interrelated (Hanf 2012).[35]

In spite of the manifold working groups, validation of non-formal and informal learning so far is "no major priority" (interview DE_PUBL-2) and many questions remain unanswered. First, although the working groups' recommendations are based on a very comprehensive understanding of validation, they lack a clear overall route for the implementation of validation procedures. They recommend establishing competent bodies, but their set-up and role is not specified. While competent bodies are supposed to accredit non-formal learning programmes, at the same time they should oversee the validation of informal learning. Second, it is not specified who pays for validation procedures. Voluntary examiners will not be able to fulfil this task, so that privatisation might be a consequence (interview DE_PUBL-4). Third, because of political reasons, primary and secondary education were left out of the DQR (see Sect. 4.2.2)—this however is a contradiction to the broad understanding of competences in validation processes which now exclude general education qualifications. Can language certificates be linked to the DQR if obtained through non-formal education, but not if language skills have been acquired at schools? Finally, it is not yet clear if validation shall be a tool for the accreditation towards full qualifications or if validation procedures should also be carried out for small individual competences. Civil society organisations demand the latter: for example, qualifications obtained as a trainer in sport associations should be validated and linked to the DQR. This view is supported by experts, for example Deissinger et al. (2011: 399). Other experts argue that relating learning outcomes to qualifications is a precondition for referencing informal learning to the DQR (Gutschow and Seidel 2010) and that the recognition of non-formal and informal qualifications should be based on existing (initial and continuing) VET professions (Kremer 2007: 38).

---

[34]Original: "Gesetz zur Verbesserung der Feststellung und Anerkennung im Ausland erworbener Berufsqualifikationen."

[35]Hanf (2012) moreover points out that in many ways, the law relates to the European directive 2005/36/EC (see Chap. 2). In this sense, the new law amplifies recognition procedures to non-restricted occupations (ibid).

Politics of Reform and Actors' Positions

In the view of the government, it is necessary to keep the high quality of VET. Validation mechanisms should always lead to full qualifications (interview DE_PUBL-1). Procedures already exist, and it is questionable if a sufficient number of participants would make use of further validation mechanisms. Still, it would be possible to install a coherent and comprehensive system such as the one already existing in Switzerland or to amplify those procedures established by the Act for the assessment and recognition of VET qualifications acquired abroad (ibid). In general, as pointed out above, validation has not been made a "major priority" in Germany (interview DE_PUBL-2).

Employers in general support procedures for validating non-formal and informal learning since it allows them to better evaluate the competences of applicants and employees. However, preferences differ across employers' organisations. While the BDA believes that new validation procedures should be tested (interview DE_PRIV-3), the DIHK does not see any need for additional practices within VET (Lambertz 2012). The Chambers refer to experiences in other countries which point at a rather small take-up of validation procedures and that in other countries individual learning outcomes are not linked to the national qualifications framework directly. In the view of the ZDH, validation should be introduced only for specific target groups, focussing on subsequent participation in the formal system (interview DE_PRIV-2). Otherwise, validation might lead to an erosion of the formal system: especially large companies might hire unskilled workers, and have some of their skills validated after a few years on the job (ibid). This already takes place occasionally at large firms; employees are then registered for the Chambers' VET examinations as an external candidate (interview DE_PRIV-3).

Trade unions stress that social partners should be included in the development of validation procedures and that a "cooperative model" should be developed for validation of non-formal and informal learning (Nehls 2012). In spite of this positive view on validation, trade unions also point out critical factors. When it comes to preparatory vocational qualifications, firms will most likely not be required to recognise them in subsequent apprenticeships, which would reduce the utility of validation processes. Nehls underlines the importance of occupational proficiency (*berufliche Handlungsfähigkeit*), which should also be kept for validation procedures. Moreover, he demands that individuals should not have to pay for validation procedures (ibid). In general, procedures for assessing competences will be highly complex, so that the cost-benefit relationship of such proceedings might be questionable (interview DE_UN-1). Trade unions do not support validation of competences below the threshold of apprenticeships, since experience shows that many participants do not continue their education (ibid).

Brief Evaluation

Validation of non-formal and informal learning is weakly developed in Germany; notable exceptions are the option to take part in the Chambers' apprenticeship examinations as an external candidate and the recognition of previously acquired competences within upgrade training. The further path is still unclear, although discussions were steered by the DQR and several working groups dealt with the issue. Especially, it is unclear how costs for validation procedures are shared, if recognition and examination bodies are to be set up in a corporatist way, and which qualifications should be linked to the DQR.

For the focus of this book, several aspects are important: First, there is a risk that validation mechanisms lead to de facto sub-qualifications—and hence to de-standardisation. Firms might hire school graduates as unskilled workers, train them on the job and have their skills validated without full apprenticeships. While some large firms already pursue such strategies, this might be extended with the introduction of additional validation procedures. Such firms might then back out of the dual system. The BDA supports testing new procedures, while Chambers believe that currently existing options are sufficient and the crafts sector supports the introduction of new procedures for specific target groups only. The latter two organisations have self-interest in keeping exams since they are responsible for them. Trade unions argue that validation should always be orientated towards full qualifications. Second, it will be important to observe if partial qualifications or individual competences are linked to the DQR via validation of non-formal and informal learning. Such a way of implementation might steer the further differentiation of VET. Third, although final examinations comprise the VET schools' curriculum as far as it is "essential" for the apprenticeship,[36] examinations prioritise company-based VET and do usually not cover general education subjects that are taught at VET schools during apprenticeships. Therefore, the balance of skills changes with the introduction of validation procedures. Fourth, since it is not clear how competent bodies for validation of non-formal and informal learning could look like, validation procedures might also be carried out by private actors. This would imply a marketisation of VET and decrease the involvement of employer organisations. Yet, with all of these risks, it will largely depend on how validation of informal and non-formal learning will be implemented in Germany; so far, stakeholders' preferences do not point at a conflict with fundamental pillars of the dual system.

---

[36]The Vocational Training Act specifies in §38 that the final examination shall test—next to other skills—the familiarity "with the content of the curriculum to be taught at vocational schools that is essential for the apprenticeship." Original: "In ihr [der Abschlussprüfung, C.A.] soll der Prüfling nachweisen, dass er (...) mit dem im Berufsschulunterricht vermittelnden, für die Berufsausbildung wesentlichen Lehrstoff vertraut ist."

3.2.6 Quality Assurance

Quality procedures in German VET are mostly focused on standards such as standardised definitions of broad and holistic competences, and on training meeting the demands of the labour market. Against this background, the duality of learning places is of central importance. Training ordinances are continuously modernised in order to meet new market needs or technological advancements. The modernisation of training ordinances lies in the responsibility of the Federal Ministry of Economics and Technology, and is carried out in close co-operation with social partners and the *Länder*. Federal training ordinances set standards and create common rights and duties for all actors involved in dual VET. Examinations assure a common standard and the portability of qualifications. The responsibility for examinations lies with independent committees of the local Chambers and they are carried out by practitioners that equally represent employers, employees and VET school teachers. It is a rule that examiners do not test their own trainees or students, so that the skills of apprentices and the quality of apprenticeships are often assessed by a company's competitors (interview DE_PRIV-2). Comprehensive statistics are provided by the annual reports on VET and national education reports. While quality assurance mechanisms exist for VET schools—such as standards, common curricula as well as inspections of schools, classes and examinations (interview DE_PUBL-4)—quality of training by firms is monitored by the Chambers. Moreover, in order to be eligible for training apprentices, trainers have to fulfil certain criteria defined by decree. In particular in large firms, comprehensive internal quality management tools are commonly used (Küßner 2009). Apprentices keep minutes of the training throughout the apprenticeship as a precondition for taking part in examinations.

Quality management procedures have not been on the top of the agenda (Euler 2006). A vast debate on quality of VET took place in the 1970s—at that time, studies had shown that the quality of apprenticeships differs across occupations, sectors and firms. Currently, the debate mostly focuses on the argument that the German VET system is a quality standard in itself, and therefore there are no pressures to introduce changes in this area (Werner and Rothe 2011a: 3).

Still, the quality of VET is subject to critique in national debates, which is voiced by several experts and by trade unions. Euler (2006) argues that several indicators show a need for quality management procedures in work-based training. A high number of contracts are terminated before the completion of the apprenticeship. In a substantial number of cases, training in companies is not carried out according to the firm's training plan—sometimes apprentices are not even familiar with it. Much of the training of apprentices is de facto carried out by personnel that have not been trained for this task, for example journeymen (ibid). Moreover, a substantial number of graduates do not find employment in the occupation they have been trained for. The double function of the Chambers to both consult and monitor firms might lead to a conflict of interest. Another point of critique is geared towards the quality of training at schools, which is often criticised by employers. Critique often points at inadequate structures, didactics, schools lacking modern technological equipment, little practical relevance, and small-scale co-operation with firms. Euler (2006) observes that social partners address the issue of quality only if it is beyond the scope of their own responsibility. As a final point, quality of training in firms is not studied to a sufficient degree (Nickolaus 2009). There is no coherent strategy for the system as a whole and there is no systematic evaluation of existing practices. In sum, while the quality assurance of German VET focuses on standards, there are a few points of critique which are not systematically addressed. Much of this critique focuses on the quality of training on the provider level.

The implementation of European instruments for quality assurance is still at its beginning. In 2008, a reference point for quality assurance in VET (DEQA-VET) was launched and is located at the BIBB. It aims at promoting a "culture of quality assurance" by developing measures for supporting quality assurance, fostering networks among national actors and institutions, providing information on quality assurance and on best practices, and by organising expert meetings and conferences (DEQA-VET 2010). However, the reference point's tasks do neither include the creation of a coherent strategy on quality assurance nor the implementation of the EQARF quality circle. In addition to establishing DEQA-VET, Germany took part in two peer learning activities on quality assurance in the dual system in 2007 and 2009 (Küßner 2009) and organised a European expert conference on "work-based learning—meeting demands of labour market and lifelong learning".

Politics of Reform and Actors' Positions

In general, the government does not see need for action in the field of quality assurance. In a response to a minor interpellation on the question what problems exist regarding the quality of VET and how the government aims to address these, the government answered that "since surveys show a high satisfaction of apprentices with their education, in the view of the federal government there is no urgent need for action at the moment" (Deutscher Bundestag 2010b: 2).[37]

While the government supports EQARF, it does not seem to put a lot of effort into implementing it. On the one hand, the government believes that the instrument "provides an opportunity to show the manifold activities and established procedures that already exist in Germany as well as to further support the cooperation of actors in the field of education" (Küßner 2009: 7).[38] Existing approaches of quality assurance shall be developed further in order to establish a national strategy, and experiences on quality mechanisms shall be subject to exchange on the national and

---

[37]Original: „Angesichts der Tatsache, dass lediglich etwa 7 bis 8 Prozent mit ihrer Ausbildung eher oder gar sehr unzufrieden waren, besteht nach Auffassung der Bundesregierung derzeit kein akuter Handlungsbedarf (Deutscher Bundestag 2010b: 2).

[38]Original: "Sie [die Empfehlung zur Einrichtung eines europäischen Bezugsrahmens für Qualitätssicherung, C.A.] bietet vor allem die Chance, die in Deutschland bereits vorhandenen vielfältigen Aktivitäten und bewährten Verfahren sichtbar zu machen und die Zusammenarbeit der Bildungsakteure weiter zu fördern."

European level. (Deutscher Bundestag 2010b). On the other hand, interview partners expect European quality assurance policies to have little or even no impact at all. An interview partner from the federal administration believes that major changes are unlikely (interview DE_PUBL-1). As another interview partner from the federal administration puts it: EQARF and EQAVET are "tolerated, and one is a bit obligated to do something, but also the link to national politics (...) is not that elaborated" (interview DE_PUBL-2).[39] This is confirmed by an interview partner from an employers' organisation: in his view, the BMBF does not put a lot of effort into implementing EQARF (interview DE_PRIV-3). The national reference point for quality assurance is smaller than in other European countries and has fewer competences (Früh 2010). An interview partner from a trade union argues that the reference point and its network are "toothless" (interview DE_UN-1). Matters are further complicated by the fact that *Länder* are responsible for VET schools, so that the federal government cannot introduce common structures.

The German government actively influenced the European processes according to their preferences. At the European level, the government opposed the introduction of indicators as benchmarks for comparisons and instead highlighted the nature of the indicators as a "toolbox" (Küßner 2009: 7). Meanwhile, the vagueness of indicators is used to adjust the reporting in a way that indicators are met best (interview DE_PUBL-6).

It is worthwhile to take a closer look at an argument an interview partner from the federal administration brings forward regarding the unlikeliness of introducing a policy cycle for quality management (interview DE_PUBL-2). In his view, the hesitation stems from the far-reaching consequences the instrument could unfold. He gives the example of drop-outs from the apprenticeship system: with a quality cycle it would be necessary to analyse at what point and why apprentices left the system. Such an analysis would require the establishment of causal chains on the reasons of drop-outs. At this point, however, actors of the system would need to admit that the system is not working as it should. Yet, as the interview partner argues, employers "do not allow interferences"[40] in the sense that they should, for example, increase investments in trainers by a certain amount. Hence, a demand like this would never be brought forward in policy papers. For employers, it is easier to say that outside of the dual system young persons are not being well-prepared for an apprenticeship. That is why in the view of the interview partner, actors are not interested in evidence-based policy: "If transparency becomes high enough, snugness ends"[41] (ibid). In the end, because employers fear costs and follow-up efforts from addressing problems of the system such as the number of apprenticeship drop-outs, the introduction of a cycle of quality management is unlikely.

---

[39]Original: "geduldet, man ist ein bisschen verpflichtet, was zu machen, aber der Link zur nationalen Politik (...), der ist nicht so elaboriert."

[40]Original: "Lassen sich nicht reinreden."

[41]Original: "Wenn die Transparenz groß genug wird, hört die Gemütlichkeit auf."

Employers argue that European instruments should be implemented within and in accordance with existing structures and without new bureaucracy or costs for companies—regarding both the content of qualifications and quality assurance (KWB 2010). In their understanding, EQARF can serve as a voluntary tool; descriptors and procedures should by no means be compulsory (KWB 2008b). Only relevant indicators should be used in Germany (interview DE_PUBL-6). In general, quality assurance mechanisms are seen to be well-established in Germany but will need to be adjusted to learning outcomes. Efforts made for implementing EQARF and for reporting to the Commission on the instrument should not exceed the benefits of the instrument (ibid). On the European level, employers' organisations had criticised that EQARF asks for quality management systems at provider level (see Chap. 2), especially against the background that in some countries, companies are VET providers. In Germany, it would be difficult especially for SMEs to install comprehensive new quality mechanisms (interview DE_PRIV-3). In sum, employers believe that EQARF can support the quality of the system (ibid), but clearly prefer an instrument with little implementation costs and few compulsory elements.

Trade unions continuously criticise the quality of apprenticeships in several regards. The trade union's youth organisation regularly publishes a VET report in which apprentices are surveyed on the quality and conditions of their training (DGB 2012). In all of these reports, they find problems related to the violation of regulations, for example on working hours, health and safety regulations for underage workers. Problems vary across occupations and with the size of the training firm. Trade unions criticise that the Chambers' training consultants who monitor the quality of training in firms are overstrained and cannot sufficiently fulfil their task (interview DE_UN-1). They argue that once a firm is admitted as a training company, monitoring is low, and that a coherent approach to quality is missing (ibid). Unions also criticise a lack of resources at VET schools regarding the modernity of material and machines as well as concerning the availability of teachers (DGB 2012). Regarding EQARF, trade unions prefer to use all 10 indicators (interview DE_PUBL-6). They support the introduction of a quality circle and argue that especially two elements, evaluation and reflexion, are not pronounced features of the German VET system (interview DE_UN-1). In the trade unions' view, firms fulfil a societal and public function in training, so that they have to take quality criteria into account also beyond managerial logics (ibid).

Brief Evaluation

German VET focuses on standards, procedures and certification, but largely lacks comprehensive quality management. Apart from the establishment of a national reference point with very limited powers, European processes have not lead to any changes in quality assurance so far. Although the government in principle supports initiatives on quality assurance on the basis of existing instruments, it believes that quality in VET is already very high so that there is limited need for action. The government highlights that EQARF indicators are a 'toolbox' and that their use is voluntary: Germany had opposed to introduce them as benchmarks. Employers oppose any additional regulation on quality that is not voluntary, since this would interfere with their training arrangements as VET providers, and increase costs. Especially SMEs might have difficulties to deal with additional quality requirements, while large firms often have comprehensive quality mechanisms in place. An interview partner from the federal administration argues that the introduction of a policy cycle for quality management is unlikely, since it might interfere with the way training is carried out and hence might lead to higher costs. Trade unions criticise that current regulation is both insufficient and often not followed; they actively lobby for improving the quality of VET.

3.3 Conclusions

The discussion on the Copenhagen process has been very controversial in Germany. In the words of Rauner (2005), the introduction of a qualifications framework would mean to "sacrifice a highlight of German business culture for an inferior European solution." At the beginning of the debate it was largely believed that implementing Copenhagen would require the modularisation of the German VET system. Several authors believed that the implementation of the Copenhagen process would also lead to the introduction of a "à la carte" system in the direction of the British market-led training regime. On the other hand, Kremer (2007), for instance, believed that units were necessary for the implementation of EQF/ECVET but could be established within nationally regulated full qualifications—and hence in line with the fundamental pillars of VET. How did the instruments of the Copenhagen process impact the German VET system in practice?

In 2011, a q*ualifications framework,* the DQR, was introduced in Germany. The process was steered by the federal and *Länder* administrations, and involved a broad range of stakeholders, including social partners. The framework was passed in consensus. Long discussions on the design of the DQR improved the mutual understanding among actors across education subsystems. The descriptors for the DQR have been adjusted to reflect the distinct balance between broad and specific skills of the German VET system. VET qualifications are referenced to the DQR as follows: vocational preparation schemes—level 1 and 2, 2-year apprenticeships—level 3, "standard apprenticeships" lasting 3 or 3½ years—level 4, and upgrade training (such as *Meister* qualifications)—level 6 together with the bachelor's degree. All DQR levels are open for occupational qualifications. Referencing for secondary school qualifications will be carried out in 2017. This is a compromise stemming from a conflict in which *Länder* education ministers had argued that the general school leaving certificate should be referenced to level 5 together with high-ranking apprenticeships; however, they remained isolated with this position. Open questions remain, most importantly regarding the future referencing process, the referencing of high-value VET qualifications such as speech therapy, and a

3.3 Conclusions

potential impact on the design of training ordinances which could be aligned to meet criteria for certain DQR levels. So far, referencing has not been carried out according to learning outcomes or competences but based on input criteria.

While Powell and Trampusch (2011: 294) assume that NQFs steer reforms "also by indirectly inducing change in the national vocational training institutions, for example through enhanced modularization", such tendencies have not been observed in my analysis. The DQR maps the education system rather than impacts it. In line with Busemeyer (2012), the analysis shows that the DQR hardly achieve the objective to increase permeability, since it does not change admission procedures. While most VET qualifications are still grouped on the lower DQR levels (Busemeyer 2012), the standing of VET is improved by referencing upgrade training qualifications and bachelor's degrees to the same level and by opening all DQR levels for VET qualifications. Moreover, although the DQR encompasses all educational pathways, the departments dealing with VET took the lead in the process. The differentiation of VET is increased by assigning different levels to 2-year and "standard" apprenticeships.

The concept of *learning outcomes* is largely understood as "competences" in Germany and thus has been adjusted to reflect the specific balance of skills of the German dual system. The Copenhagen process is likely to speed up the reform towards a competence-based orientation of training ordinances and curricula that has been ongoing but is far from being completed. The government argues that the European focus on learning outcomes can advance the status of VET in relation to higher education. Trade unions believe that a shift towards learning outcomes can blur the mix between specific and general skills, a core feature of the German system, since the German balance of skills is also based on the duality of learning as well as on learning methods and training contents. However, with the adjustment of the concept to the idea of competences and the reform of ordinances and curricula that have been ongoing in the past without challenging the dual principle, such an impact is highly unlikely.

ECVET has been implemented in two different ways. First, the establishment of a national coordination point and the provision of funding for mobility experiences via the Leonardo da Vinci programme focus on a bottom-up implementation of ECVET. The instrument is a means to foster transnational mobility. Second, the DECVET initiative actively fosters modularisation, flexibility and permeability of the national VET system. The objective is to improve transitions within VET and across educational strands by measuring, transferring and crediting competences. While the first taking of ECVET is unlikely to have an influence on the core features of VET, DECVET might affect portability and certification by flexibilising exam preparation and admission. Since DECVET is based on pilot projects, its effects so far have been limited to these.

A national reference point for *quality assurance* in VET (DEQA-VET) has been established that aims at fostering a culture of quality. DEQA-VET has limited powers. A policy cycle for quality management has not been established. While fostering quality assurance could help to address malfunctionings of the system, from a political economy perspective it also potentially raises costs for firms, especially for SMEs. This could lead to a decreasing number of training firms, and hence would affect a core pillar of the German VET system. In one of my interviews, a public official clearly stated that it is the potential impact of quality assurance on firms that makes firms lobby the government to not stress quality assurance too much—and the government follows. However, a certain scope for fostering quality at the provider level should exist without making firms drop out of the training system. My analysis shows that so far, the impact of EQARF and ENQAVET is marginal.

No changes have been introduced in the field of *validation of non-formal and informal learning*. It was agreed to deal with the topic after the development of the DQR, which explicitly comprises all formal, non-formal and informal qualifications. Although the DQR steered discussions on the topic and two working groups dealt with the issue, further development is still unclear.

Politics of Reform and Actors' Positions
The government proactively fostered modularisation and flexibility of the VET system. As an interview partner from the federal administration puts it: "Another thing is the question how you can use Europe as an instigator and respectively sometimes as a punching bag, you do that according to requirements. (...) Sometimes, Europe simply is the battering ram which allows us to breathe some fresh air into encrusted national debates during discussions, and we actively make use of that" (interview DE_PUBL-1).[42] As the above analysis shows, at the early stage of the discussion the government actively fostered change by launching the so-called innovation circle which developed reform proposals. Here, Europeanisation was brought forward as an argument of why change would be necessary. Subsequently, pilot programmes on "building blocks" ("modules") were introduced. The DECVET initiative fosters modularisation and flexibility, while such an understanding of ECVET originally had not been intended by the Commission. An interview partner from an employers' organisation underlines the active role of the federal administration: "Somebody at the ministry simply wanted to set a monument for himself."[43] The government actively used the Copenhagen process as a justification for fostering reforms. This finding is in line with existing literature: Trampusch (2008) also shows that the government used the Europeanisation of VET to strengthen its role in the policy process. Still, because of lacking support (see below) and the limited role assigned to the federal government in VET, initiatives mostly take the form of pilot projects whose impact remains to be seen.

---

[42]Original: "Das andere ist die Frage, wie kann man Europa nutzen als Impulsgeber beziehungsweise manchmal auch als Prügelknabe, das macht man dann je nach Bedarf. Aber wichtig ist, dass man überhaupt einen Ankerpunkt hat. Europa ist manchmal einfach der Rammbock, der uns erlaubt, bei verkrusteten nationalen Debatten frischen Wind reinzubringen in den Diskussionen, und das nutzen wir auch aktiv."

[43]Context: "One thing I find unfortunate in general is that now one says: the one thing only transnational mobility, the other only permeability, just because one writes a "D" in front of it. (...) Somebody at the ministry simply wanted to set a monument for themselves." Original: "Ich finde es grundsätzlich unglücklich, dass man jetzt dann sagt: das eine nur transnationale Mobilität, das andere Durchlässigkeit, nur weil man ein "D" davor schreibt. (...) Da wollte sich halt jemand im Ministerium ein Denkmal setzen."

3.3 Conclusions

The government mentions the following reasons for fostering modularisation and flexibility: improving transitions from school to apprenticeships; preventing that the same training contents are learned twice in different programmes, which artificially prolongs the duration of training; and improving the situation of dropouts. The "holistic" German system is seen as being too "inflexible" to accommodate these quests (interview DE_PUBL-2). Yet, two aspects are striking. First, it is questionable if modularisation is the right policy tool for solving these problems, especially regarding the transitions from school to apprenticeships, which constitute a profound malfunction of the German training regime and a vast inclusion problem (see Sect. 3.1). Firms actually oppose an automatic recognition of prior competences because it is against their business case for training. Hence, if the recognition of prior training takes place automatically, firms might hire fewer graduates of vocational preparation schemes; if it is voluntary, the impact is likely to be low. Second, alternative policies exist. The government could, for example, increase the number of extra-company training places and thus enable every school leaver to start an apprenticeship or increase support during apprenticeships such as additional coaching. The quest for modularisation and thus flexibility therefore has to be understood as a political choice. It is in line with demands voiced by large employers.

The government does not support a full liberalisation of VET. When it comes to modularisation, there is the agreement that units should not be too small (interview DE_PUBL-2). There is a large consensus that final examinations should be kept (ibid). The government has proactively limited the impact of the Copenhagen process on Germany. During European negotiations, Germany opposed the idea of an automatic accumulation of partial qualifications across Europe that could lead to full VET qualifications as well as the automatic accumulation of learning outcomes across countries ('Mr X'). Such shaping of policies on the European level also took place with quality assurance policies; Germany opposed to use quality indicators as benchmarks. The government, moreover, reinterprets terms used on the European level, such as "flexible pathways": "We interpret that [flexible pathways, C.A.] never in a way that it is an 'à la carte' system in a training sector, but that permeability shall be increased" (interview DE_PUBL-2).[44] The reason for this might be that the government wants to present itself as "good Europeans" and as a leading actor in Europe—a motivation an interview partner (DE_PUBL-1) from the federal administration had mentioned several times.

In the early stage of the discussion on the impact of the Copenhagen process, employers believed that modularisation would be a necessary consequence from European proceedings. At that time they made a proposal for an integrated EQF-ECVET system that would require modularisation, but is in line with the fundamental pillars of the system. The ongoing shift towards a competence-orientation of training ordinances is supported. Employers are largely satisfied

---

[44]Original: "wir interpretieren das nie so, dass das ein ‚à la carte'-System in einem Ausbildungsbereich ist, sondern dass die Durchlässigkeit gesteigert werden soll."

with the application of descriptors to the national realm and believe that the DQR helps firms at the first stage of assessing applicants' qualifications. ECVET is seen as being too abstract and incomprehensive and should be implemented bottom-up. Because costs would increase, they do not support automatic recognition of prior competences that lead to a shortening of the duration of apprenticeships. The same holds for additional non-voluntary regulation on quality.

Employers' positions on modularisation and flexibilisation diverged. In the view of the BDA, sectors should have more flexibility in deciding on the design of dual training. While keeping final examinations, this includes options as introducing modularisation, reducing the duration of training, and carrying out examinations for "building blocks" at the firm level. This view challenges the certification and portability of skills and deregulates the VET system. Chambers propose a reform that bundles training in related occupations in the first 2 years of an apprenticeship, and then offers a choice of modules for more specialised training in the third year. This adjustment would make skills broader and more firm-specific at the same time, while being largely in line with the fundamental pillars of dual VET. The crafts sector opposes modularisation, since it would reduce the flexibility of firms to integrate training into their business routine. In their opinion, modules should be limited to specific target groups. Because of the business case of the crafts sector for apprenticeships, the duration of training should not be reduced. The diverging preferences of employers were also reflected in the DQR referencing process: With the support of the BDA, employers from several sectors (IT, metal, machine building and high tech) had demanded to reference apprenticeships to three levels, while ZDH and DIHK oppose such a differentiation. Regarding the validation of non-formal and informal learning, the BDA supports testing new procedures while the craft sector supports this for specific target groups only and Chambers believe that existing options are sufficient. In general, the latter two organisations have a strong self-interest in keeping final examinations, since they constitute a core task of the organisations (Busemeyer 2009b; Thelen and Busemeyer 2008; Trampusch 2010b). Complementing or replacing final exams with exams carried out at firm-level is also more costly for SMEs (Busemeyer and Trampusch 2011b).

Trade unions oppose modularisation as well as any changes that would challenge the fundamental pillars of dual VET. They aim at foreclosing the introduction of an 'à la carte' system, an understanding of education that is solely based on economic considerations, and a further differentiation of apprenticeships. The latter is why they had originally proposed a five-level-structure for the DQR, in which all apprenticeships are grouped on the lowest level. Although unions support the DQR in its current form and were in favour of adjusting descriptors to better reflect occupational proficiency (*berufliche Handlungsfähigkeit*), they are concerned that the DQR might strengthen the standing of qualifications below the level of skilled workers and that firms could back out of standardised apprenticeships. Therefore, validation should be orientated towards full qualifications. In their view, with a shift towards learning outcomes, learning methods become arbitrary; moreover, there is the risk that learning outcomes refer to a narrower set of qualifications. Regarding ECVET, they support an understanding of the instrument that fosters transnational

3.3 Conclusions

mobility by setting standards. However, unions are critical towards implementing ECVET in a way that could lead to focussing solely on creditable learning outcomes, modularisation or certification of single units. For many years, unions have moreover criticised that current regulation on quality assurance is both insufficient and often not abided.

My analysis therefore shows that when it comes to modularisation and certification of single units (not final examinations) at the firm level, VET stakeholders are divided into two coalitions. These actors' coalitions have already been described in the literature (Busemeyer 2012; Trampusch 2010b). On the one hand, large firms lobby for reform in this direction. They cooperate with public administration in order to steer institutional change in the direction of modularisation and increasing flexibility of training. On the other hand, an "alliance of preservers" (Busemeyer 2012) of Chambers, the craft sector and trade unions opposes these steps. However, contrary to the predictions mentioned in the literature that had foreseen a fundamental transformation of the German VET system in the direction of modularisation and flexibility, my analysis shows that the coalition between some employers and the public sector so far has not been successful in steering institutional change.

Chapter 4
The Impact of the Copenhagen Process on the Dutch Training Regime

4.1 The Dutch Vocational Education and Training System

The Dutch VET system dates back to employers' initiatives during industrialisation in the nineteenth and twentieth centuries. There is a historically grown division between general and academic education (*algemeen onderwijs*) and vocational education (*beroepsonderwijs*) (Anderson and Hassel 2013). An important reform of the VET system took place in 1996 with the introduction of the Adult and Vocational Education Act (*Wet educatie beroepsvorming*, WEB). An objective of the law was to bring VET closer to the needs of the labour market, since in the late 1970s and the early 1980s employers often complained that graduates were not even able to hold a hammer (Brandsma 2006). Several high-ranking advisory commissions—the Wagner Commission (1983), the Rauwenhoff Commission (1990) and the Van Veen Commission (1993)—had recommended to improve the standing of business within VET decision-making structures and increase the time spent at workplace-based learning (Hövels and Roelofs 2007: 4). One reform proposal which would have dissolved the apprenticeship system was opposed by social partners (Anderson and Hassel 2013: 185). Instead, and as outlined below, the WEB integrated the school-based VET system and apprenticeships as distinct pathways under one roof. The reform strengthened the influence of employers, which before had been limited mostly to the apprenticeship system. Instead, it installed a system of shared responsibility between the state, educational institutions and social partners. The WEB reform has strengthened workplace-based learning within VET (Van Lieshout 2007; Anderson and Hassel 2013). Schools gained more autonomy and have a strong standing in the system.

It is often stated that the objective of VET in the Netherlands is threefold: firstly to acquire occupational competences that are necessary for entering the labour market, secondly to establish the basis for continuing (vocational) education and training, and thirdly to equip participants with societal and cultural competences in the sense of citizenship training (Hövels and Roelofs 2007: 7; Visser et al. 2009).

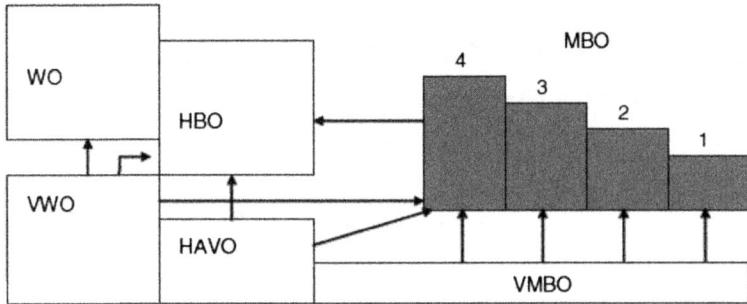

Fig. 4.1 Secondary education, VET and higher education in the Netherlands. *Source*: Hövels and Roelofs (2007: 2), own adjustments

The Qualification Structure

After primary education, at the age of 12, students choose between three secondary education pathways:

- "Pre-university education" (*voorbereidend wetenschappelijk onderwijs*, VWO) lasts 6 years and leads to a higher education entrance qualification. Many students also continue their education by enrolling in professional education at the tertiary level (HBO, see below);
- "General secondary education" (*hoger algemeen voortgezet onderwijs*, HAVO) lasts 5 years. It offers access to tertiary professional education, but many participants also continue with a MBO (see below);
- "Pre-vocational secondary education" (*voorbereidend middelbaar beroepsonderwijs*, VMBO) lasts 4 years and combines vocational and general education. Four different learning paths exist within VMBO which differ regarding their combinations of *leren* (theory) and *werken* (practice). Three of these programmes prepare for MBO on level 3 or 4 with different mixtures of general and pre-vocational training, and the fourth pathway prepares for MBO on level 2. After finishing VMBO, students can study for additional 2 years in HAVO; the same is possible for HAVO graduates who wish to graduate from school with a VWO (Fig. 4.1).

Secondary vocational education (*middelbaar beroepsonderwijs*, MBO) and adult education are regulated by the WEB. With about 75 % of VMBO graduates and many HAVO graduates entering MBO, it is the most popular education pathway after secondary education (Anderson and Oude Nijhuis 2011). MBO comprises two pathways:

- BOL (*beroepsopleidende leerweg*), which could be translated with extra-company training. BOL is school-based VET. The government has fostered the relative importance of workplace-based learning within the BOL track, so that it now involves between 20 and 60 % training at the workplace in the form of BVPs (*beroepspraktijkvorming, BVP*) (Anderson and Oude Nijhuis 2011). It is possible to study the programme full-time or part-time. The participant has to receive at least 850 hours of qualified training at school during the time of her study; and

- BBL (*beroepsbegeleidende leerweg*), which is a dual apprenticeship system. Usually, 1 day is spent at school and 4 days are spent at the training company. The apprentice has a contract with the training company.

In principle, it is possible to change between the two pathways during VET.[1] General skills—such as related to citizenship, entrepreneurship, Dutch, and on MBO 4 a foreign language—are part of all MBO courses. This is regulated by a national framework (interview NL_PUBL-3).

There are several differences between the two programmes. With about 70 % of all MBO students, BOL has more participants than BBL (MOCW 2012: 119). While most BOL participants enter the programme directly after completing secondary education, almost half of all BBL participants are older than 24 (ibid). Therefore, BBL can be an option for low qualified workers to acquire a VET qualification at the upper secondary level at a later stage (Hövels and Roelofs 2007: 29). After graduation, BBL graduates find employment more easily and have higher salaries (Visser 2010a). Visser relates this to higher levels of practical experience and to the fact that most participants are employed already. For BOL graduates, employment chances increase with the level of the MBO (MOCW 2012). Plug and Groot (1998: 14) have found that in the long run, income and employment opportunities hardly differ between BOL and BBL graduates. This is because BOL graduates have more upwards mobility and can shift more easily to higher education (Van Lieshout 2007; interview NL_PUBL-1). Moreover, studies have found that the jobs of BOL graduates usually match their qualification levels and occupations better (Van Lieshout 2007).

In general, the status of BOL is higher than the status of BBL (Anderson and Hassel 2013; Van Lieshout 2007: 322; interviews NL_PUBL-4, NL_MIXED-5). Still, BBL is a widely accepted educational route (Anderson and Hassel 2013) and employers have a strong liking for the BBL track (interview NL_PRIV-1). However, the interview partner also stressed that this is most valid in the field of technology, and that firms have different preferences, so that the strength of the system lies in the duality of the pathways (ibid). Both pathways comprise work-based and theoretical learning—but the balance differs, and so does the balance between broad and specific skills. Since more students participate in the BOL track, the workforce overall has broader and less specific skills than in Germany.

---

[1]There are certain obstacles: for example, the respective qualification might not be offered in the other pathway on the same level, the local ROC decided not to offer it, or curricula might differ (see Hövels and Roelofs (2007).

Four different MBO levels exist which prepare for occupations with different levels of competence regarding the level of responsibility, the complexity of tasks, and the ability to transfer abilities and skills to new situations (Brandsma 2006: 97):[2]

- Level 1 (*assistentenopleiding*): assistant worker, which comprises vocational preparation schemes and enables graduates to carry out simple tasks under supervision. VET on this level lasts between ½ year and 1 year. Graduates can progress to MBO level 2;
- Level 2 (*basisberoepsopleiding*): basic vocational training, which lasts between 2 and 3 years. Graduates are skilled workers that mostly work under supervision. Graduates can move on to MBO level 3 and, under certain conditions, to MBO level 4;
- Level 3 (*vakopleiding*): professional training, which trains participants for skilled workers' positions in which they perform tasks autonomously. Training lasts between 2 and 4 years. Graduates can move on to MBO level 4; and
- Level 4 (*middenkaderopleiding* or *specialistenopleiding*): middle management training, which usually lasts 4 years and prepares participants to perform tasks autonomously and with higher responsibility than on MBO level 3. Specialist training lasts 1 or 2 years; participants need to have completed MBO studies at level 3 (or 4). It allows graduates to enter HBO (see below), a route that more than half of MBO 4 graduates take.[3]

While more than two thirds of MBO students graduate with an MBO on level 4, only 2 % leave the MBO system with an MBO on level 1 (MOCW 2012: 8).[4] In 2011, only 4 % of MBO students participated in a programme on level 1 and 24 % in one on level 2, while 28 % were enrolled in a programme on level 3 and the remaining 45 % in a MBO 4 programme.[5] BBL has a stronger focus on levels 1 and 2 (Visser 2010a). The general conception is that level 1 does not have a high value on the labour market (NL_MIXED-9). Social partners believe that as many young persons as possible should obtain at least a MBO 3 qualification (StvdA 2008: 9). It has been criticised that the qualification structure is too complex, and that the differentiation between the levels is not always clear-cut (Van Lieshout 2007).

On the tertiary level, "professional higher education" (*hoger beroepsonderwijs*, HBO) programmes usually combine theoretical knowledge and specific skills and are geared towards a specific occupation or occupational field. Programmes are

---

[2]I took English translations for the level descriptions from Brandsma (2006) and details on the content from Hoppe (2005).

[3]An interview partner from an employer organisation remarks that many of those participants that enter HBO after completing MBO on level 4 fail to complete the programme (interview NL_PRIV-1).

[4]For a detailed analysis on school careers within the MBO track see MOCW (2012: 34–35).

[5]Own calculation with rounded percentages on the basis of figures provided by the MOCW (2012: 119).

offered by approximately 40 universities of applied sciences (*hogescholen*) and often involve work experience placements. Qualifications run through an accreditation procedure, degrees are then awarded by the *hogescholen* themselves. Private providers can also offer HBO courses under the condition that they have the necessary accreditation for their programmes. After 1 year in HBO, students can choose to enter university programmes. With a HBO bachelor's degree, it is possible to continue studying for a master's degree at a university; often universities offer bridging programmes (interview NL_MIXED-2). Students pay tuition fees and are eligible for financial support from the age of 18.

Following demands from employers—especially SMEs (MOCW 2009; Duvekot 2010: 2)—pilot projects on "Associate Degree" programmes were launched in 2006 and made a regular degree of higher education in 2011. These short cycle degrees last 2 years; during the second year a work-based training component is compulsory (IKEI 2012). In 2011, about 1.5 % of students that started a HBO degree enrolled in an associate degree programme (Gans 2013). Compared to other tertiary study programmes, more students came from the MBO track and more students work part-time (ibid). Entry requirements are similar to other HBO programmes. It is possible to continue studying for a bachelor's degree.

Continuing VET is largely market-driven. It is often criticised that the private sector for continuing (vocational) education is largely lacking a sufficient degree of transparency (Van Lieshout 2007; interviews NL_MIXED-9, NL_MIXED-10). It is more common in the Netherlands that secondary education VET pathways serve as continuing VET for individuals than it is in other countries, such as Germany. Continuing VET can be financed by Sectoral Training Funds (*Onderzoek en Ontwikkelingsfondsen*, "O & O fondsen"). In general, continuing VET in the Netherlands is "strongly regulated by collective agreements" (Trampusch et al. 2010), leading to social partners being more involved in this field than in Germany (Van Lieshout 2007: 278).

In comparison to other countries, the status of VET is high—yet it is lower than in countries in which dual VET systems predominate. The government aims at increasing the percentage of the professional population that holds a higher education degree to 50 % (Onderwijsraad 2005). Social partners clearly value VET and argue that against the background of the knowledge economy, the government should not only concentrate on tertiary education but on the entire spectrum of education and lifelong learning (StvdA 2005, 2006). An interview partner from an employers' organisation stressed that the MBO is an essential part of firms' recruitment strategies with its own importance next to and in relation with higher education (interview NL_PRIV-1).

Qualification Files
It is a strength of the Dutch VET system that qualifications have a strong relevance on the labour market. The strong involvement of social partners in the development process of qualifications is an important reason for this. As Fig. 4.2 shows, the first step for the development of a qualification is that social partners develop an occupation profile (*beroepscompetentieprofiel*) that reflects professional practices.

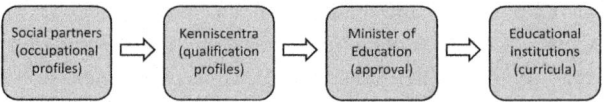

Fig. 4.2 Development process of qualification files in the Netherlands. *Source*: Colo (2008: 5); own adjustments

The initiative for the development of a new qualification can stem from both social partners and educational institutions (Visser 2010b: 13). On this basis, the respective *kenniscentrum* (Centres of Expertise, see below) draws up a qualification file (*kwalificatieprofiel*) (Colo 2008: 5). In a third step, the quality of qualification profiles is assessed by the Coordination Centre for Senior Secondary Vocational Education Qualifications, an independent institution under the authority of the Ministry of Education, Culture and Science (*Ministerie van Onderwijs, Cultuur en Wetenschappen*, MOCW) (Colo 2008: 5). On this basis, the Ministry officially approves the qualification file. Finally, the curriculum for a qualification is developed by the Regional Training Centres (*Regionaal Opleidingscentrum*, ROCs) (the general role of ROCs is described below).

A national framework sets criteria for qualifications in the sense of "selective flexibility" aiming at establishing occupational qualifications which are broad and persisting (Hövels and Roelofs 2007: 7). Since the development of qualifications is carried out on the national level, qualifications are portable. An interview partner from a *kenniscentrum* has argued that pressures exist to develop qualifications that are very specific (interview NL_MIXED-1). For example, there is a qualification for a general salesman, but also more specialised qualifications, for example for bicycle salesmen (ibid). Van Lieshout (2007: 304) argues that some qualification profiles are too narrow. The MOCW decides which qualification is offered on which level (Hövels and Roelofs 2007: 33). About half of the qualifications are offered for both pathways and on all levels. In total, more than 600 qualifications exist (interview NL_MIXED-2). Both BOL and BBL are based on the same qualification profile and formally lead to the same qualification.

Van Lieshout (2007: 314) highlights the nature of the Dutch training regime as a high skill equilibrium. "Both individuals and firms routinely invest in substantial, multi-year, initial, senior secondary VET tracks" (ibid). Following Lieshout, empirical studies show that the way work is organised in (larger) firms is closer to the work organisation in German firms than in American firms. The idea of craftsmanship (*vakman*) exists but is not as pronounced as in Germany (Van Lieshout 2007: 324). The level of autonomy with which an employee performs her task depends much on the level of the MBO. Since about three quarters of participants take part in level 3 or level 4 programmes (MOCW 2012: 119) and these prepare for tasks characterised by a substantial level of autonomy, it can be concluded that the ability to perform tasks independently is a widespread feature of Dutch VET.

While in the German training system VET skills are mostly acquired in apprenticeships, in the Netherlands the school-based track with work placements is the dominant form, and this has consequences for the kind of skills prevalent in the work force. Against the background of Streeck's (2011) distinction, VET skills in the Netherlands are occupational, portable, and have a distinct balance between broad and specific skills. The occupational nature of skills is strengthened by the strong selection of secondary general education, with a demanding university entrance qualification acquired by merely 15 % of a cohort (interview NL_PUBL-4), as well as by the strong status of occupation-related education on the tertiary level (HBO). Portability is high since national standards safeguard comparability. Because of employers' involvement, VET qualifications are highly recognised on the labour market. With the involvement of social partners in setting the content of training, skills can be described as industry-specific and occupational in spite of the higher share of school-based VET than in dual training regimes such as the German one (Anderson and Hassel 2013). As Anderson and Hassel (2013: 177) put it: "To the extent that employers and unions decide on the content of occupational skills, skills tend to be more industry-specific and therefore similarly occupational as in workplace-based regimes." Although the main responsibility for training lies with vocational schools and not with firms, schools have access to employers which helps them to find BVP placements.

However, because of the level structure, training is more closely fitted to the needs of employers. Arguably, the employability therefore is lower than in the more standardised German system: while a worker with a MBO on level 2 can expect that employers throughout the country will recognise her MBO for a job on the same level, she is unlikely to be suited for a position that requires a MBO on level 3. Larger, international firms mostly have a stronger preference for general education (interviews NL_MIXED-5, NL_PRIV-1). SMEs prefer more specific skills (interview NL_PRIV-1). Le Deist and Winterton (2011: 21) argue that—similar to the German craft sector—small firms often primarily regard VET participants as cheap labour. As a consequence, qualifications are a compromise between these different interests (interview NL_MIXED-5).

Actors and Institutions
There are 17 sector-level *kenniscentra* that serve as sector councils for VET. They fulfil an important role by linking VET providers with the labour market (Anderson and Oude Nijhuis 2011: 105). Employers' organisations, unions and the MBO Raad[6] have an equal number of seats on their boards. *Kenniscentra* accredit firms as training companies, monitor the quality of training, and support firms with the provision of training. For the latter, they offer courses for firms' trainers and facilitate the communication between ROCs and between training companies. It is in their responsibility that the number of BVP placements is sufficient. Reuling (2000: 135) argues that this undermines the quality of workplace-based training: the quality demands kenniscentra bring forward tend to be low, since otherwise not enough training places might be

---

[6]The MBO Raad (MBO Council) is the national association of VET colleges which represents all government-funded colleges for secondary VET and adult education. There is, moreover, an Agricultural Education Council which is the association of the institutions funded by the Department of Agriculture.

found. *Kenniscentra* moreover carry out labour market research. On the national level, the Foundation for Cooperation between Vocational Education, Training and the Labour Market (*Stichting Samenwerking Berofsonderwijs Bedrijfsleven*, SBB) brings together MBO education and the organised labour market.

VET schools play an important role in the VET system and have a high degree of autonomy. There are 43 Regional Training Centres (*Regionaal Opleidingscentrum*, ROC) throughout the Netherlands. Schools develop the curriculum on the basis of qualification profiles. ROCs can adjust courses to the needs of the local labour market with a scope of about 20 % of the curriculum (Hövels and Roelofs 2007: 5). On the basis of national regulation, they decide on didactics and on the question which content is completed at what location of learning. Schools decide which VET qualifications they offer, including the level of the occupation. In the future, however, it is planned that employers will have more influence on this decision (interview NL_PRIV-1). ROCs can carry out educational activities for third parties and are active in adult education. In the field of agriculture, there are twelve separate Training Centres (*Agrarische opleidingscentra*). Moreover, there are twelve professional colleges for specialised branches (*vakschool*), for example for shipping or graphics. Private providers of MBO also exist but are rare. Their programmes have to be recognised by the MOCW. The quality of education at ROCs and of private providers is monitored by the Education Inspectorate (*onderwijsinspectie*) (see also Sect. 5.2.5).

Final examinations are carried out by ROCs or the respective education provider on the basis of national standards. They are required to cooperate with trainers from firms. Examination methods are chosen by the ROCs, and often take the form of aptitude tests with simulations or employment tests (Van der Sanden et al. 2012). Content that was taught during BVPs is usually assessed at the place of learning in firms (interview NL_PRIV-2). The education inspectorate monitors the quality of assessments regarding their content, their level and the underlying procedures of the programme level (Visser 2010a: 42). Employers are not very satisfied with the quality of exams (interview NL_PRIV-1). In the future, the law will be changed so that employers will be more influential regarding final examinations (interview NL_PRIV-1).

ROCs work together with other actors in the regions and are involved in finding BVP placements. They can accept participants for their courses only if sufficient BVP placements are available. In BOL, schools are required to keep in contact with firms during phases of training in the company (interview NL_PUBL-2). These links between employers and schools are important for matching skills with the labour market (Anderson and Hassel 2013), especially because schools have some scope for action regarding the content of skills. However, according to Van Lieshout (2007), sometimes the quality of BVP places can be insufficient. This is underpinned by empirical studies such as Detmar and De Vries (2009). It is criticised that the linkages between learning in schools and learning at the workplace are often not close enough (Hövels and Roelofs 2007: 30). Moreover, Van Lieshout (2007: 305) remarks that it is not without problems that the responsibility for BVPs is shared between *kenniscentra*, ROCs and firms. As Reuling (2000: 135) puts it, because ROCs are dependent on placements offered by firms, "it is questionable if ROCs are in reality as dominant as it formally seems."

Social partners are involved in VET in numerous ways. As outlined above, social partners play an important role in the development of qualifications and occupy half of the seats on the board of *kenniscentra*. Employers provide work-based training and are involved in examinations. Firms also serve as members of vocational schools' supervisory boards. Social partners are members of several councils and bodies at the national and regional level. The influential Socio-Economic Council (*Sociaal-Economische Raad*) advises the government and the parliament on social and economic policy. The SER is composed in a tripartite way and has 33 members-employer representatives, union representatives and independent experts. The Labour Foundation (*Stichting van de Arbeid*) serves as a forum for social partners and comprises three peak employer organisations and three peak trade union federations. Social partners use this influential platform to issue advice or make agreements on labour market policies, including VET. Twice a year, the Labour Foundation meets with the government. Social partners moreover installed a steering group on VET (*Stuurgroep Impuls Beroepsonderwijs*) with the aim to strengthen VET, establish a joint responsibility for training, and develop training initiatives. On the regional level, social partners are often members of the ROCs' supervisory board. The influence of employers will further increase when, as pointed out above, employers will have more influence on exams and on the question which qualifications are offered in which region. This constitutes a "huge step" and will also increase employer satisfaction with the training system (interview NL_PRIV-1). Overall and notwithstanding options for improvements exist, the interviewed firms are in general satisfied with the VET system (interviews NL_PRIV-2, NL_PRIV-3, NL_PRIV-4, NL_PRIV-5).

As already pointed out, firms offer apprenticeships in the BBL track and BVP placements in the BOL track. Currently, around 223,000 firms are accredited for VET training (*erkend leerbedrijf*) (IKEI 2012).[7] Drawing on own material and on calculations carried out by other researchers, Van Lieshout (2007) estimates the number of firms offering BBL places is around 9 %, and that 30 % of these firms and 20 % of remaining firms offer BVP placements. Training behaviour differs considerably across sectors and firm sizes (ibid). Larger firms sometimes have separate training facilities and VET participants enter the production process at a later stage (interview NL_PRIV-1). Since firms can rely on an external labour market from BOL, the incentive to engage in apprenticeship training is lower than in dual VET systems (Van Lieshout 2007: 317). Companies largely use work placements as a recruitment strategy: a remarkable 75 % of VET participants start working at the work placement company after completing VET (Colo 2011: 2). Firms receive tax reductions for offering training. Visser (2010a: 46) states that on average firms

---

[7]A training company has to meet the following requirements: A practice trainer (*praktijkopleider*) must be working at the firm who can prove that he is able to train the participant; facilities have to be adequate; the tasks of the participant have to be adequate for the respective VET programme; the firm has to establish a cooperation with a VET school and with the consultant of the *kenniscentrum* (IKEI 2012). There are around 300,000 trainers.

spend 8,400 euros per year for each BBL participant and 1,750 on providing BVP places to BOL students. Studies have found that firms believe apprentices in the BBL track recover their costs (see Hövels and Roelofs 2007: 45). Yet, research on the costs and benefits of training for firms is insufficient (Van Lieshout 2007: 315).

Social partners have created the sectoral O & O funds which experienced a rapid growth during the 1980s. In some branches, such funds had already existed, in others they were introduced around that time because the Ministry of Social Affairs tied subsidies to the funds (ibid). The funds are based on collective agreements and run bipartitely. Social partners can request that the funds are declared collectively binding by the Ministry of Social Affairs and Employment (Trampusch et al. 2010). O & O funds mainly serve to fund continuing (vocational) education and training and hereby strengthen sectoral labour markets (ibid). Firms pay a certain percentage of the gross wage bill (ibid). Approximately 140 O & O funds exist that cover approximately 85 % of employees (Visser 2010a: 35) and differ considerably in size (interview NL_MIXED-9). They do not cover continuing VET for those who want to change sectors (interviews NL_MIXED-9, NL_MIXED-10).

Unions are "flexible on the issue of matching VT content and skill certification to labor market needs and care more about issues such as apprentice pay, working conditions, and employability" (Anderson and Hassel 2013: 185–186). They do not oppose VET qualifications being offered on a variety of levels and, related to this, have a less 'monolithic' understanding of VET. Unions perceive drop-outs and the access of older workers to VET as problems of the VET system (interview NL_UN-1). Validation of non-formal and informal learning is seen as an important instrument to tackle these problems (see Sect. 5.2.4) but in the unions' view, schools also need to become more flexible for workers with experience, for example by providing classes in the evening (ibid).

The state has a stronger role in financing VET than in Germany. Employers argue that initial training is the responsibility of the government (Van Lieshout 2007: 320; NL_PUBL-4). At the end of the 1990s, the government tried to increase the role of employers in education and especially in VET, but could not overcome employers' opposition (interview NL_PUBL-4). VET participants contribute more to the financing of training than in Germany. In the dominant BOL track, participants are "students" rather than employees or apprentices. Students pay tuition fees; however, until the age of 18 parents are entitled to child allowance and educational grants are available for full-time students in the BOL pathway. This makes training less costly for firms and less coupled to individual apprentices but at the same time more costly for students. In the BBL pathway, apprentices receive salaries that are negotiated in collective agreements and are at least as high as the (youth) minimum wage.

In sum, the Dutch VET system has several characteristics that position it between the corporatist German dual system and the market-based British training regime. The involvement of employers in the development of qualifications can also be found in the corporatist German skill regime. The status of VET is high but not as high as in Germany. Qualifications have a high degree of standardisation which is closer to the German case than to the British one, although the level structure and the autonomy of schools differ from the German VET system. The stronger status of schoolbased training also leads to a mix of skills which is more general than the German case but still industry-specific (Anderson and Hassel 2013). The level structure leads to more tailor-made skills for firms, but also limits the employability across levels. Because of the existence of the two pathways, the VET system is less vulnerable to economic cycles (although economic cycles also affect the provision of BVPs), risk groups are included better, and the permeability towards higher education is higher (Hövels and Roelofs 2007: 44). Financing of initial VET relies more on the state and on VET participants. Finally, in line with observations by Anderson and Hassel (2013) and van Lieshout (2007: 261) the above analysis shows that there is a high degree of institutional innovation in the Netherlands, especially when compared to the institutional stability redominating in Germany. Van Lieshout (ibid) remarks that "at the same time, dominant governing principles as well as the underlying choices of individuals and firms show more continuity than those vast policy efforts would suggest."

With this mixture between elements from CMEs and LMEs, the Dutch VET system resembles other political-economic institutions in the Netherlands which also can be considered as a hybrid type. In an empirical analysis on the basis of longitudinal data, Schneider and Paunescu (2012) find that the Dutch economy has moved closer to an LME over the last 20 years. Corporate governance has shifted towards shareholders due to privatisation, liberalisation and deregulation policies (Houwing and Vandaele 2011). Furthermore, the economic structure of the Netherlands is more characterised by trade than by manufacturing. Industrial relations are corporatist; in comparison to Germany, tripartite governance and the roles of national peak associations are more pronounced (Van Lieshout 2007; Van Klaveren et al. 2009). Houwing and Vandaele (2011: 132) conclude: "Dutch corporatism has been relatively stable." However, changes take place: "Wage bargaining has the form of guided decentralisation (or indirect centralisation), cuts to welfare have taken place, and shareholder capitalism has grown stronger in this country with many—some large—multinational companies" (ibid: 147). Yet, in sum, "reforms took place in a policy environment still largely characterised by high trust, coupled with a discourse on vulnerability to global pressures and the unavoidability of adjusting the Dutch political economy in line with these pressures" (ibid: 148).

Core Features of the Dutch training regime
The following four aspects are defined as core features of the Dutch training regime: a strong role of the state in the regulation and financing of VET with an institutionalised participation of social partners; broad VET skills on an intermediate level with a mixed balance between general and industry-specific skills due to a mix of the dominating school-based learning with workplace-based learning; mostly standardised training content and certification leading to a high portability; and a medium to high status of VET as a viable educational path after secondary

education.[8] The following section will trace the implementation of the Copenhagen process in Germany and analyse in how far central pillars of the German VET systems have potentially and actually been affected by them.

4.2 Implementation of the Copenhagen Process in the Netherlands

This subchapter discusses the implementation of the instruments and principles developed within the realm of the Copenhagen process in the Netherlands. For each of these, a separate subsection analyses the implementation process.

4.2.1 Learning Outcomes

Recent reform has made Dutch VET based on competences (*competentie*), an approach that closely resembles the idea of learning outcomes. As Duvekot (2010: 4) puts it: "VET is based on a learning outcomes approach in theory. This is called the competence-base of VET in which all national standards embedded in VET are formulated in terms of competences." Interview partners remark that the competence-based approach and learning outcomes are very similar (interviews NL_MIXED-1, NL_MIXED-2). The understanding of competences resembles the Dutch mix between broad and specific skills. Biemans et al. (2004: 5) stress that in contrast to the understanding of the term 'competences' in the Anglo-Saxon world, in the Netherlands and in Germany "a more holistic approach is advocated (...). In these discussions, competence is regarded as the integrated abilities required to cope with complex tasks." Workers are able to reflect on their job and its context (ibid). Competences are defined as "the ability to use and apply a set of knowledge, skills, attitudes (and personal qualities) for the execution of tasks in an adequate way. (...) The competence level connects with the amount of autonomy and responsibility concerning the execution of tasks" (Visser 2010a: 11). Competences focus on problem solving, which shall enable graduates to apply their competences in different situations. The focus is on the individual learner (EACEA 2009: 148; Brandsma 2006: 112).

With the reform, qualifications regulated by the ministry are based on a matrix with descriptors for learning results (Van der Sanden et al. 2012: 28). The qualification structure (Kwalificatiestructuur Beroepsonderwijs) is fully based on

---

[8]Anderson and Oude Nijhuis (2011: 103) define three key features: "The outstanding features of the Dutch VET system are the dominance and higher status of school-based education, strong state involvement in terms of regulation and financing, and the institutionalised participation of unions and employers."

competences and led by objectives (Visser 2010a: 12). It refers to broad types of qualification (i.e. it regulates what competences a graduate with a MBO degree on level 4 should have obtained) and not to the content of a specific occupation (e.g. what competences a "general salesman" on MBO level 3 should have). In higher vocational education, most programmes are also focused on competences (Biemans et al. 2004: 1). The new structure is more abstract and therefore leaves more scope for action to ROCS when choosing their own pedagogical and didactical tools (Maes 2004: 17; Hövels and Roelofs 2007: 34). In sum, it becomes obvious that, similar to the German case, the focus of competences is on "a more holistic perspective on individuals with both theoretical knowledge and practical experience" (Powell and Trampusch 2011: 304).

The shift towards a competence-based system was initiated prior to the Copenhagen process. First proposals for a new competence-based qualification structure were presented in 2002 (Brandsma 2006: 111) and in 2006 schools started to work with the competence-based approach (Wesselink et al. 2007). The descriptors were developed in a broad process which included two consultation phases with stakeholders from the system (Van der Sanden et al. 2012). Colo, which was the association of kenniscentra until it was integrated into SBB in 2012, coordinated the development of a new qualification structure (Maes 2004). Although the implementation took longer than originally envisioned and involved many experiments on the local level (Brandsma 2006), now almost all VET programmes are competence-based (IKEI 2012). The competence approach has become "the leading paradigm for innovation, both at the system level and at the level of learning environments" (Biemans et al. 2004: 1). The introduction of competence-based qualifications is closely related to changes in the world of work, with the idea that such changes require different skills including social skills, entrepreneurship, and problem solving (Biemans et al. 2004). The reform aims at improving the match between VET and the labour market as well as facilitating taking up studies on the tertiary level (EACEA 2009; cf. Biemans et al. 2004; Wesselink et al. 2007).

The shift towards a competence-based qualification structure has been accompanied by an "intense debate" (StvdA 2007: 3; cf. Wesselink et al. 2007). First, Brandsma (2006: 110), Biemans et al. (2004: 7) and Wesselink et al. (2007: 42) argue that a clear definition of the concept of competence is lacking. Providers use different descriptors, which reduces the trustworthiness of the approach (Biemans et al. 2004: 8). Several aspects, such as the distinction between key problems and key tasks, are criticised to be blurry, and Brandsma (2006) doubts that competences can be derived from them. Second, both experts and employers have argued that competence-orientated qualifications are a burden for SMEs, since they require more mentoring and supervision (Hövels and Roelofs 2007: 37). Third, Hövels and Roelofs (2007: 30) remark that there are problems related to the implementation of "interdisciplinary requirements" associated with the concept. Fourth, Biemans et al. (2004) argue that there can be dilemmas between local flexibility and standardisation on national level. Descriptions and abstract standardisations often do not meet the reality of the workplace. Moreover, in their view it is crucial how the shift towards competence-based education is implemented at schools. The role of teachers changes towards coaching and guiding learning processes (Biemans et al. 2004). Yet, an interview partner argues that schools are left alone with the implementation process (interview NL_MIXED-4). The reform process coincided with the organisational reform of schools so that they had to handle both reforms at the same time (ibid). Finally, examinations of competence-based learning are more difficult and require more time and labour resources; therefore this point can be regarded as the weak spot of the concept (Wesselink et al. 2007: 42). New examination tools have to be developed (Biemans et al. 2004: 9), which is crucial since if the qualification structure focuses on competences or learning outcomes rather than on input, examinations gain in importance (interview NL_MIXED-8).

Politics of Reform and Actors' Positions

Social partners had started voicing demands for redesigning the qualification structure in a competence-orientated manner together with the education communities (EACEA 2009: 148; StvdA 2007: 3) and thus contributed to initiating the shift. Social partners made an agreement in which they called for the introduction of a competence-orientated qualification structure in 2006 with a memorandum published under the realm of the Labour Foundation (ibid). An interview partner from an employers' organisation confirms that employers were in favour of a change towards a competence-based approach (interview NL_PRIV-1). The reason for their engagement is their belief that in the future skills need to be orientated towards an independent and demand-oriented work style (ibid). The reform therefore strengthens the role of social skills within VET (IKEI 2012). VET is now more aligned with actual work processes, which changes the way training is carried out and lessons are held (interview NL_PRIV-1). This holds especially for BOL, since the focus on these aspects is already more pronounced in the BBL pathways (ibid). The actual implementation of the process also met critique from the employers' side. The critique was directed at the way the reform was implemented, but also employers demanded more attention for social skills (ibid). Since 2009, less critique has been voiced, and employers are now more satisfied with the balance between social skills and work-related skills (ibid). Unions also support the shift towards competence-based VET (interview NL_UN-1). In their view, it brings VET closer to the labour market and fosters employability, since graduates acquire skills they can use in other, related jobs (ibid).

Brief Evaluation

A shift towards a competence-based qualification structure had been initiated prior to and hence independent of the Copenhagen process. As a consequence of the reform, the Dutch VET system is largely outcome-orientated. The understanding of competencies largely resembles a CME understanding of skills based on a holistic approach. The concept is criticised to be blurry and demanding to implement for SMEs. The importance of examinations increases, while in practice it can be challenging to assure the quality of examinations which are based on learning outcomes (see Sect. 5.2.5). Employers called for the shift and believe that VET, especially the BOL track, is now more closely related to actual work process and therefore closer to the labour market.

4.2.2 The Dutch National Qualifications Framework (NLQF)

Following the EQF recommendation, the Netherlands decided to develop the Dutch National Qualifications Framework (*Nederlands national kwalificatiekader*, NLQF). In 2007, a steering group was set up that comprised members from various departments of the MOCW (2007: 8). The ministry commissioned a study on the implementation of the EQF (Westerhuis 2009: 3). This report proposed an eight-level-framework which covered only tertiary education and VET—for that reason it was not believed to be an adequate starting point for the discussion (ibid). The proposal moreover had been published without building consensus beforehand, which is unusual in a country which traditionally relies on the consensus-built "polder model" (interview NL_MIXED-5). The proposal therefore contributed to the opposition voiced by VET and higher education actors.

The process did not really proceed—in the words of Westerhuis (2009: 3): "To put it mildly, the Netherlands were not in the forefront in terms of implementing the European Framework for Life Long Learning." In the words of an interview partner, the MOCW opted for a "wait and see" approach (interview NL_MIXED-3). This was also related to the fact that the change towards competence-based learning was still going on (see Sect. 5.2.1) so that actors did not feel the need to steer the development of another framework (interview NL_MIXED-5). This reluctance has been noted both on the European level and within the Netherlands (Westerhuis 2009: 3). Awareness increased that it would be not be sufficient to link subsystems—such as the four level structure of VET—to the EQF but that it would be necessary to develop a national qualifications framework (ibid). An interview partner from the public administration points out that in a report on the implementation of qualifications frameworks, the Netherlands were lagging behind and the parliament had begun to ask questions, which prompted the minister to speed up the process (interview NL_PUBL-4). To conclude, the Netherlands had a slow start regarding the implementation of the EQF and the development of a national qualifications framework.

In 2009, the ministry's Director General of Higher Education and VET, Science and Emancipation at the MOCW launched the development of the NLQF (Van der Sanden et al. 2012: 26). At that point, the Centre for Innovation in Education and Training (*Centrum voor innovatie van opleidingen*, CINOP) had proactively developed a plan for the implementation of a framework that comprises all education sectors, public and privately funded qualifications, as well as formal, non-formal and informal learning (interview NL_MIXED-3). The MOCW adopted seven principles for a NLQF: the NLQF should bridge the EQF with the national system while not replacing traditional descriptors prevalent in the subsystems; the number of levels should be open and not a priori limited to eight; it should be used for comparing qualifications but not for establishing rights or duties on admission; it should comprise all sectors of education including non-formal education; higher levels should be open to qualifications not formally registered as higher education qualifications; experts should give advice on the design of descriptors; and the MOCW should decide if a national coordination point should be run by private or by public actors (Westerhuis 2009: 3–4).

The ministry established an organisational structure for the development of the NLQF. A project leader from the MOCW was appointed and several groups and committees were established (ibid). Within the MOCW, the VET division was made responsible (interview NL_PUBL-4). A steering group guided the process. It comprised directors of the ministry's VET, higher education, secondary education and learning and working directorates as well as the director of the knowledge department from the Ministry of Economic Affairs, Agriculture and Innovation. Moreover, an internal working group brought together the policy staff of the VET, higher education and secondary education and learning directorates. A group of experts from several stakeholders[9] was asked to develop descriptor elements, the NLQF's level descriptors and a proposal for the referencing of the NLQF to the EQF. It was also the task of the expert group to develop descriptions for regulated qualifications in terms of learning outcomes. The group held meetings with stakeholders and representatives from the education sectors and participated in field testing.

In November, the results were handed over to the Leijnse Committee. The Leijnse Committee was established with the task to monitor the development of the NLQF and to give advice on questions such as the accurateness of the NLQF, the referencing process, the establishment of a national coordination point, and the inclusion of non-formal and informal learning (interview NL_MIXED-8). The committee's chair, Frans Leijnse, is a professor at the Open University in Herleen and a former politician; further members included professors from different universities. In eight meetings, the Committee reviewed the expert group's proposal. Subsequently, a new consultation phase was launched in which the Leijnse Committee met with national stakeholders as well as with international experts from Cedefop and other countries. In May 2011, the Committee presented its conclusions to the minister.[10]

---

[9]These included SLO (an independent, non-commercial research centre), MBO Raad, Colo, the Dutch-Flemish accreditation agency, and PAEPON/NRTO (Tweede Kamer der Staten-Generaal 2011a).

[10]The advice of the Leijnse Commission is available for download in Dutch at http://www.nlqf.nl/images/downloads/NLQF/c_Het_advies_van_de_Commissie.pdf [last accessed 2 April 2013].

Stakeholders from all education sectors and all levels have been involved in the process. This made the process complex (Van der Sanden et al. 2012: 27) and long (interviews NL_PUBL-4, NL_MIXED-5). Six round tables with more than 200 participants—representatives from education institutions, policy makers, social partners, teachers and trainers—took place in autumn 2010 (Van der Sanden et al. 2012). Subsequently, an online consultation was launched (ibid). Yet, the vast involvement of stakeholders has also been a huge advantage (interview NL_MIXED-8). The input gained during the consultation phase was incorporated into the proposal on the introduction of the NQF (ibid).

In July 2011, the minister wrote a letter to the Dutch Parliament in which she forwarded the advice of the Leijnse Commission (Tweede Kamer der Staten-Generaal 2011a). The parliament asked several questions on the instrument and its implementation in written form, to which the minister replied in another letter in November 2011 (Tweede Kamer der Staten-Generaal 2011b). A national coordination point for the NLQF (*national coördinatiepunkt NLQF*) has been established at the MOCW and has subsequently been transformed into an independent organisation. In international comparison, its competences are quite vast (Schöpf in Van der Sanden et al. 2012: 73). It is financed by the MOCW and the European Commission. The coordination point will be in charge of referencing non-regulated qualifications to the NLQF, evaluating the NLQF against its objectives to increase transparency as well as to foster mobility and lifelong learning (ibid, 65). Informal and non-formal learning qualifications will not be linked to the NLQF directly but only via distinct procedures (see Sect. 5.2.4) (interview NL_MIXED-6).

The objective of the NLQF is to foster transparency and comparability of qualifications both within the country and across Europe (Van der Sanden et al. 2012: 26). Moreover, it seeks to facilitate communication across the educational sector and the labour market (ibid). The framework is perceived as a "systematic classification of all qualification levels in the Netherlands" (Van der Sanden et al. 2012: 1), meaning that it is "**not** a revision of the Dutch education system" (ibid, 25; bold in the original) or replacing any existing legislation (ibid, 31). The NLQF does not establish entitlements to degrees or admission rights (ibid, 25). Moreover, it is stressed that not all NLQF levels should be regarded as entry qualifications for the labour market (ibid).[11]

The NLQF descriptors highly reflect existing qualifications and their characteristics. The learning outcomes of HAVO, MBO level 4 and doctorates were used as a starting point for developing the NLQF structure, since these qualifications were seen as having high social recognition and therefore fixed values (Van der Sanden et al. 2012: 28). A conceptual framework was established on the basis of the matrix

---

[11]As pointed out in Sect. 4.1, neither VMBO qualifications nor MBO level 1 are considered to sufficiently equip individuals for finding sustainable work, with the "qualification duty" marking this threshold. The advantage of the framework is seen in offering an overview on available qualifications and showing in what way they might add to advance an individual's position on the labour market (Van der Sanden et al. 2012).

of learning outcomes developed by the MOCW for the regulated qualifications (see Sect. 5.2.1) as well as on the basis of EQF descriptors and other NQFs (ibid). Four descriptors were developed: context, knowledge, responsibility and independence, and skills. The latter descriptor further distinguishes between the application of knowledge, problem-solving, learning and development on the one hand, as well as information and communication skills on the other hand (ibid, 30). The descriptors accentuate soft skills and structural or procedural skills (applying knowledge and problem-solving); responsibility and independence are distinct descriptors. Descriptor levels show "within what context and with what type of knowledge" a person can apply these skills and on what responsibility level she can act (ibid). Descriptors thus serve as a point of reference rather than a complete description of a specific qualification (ibid). It has been criticised that descriptors are blurry and that levels 1–4 are too similar (Van der Sanden et al. 2012). To conclude, descriptors are more complex, or "detailed" (interview NL_MIXED-8) than in other qualifications frameworks. The NLQF and its underlying understanding of education focus more on holistic qualifications than the EQF. The EQF and its descriptors were adjusted to the national realm (Tables 4.1 and 4.2).

The NLQF has nine levels: eight levels and one entry level. Level 4 distinguishes between level 4 and level 4+. Each level builds on the lower levels (Van der Sanden et al. 2012: 31). All levels are open to all education sectors. Levels 5–8 are based on descriptors that reflect both the EQF and the 'Dublin descriptors' of the Higher

Table 4.1 Descriptor elements describing the Dutch qualification levels

Context	The descriptions of the contexts are, together with the described knowledge, determining the level of difficulty of the skills
Knowledge	Knowledge is the totality of facts, principles, theories and ways of practice, related to an occupation or a knowledge domain
Skills	Cognitive capabilities (logic, intuitive and creative thinking) and practical capabilities (psychomotor skills in the use of methods, materials, aid and instruments) applied within a given context:
Applying knowledge	• Reproduce, analyse, integrate, evaluate, combine and apply knowledge in an occupation or a knowledge domain
Problem solving skills	• Comprehend, recognize or identify and solve problems
Learning and development skills	• Personal development, autonomously or under supervision
Information skills Communication skills	• Obtain, collect, process, combine, analyse and assess information • Communicate based on context-relevant conventions
Responsibility and Independence	The proven capability to collaborate with others and being responsible for own work or study results or of others

Source: Van der Sanden et al. (2012: 85).

Table 4.2 NLQF scheme

EQF	NLQF	Adult Education	Vmbo	Mbo	Havo/Vwo	Higher education
8	8					PhD / Designer / medical specialist
7	7					Master
6	6					Bachelor
5	5					Associate Degree
4	4+	Vwo			Vwo	
	4	Havo		MBO-4	Havo	
3	3			MBO-3		
2	2	Vmbo Basis Education 3	Vmbo	MBO-2		
1	1	Basis Education 2	Vmbo (bb track)	MBO-1		
	Entry level	Basis Education 1				

Source: Van der Sanden et al. (2012: 32), own adjustments.

Education Qualifications Framework (ibid, 34). NLQF levels are consistent with EQF levels. Referencing took place on the basis of a 'best fit', meaning that a qualification does not have to meet all aspects of a level, but that it is linked to the level it fits best. Qualifications were referenced to the NLQF as follows. The different levels of MBO degrees are referenced accordingly to the respective NLQF level: MBO 1 to level 1, MBO 2 to level 2, and so on. The different pathways of the general secondary education VMBO are referenced to level 1 and to level 2. HAVO is referenced to level 4 and VWO to level 4+. The Associate Degree, Bachelor, Master and Doctorate are referenced to the levels 5–8. Basic education qualifications (*BasisEducatie*) 1–3 within the adult education sector are qualifications that focus on basic and social skills (Van der Sanden et al. 2012: 32). Level 1 is below EQF level 1 and therefore cannot be referenced to the EQF; for this reason, an entry level was created (ibid).

Several aspects of the referencing process have been subject to discussions. First, the decision to reference the three advanced VMBO pathways to level 2 together with the MBO-2 has been contested, since the VMBO is not seen as being sufficient for entering the labour market. Yet, it is argued that levels are based on learning outcomes and not on types of education (Van der Sanden et al. 2012: 63). Second, as mentioned above, referencing was carried out on the basis of existing qualifications, not on learning outcomes. This procedure was chosen for practical reasons because of the multitude of existing qualifications (interviews NL_PUBL-3; NL_MIXED-4, NL_MIXED-8). Third, discussions arose regarding the referencing of MBO qualifications. The MBO-4 was seen to also fulfil important criteria for level 5. As a solution, education providers will be able to request that MBO-4 programmes are referenced to level 5, and decisions will depend on the learning outcomes of the programme (ibid). An interview partner from a *kenniscentrum* argues that it was not politically feasible to position MBO-4 on level 5 because it is a VET qualification (interview NL_MIXED-1). Moreover, interview partners have pointed out that differences between the MBO levels are not always big enough to justify a one level-difference (interviews NL_PUBL-3, NL_MIXED-1). A government report on the referencing process (Van der Sanden et al. 2012), however argues that studies had shown a high internal consistency of MBO levels. Fourth, it is sometimes criticised that VET qualifications are referenced on too low levels or in a "conservative" manner (interview NL_MIXED-8). In the view of an interview partner, other countries reference qualifications that are similar to MBO-4 to level 5 (ibid). In the more drastic words of another interview partner: "intellectuals have done this work so they punished the lower-qualified" (interview NL_MIXED-2). Yet another interview partner remarks, similar to an argument brought forward in Germany, that some of the VET qualifications positioned on the higher levels of MBO in the Netherlands are taught at university in other countries, for example MBO 4 in nursing (NL_MIXED-7). She argues that the NLQF process has been carried out by national experts and has focused less on the international consequences of having such a framework (ibid).

The most vivid discussion was concerned with the referencing of the VWO qualification. This debate mostly focused on the question of how to relate general education and VET to one another. Originally, the expert group had proposed to position the VWO on level 4. The Leijnse Committee then advised to reference it to level 5, arguing that the difference between HAVO and VWO is considerable (Van der Sanden et al. 2012: 33). Only 15 % of students participate in VWO, which shows that it is a demanding qualification (interviews NL_PUBL-4, NL_MIXED-8). It is seen as a pathway for above-average students (Tweede Kamer der Staten-Generaal 2011a: 5). An interview partner argues that it is higher-ranking than, for example, the British A-Levels (interview NL_MIXED-2). After receiving the proposal of the Leijnse Committee, the minister tentatively took the Committee's advice and remarked that the referencing of VWO differs from ISCED levels and the European perspective should be taken into account (ibid). On the European level, criticism on the referencing of VWO was voiced in the EQF advisory group after a presentation of the Dutch representatives (DE_PRIV-1, Van der Sanden et al. 2012: 33). A participant of the meeting reported that—untypical for the nature of the meetings—"feelings ran high"[12] (DE_PRIV-1). Other member states and the Commission concordantly suggested reviewing the Dutch referencing of the VWO qualification; it was argued that a "coherent approach" across countries is necessary (ibid). An interview partner from the EU level has described this discussion as

---

[12]Original: „Es ging hoch her."

"very tough", with the advisory group being "very critical" (interview EU_PUBL-4). "Due to this problem and after consulting the Dutch expert group again the Minister decided to put the VWO school leaving certificate on level 4+" (Van der Sanden et al. 2012: 33). The difference between HAVO and VWO is therefore accounted for by subdividing the level (Van der Sanden et al. 2012: 33). The creation of a level 4+ underlines that the government aimed at establishing an eight-level-structure that facilitates comparisons with the EQF (Van der Sanden et al. 2012). As interview partners remark, this has been a political choice (interviews NL_MIXED-1, NL_MIXED-2) in order to make the connection between NLQF and EQF clear and without ambiguity (interview NL_MIXED-8). This is also why an entry level has been established (interview NL_MIXED-2). The referencing and the NLQF in general will be subject to a complete evaluation after 2 years (Van der Sanden et al. 2012).

The referencing of qualifications that are offered by private providers is an important aspect of the NLQF. The procedures and criteria for this were subject of discussion both regarding minimum requirements for those qualifications and regarding administrative efficiency (Tweede Kamer der Staten-Generaal 2011b). It has been agreed that education providers can apply for their qualifications to be referenced to the NLQF in two steps. First, the provider itself will be subject to a procedure evaluating the quality assurance management, continuity, and legal personality. In case of a positive evaluation, in a second step the NLQF coordination point will decide if qualification(s) fulfil requirements for the respective NLQF level. The coordination point will bring the applications to the attention of a group of experts and decide based on their opinion (Van der Sanden et al. 2012). An Appeals Committee can review the decision made by the coordination point on request of the competent body (ibid, 66). Private providers pay a fee for the classification of their qualifications (NLQF Nationaal Coördinatiepunt 2012: 7). The procedure will only be carried out for those qualifications that are described in learning outcomes and "have a clear civil effect on the labour market" (Van der Sanden et al. 2012), including a significant volume of learning around a critical limit of about 400 hours (ibid, 107). The NLQF provides a picture of qualifications existing in the Netherlands and how they relate to each other (ibid, 25), which is believed to be an important impact (interviews NL_MIXED-7, NL_PUBL-4, Westerhuis 2009: 4). In sum, the NLQF comprises not only those qualifications regulated by the state; efforts have been made to also include qualifications offered by private providers.

In contrast to Germany, discussions on the NLQF did not focus much on the question of permeability. Interview partners argued that the VET system is already permeable, since there are "ongoing learning lines", as it is called in the Netherlands (interview NL_PUBL-4, c.f. interviews NL_MIXED-2, Visser 2010b). The topic of permeability had already been high on the agenda and a small committee, the Boekhoud Commissie, had issued a Transfer Agenda in Vocational Education (Doorstroomagenda Beroepsonderwijs) in March 2001 (Advies Commissie Boekhoud 2001). The focus of this paper is the individual's education career, including an alternative route to higher education via VET (Visser 2010b: 19).

The Agenda guided and impacted improvements in the VET sector, for example regarding the funding of VET schools (ibid). Yet, limits and critical points also exist regarding the permeability of Dutch VET. Moving from one MBO to another can take very long, since usually no prior contents are recognised[13] and it is in the power of schools to decide on these matters (interview NL_MIXED_2, NL_MIXED-5). An interview partner points out that the permeability to tertiary education is higher for BOL graduates (interview NL_MIXED-5). A research project report argued that a qualifications framework in the Netherlands can still support the objective of permeability by making visible gaps between educational subsystems and by attuning educational subsystems (Transeqframe 2005: 2). An interview partner from the national administration however points out that the NLQF will not change the Dutch education system and hence will not steer changes regarding the permeability of existing qualifications (interview NL_PUBL-4).

Open questions remain. Schöpf (in Van der Sanden et al. 2012: 73) remarks that the legal status of the NLQF is still unclear. Changing legislation is required in order to establish a legal basis and mention NLQF levels on qualification files (NLQF Nationaal Coördinatiepunt 2012: 2). Schöpf (in Van der Sanden et al. 2012: 73) furthermore questions the necessity of having an entry level at all (ibid). Effects on quality assurance are unclear; efforts on implementing quality mechanisms could increase (ibid). Moreover, whether the NLQF changes the status of VET is an open question. During the consultation phase, some respondents remarked that descriptors focus too much on cognitive skills, "and because of this weighting general education appears to be valued more highly than VET in the framework" (ibid, 115). This might also be a disadvantage for applying APL procedures (ibid, 117). Finally, the government report on the NLQF argues that one of the objectives of the NLQF is to "stimulate thinking in terms of learning outcomes as building blocks of qualifications" (Van der Sanden et al. 2012: 26). It is not yet clear if and how this aspect will be fostered, in particular against the background of the discussion on contradictions between the newly-introduced competency-based approach and units (see Sect. 5.2.1 for a full discussion).

Politics of Reform and Actors' Positions

A study on the implementation of the EQF commissioned in 2007 found that at that time, stakeholders had a "distinct lack of knowledge about the EQF initiative" (Westerhuis 2009: 3). The report also highlighted that "many stakeholders foresaw implications at system level when implementing the eight EQF levels, and as system discussions are extremely sensitive in this country, the EQF implementation had to be carefully orchestrated" (ibid). Another report had argued that "the predominant opinion is that the Netherlands does not need a new National Qualifications Framework as a response to the launching of EQF" (Transeqframe 2005: 1). As pointed out above, the development of the NLQF gained momentum only

---

[13]Unless in a procedure on the recognition of non-formal and informal learning, see Sect. 4.2.4.

4.2 Implementation of the Copenhagen Process in the Netherlands

when a European report found that the Netherlands were lagging behind with the EQF implementation. Since stakeholder involvement was vast and mostly consensus-led, the outcome of the process in the end is widely recognised (interview NL_MIXED-8).

The MOCW believes that the qualifications framework is a means for improving the transparency of qualifications and for relating them to each other within the country and across Europe (Transeqframe 2005: 1; interview NL_PUBL-4). It should not have any other purpose or replace the national system (ibid). This view is supported by national stakeholders, including social partners, the MBO Raad, and higher education stakeholders (Transeqframe 2005).

Employers support the development and the implementation of the NLQF. They hope that the instrument will contribute to increasing labour mobility, especially if combined with the validation of non-formal and informal learning (see Sect. 5.2.4) and quality assurance (see Sect. 5.2.5) (Van der Sanden et al. 2012: 69). Employers hope that this will foster lifelong learning, whether skills are acquired via formal or private education and training (ibid). The referencing of the three higher VMBO pathways on the same level with MBO-2 has been criticised by employers, since in their view only the latter qualifies for entering the labour market (Tweede Kamer der Staten-Generaal 2011a). Within employers' organisations, the association of private education and training providers (*Nederlandse Raad voor Training en Opleiding, NRTO*) is well-positioned on the topic and has been the most active within employers' organisations (interview NL_MIXED-8); their experts sometimes served as the experts for employers' organisations in general (ibid). The largest employers' organisation VNO-NCW and the organisation of SMEs, MKB, are "not interested very much" in the process, as an interview partner from an employers' organisation reports (NL_PRIV-1). An internal meeting on the topic took place but the organisations did not recognise any substantial relevance of the instrument for their work (ibid), in particular since the NLQF refers to learning outcomes and not to the labour market (interview NL_PUBL-4). They argue that firms already know what different educational tracks are worth (ibid) and in the border regions firms already know what the systems in neighbouring countries are worth (interview NL_PRIV-1). The NRTO requested to have their qualifications referenced to the NLQF with "eagerness" (NLQF Nationaal Coördinatiepunt 2012: 2). Naturally, they have a self-interest that motivates them to engage on the topic. The association of private education providers (*Nederlandse Raad vor Training en Opleiding*, NRTO) believes that this will increase the standing of their qualifications and certificates (Van der Sanden et al. 2012: 69). The private sector does not oppose the request that all qualifications, including those developed by the private sector, have to be described in terms of learning outcomes in order to be linked to the NLQF.

Unions also support the development and implementation of the NLQF. In their opinion, the instrument contributes to fostering lifelong learning, employability, mobility, and the transparency of sector qualifications (Van der Sanden et al. 2012, interview NL_UN-1). It can therefore help individuals to move within and across sectors. Moreover, it could improve the quality and standing of non-formal and informal education and training, since the benefit of validation procedures (see Sect. 5.2.4) is not always clear to individuals (interview NL_UN-1). In the unions' view, the NLQF can help choose the right programme and can contribute to spending money on training effectively (Van der Sanden et al. 2012). Finally, the NLQF could motivate low-skilled workers by showing them the qualification level they already have accomplished and provide an incentive to attend further education and training (ibid). In the view of the unions, the success of the instrument will depend on its inclusion in a coherent employability strategy that also involves APL as well as overall learning strategies (ibid).

Higher education institutions such as the organisation for accreditation, which is an independent accreditation organisation providing expert judgement on the quality of higher education programmes in Flanders and the Netherlands, had demanded that only higher education qualifications should be referenced to the levels 5–8 (Van der Sanden et al. 2012: 68) and that higher education and VET should be clearly distinguished (interview NL_MIXED-3). The sector fears to lose its status if permeability increases (ibid). This position was isolated and did not prevail. In general, however, the higher education sector mostly kept out of the process, since the European Qualifications Framework for Higher Education had already been established; for them, the most important aspect was that this framework would not be changed but incorporated into the NLQF (interviews NL_MIXED-5, NL_MIXED-8).

The MBO Raad argued that with the qualification structure, a framework already exists for VET (interview NL_MIXED-5). In their view, it was important that all NLQF levels are open for all qualifications (interview NL_PUBL-3). The organisation welcomed the option to have MBO 4 programmes referenced to level 5 (Van der Sanden et al. 2012: 69). In general, schools are satisfied with the implementation of the NLQF (interview NL_PUBL-3).

Brief Evaluation

The Netherlands developed a NQF as a response to the EQF in a process that involved stakeholders and was largely consensus-led. The process gained momentum only when a European report showed that the Netherlands were lagging behind in the implementation of the EQF, which steered political will to speed up the process. The framework excludes any changes of the existing education system and is perceived as a tool for comparability and transparency both on the European and national level. As an interview partner sector puts it, "In fact, nothing has changed" (interview NL_PUBL-3). Discussions on the referencing mostly focused on the relationship between general education qualifications and VET. European critique has led to the re-positioning of the general university entrance qualification. Several interview partners remarked that the referencing has been "conservative" regarding the positioning of VET qualifications, yet the highest MBO qualification is now on the same EQF level with VWO. On the national level, the system makes the different educational pathways and options for transitions transparent. Procedures have been developed to reference qualifications offered by private providers to the NLQF, which fosters the comprehensiveness of the framework also with respect to the market for continuing VET. Private providers developed self-interest in the process; in combination with a lack of interest of the two umbrella organisations, they became the most important voice of employers' organisations in the process. While the eight-level-structure of the framework can be considered a political choice that shall facilitate comparability with the EQF, descriptors have been adjusted to reflect the Dutch system, including a focus on autonomy and a holistic approach to VET. In sum, the core institutions of the Dutch VET systems have not been challenged at all. The process did, however, steer discussions on the relative weighting of different educational strands. If there are effects on the status of VET, these should not be overestimated and are unlikely to change the core institutions of Dutch VET.

4.2.3 The European Credit System for Vocational Education and Training

The mobility of MBO participants is still low: only 0.64 % of MBO students registered a stay abroad in 2010 (MOCW 2012: 62). This percentage rises continuously but only slightly (Van IJsselmuiden 2009). Most exchange experiences take place within European mobility programmes which are carried out by CINOP (ibid). Moreover, small-scale exchange programmes exist with Germany and Flanders. Eighty-six percent of ROCs and Agricultural Training Centres have mobility partnerships, on average with 19 partner institutions abroad (MOCW 2012: 62). About 3500 foreign companies offer BPV placements and Dutch companies increasingly provide placements in their foreign establishments (Van IJsselmuiden 2009). An MBO Internationalisation Agenda has been developed in order to foster international competences of MBO participants, especially on level 3 and 4, against the background of increasing levels of globalisation of the Dutch economy (ibid). The strategy aims at increasing the international orientation of the MBO curriculum, fostering incoming and outgoing mobility, continuing cooperation in VET on the European level, and increasing the image of Dutch VET abroad (ibid).

Few efforts have been taken to implement ECVET. The Netherlands conducted a consultation on ECVET and reported the results of a national consultation to the European Commission in April 2007 (Van Bijsterveldt-Vliegenthart 2007). Educational institutions, social partners, sectoral organisations and experts took part in the consultation process (ibid). In 2010, the Netherlands established a national coordination point for ECVET; this task is planned to be taken over by the reference point for quality assurance, which will serve as a national coordination point for both instruments and is set up at the CINOP International Agency (Visser 2010b: 10). The task of the coordination point has been to monitor existing developments and initiatives (interview NL_MIXED-3).

Van IJsselmuiden (2009: 31), a government official, points out that concerning ECVET "the Netherlands was at the cradle of this idea, which was part of the Maastricht Communiqué in 2004." However, he continues, "Upon further investigation it is questionable whether it is worth the effort, in view of the still slight international mobility of MBO participants. ECVET is rather something for the long(er) term, once the EQF has been properly implemented" (ibid). At that point in time, van IJsselmuiden argues that if the European Commission sticks to the instruments and its time plan for implementation, the focus of the Netherlands will primarily be on those MBO courses with a high mobility (ibid).

The Dutch way of dealing with ECVET hence has been described as a "wait and see" approach (interviews DE_PUBL-2, NL_MIXED-3). In line with this, the resources of the coordination point are "modest in size" (Visser 2010b: 10; cf. interview DE_PUBL-2). Indeed, the annual budget of the coordination point is 100,000 euros, which is insufficient for implementing a complex instrument (interview NL_MIXED-2). An interview partner argues that while the ministry felt the necessity to show some action, it adapted the organisational structures for the implementation of ECVET to the low priority it assigned to the instrument (ibid). The implementation of ECVET therefore mostly focuses on a bottom-up approach (Van Bruggen 2011). Several pilot projects on the practical use of ECVET have been carried out in line with such an approach (ibid). An impact on the system itself is unlikely.

The limited effect of ECVET is also caused by the unsuitability of the unit-concept for the Dutch approach to restructuring the VET system on the basis of competences. While I outlined that the competence approach is also geared towards outcomes rather than incomes, it still differs from a unit-approach. In a letter to the Commission, State Secretary for Education, Culture and Science Van Bijsterveldt-Vliegenhardt[14] (2007) points out that a unit-based system is not in line with the Dutch qualification structure, since the system just moved away from the concept of units. Prior to the shift towards competences, qualifications had been defined as partial qualifications (*deelkwalificaties*) which could be described as modules—this system would have had a good fit with ECVET (interview NL_MIXED-3). With the competence-based approach, only some qualifications have partial qualifications—a prerequisite for this is that *deelkwalificaties* have an autonomous meaning for the labour market (NL_MIXED-2). During a discussion in parliament, the question arose why partial qualifications were not introduced for all qualifications (ibid). The minister replied that this is not desirable, since every student should receive a full diploma (ibid). Yet, of course it would be possible to develop units solely for the purpose of facilitating mobility (NL_MIXED-1) or transform core tasks into units (interview NL_MIXED-7). This would mean to implement ECVET within qualifications (interview NL_MIXED-7).

---

[14]Maja Bijsterveldt-Vliegenthart was State Secretary for Education, Culture and Science from 2007 to 2010 and Minister for Education, Culture and Science from 2010 to 2012.

Politics of Reform and Actors' Positions

On the basis of the conducted consultation, the State Secretary concludes "that the organisations involved in secondary VET subscribe in full to the goals ECVET is seeking to achieve. The ambition to create more mobility in the European educational- and labour market [sic] will benefit from a greater transparency in the qualification structures and education systems across Europe (Marja Van Bijsterveldt-Vliegenthart 2007: 1)." The positive evaluation is that the instrument fosters partnerships between education providers across member states and international mobility.

The State Secretary also points out that "a surprisingly large number of respondents address the question of whether ECVET is the appropriate tool for achieving these goals" (ibid, underlined as in original). Most stakeholders believe that the instrument is not well-suited to address the objectives the Commission has outlined in the consultation document. In the words of Visser (2010b: 10): "from a pragmatic point of view, the question can be raised whether the combination NLQF/EQF—Europass (possibly a refined version hereof) would not suffice to promote the transparency of and communication about qualifications and acquired competences." As the State Secretary writes in her letter to the Commission, "the practical problems involved in defining equivalent occupational units at European level, the linking of ECVET credit points with learning outcomes and the administrative burden that the full-scale implementation of ECVET may imply, serve only to reinforce these doubts" (Van Bijsterveldt-Vliegenthart 2007). The Netherlands are sceptical regarding the effectiveness of the system: "Without a European qualification system, the ECVET can never be better than the national qualification systems on which it is based, and the quality of these systems differ greatly" (ibid). Moreover, the State Secretary "strongly endorses" the recommendation voiced by Dutch stakeholders to better align ECVET with EQF and Europass (ibid). Finally, while in her view the relation of the qualifications structure to the business community is a strong asset of the Dutch VET system, "relevance for the labour market is an aspect I would like to see more reflected in ECVET" (ibid). In the long run, from a Dutch perspective, ECVET could be adjusted to serve as a quality standard for learning outcomes acquired abroad (Van Bijsterveldt-Vliegenthart 2007). This understanding is in line with a bottom-up implementation of ECVET in the Netherlands.

The government subscribes to the goals of ECVET but is sceptical of the effectiveness of the instrument. According to an interview partner, the minister stated several times that there will not be a change of the system because of ECVET (interview NL_PUBL-3). This is underlined by an interview partner in the national administration who believes that such a change would be highly unlikely (interview NL_PUBL-4). As pointed out above, Van IJsselmuiden (2009), a government official, argues that ECVET might not be worth the effort. Interview partners remark that the instrument still has to be developed (interviews

NL_PUBL-4, NL_MIXED-3). That the idea was part of the Maastricht Communiqué during the Dutch presidency "gives some obligation to bring the idea further" (interview NL_PUBL-4). Therefore, the government waits for the results of ECVET projects and has indicated that it would be a good approach to first implement EQF and then ECVET (ibid). In the long run, it should be merged with ECTS (Van IJsselmuiden 2009). In practice, the way the government approaches the issue and the way the ECVET coordination point is designed shows that ECVET shall not have any impact on the system (interview NL_MIXED-2).

An interview partner from an employers' organisation points out that employers in general are not very interested in the ECVET instrument (interview NL_PRIV-1). Firms have no knowledge of the instrument (interviews NL_PRIV-2, NL_PRIV-3, NL_MIXED-1, NL_MIXED-7). Employers prefer standardised qualifications with a clear market value (ibid). At MBO level, firms mostly look at the Dutch labour market for recruitment (ibid). Incoming mobility is limited, since in many professions Dutch language skills are very important for firms (interviews NL_PRIV-2, NL_PRIV-3, NL_PRIV-4). At the same time, language skills are also important for outgoing mobility; employers, especially those active in the BBL track, would oppose more time spent in school (interview NL_MIXED-1). An interview partner from the national administration points out that social partners are highly supportive of increasing mobility but do not want to cover the costs (interview NL_PUBL-4). Exceptions for an active taking on VET are the health and welfare sectors, which will start experimenting with units. This is perceived as a step back to the old system by others (interview NL_PUBL-3). Still, these sectors fear skill shortages and believe that ECVET could support efforts to recruit employees from other sectors and from abroad (interview NL_MIXED-3). ECVET has not yet been discussed within unions (interview NL_UN-1).

In a meeting on ECVET, it became clear that other stakeholders—such as Colo or the MBO Raad—are more enthusiastic about ECVET than the MOCW (interview NL_MIXED-3). While some actors proposed to evaluate how ECVET could be included in plans to reform the duration of several MBO programmes from 4 years to 3 years, the MOCW has been reluctant (ibid). However, defining units on the national level would be a threat to school autonomy, as an interview partner remarks (interview NL_PUBL-3), since the design of curricula and examinations lies within their responsibility. An interview partner from a school stressed that although ECVET has to be implemented most importantly via schools,[15] nobody at the school-level talks about the instrument (interview NL_PUBL-2). At his school, ECVET is not used since it does not yet have a market value (ibid). Moreover, if schools are responsible for the quality of education, even if participants go abroad, it is not clear why a European instrument is needed (ibid). The instrument is not yet

---

[15]*Kenniscentra* are also involved in assuring the quality of workplace-based training during mobility phases (interview NL_MIXED-1).

in the mind of *kenniscentra*, although in the view of Colo they should be responsible for the implementation of ECVET, since they develop qualifications (interview NL_MIXED-7). If each school creates units, this could undermine transparency and mobility rather than facilitate it (ibid).

The only advocate for an 'à la carte' system is the CINOP International Agency, where the coordination point has been set up (interview NL_MIXED-3). It is argued that such an approach would better fit the needs of employers and reduce costs. Moreover, in their view, such a system could reduce training time spent on learning content that is already familiar when participants go abroad, change MBO tracks or start with another qualification after graduating from MBO (ibid). The national coordination point for ECVET tries to advocate the use of credit points because they can facilitate transfers; for this, learning outcomes and flexible pathways are essential (ibid). Other actors do not share the point of view of the international agency, and it is widely believed that an 'à la carte' system would undermine the demand for skilled workers (*vakman*) (interview NL_MIXED-7). For example, an interview partner from a school argues that it is the social function of education that is not in line with an 'à la carte' system, although in VET there is always a tension between the objectives to foster personal development and to meet the demands of labour markets (interview NL_PUBL-2). Moreover, he points out that if education becomes too individualised it is not efficient, since participant numbers might be too low (ibid).

Brief Evaluation

The implementation of ECVET has been subject to a 'wait and see' approach. The government opted to implement the NLQF first, and questions if the implementation of ECVET is worth the effort at all. The government feels obligated to show good will, since compromise on the instrument was reached in Maastricht during the Dutch presidency. A coordination point for ECVET was created at the CINOP International Agency but has limited means. The implementation of a unit approach is complicated by the recent shift away from a unit-based VET system towards a competence-based qualification structure, which is based on core tasks. It is widely believed that a change back to units is not desirable. Schools are responsible for the curricula and examinations and hence would need to implement the ECVET in the sense of the currently envisioned bottom-up approach. If units were defined on the national level, schools' autonomy would be massively cut. However, it would be possible to have *kenniscentra* include units in the existing qualification structure with the sole focus on mobility or transforming core tasks into units. The International Agency is the only advocate for a system change towards an 'à la carte' system; other actors oppose such an idea. Social partners have not been very interested in the instrument thus far. Only in the health and welfare sector, employers started to look towards ECVET as an instrument to prevent skill shortages by facilitating mobility of employees from other sectors and from abroad. In general, international mobility in VET is very low. In sum, the ECVET is highly likely to be implemented solely as an instrument for mobility. Whether a bottom-up approach is chosen or whether *kenniscentra* develop units for mobility, both ways of implementation are highly unlikely to lead to changes of the system's core institutions.

4.2.4 Validation of Non-formal and Informal Learning

In the Netherlands, a well-developed system for the validation of non-formal and informal qualifications (usually termed "accreditation of prior learning"; or, in Dutch *Erkenning van Verworven Competenties*, EVC) exists. EVC has been on the agenda in the Netherlands since the 1980s (Maes 2004: 50). Taking part in examinations as an external candidate had been possible even prior to that (ibid). While in the beginning EVC was used in a few sectors and settings, it was soon used more widely (ibid). According to the law, the qualification structure should facilitate the recognition of skills that have been acquired previously in the formal, non-formal or informal sector (Duvekot 2010). In 2000, a publication on EVC was issued and a working group formulated a strategy for EVC (ibid). A kenniscentrum EVC was created in 2001 to foster the use of EVC procedures, disseminate best practices and provide expertise on the topic.

ROCs, higher education institutions, private education providers or private companies that provide career advising can serve as EVC providers (interview NL_MIXED-6). Those carried out by private providers are not always recognised by ROCs, although in numbers private providers carry out more procedures (ibid). For publicly financed institutions, EVC procedures are contract activities (ibid). Assessment agencies regularly monitor provider compliance with the code and accredit their eligibility to offer EVC for specific qualification standards (interview NL_MIXED-6). Previously, this task was carried out by the Inspectorate; now seven such institutions exist and more quality assurance is needed to meet their assessments (ibid). In 2009, 15,700 *Evaringscertificaten* (certificate of prior learning) have been carried out, mostly in the MBO sector (Duvekot 2010: 8). Between 2007 and 2009 the number has increased by more than 60 % (ibid). Still, the number of EVC procedures does not meet the target of 50,000 procedures in 2010, which was formulated in the Plan of Action in 2004 (Advies et al. 2007: 22). EVC procedures are used more often in bigger companies (interview NL_PRIV-3). Procedures can cost up to a few thousand euros (Advies et al. 2007). Most often, the employer, O & O funds or local authorities[16] pay for the costs of EVC programmes so that candidates usually do not need to finance the procedures (Advies et al. 2007: 38–39). The state subsidises EVC procedures by tax measures both for employers and for individuals, as laid down in the 2007 Tax Relief APL

---

[16]Municipalities pay for EVC procedures for the unemployed; funding has been cut recently (interview NL_MIXED-6).

Procedures Act (Wet Vermindering Afdracht Erkenning Verworven Competenties).

The procedures aim at providing a "picture of an individual's knowledge, skills and competences against a chosen (qualification) profile" (Van der Sanden et al. 2012: 20). Standardised qualification profiles, including regulated VET qualifications and sector qualifications that have been developed by branches,[17] enable recognition of EVC certificates on the labour market (ibid). In 2012, a new covenant has been signed by social partners and the government that highlights the nature of EVC as a labour market instrument that can improve an individual's standing on the labour market or shorten educational programmes (StvdA 2012: 19). Two kinds of procedures exist: In addition to EVC procedures leading to an *Evaringscertificaat* in which the candidate's profile is assessed against a qualification, it is also possible to undergo a procedure with the objective to set up a generic personal portfolio (*Evaringsprofiel*) (Duvekot 2010). Here, all of a candidate's qualifications are assessed; the focus is on the recognition and not on the accreditation of prior learning (ibid). Moreover, EVC procedures exist not also in higher education.

Procedures follow four steps:[18]

1. Information on the procedure is provided and an agreement is signed by the candidate and the education and training institution that specifies the standard against which the procedure is carried out;
2. A portfolio is drafted that shows the knowledge, skills and competences of the candidate. The candidate provides evidence when filling out the portfolio. In addition, it is possible that skills are demonstrated in an interview or at the workplace. Often, a mix of methods is used (Duvekot 2010: 22);
3. A professional evaluates the portfolio of the candidate and determines the fit between the applicant's skills and the chosen qualification profile;
4. The candidate receives a certificate of experience (*Ervaringscertificaat*) in which the skills and their evaluation are described, as well as the way the skills have been demonstrated.

A quality covenant for EVC procedures was established in 2006 and subsequently a quality code (Kwaliteitscode EVC) was developed by the kenniscentrum EVC, in which the European guidelines on the validation of informal and non-formal learning (Council of the European Union 2004b) were incorporated (interview NL_MIXED-6). EVC started as a bottom-up initiative with a lot of diversity, and it was felt at that point that more regulation was needed in order to improve quality (interview NL_MIXED-6). However, it was believed that the quality code does not clearly enough address the division of responsibilities, and

---

[17]Government and social partners decide together which branch qualifications are suitable as EVC standards (interview NL_MIXED-6).

[18]The steps of the APL procedure are as described in Van der Sanden et al. (2012: 20), if not indicated otherwise.

so stakeholders commissioned the government to develop basic quality standards and assurance arrangements (StvdA 2011: 20). As a consequence of a government regulation issued in 2009, providers that do not fulfil the required quality criteria lose their recognition; costs for EVC procedures with these providers are no longer tax-deductible (Van der Sanden et al. 2012: 21).

Critique on the EVC procedures is brought forward, since EVC certificates are not always recognised by other education providers (Advies et al. 2007, interviews NL_MIXED-8, NL_MIXED-2, NL_PRIV-1). Schools evaluate if EVC results can be accredited to qualification programmes, since they are also responsible for issuing certificates (interview NL_MIXED-8). It is difficult to establish comparability of the assessments carried out during EVC procedures (Duvekot 2010: 23). It is therefore important to assure high competences of the supervisors and assessors of EVC procedures (ibid). The inspectorate has been very critical on EVC (interviews NL_MIXED-2, NL_MIXED-6). Finally, since the importance of general subjects grew within MBO qualifications (see Sect. 5.1), these also have to be accessed by EVC procedures (interview NL_MIXED-6). These new requirements will be harder to fulfil, especially for those candidates who have worked before taking part in EVC procedures (interview NL_MIXED-6).

From a Dutch perspective, the link to the NLQF should not be overestimated: The "(...) successful integration of learning outcomes of informal and non-formal learning in an NQF (...) and their validation by schools will not so much depend on the fact that an NQF is in place, but much more on the fact that procedures to validate the outcomes of informal and non-formal learning are in place" (Transeqframe 2005: 1–2). Moreover, the description of learning outcomes and competences is seen as too abstract focussing too much on educational terms for serving as references for EVC (ibid). EVC procedures serve as a description of to what extent an individual's competences meet the standards of a qualification; education providers decide if the candidate has to undergo additional education or—which is rare—if skills are already equivalent to a qualification (interview NL_MIXED-6). The referencing of EVC to the NLQF therefore has to take place via an education provider (ibid). Still, synergy effects can be derived between EVC procedures and the shift towards competence-based qualifications (Maes 2004: 51) and the NLQF (Tweede Kamer der Staten-Generaal 2011b: 5).

Politics of Reform and Actors' Positions

The State Secretary for Education, Culture and Science assesses the experiences with EVC as positive and believes that trust and agreements between the stakeholders are important for the functioning of the system (Van Bijsterveldt-Vliegenthart 2007: 2). The government has supported EVC procedures with tax facilities and with an institutional infrastructure. However, an interview partner argued that the number of EVC procedures grows slowly and that the promotion of EVC has been "very fake" (interview NL_MIXED-9).

4.2 Implementation of the Copenhagen Process in the Netherlands 155

Social partners support the use of EVC procedures, especially as a labour market instrument and as a part of collective agreements (StvdA 2012) in which sometimes it is agreed that O & O funds can be used to fund EVC procedures (Duvekot 2010). They believe it is especially useful to strengthen an individual's standing on the labour market and career development (ibid), in particular for individuals with lower education (interview NL_MIXED-6). Several sectors moreover launched EVC initiatives which involve social partners, kenniscentra and ROCs (ibid). These support a bottom-up approach for the introduction of EVC procedures (Duvekot 2010: 2) and can include agreements on their recognition (interview NL_PUBL-3). The care sector is not only active in ECVET but also in EVC procedures (interview NL_PRIV-1); they believe that they are a tool to overcome skill shortages in the short and in the long run (interview NL_MIXED-6). Employers demand that the results of EVC procedures should be acknowledged by all schools (interview NL_PRIV-1). While employers believe that EVC procedures can help address shortages of qualified personnel, trade unions are concerned with the employability of employees (Advies et al. 2007: 24). Unions stress that the initiatives for improving quality are important and that the instrument is not suited for every worker but is particularly important for older workers or the unemployed (interview NL_UN-1). A union interview partner also stressed that increasing the general skills component within the procedures might make it difficult for individuals to master the requirements (ibid).

Brief Evaluation

The introduction of EVC procedures preceded the Copenhagen process and has been carried out for reasons to be found in the national arena rather than in the European one (interviews NL_MIXED-2, NL_UN-1). However, European guidelines were incorporated into the quality code for EVC procedures. While in the beginning procedures were very diverse, they became more standardised. Both publicly funded education providers such as ROCs and private providers can carry out EVC procedures. They are not always recognised by the local schools, which remains a problem. Numbers are small, so that the EVC procedures will not undermine the system as such (interview NL_MIXED-6). The incorporation of general skills remains a challenge. Validation procedures can focus on providing a generic profile of a candidate's skills (recognition) or on the accreditation of her skills against a recognised qualification in order to shorten the duration of education (accreditation). Referencing to the NLQF can only take place via the accreditation of schools that have to determine that the individual's competences meet the standards for the qualification which served as a standard for the EVC procedure. All stakeholders support EVC procedures; costs for procedures are mostly paid for by employers or (in the case of unemployed and with decreasing funds) by the state, which also provides a general infrastructure.

4.2.5 Quality Assurance

Much attention is paid to quality assurance in the Dutch education system. VET providers have a large responsibility for quality assurance themselves: "Schools determine, assess, assure and improve the quality of their vocational training courses" (Van den Boom 2011: 3). The institutions are free to choose their quality assurance methods and instruments but must adhere to the following criteria: setting adequate policies and objectives; establishing a policy, planning and control cycle in which quality assurance is a central and systematic element; involving stakeholders in a dialogue on these policy goals; involving stakeholders in assessing quality; cooperating with independent experts in assessing quality; and communicating with and reporting to concerned actors (ibid). Public accountability is an important aspect of quality assurance. The MOCW commissions independent research on the satisfaction of VET participants both at the system level and at the institutional level. This data is also used by the ROCs to improve quality. Moreover, up to a fifth of public funding is based on the performance of institutions.

The Inspectorate of Education monitors public and private VET providers and visits the training institutions at least once a year. The supervision is risk-based, meaning that the intensity of monitoring depends on how well-functioning the quality system of the respective provider is (IKEI 2012). The monitoring process is based on the providers' annual reports and comprises three phases (Van der Sanden et al. 2012: 12). First, a review of the institutions is carried out in order to observe deficiencies in the quality of education or the management. Second, in case deficiencies are found, the Inspectorate analyses these more closely. These can, for example, include the delivery of programmes, examinations, the governance capacity, accessibility and contents of the programmes, completion rates and drop outs, satisfaction of the participants, the compliance with financial or legal matters, and—a subject that receives increased attention—the norm of 850 hours of supervised training for upper secondary VET (Van der Sanden et al. 2012: 12; Visser 2010b: 18). Third, the Inspectorate makes an agreement with the institutions in order to determine how shortcomings can be addressed (Van der Sanden et al. 2012: 12). The progress is monitored by the Inspectorate after 1 year. In case insufficient progress is observed in addressing the deficiencies, the Inspectorate can forward the case to the Minister, who can review the financial basis of the institution or withdraw its license for offering VET programmes and carrying out examinations. Reports and improvement policies are subject to a discussion by the Minister and the State Secretary in the Parliament. The Inspectorate regularly publishes a report on the results of their inspections and on the state of the education system on the internet.

In 2008 the MBO Raad and Colo made a proposal on the standardisation of examinations, which led to the introduction of examination profiles. These are standards for the process and the conditions of examinations (IKEI 2012). ROCs develop examination regulations on the basis of these national qualification profiles. The Inspectorate then monitors the quality of examinations. Every year, the Inspectorate draws a sample of all courses offered at each school and controls whether the exams meet the national standards and if they are reliable (ibid). Examinations have been seen as a deficiency in the quality assurance system, and efforts have been made to improve their quality, for example by increased supervision or by training teachers (interview NL_PUBL-1).

The quality of BVP placements and apprenticeships is monitored by the *kenniscentra*. Firms need to be approved by *kenniscentra* as training firms, according to the criteria which are mostly set by the respective *kenniscentra* on the basis of minimum criteria enacted by the SBB. Hence, criteria differ across sectors; some, for example, require trainers to undergo a special training course (Smits 2005). Moreover, *kenniscentra* employ about 800 education advisors (*opleiding-sadviseurs*) who support firms that offer placements by regular visits, supporting trainers, and providing information and building networks of training companies (IKEI 2012). The arrangement that *kenniscentra* are responsible for both the quantity and the quality of BVP placements is subject to criticism (Le Deist and Winterton 2011: 21; Smits 2005). Apparently, in sectors in which firms are less eager to offer BVP placements, the criteria for approval seems easier to fulfil—therefore, the quality of training differs (ibid). ROCs are formally responsible for participants during their BVP placements, but lack resources to monitor the quality of the training in firms (ibid). Empirical studies have found that the quality of training in firms is insufficient (Le Deist and Winterton 2011: 21). Problems include subordination of training under production, participants may not have the opportunity to accomplish their training tasks, and tasks assigned to them may not be related to their training (ibid).

Quality assurance in higher professional education is based on self-evaluation, review, and accreditation of programmes (Visser 2010b: 10). In HBO, there is an agreement that programmes are based on national profiles, which are legitimised by the HBO Raad[19] and validated by sectoral or professional bodies (Transeqframe 2005). Accreditation procedures are carried out by the Dutch-Flemish Accreditation Organisation (*Nederlands-Vlaamse Accreditatie Organisatie*) and are based on the same national profiles (ibid). Examinations fall under the responsibility of the educational institution (ibid). Institutions also install quality assurance mechanisms and organise peer to peer quality assessments (ibid).

As Van der Sanden et al. (2012: 12) remark in an official report on the referencing process of the NLQF to the EQF, "the quality framework EQAVET is largely in line with the existing quality assurance in VET. Both use a model (...) containing four phases: plan, do, check and act." Such a quality cycle has already been included in the 1996 WEB (interview NL_PUBL-1). European indicators are

---

[19]The HBO Raad (*HBO Council*) is the association of government-funded universities of applied sciences.

largely met (Visser 2010b: 10). This is confirmed by an interview partner in the national administration, who also points out that definitions sometimes differ (interview NL_PUBL-1). The interview partner argues that the Netherlands already meet about 90 % of European proposals on quality (interview NL_PUBL-1).

A National Coordination Point for EQAVET has been established at the CINOP International Agency with the aim to link European and national policy developments. Its tasks are to promote quality assurance, establish a network between different stakeholders, disseminate information on EQAVET, issue reports and action plans, and represent the Netherlands in the European EQAVET network. While Visser (2010b: 10) argues that the coordination point is "fairly small", an interview partner from the MOCW points out that its task is mostly to match the national with the European level. Since at the national level an elaborated quality assurance system already exists, funding is sufficient for this task (interview NL_PUBL-1). In January 2011, the NLQAVET project was launched. It aims at promoting EU policies in the national arena, creating an inventory of quality assurance systems, improving the quality assurance culture at provider level, and involving all stakeholders in quality assurance. An action plan for referencing the quality assurance system to EQAVET was being developed in 2012 by a working group (Van der Sanden et al. 2012: 12). The latter comprises members from the MOCW, the MBO Raad, Colo, trade unions, the NRTO, the Inspectorate, and the Youth Organisation for Vocational Education (ibid). Five pilot projects were launched with the objective to search for ways to implement EQAVET on the provider level (interview NL_MIXED-3). This is seen as especially important, since quality assurance mostly focuses on the management level but is not present on the floor (ibid).

While the Netherlands already largely fulfil requirements from the EU level regarding quality assurance, the NLQF can steer the ongoing discussion on the quality of examinations, since it focuses on outcomes, and such a focus fosters the importance of examinations (interview NL_MIXED-8). An interview partner from the national administration believes that EQAVET mostly brings together stakeholders in the Netherlands in the sense of a platform on the national level (interview NL_PUBL-4). In this sense, it has a structuring effect (interview NL_MIXED-7). As another interview partner from the national administration puts it: "The impact of the European part is very small, because we are already thinking, and revising, and stimulating" (interview NL_PUBL-1). In very specific areas, "small exchanges" are fostered by the European cooperation—for example, regarding performance-based financing an interchange with Finland has been launched (interview NL_PUBL-1). European guidelines are used only if they match national needs: "You take what can be useful for your country" (interview NL_PUBl-1). Instead of the European level influencing Dutch quality assurance, an interview partner from the national administration points out that "EQARF is inspired by us, also by some other countries" (interview NL_PUBL-1).

Politics of Reform and Actors' Positions

Quality assurance is high on the MOCW's agenda and improvements are regularly being made. An interview partner from the national administration points out that although quality assurance mechanisms are already well-defined, in practice the feedback loop is not elaborated enough, which will be addressed with new instruments [September 2011] (interview NL_PUBL-1). In large schools, quality assurance is mostly a subject for the management but always leads to improvements in the classrooms (ibid). Together with European partners, pilot projects are carried out in order to bring quality initiatives down to the teacher level (ibid). The interview partner moreover sees room for improvement regarding the supervision of private education providers and firms offering BVP or apprenticeships (ibid).

Employers believe that the quality of Dutch VET is already very high (interview NL_PRIV-1). Still, improvements are necessary and on their way: In the realm of the SBB, agreements on BVP placements in MBO will be made [September 2011]. These agreements will also request more quality assurance from firms, since "both sides have to increase quality" and firms should provide good guidance to VET participants (ibid). Moreover, employers welcome recent initiatives to monitor the provision of hours in schools more closely (see above), since schools too often fail to provide the agreed learning hours in practice (ibid). The interview partner admits that there are firms that use participants to accomplish easy tasks but are not involved enough in providing the training of relevant contents (ibid). Employers' organisations articulate this position to firms (ibid). An interview partner, however, stresses that EQAVET itself is not present in the mind-set of *kenniscentra* or companies (interview NL_MIXED-7).

Unions highlight the importance of quality assurance and continuously lobby for improving the quality of Dutch VET. An interview partner from the unions argues that the topic is on the agenda—however, there is hardly any influence from European initiatives other than the organisation of meetings (interview NL_UN-1). The interview partner stresses that some schools have management problems, and that the quality of VET differs across firms. Therefore, agreements in which each stakeholder commits to carry out improvements are very important for fostering quality (ibid). Evaluations are a good tool to monitor the development (ibid).

Brief Evaluation

The Netherlands have a much elaborated quality assurance system that is based on quality assurance by the providers themselves, monitoring by the Education Inspectorate, agreements with stakeholders including firms, a policy cycle on quality assurance and continuous revision of the system itself. In contrast to Germany, schools are responsible for the quality of their VET courses and need to have quality assurance mechanisms. Firms are included into quality assurance by agreements and monitoring, yet problems seem to prevail. Employers' organisations address the need for high quality in workplace-based learning more openly than their German counterparts and demand improvements from firms. The proposals by EQARF and EQAVET are largely met. A national coordination point has been established that mostly steers a debate on the national level. The ministry selects useful elements for the national arena and initiates learning processes on specific issues from other countries. The government itself has influenced policy developments on the European level in the way the Dutch system of quality assurance is organised.

4.3 Conclusions

Visser (2010b: 5) summarises the impact of EU VET policies on the Dutch system as follows: "In short, while 'Europe' is key to the Dutch situation, its impact on the Dutch VET system as such should not be overestimated (not underestimated for that matter)." Powell and Trampusch (2011: 304) observe that "the Netherlands had already begun moving in the direction of skill formation reform favoured in Europe in the decade prior to 2002."

Powell and Trampusch (2011) argue that the 1996 WEB law "shifted attention toward an outcome-based and modularized qualification system, which is now advocated strongly within the Copenhagen Process." My analysis confirms that before the Copenhagen process a shift towards competence-based learning was already launched that focuses on core tasks and is largely similar to *learning outcomes*. However, interview partners stressed that while the system was based on units, with the recent shift towards competence-based learning it is no longer. Interview partners argued that implementing *ECVET* in a system-orientated way is therefore unlikely, since the system just moved away from a unit-based approach. It is thus believed that ECVET will be implemented in a bottom-up manner to foster mobility. Schools are responsible for curricula and examinations and hence would implement ECVET—otherwise their autonomy would be massively diminished. An alternative route to implementing ECVET could be involve *kenniscentra*: They could develop units or transform core tasks into units for mobility purposes, so that a unit-based approach would not be installed on system-level but only as a basis for fostering mobility. So far, the government opted for a 'wait and see' approach towards the instrument. A national coordination point has been installed, but is equipped with limited means. In contrast to the German case, it is not discussed how units could improve permeability within the system.

The development of a *Dutch qualifications framework* in the Netherlands (NLQF) as a response to the EQF has been caused by the Copenhagen process. Yet, similar to the German case, the NLQF maps the system and hence fosters comparability and transparency at the national and European level but impacts the VET regime only to a very limited degree. Any changes on admission procedures are excluded. Discussions regarding the referencing of qualifications mostly concerned the relationship between VET and general education. The NLQF has

4.3 Conclusions 161

eight levels, which can be seen as a political choice to foster comparability between EQF and NLQF. Descriptors have been adjusted to reflect the Dutch system, including a focus on autonomy and a holistic approach to VET. Interview partners have argued in the referencing process that VET qualifications were referenced to lower levels than in other countries, which took place to the disadvantage of VET qualifications. The procedure has been consensus-led and stakeholders are in general satisfied with the outcome.

Procedures on the *accreditation of prior learning* (*EVC*) existed prior to the Copenhagen process. Yet, European guidelines were incorporated when a quality code for EVC procedures was developed. While procedures had been very diverse in the beginning, the level of standards was increased. It is possible to use validation procedures as a generic procedure to show an individual's skills, or to evaluate in how far the skills meet a qualification and carry out an accreditation. The number of procedures that are carried out is still small, so that they are unlikely to undermine the system.

The Netherlands have a much elaborated *quality assurance* system that is based on the providers' quality assurance systems, monitoring carried out by the Inspectorate, agreements with stakeholders including firms, a policy cycle on quality assurance and continuous revision of the system itself. The system largely fulfils provisions of EQARF and EQAVET. A national coordination point has been established that mainly structures debates on the national level.

Politics of Reform and Actors' Positions
In contrast to the German case, in the Netherlands national discussions on EU VET policies and their implementation did not take place. As an interview partner puts it, "The Copenhagen process is still not very known" (interview NL_MIXED-2). Decisions are mostly taken by a small elite (ibid, interview NL_MIXED-4).

An interview partner argues that the MOCW mostly deals with European initiatives in VET only if they interfere with national policies (interview NL_PUBL-3). An Interview partner from the MOCW stresses that the pace of European initiatives increases, while the staff in the ministry is limited (interview NL_PUBL-4).

The government has taken a critical stand on ECVET and kept implementation efforts to a minimum, but feels committed to the instrument, since it was agreed upon during the Dutch presidency. The NLQF gained momentum only when a European report showed that the Netherlands were lagging behind in the implementation of the EQF. This steered political will to foster the process. Regarding quality assurance, the ministry takes a selective approach by choosing useful elements for the national arena and initiating selective learning processes on specific issues from other countries. The government has, moreover, influenced policy developments on the European level in the way the Dutch system of quality assurance is organised.

The CINOP International Agency takes a special role in the national debate, since it is the only actor to advocate a flexible 'àla carte' system for VET. The impact of such efforts is hard to assess and, moreover, contested, An interview partner pointed out that impact of the agency is very limited (interview NL_MIXED-2).

Employers' organisations "are not very enthusiastic about the European systems" (interview NL_PRIV-1). The shift towards making the VET system more competence-based was called for by employers, and they believe that now VET more closely resembles the labour market. Employers support EVC procedures. The quality of work-based training seems to differ across firms, and employers' organisations address this issue more openly than their German counterparts and enter agreements to improve the quality. The MBO is seen to focus mostly on the national arena, in contrast to higher education (ibid). In the words of another interview partner: "Employers are very inward-looking" (interview NL_MIXED-4). An exception is the health and welfare sector, which has been active in developing pilot projects on ECVET—including the creation of units—with the idea that a combination of ECVET and EVC procedures can be used as a means to address the arising problem of a shortage of labour in these professions by facilitating inflow from other sectors and from abroad. Private training providers have been active in the development of the NLQF, since they perceive the instrument as an option to improve the standing of their qualifications offered in continuing VET.

Unions support the shift towards a competence-based VET system and argue that the shift brings VET closer to the labour market and fosters the employability of graduates, since they can better make use of their skills in related jobs. When the NLQF was initiated as a response to the European initiative, unions supported the instruments. In their view, the NLQF fosters lifelong learning, employability, mobility, the transparency of sector qualifications, and the motivation of low-skilled workers by showing levels they have already accomplished and making educational routes transparent. In their view, an advantage is that the NLQF can strengthen the visibility and standing of validation procedures. Unions support EVC procedures. From their perspective, improvements can be made by fostering quality and focussing on the right target groups—such as older workers or the unemployed. While quality assurance is high on the unions' agenda, they believe that European policies are not very far-reaching. Unions believe that the quality of training differs across training firms and also lobby for improvements in the schools' management.

In the first section, core features of the Dutch training regime have been defined. These are hardly impacted by the way the Copenhagen process is implemented. Minor impacts concern the standing of VET: It has been argued that VET qualifications were referenced to lower levels than in other countries, which might weaken the status of VET compared to general secondary and higher education. Moreover, the general university entrance qualification has been positioned above VET courses, a decision that has been reconsidered only after criticism from other member states and the Commission. However, this impact surely should not be overrated. The remaining core features remain unaffected: the dominance and higher status of school-based VET, the integration of workplace-based training into school-based VET and the resulting balance between broad and specific skills, strong state involvement in regulation and financing, and the institutionalised participation of social partners all were not influenced by the instruments and principles developed by the Copenhagen process.

Chapter 5
The Impact of the Copenhagen Process on the English Training Regime

The case study on the UK focuses on England.[1] In the following sections, the English VET system will first be laid out by presenting the different qualifications, analysing the institutions of the English VET system, and highlighting four main features. The second subsection addresses the implementation of the principles and instruments of the Copenhagen process. The conclusion discusses actors' role and positions as well as main findings of the case study against the background of the core features of the system.

5.1 The English Vocational Education and Training System

The British VET system is market-led. The state operates as a regulator for the market. Apprenticeships in the UK have historically been contested and subject to a lack of coordination and credible commitment (Thelen 2004). Employers and unions were not able to coordinate and create common standards, so that in combination with long durations of training and poaching training became a less and less viable option (ibid). Relying on a workforce with low skills and low-quality production, in the political economy literature the British VET system has been characterised as a "low skill equilibrium" (Soskice 1994; Finegold and Soskice 1988). The British economy is focused on standardised mass products rather than on products that require higher degrees of innovation and a skilled labour force (ibid, 27). This equilibrium is a free ride or public good problem, since it is cheaper for firms to hire skilled workers than to invest in their training themselves when VET graduates might then be poached by other companies (ibid, 25). Therefore, in their seminal article Finegold and Soskice (1988) see the "failure of training" as both a

---

[1] See Sect. 1.2 for details on my case selection.

consequence of the country's focus on mass production as the first industrialised country and—having a lower educational attainment than other industrialised countries—as a cause for difficulties in adapting to changing economic conditions.

Overcoming the low skill equilibrium has been high on the agenda for decades. In the 1940s and 1950s, apprenticeship training was strengthened due to skill shortages (Thelen 2004). Many policy initiatives on upskilling were launched in the 1970s, 1980s, and 1990s (Deissinger et al. 2011: 400). In spite of government policies such as a training levy and a tripartite structure for apprenticeships, the number of apprenticeships decreased from about 120,000 in 1970 to about 30,000 in 1983 (ibid, 147). The government remained highly active in the policy field: In the 1980s alone, there have been as many as 43 new initiatives (Milner 1998: 169). In spite of these efforts, Streeck (2011: 323) argues that "in fact, in the 1990s at the latest, the United States and Britain finally gave up on industrial upskilling and, with it, on the industrial working class". Instead, the two countries fostered the supply of skills for the service sector, especially for the financial sector (Streeck 2011). As a result, it can be seen empirically that in the UK, fewer employees work in manufacturing, while employment in the service sector is higher than average in the EU (Cedefop Refernet 2011: 7). The UK followed a strategy of mass higher education. For the individual, this bears a certain risk of over-qualification (Hillmert 2008; Roberts 2004), especially since the expansion of higher education took place mostly in "soft" subjects and not in technical fields (Hillmert 2008). Still, returns on training have remained stable (Hillmert 2008: 71) and returns on higher education are higher in England than in most European countries (Wolf 2011: 31). The rising number of higher education graduates is contrasted by a lack of intermediate skills in the workforce. This is, as will be analysed in more detail below, in spite of continuous efforts to reform the VET system. According to Unwin (2006), this "hourglass economy" is characterised by high demand for jobs on the higher and lower levels but without a matching level of intermediary skills.

Still today, as will be seen later, change is a constant in British VET policies, leading to a highly multi-facetted and continuously changing training regime.[2] Upskilling is a key priority in a recent skills strategy from the Department for Business, Innovation and Skills (BIS). The strategy underlines the dimension of the challenge: "There should be no illusions about the scale of the challenge we face. Our working age population is less skilled than that of France, Germany and the US and this contributes to the UK being at least 15 per cent less productive than those countries" (BIS 2010: 4). An example for the focus on upskilling is the influential Leitch Review (Her Majesty's Treasury 2006) which recommended that 90 % of the population should gain skills on level 2 (see below), an additional 1.9 million should attain a level 3 qualification and 40 % of the population should have skills

---

[2]Kohlrausch (2009: 68) remarks: "A systematic overview of the current training schemes can hardly be provided, since the structure of the UK VET-system stands out because of its high diversity." This chapter therefore will not attempt to reflect all changes in the past years, but rather highlight changes in a few selected areas.

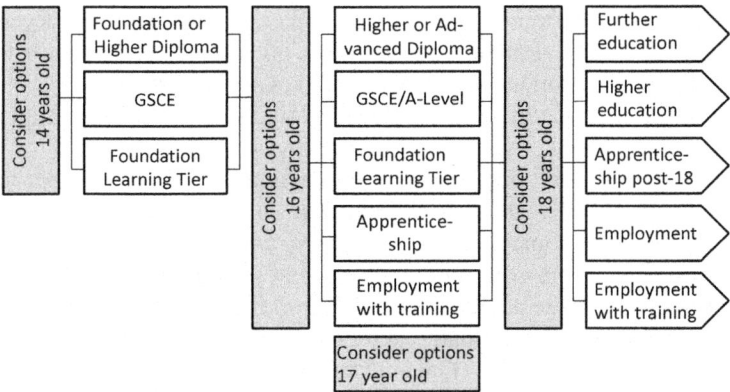

Fig. 5.1 Choices in 14–19 education and training in England. *Source*: Cedefop Refernet (2011: 42). Public sector information licensed under the Open Government Licence v2.0. For more information, see: http://www.nationalarchives.gov.uk/doc/open-government-licence/version/2/

on level 4 or higher. The influential Wolf (2011) report critically analysed the British VET system and argued that substantial changes should be made to the system. Wolf (2011: 21) estimates that "350,000 young people in a given 16–19 cohort are poorly served by current arrangements." In her view, progression into stable employment or higher education levels is not given in an effective or consistent way (ibid).

Qualifications

In the English school system, differentiation between general and vocational education takes place at the age of 14 (Fig. 5.1). In comparison to Germany and the Netherlands, the system is less stratified (Kohlrausch 2009). At upper secondary level ("post-16"), education in the UK is much less vocationally-orientated than in other European countries (Cedefop Refernet 2011: 45): The majority of students follow general education programmes, mostly leading to the "General Certificate of Secondary Education" (GCSE), which can be acquired at the age of 16. Subsequently, the "General Certificate of Education at Advanced Level" (GCE A Level, "A-Levels") can be acquired at the age of 18. Universities often require A-Levels with a certain range of grades for admission. In 2000, vocational GSCEs and vocational A-Levels were introduced to strengthen vocational routes during secondary education (Cedefop Refernet 2011). In addition, diploma programmes exist, which combine general and vocational education as "applied learning" in economic sectors. There are Foundation, Higher and Advanced Diplomas. Foundation Learning programmes are geared towards students with lower performance and are structured around national qualifications. Many of these qualifications are very small, with a third of the qualifications lasting less than 50 hours (Wolf 2011: 72). Wolf (ibid) argues that the labour market value of these recently introduced qualifications is low. For compulsory education, there is a national curriculum. The distribution of funds, admissions, employees, and pupils' achievements are within the responsibility of

Local Education Authorities (LEAs), which makes education largely decentralised (Kohlrausch 2009: 68). Private schools make up a small percentage of student numbers but are an important part of the education system (ibid).

Students can continue their education and training at different institutions and with different directions. According to Steedman (2010), about 86 % of students stay in full-time education post-16. Of the remaining 14 % that do not participate in full-time education, only about 5 % participate in work-based learning schemes supported by the government (ibid). About 4 % are employed and the remaining 5 % are "NEET"—not in education, employment or training (Wolf 2011). Traditionally, firms recruit the majority of their workforce directly after compulsory schooling while in addition a smaller percentage of higher education graduates are hired for management positions (Finegold and Soskice 1988). However, the number of jobs available for 16 and 17 years olds has been declining (Wolf 2011: 10). At the age of 18, about a fifth of the cohort is in VET (ibid). According to Wolf (2011: 52) there are, however, many young people that move "between qualifications that provide little scope for progression, and unsatisfactory, often short-term employment or periods of unemployment" (Wolf 2011: 52).

Hardly any distinction is made between initial and continuing VET. However, different regulations and funding mechanisms exist for young persons aged between 16 and 19. While the BIS is responsible for adult learners and oversees the Skills Funding Agency (funding will be discussed below), the Department for Education (DfE) is concerned with VET for pre-19 education. Both Departments established a joint unit that coordinates and develops apprenticeship policies, and they jointly oversee the National Apprenticeship Service. The latter supports cooperation with business, deploys a field force that works on expanding the number of apprenticeships, collects data on performance, and safeguards quality. Local authorities have been made responsible and accountable for the provision of education and training for 16–19 year olds by the Apprenticeships, Skills, Children and Learning Act of 2009. In initial VET, the DfE sets the National Curriculum and determines the type of VET offered in schools. It can be part of the secondary school system and of the further education system. VET can be provided by general or specialist Further Education Colleges, Sixth Form Colleges, publicly-funded work-based learning, apprenticeships, and adult and community learning (Cedefop Refernet 2011). Next to publicly-funded schemes, there is a multitude of private training providers as well as employer-based training. It is not without problems that there is hardly any separation between initial and continuing VET: Wolf (2011) argues that qualifications which are suitable for adults are often tailor-made to their workplaces and hence might not be the right ones for young people.

Participation in lifelong learning is comparatively high in the UK. Participation largely differs across firms and sectors (Wolf 2011). A considerable proportion of 40 % of training funded by employers is turned towards achieving a full or part-qualification (ibid). Employer-funded training is supported by several government initiatives, as for example the *Growth and Innovation Fund* (ibid). In continuing VET, private training providers and employers have a high market share. Moreover, universities also offer continuing training below the Bachelor's level, such as 2-year courses or Foundation degrees. Continuing VET programmes offered by universities are often designed in cooperation between employers and higher education institutions. There are further work-related programmes, such as the 2-year Higher National Diplomas (vocational higher education degrees on the same level as foundation degrees) and the 1-year Higher National Certificates. A multitude of other vocational higher education programmes exist that can be provided by universities, other higher education institutions or further education providers.

The market-led governance of VET leads to a low standardisation of qualifications. There are, approximately, 15,500 qualifications in the UK in VET and general schooling (interview UK_MIXED-2). In addition, there are about 50,000 higher education qualifications, since every institution's qualifications are unique even if several qualifications of broadly the same type and level often exist (ibid). Qualifications are therefore characterised by a low level of portability.

In order to increase the standardisation of VET qualifications, NVQs were introduced in 1986 and expanded in the 1990s (Hillmert 2008). Employers in particular lobbied for the introduction of NVQs (Steedman 2001). In this system, qualifications are described in terms of competences. Within NVQs, "learners carry out practical, work-related tasks designed to help develop the skills and knowledge to do a job effectively and are assessed on practical assignments and a portfolio of evidence" (Cedefop Refernet 2011: 46). NVQs are mostly offered at levels 1, 2, and 3 (see Sect. 6.2.2); it is possible to continue training in further education (ibid). NVQs are designed by Sector Skill Councils (SSCs, see below) in cooperation with employers. Curricula are developed by the provider. NVQs are based on National Occupational Standards (NOS), which are very detailed (interview UK_mixed-2). "Standards are specified in the form of units, aggregated to meet qualification needs or specific occupations, which are identified by a parallel process of occupational mapping" (Cedefop Refernet 2011: 56). National Occupational Standards are revised every 3–5 years in order to reflect technological developments and innovations. VET providers are then responsible for bringing their curricula up to date and meeting labour market requirements. Examinations are carried out for each of several modules. Certificates for a certain combination of (usually 6–10) modules lead to a full qualification. It is possible to carry out assessments solely on the employers' premises (Steedman 2011).

Five levels of NVQs exist[3]:

- NVQ 1: Basic skills, preparation for activities which are routine and have a predictable character, equivalent to GSCE at grade D-G;
- NVQ 2: semi-skilled, preparation for activities that are characterised by a significant range of different work activities in a variety of contexts often carried out in cooperation with others in a group or time, equivalent to GSCE at grade A*-C;

---

[3]Level descriptions are based on Kohlrausch (2009: 72).

- NVQ 3: application of knowledge in a broad variety of activities and contexts, including to work autonomously and guide others; equivalent to the German apprenticeship as well as 1–5 A levels at grade A*-C;
- NVQ 4: similar to level 3 but involving technical and professional work activities;
- NVQ 5: preparation for activities that are carried out in a vast variety of contexts and are often unpredictable; performance are characterised by a substantial level of autonomy and significant responsibility for the work of others.

The NVQ system has a number of problems. According to Hillmert (2008), it is often criticised that NVQs qualifications suffer from low acceptance, low completion rates and long duration. Holm (2004) argues that there are problems regarding the implementation, funding, and recognition of qualifications. Moreover, the system does not establish standards on training procedures, and examination standards are weak (ibid). In addition, NVQs are highly complex. For applying the standards to the respective courses, usually the candidate and the assessor develop a plan of procedure to achieve a NVQ (Geldermann et al. 2009). The focus of NVQs on practical skills has arguably added to the divide between higher education and VET (Brockmann et al. 2008). Another point of discussion is that certificates on the lower levels 1 or 2 have a low labour market value. Kohlrausch (2009: 75) argues that as a consequence, these can be described as being mostly firm-specific. Skills equivalent to NVQ level 3 or higher on the other hand are usually of value to a variety of employers so that they are transferable in nature and hence industry-specific (ibid). General skills components are very weak on all levels. However, almost two thirds of all NVQ qualification achievements have been acquired on level 2 in 2010/2011 (Ofqual 2012).[4] The high share of lower NVQ qualifications is at odds with the labour market: the demand for qualifications on the lower level decreased over time, and the returns on training are very low for NVQs on level 1 or 2 (Wolf 2011). In fact, in case lower VET qualifications have been attained at a College or in government training schemes, the returns on training can even be negative (ibid). As an interview partner notes, the Wolf report found that many NQF qualifications "do not assist the individual to progress, they (...) are very easy to achieve—so what is the point in them?" (interview UK_mixed-2).

Different apprenticeships exist. Throughout the years, these schemes have been subject to many changes and much discussion. While there were 240,000 apprentices in the mid-1960s, the number was reduced to a fourth by 1990 (Cedefop Refernet 2011: 33). A Cedefop report (ibid) attributes the decline of apprenticeships to rising attainment in post-16 education and to lacking government effort, while Unwin (2006) also points out the role of the declining manufacturing industry. As a revitalisation programme, Modern Apprenticeships were introduced in 1994.[5] New

---

[4]In 2010/2011, NVQ qualification achievements were distributed as follows: 3 % on level 1, 63 % on level 2, 30 % on level 3, and the remaining 4 % on level 4 or 5 (Ofqual 2012).
[5]Modern Apprenticeships were roughly based on the dual system and led to a level 3 qualification after 3 years.

Labour aimed at increasing apprenticeship numbers, and fostered apprenticeships on lower levels (Steedman 2011: 2). Apprenticeships are also high on the agenda of the Coalition Government (see for example BIS 2010). In 2009, there were almost 300,000 new apprenticeships (Steedman 2010), mostly on level 2 however (IKEI 2012). As in other countries, apprenticeship training combines learning in schools and paid work-based learning. Yet, the standardisation of apprenticeships is much lower than in other countries. First, there are young apprenticeships for 14–16 years olds that last 2 years and correspond to ISCED level 2. These concentrate on general subjects, while only one tenth of subjects are vocationally-orientated with work experience that can comprise up to 2 days a week for a maximum of 50 days in total (Cedefop Refernet 2011: 48). Second, apprenticeships (12 months) and advanced apprenticeships (24 months minimum) correspond to ISCED Levels 3c (ibid, 48). The balance between general and vocational subjects differs, and so does the balance between school-based and work-based training (ibid). Sector Skills Councils (see below) currently set the frameworks for apprenticeships and act as the certifying authority (interview UK_MIXED-5). Frameworks contain knowledge-based components based on a Technical Certificate and competence-based elements that are often certified via NVQs. It has been criticised that apprenticeships largely lack general skill components (Hillmert 2008; Wolf 2011).[6]

Depending on the specific sector, about 4–8 % of firms participate in apprenticeship training (Steedman 2011: 3). Technical professions have fewer apprentices (Cedefop Refernet 2011: 50). There are differences regarding the level and quality of content across sectors: Apprenticeships in engineering, for example, are mostly offered on level 3 and are seen as higher-ranking than those in retail, which often lead to a level 2 qualification (Lanning 2012; Unwin 2006: 119). According to Steedman (2001), there is substantial evidence that apprenticeships are of good quality in several sectors that have a tradition in apprenticeship training, which however only account for about a fifth of all apprenticeships. Firms in sectors with strong apprenticeships have difficulties finding able apprentices and accessing government funds (ibid). Apprenticeship pay is higher than in continental European countries.

Minimum requirements for apprenticeships are set by the Apprenticeships, Skills, Children and Learning Act in 2009. Apprentices receive at least 280 hours of guided training per year, of which at least one third must be in the form of off-the-job training (IKEI 2012). Usually, apprentices take part in school-based training at Further Education Colleges or commercial providers 1 day a week (Lanning 2012). Apprentices have an individual learning plan which they agree upon with the training firm. There are 1100 registered training providers in England. There are around 50 large employers that train and assess their own apprentices, serving as providers themselves. Usually, providers enter contracts with the government on delivering a certain number of apprenticeships, and then establish contact with

---

[6]In a response to the Wolf report, the government promised to ensure that participants study English and maths until the age of 19. Ideally, they achieve GCSE A*-C.

employers to fill these places (Steedman 2011: 4). They also carry out examinations. Key skills are usually assessed in one examination by the training provider and in an additional examination which is externally verified by the awarding body (IKEI 2012). In contrast to apprenticeship programmes in other countries which are more standardised, "the programme is flexible and the employer decides how it is delivered and the content of the course" (Cedefop Refernet 2011: 48). Firms have a mixed picture on the quality of apprenticeships (interview UK_PRIV-1). Trade unions believe that the quality differs: in large manufacturing firms apprenticeships are usually of high quality, while in other sectors quality concerns prevail (interview UK_TU-1).

In conclusion, compared to the other two cases apprenticeships in the UK are more firm-specific, since firms have a higher influence on their content and duration. Apprenticeships are less standardised regarding procedures, the place of learning, examinations, and the balance between general and specific skills. Although the quality of training differs across institutions in all countries, this problem seems more accentuated in England. As Steedman (2001: 35) concludes: The "variability in duration, standards, achievements and funding are such that it is impossible to define apprenticeship in Britain". This leads to a "chronic information failure that cripples attempts to promote apprenticeship in the UK—and which has led in the past to apprentices who did not know they were on apprenticeship schemes and widespread confusion among employers" (ibid). Examinations are mostly organised by the training provider with additional assessments for key skills; they are hence private, largely de-standardised and potentially firm-specific. Funding for apprenticeships is channelled through providers which place participants with employers. Apprenticeships in England therefore lack a skills signalling effect (Steedman 2001; IKEI 2012). In the Netherlands, these functions are realised with the involvement of corporatist actors. At the same time, apprenticeships are more state-subsidised, so that the state shares more of the financial burden. In sum, apprenticeships in the UK are very different from those in the two other country cases, especially regarding the content of skills, the degree of standardisation, and their lacking portability.

Not only apprenticeships but VET qualifications in general are less standardised in the UK than in the Netherlands and in Germany in so far as that several forms of VET—NVQs, training at the firm, apprenticeships—exist. The different VET qualifications are less standardised regarding all content, locations of learning, and duration. Qualifications are often highly specific in nature, and the trend towards specific skills further increases (Wolf 2011: 74). Wolf argues that it is especially due to the large influence of SSCs which "have consistently promoted very specific and narrow qualifications, even though employers have not, in practice, valued these" (Wolf 2011: 75). Skills in England are much less occupation-specific (Kohlrausch 2009). Training largely lacks a general education component as prevalent in the Netherlands and in Germany. Because of the multitude of VET courses, there are no "overarching standards" (Powell and Solga 2008: 29). The unit-approach in the UK is indeed not necessarily geared towards full qualifications but organised in the form of units from which employers can pick and choose, so that often qualifications are narrow and highly specific.

Education Institutions, Education Bodies, Actors

The VET system is characterised by continuous reform, which gives rise to an ever-changing structure of agencies, regulation and funding. Many agencies are organised in the form of "quangos" to which the government devolves powers.[7] This leads to a complex system. The following example serves as an illustration. In 1993, responsibilities of the National Curriculum Council and the School Examinations and Assessment Council were transferred to the School Curriculum and Assessment Authority with the idea to combine tasks that are related to curriculum and assessment into one body. In 1997, the School Examinations and Assessment Council merged with the National Council for Vocational Qualifications into a new body, the QCA, in order to combine general and vocational education in one institution. In 2004, the QCA established the National Assessment Agency, which took over the organisation of National Curriculum assessments. Later, this agency was dissolved, and its tasks shifted back to the QCA. In 2008, the regulatory functions of the QCA were moved to the newly-created Ofqual, which also became the regulator of exams and qualifications. QCA's other tasks were transferred to the Qualifications and Curriculum Development Agency (QCDA), which was also in charge of the National Curriculum and associated examinations. It was dissolved in 2012. Some of its tasks have been taken over by the DfE. Its responsibilities regarding assessments was moved to the Standards and Testing Agency, which is regulated by Ofqual and has the status of an executive agency of the DfE. Such ever-changing settings might complicate the establishment of standardisation and quality assurance—tasks that these agencies were created to implement. In addition, the changing institutional structure can be regarded as a constant and characteristic of the VET system (Kohlrausch 2009).[8]

Only those qualifications can form part of the Qualifications and Credit Framework (QCF) that are accredited by an officially recognised awarding body. The recognition of awarding bodies is the responsibility of the government agency Ofqual (see below). In 2012, there were 175 such recognised awarding organisations, although a small number has a high market share (interviews UK_mixed-2, UK_mixed-3). Awarding bodies can vary in size and ownership—some are owned by multi-national companies and others by charities—but all are organised as private companies (interview UK_mixed-3). They develop units and submit them

---

[7]Quango is an acronym for "quasi-autonomous non-governmental organisation". They are also called non-departmental public bodies. There were 766 such non-departmental public bodies sponsored by the UK Government at the end of March 2009 (Cabinet Office N.N.). The idea is that quangos can carry out administrative functions effectively and without interferences for political reasons. Critics argue that this model lacks accountability and clear lines of authority. The complexity of administrative structures is high.

[8]Interviews for the UK case study were carried out in April and May 2012; this chapter is based on the institutional set-up at that time. The same holds for the description and analysis of the qualifications in the UK.

to the QCF database. Rules of combination specify which units have to be combined in order to achieve the respective qualification. Units are transferable between qualifications and awarding bodies. Awarding organisations develop assessment arrangements on the basis of rules of combination and are responsible for monitoring assessments and issuing certificates. Schools, colleges and training providers pay fees to the awarding bodies for using their units, and are approved and monitored by them.[9] Awarding bodies can also carry out procedures to approve independent training providers, who can then award accredited qualifications themselves. In the recent past it has become possible for employers and Further Education Colleges to award their own VET qualifications (Cedefop Refernet 2011: 33). Wolf (2011) argues that independent awarding bodies are a strength of the English VET system because they can create multiple linkages between the development of qualifications, the labour market, and even higher education.

Ofqual is a non-ministerial department set up in 2008 that regulates qualifications, examinations and tests.[10] Ofqual itself sets criteria for regulation and accreditation. Regulation is carried out by recognising and monitoring providers of qualifications and assessments. The recognition of awarding bodies is based on their capacities, expertise and resources. Ofqual monitors standards of qualifications and examinations, quality assurance mechanisms and the performance of awarding organisations, the quality of qualifications offered by them as well as the level of fees they request, National Curriculum assessments, and the grading of examinations. It observes the accessibility of qualifications and assessments. Moreover, Ofqual develops and monitors criteria for units and qualifications within the qualifications framework (see Sect. 6.2.2) and accredits qualifications to the QCF. In general, however, Ofqual increasingly prioritises recognising awarding bodies rather than individual qualifications (interview UK_mixed-2). While the overall objectives of Ofqual are to secure standards, high quality and efficiency, a regulator and accreditation body becomes necessary especially because of the multitude of VET qualifications and their low standardisation.

VoC (Hall and Soskice 2001) argues that in LMEs, the market is the main coordinator. Yet, since the early 1980s, the state has taken an increasingly active role in designing, controlling and implementing policy at all levels and on many topics (Keep 2007). The tradition of a market-led functioning of the VET system and voluntarism in training, however, reduces governments' options to pressuring employers or creating (financial) incentives (ibid, 165). Moreover, the standing and involvement of the state leads to a high complexity of the VET system: "The involvement of the central government leads to the need for simple and measurable outcomes as well as for political accountability—which explains a tendency for bureaucracy for channelling the funding" (ibid). Funding structures are both

---

[9]Providers need to have sufficient resources and capabilities to carry out VET teaching and have their own internal quality assurance systems.

[10]As a non-ministerial department, Ofqual is an independent agency accountable to the Parliament (not to the government).

complex and subject to continuous change. This is both regarding the government agencies responsible for funding as well as the levels and procedures of funding itself. Incentives can even be contradictory, and funding structures can lead to a downward pressure on standards since funding depends on the number of successful students (Wolf 2011). VET has become more centralised (Keep 2007) and micro-managed (Wolf 2011: 8). The BIS (2010: 5) notes self-critically: "We must abandon a culture of bureaucratic central planning and regulatory control. For too long, the skills system has been micromanaged from the centre, with Government setting targets for the number and type of qualifications that ought to be delivered, and with learners and colleges following funding." The multitude of qualifications contributes to the intransparency of the system. Efforts to increase standardisation have been undertaken, for example with the Learning and Skills Act in 2000 (Kohlrausch 2009), but without being very successful until now. The Wolf Report (Wolf 2011: 9) strongly recommends simplifying the system in order to make information better available to young persons, make the system more efficient and foster innovation. As a difference to the other two case studies, the training system is moreover highly political and subject to contradicting policy objectives (Steedman 2011). New governments set new priorities in VET policies, and continuous policy change costs much time and effort for all actors (interview UK_mixed-3). In comparison to the Netherlands and to Germany, VET policies change much more with changing political majorities.

Sector Skills Councils (SSCs) were established in 2002 with the objective to improve the involvement of employers in VET and hereby improve the matching of demand and supply of skills (Cedefop Refernet 2011: 67). SSCs are independent employer-led organisations that aim at representing the employers' views on skills. In some SSCs, a union representative has a seat on the board—in others not (interview UK_TU-1). SSCs moreover develop skill solutions and foster employers' ambition regarding skill investments. They are required to develop Sector Qualification Strategies and Sector Skills Agreements between employers and providers (ibid). They provide labour market data for their sectors. The 25 SSCs are overseen by the employer-led UK Commission of Employment and Skills. The Commission supports business in skills development as well as conducts research and skills audits. Wolf (2011: 63) argues that SSCs have become de-facto designers and first-line accreditors for most VET qualifications (Wolf 2011: 63). This is why they have a difficult relationship with awarding bodies, which believe that SSCs have a particular technical view on how to develop qualifications (interview UK_mixed-3). However, SSCs are far from establishing a degree of coordination among firms as closely-knit as in CMEs. In general, linkages between the VET system and the labour market remain low (Kohlrausch 2009), and social partners are still less involved in the development of qualifications than in CMEs.

Firms have a low level of coordination regarding VET policies. The Confederation of British Industry (CBI) has limited influence on its member firms over their training decisions (Keep 2007: 167). In the UK, individual firms are more powerful than central or industry-wide federations, so that organisations have less power to implement negotiated agreements. "This free-market approach, combined with the absence of strong local employers groups (...) has left British industry without an effective mechanism for overcoming the 'poaching' problem" (Finegold and Soskice 1988: 29). Moreover, the role of employers in the formation of VET policies is not formalised. Although the SSCs represent the employers' interest and, as pointed out above, assume a strong role in the development and accreditation of qualifications, they are not generically grown employers' interest representations. Keep (2007: 163) points out, "They remain state-licensed entities, receiving their core funding from government and expected to deliver national programmes and targets the design and setting of which they have played no role in whatsoever." Moreover, SSCs often focus on the representation of larger firms rather than of SMEs (Cuddy and Ward 2010).

Employers believe that work experiences during secondary education should be fostered, along with links between schools and business (CBI 2011a). Employers' organisations and firms support the expansion of apprenticeships—almost two thirds of respondents to a CBI survey believe that apprenticeships should be a priority of public funding. At the same time, however, they recommend the introduction of a "Young Britain Credit", which is a subsidy for hiring young persons for their first job in order to compensate for lower productivity—which might contradict apprenticeships (ibid). Employers also believe that pre-apprenticeship training should be strengthened, especially for vulnerable groups (CBI 2011a). Interestingly, although the qualification market in the UK is much more diverse than in the Netherlands and Germany, employers believe that externally-provided training should cater to their needs better than it currently does (ibid). Much of the training conducted by employers does not lead to government-recognised qualifications (CBI 2011b). Regarding apprenticeships, Steedman (2011: 3) argues that employers lacked interest and commitment in spite of the efforts to strengthen apprenticeships after 1994.

The low portability of qualifications in the UK is the result of both destandardised qualifications and firms' preferences towards qualifications which are not recognised by the government. According to Kohlrausch (2009: 78), the UK is characterised by gradual labour-market integration, which can often be observed in countries with strong internal labour markets. She argues that against the background of the tremendous variety of qualifications, employers tend to trust labour-market experience more than formal qualifications. This is why finding employment is more difficult for young persons. As a result, youth unemployment is distinctively higher than general unemployment (ibid). Wolf (2011: 10) even argues: "Work experiences still offer an alternative progression route, while many formal qualifications are not worth having at all."

Unions have little influence on VET policies (Keep 2007), which is perceived to be a "traditionally employer-led domain" (Cuddy and Ward 2010: 36). As a trade union official puts it, "In many cases, unions don't feel they have the ownership over the agenda" (interview UK_TU-1). Unions have difficulties to enforce agreements because of their complex membership structure (Finegold and Soskice 1988). As it is put in a Cedefop Refernet (2011: 33) report, "the link between training, access to a job, salary level and progression is less clearly defined or regulated than in countries where a social partnership approach structures these arrangements." Unions focus on lobbying for higher wages during apprenticeships (interview UK_PRIV-1). In other countries, unions also lobby for higher apprenticeship wages but prioritise lobbying for broad and general skills within VET (Germany) or on the employability of workers (Netherlands). Steedman (2001: 37) argues that while in countries with dual apprenticeships unions represent the interest of employees, in Britain "both trade unions and government have failed to provide sufficient compensatory counter-balance to the voice of employers in the design and day to day running of apprenticeships." Sectors with a tradition of apprenticeship training such as engineering and electrical contracting, as well as several large companies, are exceptions.

Learning Funds have been created by unions in order to support worker training. Moreover, the labour government established Union Learning Representatives. They have a statutory status and channel 250,000 employees into training each year (Cedefop Refernet 2011: 57). The Trade Union Congress (TUC) established "unionlearn", a learning and skills organisation, in 2006. It serves as a strategic framework and supports training and learning, especially of workers with lower skill levels. Training of unions' personnel and representatives is also integrated in the programme. It is mainly funded by the government but administered largely by unions themselves.

Social partnership in VET is hardly institutionalised but rather of voluntary nature (Cuddy and Ward 2010: 35). No standardised procedures for cooperation exist as in the Netherlands or Germany. Several corporatist arrangements that had previously existed, such as the Manpower Services Commission founded in 1973, comprising employers, trade unions, local authorities and education institutions, were abolished under Conservative administrations between 1979 and 1997. Hence, as Keep (2007: 162) argues, in the field of VET "the ability of social partners to exert serious influence on policy has also been sharply diminished". Unions remark that there is no general acceptance of social partnership in VET (interview UK_TU-1). An interview partner from the trade unions argues that in practice, only the CBI has been able to influence policies and has sometimes managed to propose policies that have influenced the policy process to the extent that they were then implemented, even if slightly changed, and funded by the state (ibid, 167). New initiatives to strengthen matching VET and labour markets—including the creation of SSCs and the UK Commission of Employment and Skills—focus on employers only. Unions have very limited options to impact firms' strategies on skills development (Cuddy and Ward 2010: 36).

Costs of training are shared differently than in CMEs, which naturally affects the interplay between actors. The most important difference is that employers invest in specific skills only (Powell and Solga 2008: 29). The government subsidises specific skills; there are debates if this produces windfall gains (interview UK_TU-1). Individuals bear the major costs of training, especially in school-based general qualifications (Powell and Solga 2008: 29). Since VET qualifications are not transferable, investment in VET has unforeseeable cost-benefit outcomes, which makes it much less attractive for the individual. This is even more the case since programmes are less standardised, which makes it more difficult to assess the returns from a specific training programme.

Core Features of the English Training Regime
In line with the above analysis, the following four aspects are defined as being constitutive for the English training regime: a market-based structure of the VET regime; low standardisation and regulation, which is carried out by a multitude of often-changing and (often quasi-autonomous) agencies with little involvement of social partners; firm-specific, narrow and low skills; a low standardisation of the qualifications landscape and of assessments leading to a low portability of qualifications on the labour market; a focus on general education in combination with a lower status of VET. The following section will trace the implementation of the Copenhagen process in England and analyse in how far central pillars of the English VET systems have potentially and actually been affected by the procceses' instruments and principles.

5.2 Implementation of the Copenhagen Process in the United Kingdom

In my interviews, I found that English stakeholders are little aware of the Copenhagen process. This outcome has also been stated in a Refernet report on the implementation of the Copenhagen process (Cuddy and Ward 2010: 24). Cuddy and Ward (ibid) conclude, "The relationship between European strategies and UK strategies is best described as a parallel set of developments."

Since stakeholders hardly follow developments on the EU level, this case study will not—unlike the case studies on Germany and the Netherlands—specify actors' positions for each instrument. Instead, the position of employers' and trade unions on the Copenhagen process will be summarised in the concluding subsection.

5.2.1 Learning Outcomes

The British VET system has been based on learning outcomes since the introduction of NVQs in 1986 and hence considerably prior to the Copenhagen process. NVQs are based on competences, which are largely in line with European concepts of learning outcomes. Apprenticeship frameworks are linked to NVQs, and therefore also competence-based. Leney (2010: 10) points out that competences are "at the heart of VET qualifications development and certification in the UK" and perceived as "given" by all stakeholders (ibid). The interviews conducted for this work underline this argument; the competence/outcome approach has never been questioned by interviewees. The main advantage of the approach is seen in the focus on the individual learner (Cedefop Refernet 2011: 70), which enables broadening the access to VET qualifications as well as accrediting non-formal and informal skills (Brockmann et al. 2008; cf. Sect. 5.2.4).

Brockmann et al. (2008: 236) argue that the introduction of the NVQ system "marked a radical break with the more holistic model of VET which remained linked to curricula", namely "from a model of VET based on knowledge to a system of 'training' oriented towards the production of skills that require little or no underpinning knowledge." The notion of "skills", which underlies the British understanding of competences, is rather narrow (Leney 2010: 19) and "functional-behaviorist" (Brockmann et al. 2008: 236). As an interview partner points out, one qualification can consist of up to 40 competencies, which can potentially be very narrow (interview UK_MIXED-1). Objectives such as the development of the individual, citizenship or societal aspects are subordinated (Brockmann et al. 2008: 229). Together with modularisation, this hampers the economy's knowledge base, which in turn reduces the capacity of innovation of the economy (interview UK_MIXED-1). Theoretical knowledge has a "marginal role" (Brockmann et al. 2008; interview UK_MIXED-1). According to Brockmann et al. (2008), the role of VET is to create "functional employability" while encompassing only a weak notion of general education. In line with this, assessment procedures are strongly related to the performance at the workplace and theoretical knowledge is seen to be already reflected in the performance of a practical task during assessments. The system therefore has been found to serve short-term needs of employers, and research has pointed out that large employers are reluctant to increase the share of general education in VET (ibid). In sum, outcome-orientation is understood as a fragmented set of task-specific requirements by employers and focused on short-term objectives.

Brief Evaluation

The principle of learning outcomes was introduced in the UK already in 1986 and thus substantially prior to the Copenhagen process. The approach is a key aspect of the English VET system. At the same time, the analysis shows that the way the approach is implemented in England is closely connected to—and partly causal for—the firm-specific and narrow skills prevalent in British VET.

5.2.2 Qualifications and Credit Frameworks

In England, qualifications frameworks had also been in place prior to the Copenhagen process. They were developed as a response to the multitude of vocational qualifications which steered confusion among participants, parents and employers (Kohlrausch 2009: 73). As such, they are a means to tackle the intransparency of the system by providing a guidance function.

The National Qualifications Framework (NQF)[11] has been a tool for coherent classification of qualifications since 1997 in England, Wales and Northern Ireland. As an overarching framework, the NQF covers both vocational and general education qualifications (Cedefop Refernet 2011). It comprises eight levels as well as an entry level.[12] Entry levels shall facilitate lifelong learning and equal opportunities. The framework was introduced with a focus on NVQs in order to classify NVQs ; objectives were to foster transfers and permeability within and between areas of competence of NVQs (Kohlrausch 2009: 73).

In addition to the NQF, the QCF was developed in 2002, introduced within a trial period in 2006 and formally launched in 2008. A public official interviewed for this work stressed that developments on the EU level hardly impacted the decision to launch the QCF (interview UK_PUBL-1). Stakeholders vastly supported the development of the QCF, since it was believed that the NQF no longer fulfilled the demands of the qualifications market (Cuddy and Ward 2010). One reason for this was that multiple qualifications and awarding bodies existed—but without flexible progression routes or options for accumulating credits (Cedefop Refernet 2011: 70). As a consequence, "the QCF is designed as an inclusive and flexible regulated framework of units and qualifications that is capable of recognising the widest possible range of quality assured learner achievements" (QCDA et al. 2009: 6). The interviewed public official argues that with the QCF, the VET system is moving towards a more flexible approach (interview UK_PUBL-1). It is believed to be a major advantage that learners can receive credit for what they achieved, and move in and out of the system flexibly (ibid). Although the NQF was supposed to phase out after the introduction of the QCF (QCDA et al. 2009), difficulties arose regarding linking all general education qualifications to the QCF, so that currently two frameworks are in place. Originally, the QCF had been intended to cover VET qualifications only as it was introduced with the Vocational Qualifications Reform Programme (interview UK_MIXED-1). Now it comprises both general and VET qualifications except academic qualifications. In total 9,700 qualifications were linked to the QCF in 2010/2011 (Ofqual 2012), which include almost all VET qualifications accredited by Ofqual (Wolf 2011).[13] Ofqual maintains the regulatory arrangements for the QCF.

The QCF comprises eight level and three entry levels (Table 5.1). With its outcome-based level-structure and a credit system, it serves as a "standard currency for achievement" (QCDA et al. 2009: 6). Different types of qualifications can be linked to the QCF: Awards, Certificates and Diplomas. These differ regarding the

---

[11] The term "National Qualifications Framework" and the abbreviation "NQF" is used both on the European level for national frameworks in general, and in the UK when referring to the specific NQF.

[12] Originally, the framework had comprised five levels, which was changed in 2004 when level 4 was subdivided into three levels (levels 4–6) and level 5 was subdivided into two levels (levels 7, 8).

[13] There is no obligation for all qualifications to be linked to the QCF. Yet, qualifications offered through publicly-funded education and training are usually included.

5.2 Implementation of the Copenhagen Process in the United Kingdom

Table 5.1 Qualifications frameworks in England

Framework for higher education qualifications in England, Wales and Northern Ireland	Level	National Qualifications Framework for England, Wales and Northern Ireland	Level	EQF Level
Doctoral Degrees	8	Vocational Qualifications level 8	8	8
Master's Degrees, Integrated Master's Degrees, Postgraduate Diplomas, Postgraduate Certificate in Education, Postgraduate Certificates	7	Fellowships, NVQ Level 5, Vocational Qualifications Level 7	7	7
Bachelor's Degrees with Honours, Bachelor's Degrees, Professional Graduate Certificate in Education, Graduate Diploma and Certificates	6	Vocational Qualifications Level 6	6	6
Foundation Degrees, Diplomas of Higher Education, Higher National Diplomas	5	NVQ Level 4, Higher National Diplomas, Higher National Certificates, Vocational Qualifications Level 5	5	5
Higher National Certificates, Certificates of Higher Education	4	Vocational Qualifications Level 4	4	
		NVQ Level 3, Vocational Qualifications Level 3, GCE AS and A Level, Advanced Diplomas	3	4
		NVQ Level 2, Vocational Qualifications Level 3, GCSEs at grade A*-C, ESOL* skills for life, Higher Diplomas, Functional skills** level 2	2	3
		NVQ Level 1, Vocational Qualifications Level 1, GCSEs at grade D-G, ESOL skills for life*, Foundation Diplomas, Functional skills** Level 1	1	2
		Entry Level Certificates Level 3, ESOL skills for life*, Functional skills** Entry Level	E 3	1
		Entry Level Certificates Level 2, ESOL skills for life*, Functional skills** Entry Level	E 2	-
		Entry Level Certificates Level 1, ESOL skills for life*, Functional skills**	E 1	-

Source: Own table on the basis of UK National Coordination Points (2010: 17, 19). The table contains public sector information licensed under the Open Government Licence v2.0. For more information, see: http://www.nationalarchives.gov.uk/doc/open-government-licence/version/2/

[a]ESOL (English for Speakers of Other Languages) skills for life certificates test English language competences of learners over the age of 16 who live, work or study in England, Wales or Northern Ireland
[b]Functional skills comprise English, mathematics, and ICT skills

credits needed for completing a qualification: an Award is made up of 1–12 credits, a Certificate of 13–36 credits, and a Diploma of at least 37 credits. One credit is equivalent to 10 hours of learning (see further Sect. 6.2.3). Qualifications referenced to the QCF have to be made up of units, and the way units have to be combined in order to form a qualification are laid down in rules of combination. Once units are placed in the QCF database, they are transferable across awarding bodies and qualifications. The QCF hence can be understood as a "unit-based credit framework" (ibid). Units associated to the QCF have a title, learning outcomes, assessment criteria, a credit value and a level (ibid). It does not matter where a unit is obtained and where learning takes place (ibid). Wolf (2011) argues that assessing each unit on the one hand makes the system more flexible for employers, as it is possible to make use of single units only, but on the other hand increases costs for those programmes targeted at 14–19 education.

In the UK, three further qualifications frameworks exist. First, higher academic qualifications are part of the Framework for Higher Education Qualifications for England, Wales and Northern Ireland. It has five levels and is based on learning outcomes. Descriptors are based on knowledge, understanding and abilities. Second, there is the Credit and Qualifications Framework for Wales. It incorporates the QCF/NQF, the higher education framework as well as Quality Assured Lifelong Learning. The latter strand is a further education component and has been developed to include all qualifications that are not covered by the other two. Third, the Scottish credit and qualifications framework was introduced in 2001 as one of the first comprehensive NQFs and is often perceived as the most successful (Raffe et al. 2008). It comprises 12 levels. For a rough overview on the way the frameworks relate to each other, see QAA et al. (2011).

Referencing Process and Implementation of the EQF

The UK was the third country, after Malta and Ireland, to complete the process of referencing its frameworks to the EQF.[14] This process was, of course, facilitated by the already existing qualifications frameworks. The English QCF as well as Welsh and Scottish frameworks were referenced to the EQF directly. The NQF is phasing out and as such is not linked to the EQF directly, but indirectly via the QCF, since QCF and NQF levels are compatible. The Framework for Higher Education Qualifications has been affirmed to be compatible with the Bologna Framework for Qualifications of the European Higher Education Area. The English higher education sector opposed such an idea, although in Scotland and Wales, higher education

---

[14]In fact, the UK already was in the process of carrying out referencing when the EQF Advisory Group on the European level established a sub-group on developing referencing criteria (UK National Coordination Points 2010). The process and referencing was cross-checked with these criteria once it had been established.

is automatically referenced to the EQF so that referencing takes place only via the higher education framework (interview UK_MIXED-2).

An EQF Coordination Point for England and Northern Ireland was established that is responsible for linking the QCF to the EQF.[15] It is led by Ofqual and the Council for Curriculum, Examinations and Assessment in Northern Ireland.[16] A stakeholder committee ("ENI group")—including representatives from education bodies and education sectors, government, awarding bodies, employers, and international experts—oversees the coordination points' executive. Next to the English one, two further Coordination Points have been created for Wales and Scotland respectively; the three coordination points co-ordinate their activities on implementing the EQF and on representing the UK in the EQF Advisory Group. For this purpose, an EQF Coordination Group was established comprising all coordination points.

The English referencing process started in July 2008 with a comparison of the QCF and EQF. Domains of the two frameworks were related and were found to be similar regarding the domain "knowledge and understanding" (QCF) respectively "knowledge" (EQF) but less fitting in other domains. On the descriptor level, the "best fit" between the levels was identified. Moreover, on this first stage, a small number of sample qualifications was referenced to both frameworks and for these, the relative positioning of levels was analysed. While referencing provided a good match between QCF and EQF on most levels, the EQF does not have counterparts to entry levels 1 and 2. Entry Level 3 was referenced to EQF level 1. In discussions of the European EQF advisory group, the argument that these entry levels provide support for learners with a low level of basic skills and encourage subsequent lifelong learning was addressed by the British EQF coordination group. Descriptors of QCF level 4 were seen to exceed EQF level 4 but to be below EQF level 5. On the basis of the descriptors, QCF level 4 would better match EQF level 4. Yet, it was believed that according to the logic of the EQF, level 4 already forms part of higher education, while level 3 marks the upper end of secondary and further education. It was proposed to link QCF level 4 to EQF level 4.

Subsequently, the referencing exercise was subject to a consultation process between November 2008 and February 2009. Advice from international experts from Slovenia and Spain was part of this process. Moreover, a broad stakeholder consultation took place, for which the coordination point took measures to encourage a broad participation from both stakeholders and a wider audience. In total, 46 formal responses were received, including from awarding bodies, SSCs, providers, social partners, government organisations, and consultants taking part in EQF-related projects. Respondents expressed concern about the referencing as well as about the EQF as such. Responses included demands for better information on

---

[15]If not stated otherwise, the following section on the referencing process is based on QCDA et al. (2009).

[16]Section 6.1 addressed the continuous change in governmental agencies. In this vein, when the coordination point was installed, it was co-led by the QCA; with QCA's abolishment its successor, Ofqual, has taken over.

the EQF and its objectives; concerns that the EQF might destabilise relations between the existing UK frameworks; difficulties of precisely referencing due to UK qualifications frameworks having more levels than the EQF; quality assurance mechanisms for the EQF being still in development; referencing criteria being framed in a broad manner; and the fact that the EQF lacks entry levels. Referencing of the QCF to the EQF was seen as being straightforward for most levels. Exceptions are the first two levels and level 4. Regarding the latter, in contrast to initial referencing, a "significant majority of respondents" (QCDA et al. 2009: 32) argued it should be referenced to level 5. It was argued that otherwise, several English qualifications would be linked to EQF level 4 while similar Scottish and Irish qualifications would be referenced to EQF level 5, herewith blurring consistency and comparability. Moreover, the difference between QCF levels 3 and 4 is believed to be greater than between QCF levels 4 and 5. As a consequence, the coordination point decided to adjust the referencing of QCF level 4 and proposed to link it to EQF level 5.

Against the background of the other two case studies, several aspects of the referencing process are interesting. First, A-Levels are referenced to level 4. Second, GSCEs are linked to two different QCF levels and in line with this to two different EQF levels, depending on the grade achieved. Such a distinction cannot be found in the other two countries. Third, the QCF is open to VET on all levels. Still, the bulk of VET qualifications that are actually obtained are those on QCF level 2/EQF level 3 (see above), while VET graduates in the Netherlands and in Germany more often obtain qualifications on higher levels. Finally, the plurality of qualifications in the UK and hence the number of different types of qualifications that are to be linked to the EQF is much higher than in the other two countries. All these observations clearly stem from differences of the three education systems.

Follow-up procedures for the implementation of the EQF were taken with five projects in 2010 and 2011. These projects included information activities on the EQF, a conference on using the EQF for validation of non-formal and informal learning, a survey on sectoral engagement, an international peer learning project, and a project on mentioning EQF levels on UK certificates (Ofqual et al. 2011). The latter had been a subject of discussion within the referencing process. While the EQF recommendation asks member states to adopt measures so that from 2012 onwards all newly-issued qualification certificates contain a reference to the appropriate EQF level, the complex structure of the UK VET system with its multitude of awarding and certification bodies does not make this an easy task. Awarding bodies opposed a mandatory provision on this topic (interview UK_MIXED-3); a survey among awarding organisations and SSCs was launched on different options to solve this issue. Options included to display the EQF level on the front or to issue a separate EQF reference leaflet. Most respondents preferred an online solution, meaning that a link to an internet database would be provided. This is the solution with the lowest impact on existing processes (Ofqual et al. 2011). In the end, it was decided that the way the EQF level is mentioned is left to the respective awarding body (interview UK_MIXED-2).

As I argue in Chap. 2, the EQF aims at both facilitating mobility across countries and at facilitating permeability within member states. In the UK, in spite of the multitude of qualifications, mobility from lower VET qualifications to qualifications on the tertiary level is low. For example, only 6 % of Advanced Apprenticeships graduates continued their study in higher education in 2004/2005 (Cuddy and Ward 2010). Data on progression is limited, since individual routes in the education system are not captured (interview UK_MIXED-3). A major obstacle can be seen in the narrow focus of VET qualifications, as the lacking general education component hinders progression (Brockmann et al. 2008). Wolf (2011: 8) argues that permeability should be improved: "Our system has no business tracking and steering 14 years olds, or 16 years olds, into programmes which are effectively dead-end. Any young person's programme of study, whether 'academic' or 'vocational', should provide for labour market and educational progress on a wide front, whether immediately or later in life." Hence, there is scope for improving the permeability within the UK, but since qualifications frameworks already existed, the EQF does not impact the UK system in this regard.

In contrast to the other two case studies and because of the market structure of the British VET system, Europeanisation of VET provides for an opportunity structure to sell qualifications abroad. Already, awarding bodies export qualifications to other European countries on a larger scale, especially to Eastern Europe (interview UK_MIXED-3). As an interview partner from Ofqual observes, larger awarding bodies increasingly believe that the EQF provides an added value in this regard (interview UK_MIXED-2). In the future, qualifications might even be developed specifically for export (ibid).

5.2.3 The European Credit System for Vocational Education and Training

For British students in initial VET programmes, studying abroad is unusual. If mobility takes place, students mostly rely on cooperation agreements between institutions or on employer programmes. In total, about 3500 students in initial VET study abroad (Cedefop Refernet 2011). As a consequence, while one quarter of jobs in the UK is connected to overseas business activities (Cuddy and Ward 2010), a study commissioned by the British Chambers of Commerce (2012) reports that export is hindered by lacking knowledge of foreign markets and foreign languages. Several projects have been launched to tackle this issue, such as institutional twinning, joint education projects, delivery of VET abroad, franchising, distance learning, and consultancy (Cedefop Refernet 2011). Some of these activities are, however, not only geared towards increasing mobility but also towards fostering business opportunities. A National Agency for European mobility programmes also supports mobility during VET and UK Naric carries out recognition procedures for qualifications acquired abroad. For such processes, a "comparability information" is compiled which confirms the recognition of the qualification and compares it to a NQF/QCF level. The procedure costs £55. In sum, however, government activities remain limited: "There is no clear Government strategy for maximizing inward and outward geographical mobility of learners and apprentices in the UK" (Cedefop Refernet 2011: 21).

Although the mobility of British VET students is comparatively low, England is still largely well-equipped for the implementation of ECVET: With the QCF (see Sect. 6.2.2), a unit-based system covering almost all VET qualifications is already in place. Qualifications referenced to the QCF have to be made up of units, which can be combined to form a full qualification. Ofqual has published guidelines for credit accumulation and transfer. NVQs are also based on a modularised structure.

Awareness on ECVET is not very high among stakeholders, and the rationale for introducing a unit-based structure hardly stems from the European level (Cuddy and Ward 2010: 26). Yet, involvement with ECVET is easy since systems on the UK and EU level are highly compatible: "Whilst the leading stakeholders probably see the first priority as being the development of credit in domestic UK systems and of equivalence across the systems, experience of credit transfer within the UK should pave the way for future involvement in ECVET" (Cuddy and Ward 2010: 26).

During the European consultation on ECVET, the government invited stakeholders to express their opinion on ECVET. After the ECVET recommendation was passed, three coordination points were established. The English ECVET contact point is run by ECCTIS, a private company. It aims at providing expertise for awarding bodies and other institutions, communicating with relevant bodies, providing and exchanging information within England, the UK and Europe, and being involved in research such as a pilot project on converting ECVET points to QCF credits. Several ECVET projects have taken place with partner countries such as Spain, Italy, Germany, the Czech Republic, and France (Cedefop Refernet 2011).

While so far I have pointed out that the unit-based structure of the English VET system is advantageous for the implementation of ECVET, two obstacles for its implementation derive from the market-led structure of the English system. First, awarding bodies are independent and privately-run, and units are their intellectual property. This makes awarding bodies "understandably reluctant to share unit specifications" (Cuddy and Ward 2010: 26). So far, however, the implementation of ECVET has not yet reached the stage at which this question becomes relevant (interview UK_MIXED-4). Second, well-developed quality assurance mechanisms are in place (see Sect. 5.2.5). These can, however, hinder the recognition of units that have been obtained abroad: only if a qualification or unit has been assessed to the English quality standards, a transfer to England is possible (interviews UK_MIXED-3; UK_MIXED-4). The national coordination point works with stakeholders on solving this issue (interview UK_MIXED-4). This problem is not prevalent in the case awarding bodies sell qualifications, since then they usually train the trainer and assure that quality mechanisms are built into the assessment (interview UK_MIXED-3). In sum, regarding both obstacles—the intellectual property on units and quality assurance mechanisms as necessary preconditions for recognitions—it is not yet clear if they will really hinder the implementation of ECVET in the long run.

5.2.4 Validation of Non-formal and Informal Learning

The validation of non-formal and informal learning is well-established in the UK. Already in the early 1980s, the "assessment of prior and experiential learning" was developed. Two motivations existed for the initiation of the instrument: to improve transitions to higher education for persons without formal entry qualifications, and the integration of adult unemployed (Cuddy and Ward 2010: 41). With the introduction of NVQs, the focus switched to the "accreditation of prior learning" (APL). This mechanism was initiated by the higher education sector and developed in the 1980s. Since the 1990s, APL is in use as a systematic and valid procedure (Geldermann et al. 2009). In the higher education sector, APL can facilitate access to programmes or even replace units of the respective qualification (ibid). The specific design of procedures is determined by the higher education institution itself. In VET, APL can enable low-skilled workers to gain formal qualifications in a flexible manner (Cedefop Refernet 2011: 57). In NVQs, the institution of learning or the amount of time spent on learning is irrelevant, so that knowledge and skills that have been obtained beforehand can be incorporated into assessments (Geldermann et al. 2009). While APL can also rely on certified learning outcomes, portfolios are often perceived as "the most valid assessment method" (Cuddy and Ward 2010: 41; c.f. Geldermann et al. 2009). Portfolios assemble skills and competences of the individual, competences are assessed on the basis of written documents, visual elements, products or observations (ibid). Procedures are orientated towards concrete functions and activities and require intensive counselling. Validation procedures are as similarly rigid as the assessments established for formal qualifications (interview UK_MIXED-1). In general, the QCF is also suitable for the validation of non-formal and informal learning, especially since it allows for credit accumulation (QCDA et al. 2009: 14).

Since current funding regimes and policies focus on accredited qualifications, there are few opportunities to have skills recognised outside of the formal qualifications framework. The Recognising and Recording Progress and Achievement scheme offers such an option of accrediting skills independently of a target qualification, and addresses the issue of quality assurance related to this objective (Cedefop Refernet 2011). Since informal learning at the workplace traditionally has a strong position in the UK, where new employees usually learn by observing and imitation, such procedures are seen as particularly valuable (Holm 2004). This is in spite of participation in non-formal education and training being higher than in other countries: In 2007, 40.3 % of people aged 25–64 took part in non-formal job-related training in the UK, while on EU average it has been only 31.3 % (ibid). Participation rates of low-skilled workers are especially high (ibid).

The idea of opening NVQs to the validation of non-formal and informal learning has been subject to criticism. Milner (1998) reports discussions arguing that the NVQ approach fosters validation of existing low-level skills rather than upskilling. Moreover, in a workshop at a conference on the EQF organised by the UK National Coordination Points (2010), it was noted that although APL procedures have been in place for many years, they are often believed to be too hard to complete. In practice, validation procedures are not used extensively, in spite of the strong tradition in the higher education sector (Leney 2010).

5.2.5 Quality Assurance

In the UK, quality assurance mechanisms were well-established prior to the Copenhagen process. As a Cedefop Refernet (2011: 23) report summarises: "UK VET quality assurance systems are in place and compatible with the EQAVET Recommendation."

The system comprises several pillars. First, a quality policy cycle had already been established at the UK level (interview UK_PUBL-2). Quality assurance mechanisms are obligatory for institutions using public funding, but providers have freedom regarding the choice of the specific quality assurance system and its indicators (ibid). Quality cycles on the provider level are not mandatory so as not to burden companies with more bureaucracy (ibid). Private companies focus on quality norms such as ISO (interview UK_PUBL-2). Second, quality is fostered by strong recognition mechanisms assigned to awarding bodies and unit submitters, as well as to the accreditation of qualifications and units (see Sect. 6.1). A third central pillar of quality assurance is inspections. With the Education and Skills Act from 2001, Ofsted[17] was made responsible for the inspection of all education programmes geared towards the 16 to 19-year-old (Kohlrausch 2009). During the last decade, inspection requirements have been "rigorous and demanding" (Cedefop Refernet 2011: 64). Subsequently, Ofsted shifted to carrying out risk-based inspections, meaning that external monitoring and support is especially high in low-performing institutions, while high-performing institutions are inspected in less detail (ibid). During the inspection, approximately 15 inspectors come to the institution for about 1 week for a sincere analysis (interview UK_PUBL-2), a procedure which is much respected by the institutions (interview UK_MIXED_1). Providers are assessed with an overall effectiveness grade, which is derived from factors such as outcomes of learners, provision quality, management, and the delivery of subjects. Inspection reports state points for improvement. Reports are made available online. Should institutions receive the lowest of four grades,

---

[17]Ofsted is a non-ministerial department. Further responsibilities include inspecting all public and private schools in England, local authorities, teacher training institutions, and youth work (Kohlrausch 2009).

restrictions can be imposed; if more than a quarter of learners are non-achieving, severe restrictions follow (interview UK_PUBL-2). Inspections for companies are adjusted in order to reduce the burden on business (ibid). The high level of inspections carried out in the UK is also known abroad (NL_PUBL-1).

The Wolf Report provides several recommendations for improving quality of VET. First, employers should become involved in quality assurance at the local level (Wolf 2011: 11). Second, Wolf argues that current funding provisions provide incentives to providers to choose qualifications that are easy to accomplish. Awarding bodies face incentives to assure the reputation of their qualifications but also to "make things easy for their customers", and current provisions tend to strengthen the latter aspect (ibid, 61). Third, Wolf reports that recently several highly recognised and occupationally-relevant qualifications have not been accredited. Wolf attributes this to the multitude of agencies in the VET system and the resulting complexity of regulation (see Sect. 6.1). SSCs have become "de facto first-line accreditation agencies for all vocational qualifications" (Wolf 2011: 97). Policy-makers and politicians cannot question the decisions on accreditations, which leads to a lack of accountability (ibid). Wolf also points out that, fourth, while Ofqual currently fulfils regulatory functions, it also sets the criteria for the regulation. Quality assurance for qualifications is often carried out in desk analyses (ibid). Fifth, providers and employers are not included in developing qualifications (ibid).[18]

Quality can be defined differently in different systems. While quality assurance in the UK is strong on the level of providers and regulations exist for qualification development processes, the British VET system might be weaker than its Dutch and German counterparts regarding the quality of outcomes. The youth unemployment rate is much higher than in the other two countries, also in relation to general unemployment. Not all VET qualifications have good labour market returns and hence do not meet labour market demand; qualifications on NVQ level 2 or below even have a negative rate of return (see Sect. 5.1).

The UK takes part in the EQAVET network and in working groups on the European level (ibid). Herewith, England covers the main working groups, while Wales and Northern Ireland tend to focus on covering subgroups. This division of tasks is an effort to work together effectively with given resources (interview UK_PUBL-2). A national reference point has been installed at the BIS. Yet, in the opinion of a public official working on quality assurance, European processes have a low impact on the UK, "Most of what we are doing is motivated by national developments" (interview UK_PUBL-1). In general, the awareness towards European quality mechanisms is low (interview UK_PUBL-2). In the British view, EQAVET indicators focus on important aspects that the government and publicly-funded providers should want to know about (ibid). Only indicator 2 (the

---

[18]Awarding bodies, Ofqual and the SSCs are involved in the development of qualifications. SSCs are supposed to represent employers, so Wolf's criticism points to problems in the fulfilment of this task.

investment in training of teachers and trainers) does not fit the UK context, since here there are no unified requirements (ibid). Rather, trainers are expected to have expertise in the respective job and to possess relevant vocational knowledge. The UK supports the EQAVET indicators (ibid). As outlined above, quality cycles already exist on the UK level but not on the provider level.

5.3 Conclusions

The influence of the Copenhagen process on the UK is very low. This refers both to the level of awareness and knowledge among stakeholders, which was mentioned in all interviews, as well as to the implementation of the instruments and principles. In fact, all instruments and principles developed within the scope of the Copenhagen process were already in place in the UK, so that the degree of impact the Copenhagen process *could* have had was very limited from the outset.

Politics of Reform and Actors' Positions
Government activities on proactively steering discussion on EU instruments and on increasing the mobility of VET students remain low. Although coordination points for the various instruments have been established so that compliance officially exists, which is in line with the good record of the British government regarding the implementation and enforcement of EU legislation in general (Allen 2005), resources put into implementing processes are low. Moreover, the government believes that the additional value of the instruments is low. As a public official puts it, "If historically you have a very developed qualifications system, it will be difficult to try and introduce all of the European initiatives" (interview UK_PUBL-1). Therefore, "it is depending on where you are in terms of developing your system, how much you will use those instruments" (ibid). The government welcomed the ECVET initiative and has no objections against it (interview UK_PUBL-1). The government, however, questions the separation of ECTS and ECVET as two instruments. Moreover, in the view of the UK, the way of allocating credits should be more clearly defined and units should not necessarily be linked to qualifications (ibid). Objectives such as increasing transparency, comparability, transferability and the recognition of learning outcomes are strongly supported (Government of the United Kingdom 2007).

Employers are not very active on the European level regarding VET policies (interview UK_PRIV-1). Their priority is to solve existing problems on the national level in the first place (ibid). CBI, the most important British business organisation, does hardly attend EU meetings or Cedefop board meetings (interview UK_TU-1). Still, in the employers' view, the EQF provides a range of benefits, such as improving mobility, transparency, clarity, quality standards, and knowledge on VET systems across Europe (Ofqual et al. 2011). On the national level, qualifications frameworks were set in place prior to Copenhagen, and were developed in cooperation with employers to meet their needs (BIS 2010). Employers believe that

5.3 Conclusions 189

the national QCF is more flexible than previous arrangements, which they support, since this improves options to pick and choose (interview UK_PRIV-1). However, in a conference on the referencing of UK frameworks to the EQF it was argued that many employers are not familiar with qualifications frameworks, and that they instead value practical experiences of employees (UK National Coordination Points 2010). A reason might be that, as I pointed out in Chap. 5, VET is less standardised than in other countries, so that formal qualifications have a weaker position. As a consequence, the EQF matters less to British employers than to employers in countries in which formal qualifications have a higher value. Employers support the unit-based value of the English VET system, since they can choose units and thus adjust training to their needs (Wolf 2011; Cuddy and Ward 2010: 47). In some sectors, units are obtained increasingly without the objective of acquiring a whole qualification, often because in-company training focuses on the specific job (Cedefop Refernet 2011: 70). In sum, employers' preferences are clearly structured around a flexible, firm-specific skills approach to VET.

Trade unions are much less involved in VET than employers. This is also the case for the implementation of European VET policies in England. In the ENI group, an advisory body to the English coordination group on EU VET policies, almost all relevant stakeholders have been involved except for trade unions. Inside unions, the knowledge on EU VET instruments is low (interview UK_TU-1). Unions believe that the English VET system is an employer-led system (ibid). This is also why they voice concerns about quality. In their view, providers often focus on selling qualifications to employers rather than on quality, and the quality of training and apprenticeships differs tremendously (ibid). Yet, the union official interviewed for this work believes that EQAVET will have very little impact (ibid). Regarding validation policies and the NVQ system, unions believe that these inherit both positive and negative aspects. On the one hand, union learning representatives have fostered learning at the workplace and some union representatives are supportive of learning at work, since it might be advantageous for business and hence increase participation. On the other hand, other union representatives criticise that assessments often focus on what employees already know and were able to do rather than on gaining new skills (ibid). In general, unions advocate the accreditation of prior learning. Especially, they believe that it is advantageous for workers that left school early and subsequently acquired skills at the workplace (ibid).

EU Instruments and Principles in England
Chronologically, the UK can hardly be challenged by the Copenhagen process in its core pillars, since instruments and principles had already been in place prior to the developments on the EU level. The concept of learning outcomes had already been implemented in the UK with the introduction of competence-based NVQs in 1986. Similarly, qualifications frameworks had been in place since the establishment of the NQF in 1997 and the introduction of the QCF in 2008. With the QCF, a unit-based system has been implemented that largely meets ECVET, since it is based on units that can be accumulated and transferred. Previously, NVQs had been based on a modularised structure. Procedures for the validation of non-formal and informal

learning had been established already in the 1980s with the introduction of the "assessment of prior and experiential learning", and a policy cycle for quality assurance had already been in place. In sum, as an interview partner and expert on the British VET system (UK_MIXED-1) puts it for the policy field of VET, "Westminster developments have nothing to do with European developments."

Activities were carried out in order to implement the Copenhagen process in the UK. A Coordination Point was established in England for linking the QCF to the EQF. The UK qualifications frameworks were referenced to the EQF as early as in 2010, following a broad consultation process. Difficulties stemming from a different level structure—the QCF has more levels than the EQF—were solved by the Coordination Point following the consultation. Several follow-up projects were carried out, such as an international peer learning project and information activities. For ECVET, a coordination point was set up in England, and several projects with partner countries took place. Similarly, a coordination point has been established for EQAVET.

The above analysis has also shown that the analysed instruments and principles are rooted in the logics of a LME. Interview partners have argued that with all of the instruments and principles, their advantages are widely seen in the flexibility they provide, both for the individual learner and for companies. Regarding outcome orientation of the system, VET skills became narrower. Qualifications frameworks and quality assurance mechanisms are instruments to tackle weaknesses of a market-based system: Qualifications frameworks were introduced as a means for increasing the transparency of qualifications. With the introduction of the QCF, qualifications frameworks became based on units and thus more flexible. Validation of non-formal and informal learning in practice increases the flexibility of the learner regarding the location and the timing of learning.

On the other hand, the market-based system leads to difficulties in meeting European developments in several aspects. First, regarding the use of ECVET as a mobility instrument, awarding bodies are hesitant to share unit specifications, since units are their intellectual property. Second, quality assurance in the UK has a stronger role, also due to low standardisation. In case units shall be transferred to the UK, quality standards have to be kept, which might pose a problem, should quality standards differ. Third, although the UK has a well-developed quality assurance system in place, it is practiced in a less rigid manner when firms are the providers of VET in order to not burden them with bureaucracy. This holds for inspections, quality policy cycles, and the training of VET trainers, which is one of the ten ENQAVET indicators. While inspections and quality cycles are also put in place with different regulations for firms in the German and the Dutch system, there are obligations for the training of trainers which are especially strong in Germany. Finally, awarding bodies opposed the mentioning of EQF level on VET certificates. As a consequence, it has been decided that it is up to the respective awarding body in what way EQF levels are mentioned on certificates, and it is possible to only provide a link to an online database on VET certificates. Yet, in sum, the potential for conflict is low and implications are unlikely to be severe. While the differences between the QCF matrix and the EQF have been addressed on the European level,

5.3 Conclusions

different understandings of training requirements for VET trainers seem to be accepted as such. Regarding the use of ECVET as a mobility instrument, in my interviews I found that stakeholders have not been aware of this misfit due to a limited knowledge of the instrument.

As a final point, European developments provide opportunities for a market-led system regarding the export of qualifications. In the UK, awarding bodies believe that the EQF provides an opportunity of growth for this business. Qualifications have already been sold for example to Eastern European counties. The profit-orientation of awarding bodies as developers of qualifications provides them with incentives for exporting qualifications, while in coordinated VET systems no such market actors exist. In the UK, the smaller size of qualifications and the fact that they are not embedded in a coordination process among corporatist actors facilitates selling them. Therefore, it seems that understanding European VET policies as a business opportunity is an aspect that is more pronounced in LMEs.

Chapter 6
Comparison and Conclusion

With the Copenhagen process, the intensity and depth of European coordination in the field of VET was taken to a new level. The European Commission concludes: "The Community education and training policy has gained a dynamic hitherto unknown" (European Commission 2004: 5). On the European level, this new level of integration was combined with an expectation of reforms taking place at the national level: "Reforms are being made to policies and structures, leading to their convergence on the main EU goals" (ibid). On the national level, the direction of such potential convergence was assumed to lead towards a liberalisation and crowding out of national VET regimes. Especially in Germany, a vivid debate took place that Kremer, former president of the BIBB, summarised as follows: "Save the skilled workers—from their European grave diggers" (Kremer 2007: 32). Authors such as Dehnbostel et al. (2009), Hanf and Rein (2006a), Rauner (2006) and Werner and Rothe (2011a, b) all believed that European instruments, especially EQF and ECVET, would fundamentally steer VET in Germany in the direction of a market-based system. Similarly, in other countries such as Switzerland with its dual VET system, the debate on European VET policy has also been contested, as EU initiatives were seen to be in contradiction with national VET systems (Powell and Trampusch 2011).

At the same time, in the political economy literature the influence of the EU on member states as a "liberalisation machine" (Streeck 2009: 196) received a lot of scholarly attention. Scharpf (1999, 2002, 2008a) argues that European integration has advanced asymmetrically, with market-making "negative integration" being enacted without similar levels of "positive integration" in the field of social policies.[1] Streeck (2009, 2013) argues that liberalisation pressure on member states

---

[1] Scharpf defines 'negative integration' as market-making policies, such as the internal market and the four freedoms (Scharpf 2008a: 51). With "positive integration", Scharpf refers to economic policies and regulation as the exercise of economic-political and regulatory competences on the level of the highest economic unit (ibid). See Sect. 1.1 for a more detailed discussion of Streeck's and Scharpf's arguments.

was advanced initially by the ECJ, and later on also by the European Commission. With the economic and financial crisis, member states subscribed to austerity policies—which again increase liberalisation pressures (ibid). Both Scharpf and Streeck argue that these developments have substantially limited the scope of action left to the national level. For example, with the monetary union, member states can no longer make use of exchange rates adjustments, and due to the stability and growth pact, compensatory strategies such as buffering unemployment with public sector employment or increasing the level of social policies have been made much more difficult. At the same time, competition between member states on attracting business is focused more on supply side policies such as taxes. In a similar line of thought, Höpner and Schäfer (2008a, b) argue that the Commission and the ECJ have proactively begun to support the liberalisation of member states towards a model of liberal market economies. The debate on the EU as a "liberalisation machine" is linked to VET policies by Trampusch (2008, 2009), who argues that EQF and ECVET are market-making and liberalising instruments.

Will liberalisation pressures lead to a convergence of member states? The VoC literature is based on the contrary idea that "nations often prosper, not by becoming more similar, but by building on their institutional differences" (Hall and Soskice 2001: 60). Firms derive comparative institutional advantages from the set-up of national economies, which makes them reluctant to changing institutions because they serve their interests. VoC expects member states to keep or strengthen their respective comparative institutional advantage as a CME or LME, rather than converge. Since VET policies are deeply rooted in the political economy and intertwined with complementary institutions, the argument brought forward by Hall and Soskice should hold for the impact of the EU on national VET policies. This is even more the case in an intergovernmental soft law process in which no sanction mechanisms exist. But then, why do assumptions prevail that the EU will liberalise national VET systems? This is the puzzle which has been the starting point for this book.

Does the Copenhagen process have an impact on member states' institutions? If so, is the impact in line with what should be expected from a VoC perspective? These are the questions this book aims to answer with a comparison of the intensity and direction of change the Copenhagen process initiated on the national level. I selected three countries as most different cases. From a detailed analysis of their training systems, I derived core features of the three skill regimes. The expectation is that Europeanisation does not change these core features.

- The German VET system is a classic example for a CME's VET systems. Its characteristics are: high involvement of employers' organisations in the organisation and financing of training and institutionalised cooperation between state and social partners; dual training mode which provides a distinct skill mix of broad and industry-specific skills on an intermediate level; highly standardised certification and training content leading to a high portability of skills; high status of VET as a viable educational pathway after secondary education.

- The Dutch VET system shares certain features of a CME, such as the involvement of social partners in the design and delivery of qualifications, but is also characterised by a strong role of the state and a mix of skills that is in between the CME and LME dichotomy. Its characteristics are: strong state involvement in the regulation and financing of VET with an institutionalised participation of social partners; broad skills on the intermediate level with a balance in between general and industry-specific skills due to a distinctive mix between the dominating school-based learning with workplace-based learning; mostly standardised training content and certification leading to a high portability of skills; high status of VET as a viable educational pathway after secondary education.
- The VET system in the UK (England) is market-led and provides firm-specific skills, as is typical in a LME. Its core features are: a market-based structure; low standardisation and regulation, which is carried out by a multitude of often-changing and (often quasi-autonomous) agencies with little involvement of social partners; firm-specific, narrow and low skills; low standardisation of the qualifications landscape and of assessments leading to a low portability of skills; a focus on general education in combination with a lower status of VET.

Political Economy of the Copenhagen Process: Bias Towards LMEs

I laid out the history of enhanced cooperation in VET on the EU level as well as the instruments and principles of the Copenhagen process in Chap. 2 and identified five key instruments and principles of the Copenhagen process:

- The principle of *learning outcomes* is a distinct way of defining what learners should know, be able to do and understand as a result of the learning process. It can be contrasted with a focus on 'learning input'.
- As an eight-level reference framework based on learning outcomes, the *European Qualifications Framework* relates qualifications to each other within countries and across Europe.
- The *European Credit System for VET* facilitates describing qualifications in terms of units in order to transfer these across partner institutions and, where appropriate, accumulate them.
- The *European Quality Assurance Reference Framework for Vocational Education and Training* includes a cycle of planning, implementation, assessment and review as well as a framework for the qualitative and quantitative analysis of VET systems.
- Guidelines for the *validation of non-formal and informal learning* have been established in order to complement the focus on learning outcomes so that it does not matter where skills have been obtained.

While these instruments and principles each have specific objectives, they are interrelated to each other.

I then developed a political economy perspective on the Copenhagen process in which I argue that instruments and principles developed in the Copenhagen process are *not* neutral technocratic instruments. Instead, they are biased towards both general skills and the liberalisation of VET systems. Important instruments and principles such as qualifications frameworks were heavily inspired by the UK, and hence by a LME. Modularisation of qualifications indeed is one policy option to facilitate the transparency and transfer of qualifications across Europe, since both activities are easier to undertake with smaller units than with long and complex qualifications which are designed differently in each country. A national system that is based on full modularisation, liberalisation and a low level of standardisation *advances* the implementation of the instruments and principles. As a consequence, European VET policies are potentially more challenging to CMEs than to LMEs. I argue that an impact on the core institutions is a possible outcome of the Copenhagen process in spite of the nature of the instruments as "soft law".

Another important conclusion of my analysis of the Copenhagen process is that the possible impact it can unfold is different than argued in much of the debate in Germany. Numerous authors in Germany argued that EQF and ECVET would require a modularisation of the system (see Chap. 3). This opens the door for and might be combined with de-standardisation of training contents and assessments, and hence ultimately might lead to a dilution of CME VET systems, since employers might stop investing in broader industry-specific skills but pick and choose only those firm-specific skills they have an immediate need for. Yet, I argue that the member states are left considerable scope for action regarding the implementation of the instruments, and therefore the concrete impact depends on the way policies are implemented. This is why EU VET policies are a *potential* challenge for CME countries. They constitute a *window of opportunity* for VET reform in the direction of LME. Similarly, even though a certain policy constitutes a challenge for a national VET regime, the degree of the challenge differs with the way of implementation. For example, modularisation could refer to the skill acquisition only while leaving skill profiles unaffected; this would interfere much less with the logics of the system from a political economy perspective (Thelen and Busemeyer 2008). However, as my interviews in Germany show (interview DE_PRIV-2), even this way of introducing modularisation still poses challenges for small firms: it would make training more costly because it decreases the flexibility with which they can approach training provision. Therefore, if modularisation was implemented in a way most congruent with the German system, it would still be a challenge for small firms—but the challenge would be much smaller than if modularisation was implemented as a de-standardisation of skill profiles.

In my analysis of potential effects of EU VET policies on different types of political economies, I argue that there are differences within the group of CME VET regimes as to what extent they are potentially challenged by European VET policies. Challenges exist in countries in which the provision of VET is school-based to a higher degree and in which the state has a more influential role, but are less profound than in states in which the coordination of firms and the involvement of employers' organisations is a more decisive feature of the VET regime. For example, the validation of non-formal and informal learning as well as the concept of learning outcomes imply that it is does not matter where a qualification has been obtained, which challenges the mix between specific and general training provided in dual VET systems, and could potentially change firms' cost-benefit relations.

Certifying small units, moreover, increases costs and might overstretch systems in which social partners are involved in the assessment of skills. In the end, if firms choose to have only single units of learning recognised instead of offering a complete VET course on a large scale, this might lead to a dilution of the system. Another example is quality assurance: the more firms are involved in VET, the more challenging the introduction of EQARF on the provider level because it increases the cost of training for firms. In sum, CME VET systems in which firms are the main provider of training do hold specificities that are more challenged by the Copenhagen process than CME VET systems in which state and schools play more decisive roles.

While I argue that there is a bias towards a LME understanding of VET policies in the way EU policies are currently designed, another important finding is that the European Commission had envisioned the instruments to be even more challenging to CMEs. In my interviews I found that in an original Commission proposal, ECVET was a system in which individuals would have had the opportunity to acquire modules in any member state or different states and have these recognised as a full qualification in any (other) member state. However, this idea was opposed by several member states, including Germany. Reports for EU organisations (such as Coles 2006) tie credit systems to qualifications frameworks on the basis of units, leading to a largely modularised system. The way the instrument had been envisioned on the European level would have led to conflicts with almost all core features of CME VET systems. In the end, European actors did not find the necessary support on the member state level for these proposals. The 2009 ECVET recommendation mostly focuses on mutual exchange, rather than on de-standardising qualifications profiles—and therefore it largely depends on the national implementation how far the *Berufsprinzip* is affected or if and what modularisation is carried out. In my interviews with the European Commission, I found that the European Commission still favours a system of "flexible pathways", a combined qualifications and credit system, and an à la carte system. The counter arguments to such policies from a CME perspective—that such processes could lead to dissolution of CME VET regimes and especially of apprenticeship systems—were either not noticed or not supported by interview partners. The preference of the European Commission towards "flexible pathways" and measures that are advancing a liberal market understanding of VET policies can also be found in documents, such as in a Communication on a new impetus of VET to support the Europe 2020 strategy (European Commission 2010).

In the following, I will firstly summarise my case studies on the impact of the Copenhagen process in a comparative perspective. By relating the case studies to each other, I will analyse if the different EU instruments had an impact, and if so in what direction and if core institutional features were affected. I will then proceed to discuss the theoretical implications of my findings, implications against the background of the recent economic and financial crisis, and avenues for further research (Table 6.1).

Table 6.1 Overview on the implementation of instruments and principles on the national level

Instrument / Principle	Germany	Netherlands	United Kingdom (England)
Learning Outcomes	Adjusted to national system	Already in place	Already in place
Qualifications Frameworks (EQF)	Adjusted to national system	Adjusted to national system	Already in place
Credit Systems (ECVET)	Used as a reform lever with small-scale effects on the national system	Adjusted to national system	Already in place
Validation of non-formal and informal learning	No change	Already in place	Already in place
Quality Assurance (EQARF)	Adjusted to national system	Already in place	Already in place

Two* levels of change: ☐ – no change of national VET systems or instrument/principles already in place
▬ – small-scale change without effects on core features of national VET systems

*A transformative change – defined as a change of one or more core features of national VET systems – has not been observed in this study.

6.1 Comparison of the Impact of the Copenhagen Process on Germany, the Netherlands and the United Kingdom (England)

In this section, I summarise and compare my findings on the impact of the Copenhagen process in Germany, the Netherlands, and the UK. Following Hall (1993) and Trampusch (2010a), I distinguish three different patterns of impact:

1. *No change*. Instances where member states already had the respective instruments and principles in place before the Copenhagen process or instances where the instruments and principles developed within the realm of the Copenhagen process have not been implemented (so far). This includes first order changes to instruments and principles that already had been in place on member state level prior to the Copenhagen process;
2. *Small-scale change*. Instances of small-scale change for which the decisive factor is that the direction of change is in line with the given institutional set-up. This degree of change includes second order changes; and
3. *Transformative change*. Instances where at least one of the core features of national VET institutions change. Such a fundamental change would constitute a "third order change" (Hall 1993) or a "transformative change" (Trampusch 2010a).

Learning Outcomes

In both the UK and the Netherlands, VET systems had been largely outcome-orientated before the Copenhagen process. In the UK, a shift towards learning outcomes took place with the introduction of the competence-based NVQs in 1986. The objective of introducing NVQs was to increase the flexibility of the VET system for both learners and firms. The process has been accompanied by a narrowing of VET skills. In the Netherlands, on the contrary, the understanding of learning outcomes as competencies largely resembles a CME understanding of skills, meaning a more holistic approach to VET. Employers pushed for the reform and argue that VET is now more closely related to actual work processes. The concept is criticised to be blurry, too demanding to implement in SMEs, and overemphasising examinations which are more difficult to safeguard in their quality. Therefore, while the approaches to learning outcomes differ in the two countries, both reflect the distinct functioning of VET systems in the respective country. Since both ways of implementation are in line with European concepts, this exemplifies the ample room left to member states. In both countries, no change was necessary since a learning outcome approach had already been implemented.

In Germany, on the contrary, the idea to define qualifications solely in terms of learning outcomes is new. It is understood as a shift towards "competences", a term that slightly differs from both the English term "competence" and the European concept of learning outcomes, as it reflects a broader and more holistic concept to VET skills. Thus, the European concept is adjusted to the specific skill mix of the German system. A reform towards a competence-based orientation of training ordinances and curricula is ongoing but—in contrast to the Netherlands and to England—is far from being completed. Reforming training ordinances is a tripartite and often tedious procedure organised by the government but largely relies on agreements between and impulses from social partners. Both the government and employers argue that the ongoing reform process fulfils the requirements of the European learning outcome approach. The government believes that the European concept can advance the status of VET in relation to higher education, since it focuses on work processes. Trade unions criticise that a shift towards learning outcomes makes learning methods and contents more arbitrary; moreover, they see a risk that skills could become narrower. This would affect a core institution of the German VET system, namely the balance between specific and general skills. In practice, this is unlikely for two reasons. First, with the focus on competences, the learning outcome approach has been adjusted to the German VET system. Second, steering ordinances and curricula towards competences is a process that had been ongoing in the past without challenging the dual principle. The Copenhagen process is likely to speed up this continuing process.

European Qualifications Framework (EQF)

Qualifications frameworks had been in place in England prior to the Copenhagen process, so that the impact of the EQF on the UK comes down to the referencing of existing frameworks to the EQF. On the contrary, in the Netherlands and in Germany qualifications frameworks were developed as a direct response to the Copenhagen process. In both countries, any effects on existing qualifications and the institutional set-up of the VET systems were explicitly excluded. Yet, the process of developing qualifications frameworks improved the understanding between actors in the different education subsystems. In sum, regarding qualifications frameworks, the Copenhagen process initiated a change in both countries which is small-scale and does not affect core institutions of the VET systems.

In England, qualifications frameworks were introduced with the establishment of the NQF in 1997 and the introduction of the QCF in 2008. The idea was that qualifications frameworks would increase the transparency of qualifications. Herewith, they tackle a problem which is strongly related to the marked-based structure of the system in which learning institutions and qualifications are much more numerous than in CME VET systems. The QCF is a unit-based and flexible qualifications framework. Stakeholders stress that this specific design of the QCF is in line with their preferences, which resembles the nature of the British VET system as a LME. The English system is very close to the design of the EQF, and only regarding minor aspects—the QCF has one more level than the EQF and entry levels—were the national and the European design of qualifications frameworks found to be different. On the basis of a broad consultation process, qualifications frameworks were referenced to the EQF as early as 2010. A coordination point for the EQF was established to coordinate processes in the UK. Several follow-up projects were carried out, such as an international peer learning project and information activities. One smaller problem was the question how to mention EQF levels on VET certificates which are in the responsibility of awarding bodies.

6.1 Comparison of the Impact of the Copenhagen Process on Germany, the... 201

It was agreed to opt for the way that would least impede the current practice by making the mention of a link to an online database on the certificate sufficient.

In the Netherlands, a qualifications framework was developed as a response to a European impetus. Stakeholder involvement and searching for consensus were important features of the implementation process, which gained momentum only when a European report showed that the Netherlands were lagging behind in the implementation process. Efforts were made to design the Dutch qualifications framework in a way least affecting the VET system; any changes to the existing education system were excluded. The instrument is seen as a means to foster comparability and transparency on the European and national level. While the eight-level-structure of the framework can be considered a political choice that shall facilitate the comparability with the EQF, descriptors have been adjusted to reflect the Dutch system, including a focus on autonomy and a holistic approach to VET. On the national level, discussions mostly focused on the positioning of single qualifications, also regarding the relationship between general education qualifications and VET. Qualifications offered by private providers are included, which increases the transparency of the continuing VET market. Private providers developed a self-interest in the process, while the two big employers' organisations lacked interest since they perceived the process as a technical procedure lacking labour market relevance. After the referencing was completed, the European EQF advisory group criticised the referencing level of the general university entrance qualification on level 5 as being too high. As a consequence, a new level was introduced in the Dutch qualifications framework, level 4+, and the qualification was re-positioned to this level.

In Germany, the implementation of a qualifications framework as a response to European stimuli started in 2006 by setting up a coordination group between the federal administration and *Länder* administrations. A second working group was established that included a vast variety of stakeholders such as social partners. An office for the qualifications framework was contracted to private companies in 2007. After a testing phase in 2009 and 2010, the working group agreed on the design of the framework in 2011. Similar to the Netherlands, while the eight-level-structure resembles the EQF, descriptors were adjusted to reflect the distinct balance between broad and specific skills of the German VET system, as well as the orientation towards full occupations of the German VET system ("*Berufsprinzip*"). The descriptor "professional competences" is subdivided into knowledge and skills, and the descriptor "personal competences" is subdivided into "social competences" and "self competence". The DQR explicitly excludes any impact on collective agreements, public sector pay scales or admission rules. In the process of linking existing VET qualifications to the framework, two aspects stand out. First, as a result of a great deal of discussion, upgrading training in VET (such as *Meister* qualifications) is linked to level 6 together with bachelor's degrees in tertiary education. Second, a conflict arose on the referencing of the general qualification for university entrance. The education ministers of the *Länder* had argued that it should be referenced to level 5 together with high-ranking apprenticeships, but were isolated with this position. As a compromise, stakeholders agreed to postpone referencing secondary school qualifications until 2017. While the qualifications framework is perceived to improve the standing of VET because all levels are open for both general education and VET qualifications, and since VET is seen to be better positioned than in other international education frameworks, this should not be overestimated. Another interesting aspect is the actors' coalition. The government understands the DQR as an instrument for increasing permeability and flexibility in the national realm and for improving mobility across Europe. Employers were divided regarding the referencing process. On the one hand, employers from several sectors—IT, metal, machine building and high tech sectors, which acted with the support from the umbrella organisation BDA—lobbied for referencing apprenticeships to three different levels. On the other hand, the craft sector and Chambers opposed this view, since they oppose a differentiation of apprenticeships. In the end, short 2-year apprenticeships were referenced to level 3 and 3 or 3.5-year apprenticeships to level 4. In general, employers have a positive view on the DQR because it is perceived to strengthen the position of VET and increase the transparency of qualifications. They demand further improvements regarding permeability between VET and tertiary education. Trade unions had originally proposed a five-level framework in which all apprenticeships would have been referenced on level 1. They oppose any further differentiation of apprenticeships and are concerned that the DQR might strengthen the standing of qualifications below the level of skilled workers at the cost of "regular" 3 or 3.5-year apprenticeships.

European Credit System (ECVET)
The impact of the ECVET differs across the three case studies. In England, where credit systems were already in place, the mobility component of the instrument is not in the focus and is hindered by private property questions and quality assurance aspects resulting from the market-led structure of the VET system. In the Netherlands, the implementation is subject to a "wait and see" approach, and it is likely that the instrument will be implemented as a means for fostering mobility, especially in border regions, without repercussions on the structure of qualifications and the VET system as a whole. In Germany, ECVET was used as a driver for reforms by the government and by some of the employers. While potential effects on core features of the VET system exist—namely on certification, standardisation and the involvement of SMEs in training—the implementation of reforms so far is limited to pilot projects, so that implications remain to be seen.

In England, since the introduction of the NVQs in 1986, the VET system is united-based and modularised. The QCF is also based on the unit approach to qualifications—within the framework, units can be transferred—and hereby facilitates an implementation of ECVET. An advantage of the unit approach is widely seen in the flexibility it provides to learners and companies, thus the logics of the instrument follow the market-led structure of the English VET system. The implementation of the ECVET is carried out through a coordination point which was set up in England; several projects with partner countries have taken place. While the English VET system therefore in general facilitates the implementation of the

ECVET, there are also obstacles to the implementation of the instrument that derive directly from the market-led structure of the English VET system. First, awarding bodies are private companies and are reluctant to share their intellectual property rights on qualifications and unit specifications. Second, in the diverse market-led system with its multitude of qualifications, providers and awarding bodies, quality mechanisms are in place that put specific requirements on units and their assessments. Only those qualifications obtained abroad which fulfil all quality mechanisms can be recognised towards a qualification in the UK. Therefore, in conclusion, while a unit approach has already been established in the UK, the recognition of units and qualifications obtained abroad is likely to be hindered by the market-led structure of the British VET system in the future.

In the Netherlands, the implementation of ECVET has been subject to a "wait and see" approach. The government questions if the implementation of ECVET is worth the effort. While the government still feels obligated to show good will and hence created a coordination point for ECVET, this coordination point in practice has very limited means. The implementation of a unit approach is complicated by the recent shift away from a unit-based VET system towards a competence-based qualification structure, which is based on core tasks. If a unit-based approach would be implemented, in the current system such a change would fall in the responsibility of schools, since they are responsible for curricula and examinations. Another option would be that *Kenniscentra* add units to the existing qualification structure solely for mobility purposes, or transform core tasks into units. However, the only supporter of a change towards a unit-based system is the International Agency, which advocates a change towards an "à la carte" system. Social partners thus far have not been very interested in ECVET. Only in the health and welfare sector, employers started to look towards ECVET as an instrument to prevent skill shortages by facilitating mobility of employees from other sectors and from abroad. In general, international mobility in VET is very low, and several smaller-scale government initiatives exist to foster mobility, especially in border regions.

In Germany, different activities have been taken to implement the ECVET. One approach is based on facilitating and funding the use of ECVET as a bottom-up tool for international mobility during VET. A national coordination point for ECVET has been established. ECVET is likely to serve as a standard for mobility experiences during VET in the medium run. This approach to ECVET is comparable to the Dutch view on the instrument. In Germany, however, the instrument is also used as a means to steer national reform in the direction of permeability, flexibility and modularisation. The DECVET initiative was launched as a pilot project with the objective to improve transitions within VET and across educational strands by measuring, transferring and crediting competences. Such a way of implementing ECVET had not originally been envisioned by the European Commission. After Germany launched this initiative, the approach to ECVET was taken up on the EU level, which underlines the proactive role the German government took on the subject.

When it comes to ECVET and its implementation in Germany, it is important to analyse national discussions that took place independently of European developments. Not only were EU initiatives developed at a time when inherent problems in the system piled up, the Copenhagen process also affects several issues that were already discussed against the background of increasing segmentalism. The federal government pushed for modularisation and flexibility. At the same time, the government opposed the Commission's activities to introduce an automatic recognition of qualifications and automatic accumulation of learning outcomes across countries. Employers are divided on the issue of modularisation. On the one hand, the BDA—an umbrella organisation that represents all companies but is skewed towards the interests of large firms—made a reform proposal for the national VET system that would increase flexibility and challenge core features of the system related to the balance of skills, certification and portability. In this concept, sectors could optionally introduce modularisation and reduce the duration of training. Firms could then decide to carry out examinations for single building blocks or hire awarding bodies to do so; final examinations would be reduced to one task that tests the holistic-occupational competence of the apprentice. On the other hand, Chambers and the craft sector oppose modularisation in this form and developed their own reform proposals. The Chambers proposed to bundle training in related occupations in the first 2 years of an apprenticeship, and then offer a choice of modules for more specialised training in the third year. The idea behind this proposal is to make skills broader and more firm-specific at the same time; it is largely in line with the fundamental pillars of dual VET. In the view of the craft sector, modules should be limited to specific target groups. The duration of training should not be reduced. This is because of the cost-benefit relation in the crafts sector, where firms invest in the training of apprentices during the first 2 years, whereas in the third year their productivity is higher than their wages. Employers agree that the way ECVET is currently designed is incomprehensive and too abstract. Trade unions oppose modularisation, as well as any further differentiation of apprenticeships, the introduction of an "à la carte" system and in general an understanding of education based only on economic considerations. They are critical towards developments that could lead to a system that focuses on creditable learning outcomes, modularisation or certification of single units only. Trade unions support an implementation of ECVET that highlights transnational mobility and serves as a standard for mobility experiences. In sum, the introduction of ECVET occurred simultaneously to reform discussions already taking place in the national realm. While large firms and the government favoured modularisation and flexibilisation of training, the craft sector and Chambers as well as trade unions opposed far-reaching reforms. DECVET was actively used to steer reforms in this direction, an approach that had not originally been intended by the Commission.

Does the implementation of DECVET in Germany challenge core features of the German VET system? While the first approach to ECVET as a bottom-up initiative is not in conflict with fundamental pillars of VET, it is important to take a closer look at the DECVET initiative in this regard. The way DECVET is designed challenges the dual training mode. This is because if any training carried out by vocational schools or preparatory VET schemes can be accredited towards apprenticeships, the balance of skills is geared towards general skills. Moreover, the portability of skills might be affected. However, several reasons exist, while DECVET still is very unlikely to affect these core pillars of the German VET system in practice. First, even if prior training is based on different standards than apprenticeships, the quality of this training might still be high. Moreover, these classes might also combine learning at schools with learning in firms. Second, this would only refer to parts of the training, so that effects per se would be limited. Third, so far there is no obligation for firms to accredit prior learning. If there was, however, this might affect firms' involvement in VET, since their costs of training might increase. In the current form, firms can therefore be expected to be highly unenthusiastic about accrediting prior learning to apprenticeships on a large scale. Moreover, large firms offer high quality training, which they are unlikely to find in other programmes. Small firms will be concerned because they integrate training in their work flow, and reducing the time an apprentice spends in the firm reduces the flexibility of the firm to cover training contents whenever it is suitable and in accordance with production processes. The craft sector especially benefits from training by using apprentices as workers fully acquainted with their work in the third year of the apprenticeship—if they accredit prior learning, there is the risk that apprentices might still need to catch up on training content in the third year. Fourth, DECVET is based on holistically occupational full VET courses, modularisation taking place within these, and is not implemented as a "pick and choose" concept. Final examinations are kept and are likely to gain in importance. Finally, the DECVET initiative is based on pilot projects, so per se it cannot affect core institutions of the system. Even if it was mainstreamed, its focus most likely would be on certain groups of apprentices only, namely those who were not able to find apprenticeships after graduating from school. It can be concluded that although DECVET runs close to affecting fundamental pillars of the German VET system, it is unlikely to do so in practice.

Validation of Non-formal and Informal Learning
The guidelines on the validation of non-formal and informal learning that were established on the European level show only limited effects on the national level. In the UK, procedures had been in place before the Copenhagen process. In the Netherlands, procedures also already existed. A reform that stemmed from the national level incorporated EU guidelines. In both countries, only a limited number of procedures are carried out in practice. In Germany, the topic was placed on the agenda by the Copenhagen process, but no reforms have been undertaken so far.

In England, procedures for the validation of non-formal and informal learning had been established already in the 1980s with the objective to create additional opportunities for progression towards higher education, as well as for integrating unemployed adults into the labour market. The instrument is moreover seen to advance the flexibility of learners, since they have more options to decide when and how learning takes place. It is also because EU instruments very much resemble the English VET system that they do not pose a challenge to the system.

In the Netherlands, a well-developed validation system exists with the EVC procedures (*Erkenning van Verworven Competenties*) since the 1980s. While in the beginning procedures were very diverse, they became more standardised and quality regulation was introduced. Validation procedures are carried out by schools or private providers. Validation procedures can focus on providing a generic profile of a candidate's skills (recognition) or on the accreditation of her skills against a recognised qualification in order to shorten the duration of education (accreditation). The incorporation of general skills remains a challenge. Since numbers are small, EVC procedures will not undermine the system as such. All stakeholders support EVC procedures. They are mostly paid by employers or (in the case of unemployed, but with decreasing funds) by the state, which also provides a general infrastructure. When a quality code for EVC procedures was developed, European guidelines were incorporated.

In Germany, procedures for the validation of non-formal and informal learning are weakly developed. The only exceptions are the option to take part in the Chambers' apprenticeship examinations as an external candidate and the recognition of previously acquired competences within upgrade training. The further route for the implementation of validation procedures is still unclear. So far, the development of the German qualifications framework have steered discussions on the subject, and two working groups have already dealt with the topic. Actors believe that the implementation is a difficult task, as several questions are still open, including who pays for validation procedures, if additional recognition and examination bodies should be set up and if so, if they will be designed in a corporatist way, and which results from validation procedures will be linked to the qualifications framework. These questions are closely connected to certification and assessment, and therefore to the involvement of firms in VET leading to full VET qualifications. This is because there is the risk that firms choose to back out of "standard" VET when they are able to hire graduates as unskilled workers, train them on the job and have their skill validated without necessarily completing a full apprenticeship. According to an interview partner from the craft sector, there are already large firms that follow this logic. In this case, it is also the school-based part of apprenticeships and therefore the specific skill mix created with dual apprenticeships which might change. Yet, regarding all of these three risks, it will be decisive how validation of informal and non-formal learning will be implemented in practice. So far, stakeholders' preferences do not point at a conflict with fundamental pillars of the dual system.

Quality Assurance
While the three countries' quality assurance systems differ tremendously, the impact of European ideas remains limited in all cases.

In England, a policy cycle for quality assurance as envisioned by the Copenhagen process was already in place prior to EU initiatives. The indicators developed on the European level do not pose a challenge for the UK with the exception of the indicator on the training of VET trainers; in this field, the UK has and will keep a more voluntary, less standardised approach. For the implementation of EQAVET, a coordination point has been established. Because of the market-based system, quality assurance has a strong role in the UK as a framework for the activities of private actors in the system. There are procedures for quality assurance of all qualifications that are linked to the qualifications framework, requirements towards providers (except private companies) for establishing their own quality assurance tools and a strong inspectorate system. Against the background of a largely de-standardised system with a large body of qualifications, a functioning quality assurance system can be seen as a prerequisite to keep the market-led system running.

The Netherlands have a much elaborated quality assurance system that addresses systematic evaluation processes as well as standards and certification. Similar to the UK, providers need to install quality assurance systems and inspections are carried out. Regional training centres are responsible for the quality of their VET courses. Moreover, a policy cycle on quality assurance exists. The system is continuously revised. Firms are included in quality assurance by agreements and monitoring; yet here, problems seem to prevail. Employers' organisations address the need for high quality in workplace-based learning more openly than their German or English counterparts and demand improvements from firms. EQARF and EQAVET are largely met. A national coordination point has been established that mostly steers debates on the national level. For selected specific issues, the ministry feeds ideas from quality assurance policies from other countries into the national arena. Moreover, the government has influenced policy developments on the European level with ideas stemming from the Dutch quality assurance system.

Quality in German VET focuses on standards, procedures and certification, but largely lacks comprehensive quality management. Aside from the establishment of a national reference point with very limited powers, European processes have not led to any changes in quality assurance in Germany thus far. The government supports improvements in quality assurance on the basis of existing instruments and argues that the quality of VET is already very high. It is often brought forward that the high quality of the VET system shows in low youth unemployment rates. Indicators are seen to have a 'toolbox' character. The government opposed the introduction of benchmarks on the European level. Employers agree with this reading, and oppose any additional regulation on quality, since it would make training more costly. They argue that especially SMEs might have difficulties to deal with additional quality requirements. An interview partner from the federal administration argues that the introduction of a policy cycle for quality management is unlikely, since it might interfere with the way training is carried out by firms or imply additional costs for firms. Trade unions, on the other hand, lobby for increasing quality assurance mechanisms and argue that current regulation is both insufficient and often ignored.

The Impact of the Copenhagen Process on Member States

In conclusion, national systems mitigate change. Policies are implemented in a way that is least disturbing to the national system. Oftentimes, change was not necessary because policies were already in place. In the UK, this is the case for all policies except ECVET,[2] in the Netherlands for learning outcomes. In Germany, the European impetus on learning outcomes met an ongoing change at the national level, and in the Netherlands European policies on validation procedures and on quality assurance were incorporated into existing national efforts and policies. When there was a 'misfit', only in one case—namely the validation of non-formal and informal learning in Germany—no changes were implemented in the time frame of my analysis. In three cases, regarding quality assurance in Germany, ECVET in the Netherlands and ECVET in the UK, efforts were kept to the absolute minimum. In the UK, while the national qualification system is unit-based already, the mobility dimension of ECVET is fostered only with limited efforts. As a follow-up to the EQF, both Germany and the Netherlands developed NQFs, but in both countries the impact on the national system was kept as small as possible. Here, the impact comes down to organising communication of actors across educational strands and providing an—arguable quite rough—framework for comparing qualifications across educational strands within countries and across Europe. The second intention of the European Commission, namely to steer reforms on the national level via the EQF, has not been fulfilled. Arguably, the German national qualifications framework strengthened the status of VET slightly. A small-scale effect can be observed regarding the implementation of ECVET in the Netherlands, where it is implemented in a bottom-up manner and has the potential to serve as a driver for mobility. All these ways of implementing the Copenhagen process are in line with what I expected against the background of the VoC framework: the implementation took place in accordance with existing institutions.

The scope for action left to member states was used to implement policies the way most in conformity with existent institutions. This holds not only for CMEs, which were challenged by the Copenhagen process in several ways and, as outlined above, ensured the implementation as being in line with existing institutions. The same mechanisms can be observed in England, although here policies had already been largely in line with existing institutions. However, the use of ECVET as a mobility instrument poses problems exactly because of the nature of the English VET system as a LME. While English policies had already been in line with many requirements of the Copenhagen process, unit specifications are the intellectual property of awarding bodies and there are several procedural regulations made by them regarding how units have to be taught and assessed. So far, the implementation of the instrument has not proceeded far enough to see how this question will be tackled. When awarding bodies had to mention the EQF level on their certificates, another problem interfering with the market-led system of the UK, discussions arose and the least disturbing route was chosen: to leave the decision on the concrete implementation to awarding bodies and allow them to only place a link to a database on certificates. Another interesting aspect is that in the UK, European

---

[2]Regarding qualifications frameworks in the UK, although this instrument was already in place, national qualifications frameworks were linked to the EQF.

developments might create business opportunities regarding the export of qualifications, a subject that is already discussed by awarding bodies. In sum, it seems that the implementation of the Copenhagen process is conducted in a way that is most in conformity with the existent system.

Only in one case, regarding the implementation of ECVET in Germany, the instrument was actively used to steer reforms in the national realm. National actors, namely large firms and the government used EU policies as a window of opportunity for reform. European proceedings here met ongoing reform discussions on the national level and ongoing changes in the field of VET (Thelen and Busemeyer 2008; Busemeyer and Thelen 2011), as well as in important complementary institutions (Streeck 2009; Busemeyer and Thelen 2011). The result from these reform pressures is, however, limited to an initiative based on pilot projects. While this initiative ("DECVET") comes very close to affecting core features of the German VET system in theory, effects are highly unlikely in practice. This is because decisions to recognise prior learning is left to firms which are unlikely to do so, but also results from the nature of the initiative based on pilot projects with a focus on special target groups. The most important conclusion for the focus of this book is that regarding any impact from the European level, national institutions so far are substantially sticky. This is the case even where the government and large employers used EU initiatives as a window of opportunity but could not overcome the opposition of a coalition of Chambers and the craft sector in conjunction with trade unions that opposed a larger reform.

6.2 Theoretical Implications

The theoretical implications of my findings relate to the questions if the EU impetus leads to a liberalisation of national institutions, how a VoC perspective can add to this discussion, how political economy research and Europeanisation research can fruitfully enrich each other's perspectives, and finally, what insights this study provides regarding SME's preferences on VET and the question of typologies in VoC. Subsequently, I will point out implications for further research. I will conclude the chapter by pointing out implications for policy discussions.

6.2.1 Is Europe Liberalising National Institutions?

In national debates, especially in Germany, it has been assumed that the Copenhagen process would unfold far-reaching consequences on national institutions towards a liberalisation of national VET systems. These assumptions are in line with discussions in the political economy literature regarding the impact of European market-making policy-making on national economies and welfare states in general (Scharpf 1999, 2002, 2008a; Streeck 2009, 2013; Höpner and Schäfer

2008a, b), as well as the impact of European VET policies in particular (Trampusch 2008, 2009). In Chap. 2, I developed a political economy perspective on the Copenhagen process against the background of VoC and argued that the Copenhagen process itself is indeed biased towards policies that advance liberal market economy skill regimes. Yet, in my case studies I found that

1. changes at member states level are small-scale;
2. member states use the scope for action left by European soft law policies to implement them in the way most in conformity with existent institutions; and
3. even in the case of ECVET in Germany, where European proceedings met ongoing reform discussions and the government and large firms tried to use EU policies as a window of opportunity for reform, national institutions have been largely sticky so far.

What does this mean for our understanding of the impetus from the European level on member states?

Explaining the Depth and Direction of Change in the Light of VoC

The impetus of the Copenhagen process is in line with what I expected from a VoC perspective. The expectation was that the difference of national institutions as prevalent in different types of capitalisms "generate different responses to a common EU-led impetus" (Menz 2003: 536). Member states were expected to respond to the common impetus from the European level in a way that is in line with existent institutions. If EU policies are used as a driver for reform, the expectation was that this is to strategically advance the further development of institutions along existing equilibria. In LMEs, the latter implies a further liberalisation and deregulation—understood as developments or processes that make VET more market-driven or focused on general skills. A policy change that advances the institutional set-up of CMEs, on the contrary, fosters the coordination among firms and supports the existing equilibrium of industry-specific skills on the intermediary level.

Indeed, in my case studies I observed that in spite of critical voices arguing that European policies would lead to a liberalisation of VET regimes in the direction of a LME VET model, such a change did not take place. The three countries developed different responses to the Copenhagen process that correspond to the respective VET regime. If there was potential for a conflict between European policies and national VET regimes—and with CMEs this was the case in numerous ways—countries chose to adapt European instruments and principles in the way most in conformity with existent institutions. In other words, European soft law in the field of VET did not lead to a re-calculation of national actors' preferences.

Actors' preferences on national institutions did not change as a consequence of the European impetus not only in regard to those instances when instruments and principles were implemented in a way most conforming to existing institutions: This argument also holds when it comes to the implementation of ECVET in Germany, the only incident in this study in which national actors used an instrument stemming from the European level to steer changes of national institutions. As such, the Copenhagen process constitutes a window of opportunity for increasing the scope for action in the national sphere and changes opportunity structures of domestic politics (Trampusch 2008). Yet, although some reform ideas would have affected core institutions of the German VET system, I argue that firstly the foundations for the actors' preferences can be found in the national realm, and secondly no VET institutions were changed. Actors that favoured a reform of national VET systems were not able to enforce reforms in spite of efforts to use EU policies as a window of opportunity. As such, ECVET does not constitute a counter-example for the focus of this study, namely the interplay between the national and the European sphere. Instead, VET institutions in Germany have been notably stable in the light of preferences for reforms of large firms and, partly, of the government. Thelen and Busemeyer (2008) have argued that the German VET system has made a segmentalist turn, which is based on modularisation, 2-year apprenticeships and exam reorganisation. A few years later, I argue that indeed the differentiation of VET has increased. This refers to 2-year apprenticeships, which form a noticeable but still small part of the apprenticeship system with 9% of apprenticeships in 2012 (BMBF 2013). In addition, dual study programmes have gained in importance and add to the differentiation among apprenticeships on the higher end by combining learning in firms, schools and applied universities. Options to include additional competences as a supplementary variant in apprenticeships have been established. Most importantly, the number of firms that participate in VET is decreasing (Busemeyer and Thelen 2011; Thelen 2007). The latter trend is likely to increase in pace with demographics, leading to fewer school graduates (Ante 2010). However, I argue that the VET system has proved largely stable against reform preferences on modularisation and examinations. Still, about 520,000 apprenticeships were started in 2015. The VET system as it is apparently still provides rents.

Arguing along the lines of Hall and Thelen (2009), large firms as entrepreneurial actors tested the boundaries of the VET system in Germany. Firms continuously bring up reform ideas in different areas of the economy (Hassel 2007). Herewith, they aim at making institutions work in their favour without necessarily abandoning them (ibid). VoC can accommodate changes or alterations of preferences when firms lobby for institutional change in order to increase returns. In the field of VET, the reasons why firms lobbied for reforms stem from the national rather than the European arena. Rising cost-consciousness against the background of globalised markets and technological advancements both lead to increases of the skill level firms seek their workforce to inherit. For large firms, such changes are easier to accommodate if VET systems are more flexible and allow for skills to be more firm-specific. Yet, their pressure for reform was not successful because the current system provided more benefits to the craft sector and Chambers as well as better meets trade unions' preferences. In line with Busemeyer (2012) and Trampusch (2010b), my analysis shows that when it comes to modularisation and the certification of single units (not final examinations) at the firm level, VET stakeholders are divided into two coalitions. On the one hand large firms lobby for reform in this direction. They cooperate with public administration in order to steer institutional change in the direction of modularisation and increasing flexibility of training. On the other hand, an "alliance of preservers" (Busemeyer 2012) between Chambers, the craft sector and trade unions opposes these steps. While large firms have not been successful with their requests for reform, in the end—also taking into account the interplay of complementary institutions—they still prefer the system as it is over opting out and shifting to internal labour markets unilaterally.

Explaining European Integration in the Light of VoC

The impact of the European policies on member states is at the centre of this book, with national institutions on the dependent variable. In an intergovernmental process of European policy-making, it is obvious that not only does the EU influence member states, but that at the same time member states themselves also influence policy-making on the European level. Ideally, Europeanisation and European integration should be thought together. While the focus of this book is on Europeanisation, I will point out a few interesting observations on European integration and derive first conclusions on the basis of my desk analysis, the 10 interviews conducted with a variety of European actors, and on the basis of the country case studies.

Such conclusions can build upon Fioretos' (2001) case study on German and British preferences on the Treaty on European Union (see Sect. 1.1). His key argument is that "the shape of multilateralism that an EC member espouses depends primarily upon the potential or actual implications of the form of multilateralism on the ability of that country to sustain the comparative institutional advantages provided by its specific variety of capitalism" (ibid, 215). A country's position on the design of European processes therefore derives from the way international cooperation will impact national institutions. Its position is formed by the aggregated national actors' preferences (ibid). The case of the TEU negotiations surely has potentially very far-reaching consequences on the national realm, whereas VET is a soft law policy area in which no formal sanctions exist. Yet, according to the logic of VoC, it is to be expected that market economies should differ in their preferences on European VET policies in a way that is consistent with the internal logics of the national VET regime and comparative advantages derived from the set-up of the respective VET system. VoC is an adequate framework for studying national preferences on EU integration in VET exactly because VET policies are rooted deeply in economic systems. While the importance of domestic politics for the determination of foreign policies has been acknowledged in the literature for decades (Katzenstein 1978), with the VoC framework it is possible to develop hypotheses on countries' preferences on EU integration. In a nutshell, LMEs should prefer policy initiatives that favour a market-based organisation of VET and advance general skills, whereas CMEs should prefer a design of European policies that focuses on coordination and industry-specific skills. At the same time, countries should lobby against initiatives which are opposed to their preferences.

6.2 Theoretical Implications

Another, more indirect way to approach the question of European integration is to compare the way European instruments and principles are designed with the way the European Commission's original preferences on policy design. If the goals of European actors are not fulfilled, it is an additional (non-sufficient) argument for the resistance of institutions against an impetus from European level. In my analysis, I found that the Commission intended changes that were far beyond the way policies and instruments were designed in the end, and, as I have argued above, far beyond the degree of change that was actually implemented by member states.

I found solid evidence that national actors voiced preferences that are in line with the institutional set-up of their VET systems as LMEs or CMEs. The UK has been strongly involved in the development of European policies: Staff from the English QCA took an active role in the conceptual work on the Copenhagen process (see Chap. 2). The Netherlands have been active in shaping the quality assurance model on the European level. Germany opposed, together with other countries, mechanisms for automatic recognition and automatic summation of VET qualifications across member states.

Regarding two important and far-reaching aspects, the Commission was not able to design ECVET the way it intended to. First, as stated above, the Commission originally aimed at installing a system which would allow an individual—in the Commission's presentations this person was named "Mr. X"—to complete different modules in different countries and have them recognised as a full qualification in any member state. Such a system would challenge CME systems. Second, the Commission originally intended to integrate ECVET and the ECTS into one common system. Member states opposed both proposals. Regarding quality assurance, the Commission originally intended to introduce benchmarks, but because of member state opposition, only a toolbox of indicators was developed. The reason was that several of these indicators would pose difficulties for the functioning of national VET systems, for example regarding quality assurance of providers, namely firms, or regarding the training of VET teachers in England.

Moreover, the Commission originally aimed to achieve a twofold objective with the introduction of qualifications frameworks. First, the comparability and transparency of qualifications was supposed to be improved. This goal was accomplished, although on a very broad frame of reference and only to a certain degree of preciseness. Second, reform expectations also focused on the national realm, with the idea that qualifications frameworks could be drivers for different objectives, such as strengthening the coherence of qualifications systems; improving permeability[3]; supporting lifelong learning; simplifying the recognition of non-formal and informal learning; strengthening the link of education and training and the labour market; enabling strategic planning; and providing a basis for wage bargaining (Coles 2006; Cedefop 2010a). Such reforms had been clearly linked to the EQF:

---

[3]It is possible that NQFs will steer processes on the national level, such as making further education more attractive in the Netherlands, or by developing new qualifications of further education in VET on higher levels So far, permeability has not improved in the analysed countries.

"The EQF also has an aim to support and promote change in national systems of qualifications" (Coles 2006: 25). While European actors were aware that they created a window of opportunity for reform, they were also aware that it was in the hands of member states themselves to decide if to make use of this opportunity. In my case studies, I found that the Netherlands and Germany did not use the EQF as a reform level, although they developed NQFs. In these two cases, the hopes of the Commission have not been fulfilled.

My Findings in Comparison to Previous Political Science Studies

Comparing the impact of the Copenhagen process on member states, I found that firstly changes at member states level are either small-scale or no changes were enacted; secondly member states use the scope for action European VET policies provide to implement them in the way most in conformity with existent institutions; and thirdly even in the case of ECVET in Germany, where European proceedings met ongoing reform discussions and the government and large firms tried to use EU policies as a window of opportunity for reform, national institutions have been largely resistant to change thus far. At the same time, states do influence European policy-making in order to bring European policies closer in line with their own institutions. This can refer both to hindering reforms that would affect core features of national VET systems, as well as to uploading institutions to the European level.

My findings share similarities but also differ from studies conducted by comparative political science scholars who have studied the Europeanisation of VET (Trampusch 2008, 2009, 2010b; Powell and Trampusch 2011; see also Thelen and Busemeyer 2008; Busemeyer and Thelen 2011). Trampusch and Powell have applied an approach that combines Europeanisation with an informed perspective of domestic politics and institutions (see Sect. 1.1 for details). Most certainly, Europeanisation of VET is a field which is in constant flux, so that analyses are always preliminary in nature, and new observations will constantly follow. The advantage of this study is that it is based on a comprehensive empirical analysis (see Sect. 1.2 on methodology) with a time frame that can accommodate implications from the implementation of the major EU-instruments on the member state level.

A finding that this study and Trampusch (2008, 2009), Powell and Trampusch (2011), Thelen and Busemeyer (2008), Busemeyer and Thelen (2011) and Busemeyer (2009b) have in common is, as I noted earlier, that Europeanisation opens a window of opportunity for reform, which the government and large firms used as an opportunity to push for reforms in Germany. This is congruent with my analysis.

However, I come to different conclusions than previous political science studies on the Europeanisation of VET regarding several points. First, I develop a political economy perspective of the Copenhagen process and lay down in detail that EU VET policies are biased towards LMEs. As a consequence, the Copenhagen process challenges CMEs more than LMEs. Second, I argue that the bias of the Copenhagen process towards LMEs affects different CMEs in different ways, and that this

6.2 Theoretical Implications

difference is based on two distinctive typologies of CME training regimes: a more state-based type as prevalent for example in the Netherlands, and a more coordinated or corporatist one prevalent for example in Germany (see Sect. 6.2.3 below). Third, while the Copenhagen process has been described as a process of liberalisation before, I come to different conclusions regarding the way its mechanisms challenge member states. This follows from diverging analyses of the Copenhagen process. Trampusch (2008, 2009) argues that modularisation is a core element of the EQF. Similarly, Powell and Trampusch (2011: 286) state that qualifications frameworks "break integrated occupations down into their component skill modules".[4] I argue that neither the EQF recommendation nor policy documents or publications on the EQF on the European level (Coles 2006; Cedefop 2010a) necessarily require modularisation. In addition, I do not find evidence for prevailing controversies on the DQR: throughout my interviews in Germany, interview partners stated that the way the DQR is designed in the end is a satisfying result or at least an acceptable compromise (see Chap. 3).[5] I find that questions of modularisation indeed have been discussed, but mostly in relation to ECVET. The Commission had envisioned a mechanism of automatic recognition and transfer of parts of qualification which would constitute a de facto modularisation. In this mechanism, individuals would have been able to conduct modules—in informal, non-formal or formal learning—in any member state or different member states, and have them recognised as a full qualification in any (other) member state. Policy documents such as Coles' report (2006) present credit systems in a way that certainly points towards a high degree of modularisation. However, the way the ECVET recommendation was designed in the end does not make modularisation mandatory and limits the use of "units" to a tool of mutual exchange in which national systems are left unaffected. Finally, Powell and Trampusch (2011: 306) come to the conclusion that "(...) the German case shows that the federal authorities and large employers can overcome the resistance of unions and craft Chambers". In their view, "the active role of the state facilitated the overcoming of resistance in Germany" (ibid, 307). My conclusion here is fundamentally different. I argue that while the government and large employers tried to use the Copenhagen process as a reform lever, they were successful only to a very small degree during the time frame of my analysis. This finding is in line with Busemeyer (2012) who concludes that changes initiated by the development and introduction of the German qualifications framework are very limited. In the Netherlands, EQF and ECVET did not change the system itself.

---

[4]In the early discussions on the impact of the Copenhagen process in Germany, several authors shared such a view; a possibly diverging impact of the two instruments EQF and ECVET has not often been distinguished. However, this discussion mostly took place before the respective recommendations were adopted in 2008 and 2009 (see Sect. 3.2).

[5]An exception is the debate on the referencing of the general qualification for university entrance; the decision has been postponed to 2017 and hence is off the agenda (see Chap. 3). This question is, however, not related to modularisation but to the relative weight of qualifications across different educational subsystems.

This different conclusion also has consequences for the assessment of soft law as a governance tool. Trampusch (2008: 605) concludes that in social and education policies, impacting the member states via European integration and European governance works without affecting the principle of sovereignty. As a consequence, in her view it is an open question of whether soft law can also constitute a more effective tool than regulation in other policy fields—especially since regulation can get entangled in court rulings exactly because it leaves less room for national interests (ibid). The results of this book, however, show that member states allow soft law to impact national systems only as much as they want it to.

Europe as a Liberalisation Machine?

What do these outcomes imply for the question of whether Europe is liberalising member states' institutions? First, my argument that the Copenhagen process is biased towards LMEs underlines the view developed in the political economy literature that the EU puts liberalisation pressure on member states. As such, it adds to the argument brought forward by Streeck (2009: 196) that the EU is a "liberalisation machine". While Streeck and Scharpf focus on the internal market, the four freedoms and austerity as drivers for liberalisation, I argue that the European level advances liberalisation in the mode of intergovernmental policies as soft law. I have shown that the Copenhagen process indeed has the potential to challenge fundamental pillars of national VET systems, especially for CMEs. Second, Höpner and Schäfer (2008a, b) argue that the Commission and the ECJ have proactively supported the liberalisation of member states towards a model of liberal market economies. In the case of VET, this is apparently also true for soft law policies which have been used as a liberalisation driver. The Commission and Cedefop seem to have actively promoted policies that are biased towards LMEs and proposed reforms that were more profoundly liberalising in their nature than those that were actually introduced in the end. Third, in contrast to Europeanisation related to the internal market, the nature of the Copenhagen process as soft law leaves member states scope for action rather than a clear-cut and definite route for change. In my case studies I found that member states used this scope of action by choosing ways to implement European policies in a way most congruent with existent national institutions, and in the case of ECVET in Germany the government and large firms actively used European proceedings as a reform lever on the national realm. Regarding the latter, both the active use of ECVET and the limited success of this manoeuvre can be traced back to the national sphere.

From my case studies, therefore an important hypothesis can be derived for education policies and welfare states in general. In these policy fields, the modus operandi—soft law intergovernmental processes—is similar. Moreover, education policies and welfare policies are closely connected, and education policies could even be regarded as a part of the welfare state. Welfare states are under pressure from European policies: the scope of action on the national level is increasingly reduced due to the internal market and austerity policies that lack counterbalancing with market-correcting positive integration on the European level. This book shows for the case of VET that the Commission advances market-making policies also in the areas of intergovernmental soft law via positive integration. My hypothesis is that the results of my work should also hold for education, social and labour market policies: If European policies of positive integration are market-making in nature also in these policy fields, member states can largely steer the intensity with which such impetus would change national institutions. They do so by influencing European policy making and by implementing European policies in a way most congruent with national systems. In this sense, welfare states may be challenged by (side-effects of) market-making economic policies rather than by policies of positive integration enacted in the respective policy fields, although these new modi operandi do put additional pressure on CMEs. In the case of VET, instead of heading towards a market-making flexible, "pick-and-choose" à la carte system, CMEs used European policies in a flexible manner: they chose what degree of transformation they want policies and instruments to have.

6.2.2 Varieties of Capitalism and the Study of Europeanisation

The Europeanisation literature studies the impact of the EU on member states. As such, it seems a natural first starting point when studying the impact of European VET policies on member states; this book, however, analyses the impact of EU VET policies against the background of the VoC framework. I argue that these two perspectives do not compete with each other. Rather, in my view they can complement and enrich one another.

Scholars of Europeanisation highlight the importance of domestic politics for the way EU policies are adapted and used. "Mediating factors" such as national institutions are seen as a precondition for an impact of EU policies on the national level, together with a "misfit" between the European and the domestic level (Börzel 2005). VoC, on the other hand, provides a comprehensive analytical framework for such mediating factors. Moreover, on the basis of the VoC framework it is possible to determine the extent of the "misfit" between European policies and national institutions. Since VoC provides a comprehensive framework for national systems, it is possible to relate European processes to these national systems. The misfit can then, in a second step, be classified according to the categories of CMEs and LMEs. For example, in this book I find that the Copenhagen process is biased towards a LME model of VET. With VoC, it is furthermore possible to deduct hypotheses on the direction and depth of change. For example, NQFs in Germany and in the Netherlands were implemented as a response to the Copenhagen process, but in a way most congruent with national education systems. It might be very well possible that such an analysis comes to different conclusions than analyses that only observe the European realm. This is because claims of national actors on the European level frequently can be seen as "bluff package debates"[6] (interview DE_PUBL-1). For example, national proceedings that develop independently from Europe are often sold to be European in nature.

At the same time, Europeanisation literature can remind VoC scholars that it is necessary to factor in behaviour of dutifulness of member states towards the EU when explaining the preferences of actors. For example, the Dutch government applied a "wait and see" approach to ECVET and undertakes minimum efforts to implement the instrument—but the government shows a certain level of activity because it feels an obligation to do so. In a similar vein, efforts to develop a NQF were undertaken only after a report showed that in comparison to other member states, the Netherlands were lagging behind. Such behaviour has been called "naming and shaming" in Europeanisation research. Van Ijsselmuiden (2009: 15), a government official, clearly remarks that although the European cooperation in VET is voluntary, "an agreement on a European notice or recommendation is, however, a political fact." At the same time, although member states might feel obligated to act in a certain way, it is necessary to analyse the depth of change, and here again VoC can be helpful since it is a framework that has a deep understanding of the working of national institutions.

By studying Europeanisation as a phenomenon of the impact of the EU on policy, polity and politics, Europeanisation research has identified several mechanisms for the way member states respond to pressures from the European level. I found examples in my case studies for several such mechanisms. The Copenhagen process, and more specifically ECVET, changed the opportunity structures in Germany and was used, albeit ultimately with little success, as a "reform lever" (Visser 2005). This phenomenon has been observed before (Erhel et al. 2005; Knill 2001; Visser 2005; see also Börzel 2005: 52). Moreover, against the background of understanding Europeanisation as a reciprocal process, the German government actively opposed policies that would be in conflict with fundamental pillars of the training regime. This refers to the automatic recognition of qualifications across countries as well as to the automatic accumulation of learning outcomes across countries ('Mr X'). Uploading took place extensively regarding the transfer of UK policies to the European level. In addition, quality assurance policies are partly inspired by Dutch instruments. Policy learning was observed to a smaller degree, for example regarding quality assurance mechanisms. Here, the Dutch government looked at best practices in other countries for very specific aspects, or regarding the referencing of qualifications to qualifications frameworks. When it came to referencing qualifications to qualifications frameworks, countries actively observed reference processes in other countries—partly with the idea to learn, and partly to gain arguments for their own preferences on referencing. However, it is not surprising that instances for policy learning can be found, since the Commission actively supports the exchange of best practices and mutual exchange, especially in the ENQAVET network on quality assurance and in the EQF advisory group.

---

[6]Original: "Mogelpackungsdebatten."

In VET policies, in practice the Commission continuously stresses that the development of NQFs are the best example for the effectiveness of its policies. With a growing literature on policy diffusion, one could easily argue that with the development and enactment of qualifications frameworks, European concepts found their way to member states. Similar arguments could be made for other instruments: for example, National Coordination Points could be seen as a sign for policy diffusion of ECVET, EQF and EQARF. However, on the basis of my case studies I argue that the Copenhagen process and its instruments—like many policies in the field of labour, social and education policies—are designed too broadly to come to such conclusions. It is therefore necessary to analyse the *intensity* and *direction* of change on the national systems in order to assess the *degree* of policy diffusion. Regarding the EQF, I found that the effect of qualifications frameworks in Germany and the Netherlands comes down to fostering the comparability of qualifications and the mutual understanding across different educational strands. As such, it influences the relative standing of the different educational strands, and it might help provide a first—albeit very rough—comparability of qualifications across Europe and within countries. These changes are firstly very small-scale and secondly, the objective of the European Commission to also steer changes of VET systems via the EQF has not been fulfilled. Hence, while EQFs were indeed enacted in a *direction* in accordance with EU instruments, the *intensity* of the change was low, so that within this broadly designed framework the *degree* of policy diffusion was small. In conclusion, for policies with a low degree of specificity and a high degree of scope of action on the member state level, policy diffusion can be verified only by relating it to the intensity and direction of change on the national level. The political economy literature in general and, more specifically the Varieties of Capitalism framework, can serve as a basis to conduct such analysis.

6.2.3 *Further Contributions to the Political Economy Literature*

From my case studies, several conclusions can be derived for the Political Economy literature. Most importantly, I have already laid out my argument and insights on the relationship between the EU and member states. I will now turn to discuss further conclusions that focus on theoretical aspects of the Varieties of Capitalism framework. This book can contribute to discussions related to two aspects: firstly the role, position, and preferences of firms and their organisations within advanced capitalisms, and secondly the typology that underlies the VoC framework, more specifically the question of the prevalence of systematic differences within the category of CMEs. These aspects are partly interrelated.

The diverging preferences of German firms on the modularisation of VET have already been analysed in the literature (Busemeyer 2009b; Busemeyer and Thelen

2011; Powell and Trampusch 2011; Thelen and Busemeyer 2008; Trampusch 2008, 2009, 2010b). Busemeyer and Thelen (2011) point out that the crafts sector opposes modularisation if it is related to shortening apprenticeships because of the sectors' cost benefit relation: in the third year of training, apprentices are already able to almost fully work as trained craftsmen, while still being paid the lower apprenticeship wage. My findings add that modularisation would actually reduce the flexibility they have as training providers. Even if modularisation is carried out within given skill profiles, it reduces the ability of firms to adjust training to their daily business routines in which they mostly integrate training in a flexible manner. In the current system there is a high degree of freedom regarding the point of time at which certain content is discussed or practiced. If the VET system would be modularised, firms would have to cover the training content of a given module within a limited time frame. While large firms often have distinctive training sites and can adjust their high quality training to such modules easily, in smaller firms, apprentices contribute to the production process. Therefore, while large firms and craft firms in Germany both support the flexibilisation of training, their preferences on how flexibility should be spelled out differs. Large firms aim at making training more firm-specific by partly flexibilising content and examinations, and craft firms aim at keeping skills industry-specific with highly standardised training content and examinations but with flexibility regarding the timing of covering specific training content.

Another interesting insight of this book is that preferences of firms regarding modularisation and flexibilisation of VET differ not only within countries as outlined above or across LMEs and CMEs, but also across CMEs. In the Netherlands, VET courses are available on four different levels and as school-based VET (with a high percent of training in companies taking the form of work placements) or dual apprenticeships. As a consequence, firms have more options to hire staff that fit their concrete skill needs on the intermediary level. Moreover, the distribution of costs between the state and firms is different than in Germany: Within the dominating school-based BOL track, firms offer work placements but costs are remarkably lower than for apprenticeships and expenses are coupled less to individual participants. VET participants also contribute more to financing their training. The state is seen to be responsible for initial training; schools organise work placements and examinations, with the participation of firms. My point is that these differences lead to different preferences on flexibility and modularisation. Before a shift towards competence-based learning took place, a unit-based system based on modularisation had been in place. In the current system, the MBO track is divided into four different levels, which makes VET more de-standardised than the German system. Both the modularised system and the differentiated level-structure are in conformity with firms' cost-benefit-relation to VET. The reason is that with BOL, firms can rely on an external labour market rather than being obligated to train themselves and invest in industry-specific skills. Diverging preferences on modularisation and flexibilisation across CMEs are therefore rooted in systematic differences on the system-level.

6.2 Theoretical Implications 221

Different VET institutions are also the reason why Germany and the Netherlands are challenged by the Copenhagen process to different degrees. In the Netherlands, the "misfit" to European policies is smaller:

- Although the Dutch system is no longer modularised in the sense of units, the qualification structure with its four MBO levels is more de-standardised than the German VET system.
- In Germany, it was widely feared that with the introduction of the EQF, more qualifications below the threshold of a "normal" 3 or 3½ year-apprenticeship would be introduced and that these might challenge the holistic approach to VET. In the Netherlands, the understanding of holistic VET qualifications is less bound to duration or course levels but only to a certain mix of skills. Such a system fits skills more closely to the differentiated needs of employers, whereas the German system still largely relies on unitary standardisation, although changes towards 2-year-apprenticeships have been introduced that point in a similar direction.
- The validation of non-formal and informal learning is easier to implement in the Netherlands than in Germany. Schools take over the responsibility for assessing to what extent prior learning can be accredited to their courses. Individuals do not have to search for an employer that recognises prior skills, since she can follow the BOL track to complete her education, and this decision is left to the schools. In a dual system, examinations are up to a Chambers' committee.
- In the Netherlands, schools are the most important providers of VET and are required to run quality assurance mechanisms; they also have to assure for the quality of workplace-based training. At the same time, when the importance of the state is combined with decentralisation, implementation of a European impetus can also become difficult. Schools are responsible for organising teaching content and would therefore be in charge for creating modules if a decision was made to implement modularisation. Yet, it is not a necessary prerequisite that state-based VET puts such an important focus on decentralisation.

In conclusion, changes leading to a de-standardisation of the qualifications structure might be easier to introduce in systems in which the state plays the major role, because this changes the cost-benefit ratio of firms as well as increases the size of the external labour market. The central role of schools facilitates the implementation of quality assurance and of procedures for the validation of non-formal and informal learning. In sum, my findings add to Anderson and Hassel's (2013) argument that across CME training regimes the role of the state is a systematic institutional difference.

6.2.4 Implications for Further Research

With small-N case study research as conducted in this book, it is always important to bear in mind that theoretical implications are tentative in nature. A first hypothesis has already been addressed above: An interesting avenue for further research is the question of whether positive integration is also used for market-making policies in other policy areas on the European level and if member states react to such a European impetus by a "pick and choose" approach when deciding on those instruments relevant for them and choosing what degree of transformation they want policies and instruments to have, as I claim in regard to European VET policies.

Regarding the selection of new empirical cases for the impact of market-making positive integration in VET, an interesting avenue might be to analyse member states with 'less developed' VET systems. The three countries analysed in my case studies have well-developed and long-established, albeit different VET systems. Is the picture similar for countries that are undertaking reforms to develop comprehensive VET systems in their countries for the first time? Has the Copenhagen process with its bias towards liberal market VET systems the potential to push such countries in the direction of a LME VET system? In more general terms, if the impact of liberalisation policies in soft law areas largely remains in the hands of member states with well-developed social democratic or conservative welfare states in the sense of Esping-Andersen's typology of welfare capitalisms, this is not to say how countries without such a historically-grown welfare state react to a European impetus. Here, an impetus focused on liberalisation might impact national institutions more. If that was the case, this again would have consequences on European integration in education and welfare policies, due to the shifting weights among different groups of welfare states and policy preferences. In order to approach such questions, it would be highly interesting to carry out case studies in Southern and Eastern European countries.

Another research gap is a complete and coherent analysis of European integration in VET with European policies and policy-making on the dependent variable. A comprehensive analysis would then need to consist of interviews with representatives from all member states, and would need to trace the process of European policy-making in as much detail as carried out here for the country cases. Such a study could address interesting questions: Are preferences of member states congruent with their national institutional set-up? How do states, firms, trade unions and other actors interact on the European level? Are firms' preferences solely dependent on the institutional set-up of national economies, or are there differences across sectors or firm sizes? Why do firms from some countries put more resources into shaping European policies than others? What are the preferences of large multinational companies and do they influence European policies?

My interview partners pointed to a few interesting insights of the mechanisms that the European Commission uses to deepen the integration without formally having influence. As a Dutch government official (interview NL_PUBL-4) remarks, the Commission has gained experience with tools for increasing European influence in a soft law policy field: first, the Commission mentions a topic in a meeting of director generals of higher education or VET policies who usually meet twice a year. In a formal meeting, the Commission then refers to this informal talk and argues that it has already discussed the topic. Subsequently, a broad conference is organised, followed by a Commission staff paper on the conclusions of the conference, then by a communication, which is subsequently distributed to various institutions such as the Education Committee and the Council of Ministers. The latter is not a legal obligation but a moral one. As a next step, monitoring procedures follow. Then national coordination points are founded which serve as a "bridge head" in the national sphere and national debates, as well as a point for providing the right data (ibid). Subsequently, the Commission aims at coupling funding to benchmarks. If there is resistance on the member states level, the Commission points out that they themselves agreed on the importance of the benchmarks, such as for example reducing early school leaving (interview DE_PUBL-2). The Commission occasionally speeds up the process and issues several papers in a short period of time, which challenges member states (interview DE_PUBL-1). Member states voice critique on the pace of the processes only in informal talks, in order not to be perceived as having anti-European sentiments or not working with the Commission (interview NL_PUBL-4). In sum, the steering role of the European Commission should not be underestimated which constitutes an important subject for political science scholars.

6.3 Implications for Policy Discussions

European VET policies ultimately have a twofold aim: firstly to contribute to the free movement of workers, and secondly, to contribute to make Europe "the most competitive and dynamic knowledge-based economy in the world" (European Council 2000). The Copenhagen process was launched in the light of Lisbon and after VET systems proved to be too diverse to achieve a closer cooperation and freedom of movement with previous strategies such as establishing equivalencies and recognition of qualifications (see Sect. 2.1).

My analysis suggests two points that are important for policy discussions. First, the instruments and principles developed within the realm of the Copenhagen process hardly seem to achieve the objectives the European Commission intended to steer. Regarding the objective to increase mobility, ECVET was made toothless by member states and its impact on mobility so far remains low. Although effects might appear over time, a significant effect seems unlikely. Qualifications frameworks will unfold medium to large scale changes in the national realm only in the long run, if at all. Since qualifications frameworks constitute a very rough grid, they help classifying qualifications—which advances mobility—only to a similarly rough degree. Regarding the objective to steer reforms on the member state level, an outcome of this study is that EQF and ECVET were implemented in a way most in conformity with the given systems. The validation of non-formal and informal learning and quality assurance mechanisms have not steered major changes, either. In addition, in practice validation procedures are not used widely in the countries where implemented prior to the Copenhagen process. On the plus side, while

ECVET in its current form might not serve as a standard for credits within VET and at the interface between VET and tertiary education, it might still become a standard for mobility experiences. With the implementation of NQFs, education systems are described partly[7] according to the same criteria across Europe and across educational strands so that it is easier to relate different qualifications to each other. At the same time, much effort was made to develop and implement the instruments at the European and the national level. Given the, arguably, small effects of the Copenhagen process on the three VET systems I studied, efficiency is low. Of course, this study observes a limited time frame, so that the Copenhagen process might serve as a basis for later developments.

Secondly, I found that the instruments and principles developed in the realm of the Copenhagen process are not neutral, technocratic instruments. On the contrary, they are biased towards policies prevalent in liberal market economies. Yet, In the light of the economic and financial crisis, it has been CME VET regimes that proved to be most resistant against the worrisome rise of youth unemployment. Diverging youth unemployment rates show that countries have been able to cope with the crisis to very different degrees. In Spain, youth unemployment rates rose to 53 % and in Greece to 52 % in 2014.[8] In the same year, the youth unemployment rate has been as high as 46 % in Croatia, 43 % in Italy, 36 % in Cyprus, and 35 % in Portugal. On the other hand, the youth unemployment rate was 7.7 % in Germany, 7.9 % in Norway, 10.3 % in Austria, and 12.6 % in Denmark. Countries in which VET policies are more detached from labour market demand and business needs—such as France (24 % youth unemployment rate in 2014), Sweden (22.9 %) or Belgium (23.2 %)—traditionally show higher youth unemployment rates, but in the crisis those remained relatively stable. Although general labour markets have also been affected differently by the crisis, this cannot explain the diverging success in keeping youth unemployment low since the correlation between unemployment and youth unemployment rates differ across countries. Rather, the different performances of countries can partially be traced back to their VET systems and complementary institutions. It is striking that those countries that managed to keep youth unemployment low all are examples for collective skill formation VET systems.[9] These countries performed best in keeping youth unemployment low (Fig. 6.1).

---

[7]Much of the referencing in practice took place according to input criteria rather than according to learning outcomes.

[8]All youth unemployment rates are taken from Eurostat, annual averages, age group below 25. See Annex III for an overview on youth unemployment rates in European countries from 2005 to 2015.

[9]The Norwegian VET system is more school-based and in this aspect, similar to the Dutch system, includes extensive phases of work-based training. In Norway, VET students first attend vocational schools for 2 years and subsequently enter an apprenticeship, which lasts another 2 years ("2+2 scheme"). Should not enough places be available in companies, schools arrange for alternative training in schools that leads to the same final examination. Intermediary associations play important roles and skills are portable as well as certified.

6.3 Implications for Policy Discussions

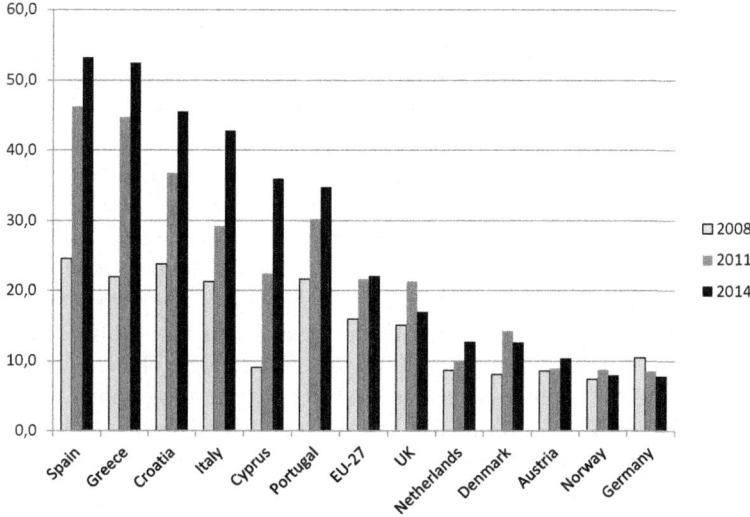

Fig. 6.1 Youth unemployment rates in selected countries in 2008, 2011, 2014. *Data source*: Eurostat; unemployment rate, annual average, age group below 25

The diverging performance of VET systems has been noted on the EU level. A German government official reports:

> "If you look at the Bruges Communiqué, the dual principle has basically been completely copied. (...) The other countries gladly transfer it because the economic and financial crisis has shown (...): these strange Germans with their crude, out-dated system have achieved a youth unemployment of 7, 8 per cent, with excellent transitions into the labour markets. (...) We carry the national debate out differently; way too many young people are in the "transition system" (...). And that was the reason why they [the Commission, C.A.] held umpteen emergency summits during the economic crisis (...) in education policy. (...) What they looked at was, how do states manage to stay strong in the economic crisis, and that was the case with us, (...) and how do they manage to keep young people in the process, in employment (...) as well as in education and training?" (Interview DE-PUBL-1).[10]

---

[10] Original: "Wenn Sie sich die Brügge-Erklärung angucken, da wird im Grunde genommen das duale Prinzip abgeschrieben von A bis Z. (...) Die anderen haben das gerne übernommen, weil die Wirtschafts- und Finanzkrise gezeigt hat: Spanien 46 Prozent Jugendarbeitslosigkeit, Griechenland über 40, Frankreich über 20, UK inzwischen über 20 – diese komischen Deutschen da mit ihrem kruden, alten System, die schaffen die Jugendarbeitslosigkeit von 7, 8 Prozent, hervorragende Übergänge in den Arbeitsmarkt. (...) National führen wir die Debatte wieder anders; im Übergangssystem viel zu viele junge Leute (...). Sie müssen das wirklich wenn Sie Europäisch diskutieren von der Metawarte aus betrachten, und die Megatrends vergleichen. Und das war der Grund, warum sie in der Wirtschaftskrise – die hatten zig Notgipfel (...) in der Bildungspolitik. (...) Worauf die geguckt haben: Wie schaffen das Staaten, in der Wirtschaftskrise erstens stark zu bleiben, und das war bei uns ja der Fall (...), und wir schaffen das, die Jugendlichen im Prozess zu halten, sowohl in der Beschäftigung (...) wie auch in der Ausbildung."

Indeed, a shift in priorities in VET on the EU level towards industry-specific skills is noticeable in several ways. Since the beginning of the economic and financial crisis, references to the dual system and work-based learning can be found in all new EU documents (interview DE_PRIV-3). The Bruges Communiqué (European Ministers for Vocational Education and Training et al. 2010) establishes priorities for VET for the next decade. The strategic objectives for 2011–2020 include the promotion of work-based learning in enterprises and of cooperation between schools and enterprises, fostering networks to increase the match between labour market needs, the development of skills, and the development of "apprenticeship-type" training (strategic objectives 1e, 1f). It is stated that "work-based learning carried out in partnership with businesses and non-profit organisations should become a feature of all initial VET courses" (strategic objective 1e). All this is clearly inspired by the dual system. In new EU programmes, apprenticeships are always named a priority. Additionally, studies on apprenticeships and work-based learning are commissioned and best practices are highlighted. A Compact for Growth and Jobs was launched in June 2012 with a budget of 120 billion euros by the European Council; one of the objectives was to fight youth unemployment. The Commission is expected to spend an additional 7.3 billion euros on projects to fight youth unemployment (BMBF 2012b). The budget of the structural funds that had not been used was reallocated to measures for SMEs and youth unemployment. As a new approach to tackle youth unemployment, the Youth Guarantee has been launched. The objective is that all young people under the age of 25 receive an offer for education or training within 4 months of leaving education or after becoming unemployed. The European Employment Initiative, which is interlinked with the Youth Guarantee, provides a funding of 6.4 billion euros for the period 2014–2020 to regions with high youth unemplyoment rates. The European Alliance for Apprenticeships has the objective to improve the quality and quantity of apprenticeships across the EU on the basis of stakeholder partnerships.

Bilateral policy learning from CME VET systems is also taking place, and is partly supported by the European Commission. Belgian, Dutch, British, Swedish and Hungarian delegations have undertaken peer learning activities in Germany (BMBF 2013). Several countries—among them Spain, Italy and Greece—signed bilateral cooperation agreements with Germany that include consultancy on VET systems, exchange of experts, study visits, and pilot projects that are developed together with business (ibid). In December 2012, Germany, Spain, Greece, Portugal, Italy, Slovakia and Latvia signed a memorandum on VET that includes measures for introducing a VET system along the lines of the German dual system. This process was supported by the European Commission and Cedefop. A German-Spanish conference on VET took place in July 2012; ministers of both countries agreed to intensify the cooperation in VET in order to increase the number of apprenticeships in Spain (BMBF 2012b). While in the past other countries often had been highly sceptical of the dual system, with the crisis this perception changed (interview DE_PUBL-1). Interview partners clearly link this to the smaller effects of the crisis on youth unemployment in dual systems (interview DE_PUBL-1; DE_PRIV-3; DE_UN-1).

As a result of this shift, EU policies may move slightly closer towards collective skill formation regimes until 2020. Such a development per se would not contradict the Copenhagen process. I have argued that although the process is biased towards LME VET systems, instruments and principles are designed in a way that leaves enough scope to CMEs to implement in a way consistent with their VET systems. Moreover, while efforts have been made to strengthen and transfer dual VET systems, such initiatives do not yet come close to the efforts made with the Copenhagen process. However, it is not only the lower degree of effort invested in transferring CME VET systems that might complicate such endeavours: such initiatives are likely to remain superficial if they do not take into account that apprenticeship systems are rooted deeply in the political economy (see Streeck 2011: 323).

Policy Options Revisited: Towards a New Approach to European VET Policies?
European VET policies face several problems. First, I have shown that doubts prevail regarding the effectiveness and efficiency of its instruments and principles. Second, while EU VET policies are biased towards those policies prevalent in LMEs, in the recent economic and financial crisis CMEs have performed best in keeping youth unemployment low. It is quite ironic that several of the original proposals stemming from the European level actually might have had serious consequences on the functioning of CME VET systems. Third, transferring dual VET to other countries faces serious obstacles because of the complex functioning of such systems.

Option 1: Transferring CME VET Systems as a Best Practice
A policy alternative to the Copenhagen process could therefore be to share best practices of CME training. Herewith, the focus should be not only on Germany but in general on CME VET regimes that have low youth unemployment rates. There is a certain divergence across CME VET systems, and each system is characterised by specific advantages and disadvantages. For example, while in Germany youth unemployment even decreased during the crisis, there is still a noticeable share of outsiders to training. VET systems as the Dutch or the Norwegian ones can accommodate better for this group as well as have mechanisms for accommodating de-industrialisation and economic cycles.

Yet, no matter what the specific design of CME VET systems, political economy scholars are sceptical of attempts to transfer such systems to countries which have different sets of institutions. As Streeck (2011) points out, over decades the United States and UK put much effort in overcoming the "low-skill equilibrium" (Finegold and Soskice 1988) with the German apprenticeship system as a model in mind. As Streeck (2011: 323) puts it, "It soon turned out, however, that the transplantation across national borders of an institution reaching as deep into the fabrics of the political economy as a collective skill formation system was a utopian project, its efficient operation being far too dependent on complementary institutions of, for example, labour market regulation and workplace interest representation, and generally on a sympathetic political, institutional, and cultural context."

The obstacles to such a project became clear during my research in England. Recently, the British government and business again directed much attention to the advantages of a German-type "dual VET system". The Failure of Training in Britain (Finegold and Soskice 1988) is still discussed today[11] and gained momentum again with diverging performances of European economies against the background of the economic and financial crisis. While the government steers debates on the topic, the English strategy remains half-hearted, with recent proposals and reforms being unlikely to suffice to achieve a policy change towards an apprenticeships system in the direction of a "dual system". On the one hand, this is because of the institutional context—such as employment regulation, financial markets, the way firms recruit personnel, the way jobs and authority structures are designed (see Finegold and Soskice 1988), the differing status and role of corporatist actors or the low skill strategies of British firms as a consequence of the low-skills VET system (Kohlrausch 2009: 67). On the other hand, recent initiatives are insufficient to transfer dual VET to England because the VET system lacks essential aspects of the dual system not tackled by recent reforms. This refers to questions such as the standardisation of qualifications, portability and certification, inclusion of social partners in the development of qualifications, and achieving a substantial involvement of employers above a certain threshold so that the risk of poaching is reduced. Recent reforms do not address these issues. As a consequence, the focus is on apprenticeships, but the way they are implemented differs tremendously from their role models. Against the background of the empirical research of this work, the most likely explanation seems to be the employers' organisations' resistance against overcoming strategies focused solely on immediate needs towards a collective system. The reasons for such resistance can be found in production strategies aligned to the given low skill equilibrium as well as in the lack of knowledge—in the sense that such strategies are outside of firms' and employers' organisations mind-set—but also in the history of social dialogue. The government facilitates this perspective by focusing on fulfilling immediate business needs. In sum, this excursus demonstrates the difficulties related to transferring VET systems. The obstacles to such an approach as a European policy are obvious.

Option 2: European Occupational Profiles

Against this background, the development of European occupational profiles seems a more promising policy approach. The basic idea is that demands on skills and knowledge of a certain profession differ less across countries than VET systems (Becker et al. 2007). Becker et al. (2007) propose a model of competence development which would make it possible to describe competences on different levels. On this basis, it is possible to develop a matrix of competences for each occupation. In a project financed by the European Commission as well as the Austrian and German federal ministries, such a matrix for the occupation of a mechatronics specialist was developed based on tasks that have to be fulfiled in practical work

---

[11] See Kohlrausch (2009) for a more comprehensive analysis on the debate. She points out that there is a general agreement on the low performance of the British VET system.

6.3 Implications for Policy Discussions

(ibid). On the basis of such matrices, it would be possible to develop common European occupational profiles. If such occupational profiles would include broader and/or general skills, their introduction would make EU VET policies more biased towards CME VET systems. Such approaches are in line with demands from the Industrial Union of Metalworkers (IG Metall 2007). In their view, European integration in VET should be based on core occupations which would combine a broad knowledge base with varying elements of more specific competences.

Such approaches are supported by empirical analysis undertaken by Brockmann et al. (2010). Carrying out an in-depth analysis of bricklaying qualifications in different European countries, they conclude that differences on the macro-level are reflected in the design of the qualifications across different countries. For example, while in Germany the bricklaying qualification is based on a broad and holistic understanding of an occupation, in the UK it refers to a rather narrow qualification. "The most basic common element is that in all eight countries the qualification requires the holder to be able to lay bricks. Beyond this, it is difficult to identify completely common elements in all eight countries, only different groups (...)" (Brockmann et al. 2010: 23). Among the eight countries that they studied—including the three cases of this work—England is an outlayer because of several points: the narrowness of the qualification, a weak knowledge base, the lacking inclusion of general or civic education, limited devotion to self management and project management, and a low acceptance on the labour market (ibid). Not surprisingly, they highlight the importance of institutions for cooperation on the European level: "(...) those countries with social partnership governance of bricklaying VET together with relatively stable firms and training institutions at the point of delivery should find it easiest to cooperate and to develop practices of mutual trust" (ibid, 23). As a consequence, it is questionable if European occupational profiles could be created across the whole European Union, since not all countries have these institutions. If carried out as positive integration in a voluntary form of intergovernmental cooperation, the approach would still be viable. Brockmann et al. conclude that for many countries, it should be possible to establish mutual trust of each other's qualifications.

As this analysis shows, creating European policies based on policies prevalent in CME VET systems is hampered by the deep rootedness of VET policies in the institutions of the national economies as well as by the manifold difficulties LMEs would face if they aimed at creating a VET system based on cooperation. It is a fundamental dilemma for supporters of a "more social Europe" that the positive integration of the welfare state required for such a project is so much more difficult to pursue than market-making negative integration. Yet, since cooperation is voluntary, creating European occupational profiles might be a viable option in the direction of a "two speed Europe" or as a module-based variant of occupational profiles.

Appendix

Annex I: The European Qualifications Framework

	Knowledge	Skills	Competence
	In the context of EQF, knowledge is described as theoretical and/or factual.	In the context of EQF, skills are described as cognitive (involving the use of logical, intuitive and creative thinking) and practical (involving manual dexterity and the use of methods, materials, tools and instruments).	In the context of EQF, competence is described in terms of responsibility and autonomy.
Level 1			
The learning outcomes relevant to Level 1 are	basic general knowledge	basic skills required to carry out simple tasks	work or study under direct supervision in a structured context
Level 2			
The learning outcomes relevant to Level 2 are	basic factual knowledge of a field of work or study	basic cognitive and practical skills required to use relevant information in order to carry out tasks and to solve routine problems using simple rules and tools	work or study under supervision with some autonomy

(continued)

	Knowledge	Skills	Competence
Level 3			
The learning outcomes relevant to Level 3 are	knowledge of facts, principles, processes and general concepts, in a field of work or study	a range of cognitive and practical skills required to accomplish tasks and solve problems by selecting and applying basic methods, tools, materials and information	take responsibility for completion of tasks in work or study
			adapt own behaviour to circumstances in solving problems
Level 4			
The learning outcomes relevant to Level 4 are	factual and theoretical knowledge in broad contexts within a field of work or study	a range of cognitive and practical skills required to generate solutions to specific problems in a field of work or study	exercise self-management within the guidelines of work or study contexts that are usually predictable, but are subject to change
			supervise the routine work of others, taking some responsibility for the evaluation and improvement of work or study activities
Level 5[a]			
The learning outcomes relevant to Level 5 are	comprehensive, specialised, factual and theoretical knowledge within a field of work or study and an awareness of the boundaries of that knowledge	a comprehensive range of cognitive and practical skills required to develop creative solutions to abstract problems	exercise management and supervision in contexts of work or study activities where there is unpredictable change
			review and develop performance of self and others
Level 6[b]			
The learning outcomes relevant to Level 6 are	advanced knowledge of a field of work or study, involving a critical understanding of theories and principles	advanced skills, demonstrating mastery and innovation, required to solve complex and unpredictable problems in a specialised field of work or study	manage complex technical or professional activities or projects, taking responsibility for decision-making in unpredictable work or study contexts
			take responsibility for managing professional development of individuals and groups

(continued)

	Knowledge	Skills	Competence
Level 7[c]			
The learning outcomes relevant to Level 7 are	highly specialised knowledge, some of which is at the forefront of knowledge in a field of work or study, as the basis for original thinking *and/or research*	specialised problem-solving skills required in research and/or innovation in order to develop new knowledge and procedures and to integrate knowledge from different fields	manage and transform work or study contexts that are complex, unpredictable and require new strategic approaches
	critical awareness of knowledge issues in a field and at the interface between different fields		take responsibility for contributing to professional knowledge and practice and/or for reviewing the strategic performance of teams
Level 8[d]			
The learning outcomes relevant to Level 8 are	knowledge at the most advanced frontier of a field of work or study and at the interface between fields	the most advanced and specialised skills and techniques, including synthesis and evaluation, required to solve critical problems in research and/or innovation and to extend and redefine existing knowledge or professional practice	demonstrate substantial authority, innovation, autonomy, scholarly and professional integrity and sustained commitment to the development of new ideas or processes at the forefront of work or study contexts including research

Compatibility with the Framework for Qualifications of the European Higher Education Area
The Framework for Qualifications of the European Higher Education Area provides descriptors for cycles
Each cycle descriptor offers a generic statement of typical expectations of achievements and abilities associated with qualifications that represent the end of that cycle
[a]The descriptor for the higher education short cycle (within or linked to the first cycle), developed by the Joint Quality Initiative as part of the Bologna process, corresponds to the learning outcomes for EQF level 5
[b]The descriptor for the first cycle in the Framework for Qualifications of the European Higher Education Area *agreed by the ministers responsible for higher education at their meeting in Bergen in May 2005 in the framework of the Bologna process* corresponds to the learning outcomes for EQF level 6
[c]The descriptor for the second cycle in the Framework for Qualifications of the European Higher Education Area *agreed by the ministers responsible for higher education at their meeting in Bergen in May 2005 in the framework of the Bologna process* corresponds to the learning outcomes for EQF level 7
[d]The descriptor for the third cycle in the Framework for Qualifications of the European Higher Education Area *agreed by the ministers responsible for higher education at their meeting in Bergen in May 2005 in the framework of the Bologna process* corresponds to the learning outcomes for EQF level 8

Annex II: The European Quality Assurance Reference Framework

European quality assurance reference framework: quality criteria

Quality criteria	Indicative descriptors at VET-system level	Indicative descriptors at VET-provider level
Planning reflects a strategic vision shared by the relevant stakeholders and includes explicit goals/objectives, actions and indicators	• Goals/objectives of VET are described for the medium and long terms, and linked to European goals • The relevant stakeholders participate in setting VET goals and objectives at the different levels • Targets are established and monitored through specific indicators (success criteria) • Mechanisms and procedures have been established to identify training needs • An information policy has been devised to ensure optimum disclosure of quality results/outcomes subject to national/regional data protection requirements • Standards and guidelines for recognition, validation and certification of competences of individuals have been defined	• European, national and regional VET policy goals/objectives are reflected in the local targets set by the VET providers • Explicit goals/objectives and targets are set and monitored • Ongoing consultation with relevant stakeholders takes place to identify specific local/individual needs • Responsibilities in quality management and development have been explicitly allocated • There is an early involvement of staff in planning, including with regard to quality development • Providers plan cooperative initiatives with other VET providers • The relevant stakeholders participate in the process of analysing local needs VET providers have an explicit and transparent quality assurance system in place
Implementation plans are devised in consultation with stakeholders and include explicit principles	• Implementation plans are established in cooperation with social partners, VET providers and other relevant stakeholders at the different levels • Implementation plans include consideration of the resources required, the capacity of the users and the tools and guidelines needed for support • Guidelines and standards have been devised for implementation at different levels Implementation plans include	• Resources are appropriately internally aligned/assigned with a view to achieving the targets set in the implementation plans • Relevant and inclusive partnerships are explicitly supported to implement the actions planned • The strategic plan for staff competence development specifies the need for training for teachers and trainers • Staff undertake regular training and develop cooperation with relevant external

(continued)

Quality criteria	Indicative descriptors at VET-system level	Indicative descriptors at VET-provider level
	specific support towards the training of teachers and trainers • VET providers' responsibilities in the implementation process are explicitly described and made transparent • A national and/or regional quality assurance framework has been devised and includes guidelines and quality standards at VET-provider level to promote continuous improvement and self-regulation	stakeholders to support capacity building and quality improvement, and to enhance performance
Evaluation of outcomes and processes is regularly carried out and supported by measurement	• A methodology for evaluation has been devised, covering internal and external evaluation • Stakeholder involvement in the monitoring and evaluation process is agreed and clearly described • The national/regional standards and processes for improving and assuring quality are relevant and proportionate to the needs of the sector • Systems are subject to self-evaluation, internal and external review, as appropriate • Early warning systems are implemented • Performance indicators are applied • Relevant, regular and coherent data collection takes place, in order to measure success and identify areas for improvement. Appropriate data collection methodologies have been devised, e.g. questionnaires and indicators/metrics	• Self-assessment/self-evaluation is periodically carried out under national and regional regulations/frameworks or at the initiative of VET providers • Evaluation and review covers processes and results/outcomes of education including the assessment of learner satisfaction as well as staff performance and satisfaction • Evaluation and review includes adequate and effective mechanisms to involve internal and external stakeholders • Early warning systems are implemented
Review	• Procedures, mechanisms and instruments for undertaking reviews are defined at all levels	• Learners' feedback is gathered on their individual learning experience and on the learning and teaching

(continued)

Quality criteria	Indicative descriptors at VET-system level	Indicative descriptors at VET-provider level
	• Processes are regularly reviewed and action plans for change devised. Systems are adjusted accordingly Information on the outcomes of evaluation is made publicly available	environment. Together with teachers' feedback this is used to inform further actions Information on the outcomes of the review is widely and publicly available • Procedures on feedback and review are part of a strategic learning process in the organisation • Results/outcomes of the evaluation process are discussed with relevant stakeholders and appropriate action plans are put in place

European quality assurance reference framework: indicators

Indicator	Type of indicator	Purpose of the policy
No 1		
Relevance of quality assurance systems for VET providers: (a) share of VET providers applying internal quality assurance systems defined by law/at own initiative (b) share of accredited VET providers	Context/input indicator	• Promote a quality improvement culture at VET-provider level • Increase the transparency of quality of training • Improve mutual trust on training provision
No 2		
Investment in training of teachers and trainers: (a) share of teachers and trainers participating in further training (b) amount of funds invested	Input/process indicator	• Promote ownership of teachers and trainers in the process of quality development in VET • Improve the responsiveness of VET to changing demands of labour market • Increase individual learning capacity building Improve learners' achievement
No 3		
Participation rate in VET programmes: Number of participants in VET programmes,[a] according to the type of programme and the individual criteria[b]	Input/process/output indicator	• Obtain basic information at VET-system and VET-provider levels on the attractiveness of VET • Target support to increase access to VET, including for disadvantaged groups

(continued)

Indicator	Type of indicator	Purpose of the policy
No 4		
Completion rate in VET programmes: Number of persons having successfully completed/abandoned VET programmes, according to the type of programme and the individual criteria	Process/output/outcome indicator	• Obtain basic information on educational achievements and the quality of training processes • Calculate drop-out rates compared to participation rate • Support successful completion as one of the main objectives for quality in VET • Support adapted training provision, including for disadvantaged groups
No 5		
Placement rate in VET programmes: (a) destination of VET learners at a designated point in time after completion of training, according to the type of programme and the individual criteria[c] (b) share of employed learners at a designated point in time after completion of training, according to the type of programme and the individual criteria	Outcome indicator	• Support employability • Improve responsiveness of VET to the changing demands in the labour market • Support adapted training provision, including for disadvantaged groups
No 6		
Utilisation of acquired skills at the workplace: (a) information on occupation obtained by individuals after completion of training, according to type of training and individual criteria (b) satisfaction rate of individuals and employers with acquired skills/competences	Outcome indicator (mix of qualitative and quantitative data)	• Increase employability • Improve responsiveness of VET to changing demands in the labour market • Support adapted training provision, including for disadvantaged groups
No 7		
Unemployment rate[d] according to individual criteria	Context indicator	• Background information for policy decision-making at VET-system level
No 8		
Prevalence of vulnerable groups: (a) percentage of participants in VET classified as disadvantaged groups (in a defined region or catchment area) according to age and gender	Context indicator	• Background information for policy decision-making at VET-system level • Support access to VET for disadvantaged groups

(continued)

Indicator	Type of indicator	Purpose of the policy
(b) success rate of disadvantaged groups according to age and gender		• Support adapted training provision for disadvantaged groups
No 9		
Mechanisms to identify training needs in the labour market: (a) information on mechanisms set up to identify changing demands at different levels (b) evidence of their effectiveness	Context/input indicator (qualitative information)	• Improve responsiveness of VET to changing demands in the labour market • Support employability
No 10		
Schemes used to promote better access to VET: (a) information on existing schemes at different levels (b) evidence of their effectiveness	Process indicator (qualitative information)	• Promote access to VET, including for disadvantaged groups • Support adapted training provision

[a]For IVT: a period of 6 weeks of training is needed before a learner is counted as a participant. For lifelong learning: percentage of population admitted to formal VET programmes
[b]Besides basic information on gender and age, other social criteria might be applied, e.g. early school leavers, highest educational achievement, migrants, persons with disabilities, length of unemployment
[c]For IVT: including information on the destination of learners who have dropped out
[d]Definition according to ILO and OECD: individuals aged 15–74 without work, actively seeking employment and ready to start work

Annex III: Youth Unemployment Rates in European Countries

	2005	2006	2007	2008	2009	2010	2011	2012	2013	2014	2015
Austria	11.0	9.8	9.4	8.5	10.7	9.5	8.9	9.4	9.7	10.3	*
Belgium	21.5	20.5	18.8	18.0	21.9	22.4	18.7	19.8	23.7	23.2	21.2
Bulgaria	21.0	18.3	14.1	11.9	15.1	21.8	25.0	28.1	28.4	23.8	21.5
Croatia	31.9	28.8	25.2	23.7	25.2	32.4	36.7	42.1	50.0	45.5	44.6
Cyprus	13.9	10.0	10.2	9.0	13.8	16.6	22.4	27.7	38.9	35.9	33.2
Czeck Republic	19.3	17.5	10.7	9.9	16.6	18.3	18.1	19.5	18.9	15.9	12.6
Denmark	8.6	7.7	7.5	8.0	11.8	13.9	14.2	14.1	13.0	12.6	10.5
Estonia	15.1	12.1	10.1	12.0	27.4	32.9	22.4	20.9	18.7	15.0	*
Finland	20.1	18.7	16.5	16.5	21.5	21.4	20.1	19.0	19.9	20.5	22.4
France	21.0	22.0	19.5	19.0	23.6	23.3	22.6	24.4	24.8	24.1	25.1
Germany	15.4	13.6	11.8	10.4	11.1	9.8	8.5	8.0	7.8	7.7	7.3

(continued)

	2005	2006	2007	2008	2009	2010	2011	2012	2013	2014	2015
Greece	25.8	25.0	22.7	21.9	25.7	33.0	44.7	55.3	58.3	52.4	*
Hungary	19.4	19.1	18.1	19.5	26.4	26.4	26.0	28.2	26.6	20.4	*
Ireland	8.6	8.7	9.1	13.3	24.0	27.6	29.1	30.4	26.8	23.9	20.6
Italy	24.1	21.8	20.4	21.2	25.3	27.9	29.2	35.3	40.0	42.7	*
Latvia	15.1	13.6	10.6	13.6	33.3	36.2	31.2	28.5	23.2	19.6	*
Lithuania	15.8	10.0	8.4	13.3	29.6	35.7	32.6	26.7	21.9	19.3	16.6
Luxembourg	14.6	15.5	15.6	17.3	16.5	15.8	16.4	18.0	16.9	21.2	14.0
Malta	16.1	15.5	13.5	11.7	14.5	13.2	13.3	14.1	13.0	11.8	12.1
The Netherlands	11.8	10.0	9.4	8.6	10.2	11.1	10.0	11.7	13.2	12.7	11.3
Poland	36.9	29.8	21.6	17.2	20.6	23.7	25.8	26.5	27.3	23.9	20.9
Portugal	20.8	21.2	21.4	21.6	25.3	28.2	30.2	38.0	38.1	34.7	32.0
Rumania	19.1	20.2	19.3	17.6	20.0	22.1	23.9	22.6	23.7	24.0	21.4
Slovakia	30.4	27.0	20.6	19.3	27.6	33.9	33.7	34.0	33.7	29.7	26.4
Slovenia	15.9	13.9	10.1	10.4	13.6	14.7	15.7	20.6	21.6	20.2	15.7
Spain	19.6	17.9	18.1	24.5	37.7	41.5	46.2	52.9	55.5	53.2	48.3
Sweden	22.6	21.5	19.2	20.2	25.0	24.8	22.8	23.7	23.6	22.9	20.4
United Kingdom	12.8	13.9	14.3	15.0	19.1	19.9	21.3	21.2	20.7	16.9	*
EU-27	18.9	17.6	15.8	15.9	20.2	21.3	21.6	23.1	23.6	22.0	20.2
Norway	11.4	8.8	7.2	7.3	9.2	9.2	8.7	8.6	9.1	7.9	*

Asterisk indicates no data available yet for 2015. *Source*: Eurostat. Annual Average, age group below 2

Bibliography

Advies commissie Boekhoud (2001) Doorstroomagenda beroepsonderwijs. MOCW, Den Haag

Advies R, Hagens K, Van den Hout T, Kraaijvanger H (2007) OECD thematic review on recognition of non-formal and informal learning. Background report for the Netherlands. Final report, 24 Feb 2007

Aff J (2005) Berufliche Bildung in Vollzeitschulen – konjunkturabhängige Hebamme des dualen Systems oder eigenständige bildungspolitische Option? In: Eckert M, Zöller A (eds) Der europäische Berufsbildungsraum – Beiträge der Berufsbildungsforschung. Bundesinstitut für Berufsbildung, Bonn, pp 125–138

AK DQR (Arbeitskreis Deutscher Qualifikationsrahmen) (2012) Einbeziehung nicht-formal und informell erworbener Kompetenzen in den DQR, Stellungnahme des AK DQR zu den Empfehlungen der Arbeitsgruppen vom 22.11.2011

Allen D (2005) The United Kingdom: a *Europeanized* government in a *non*-Europeanized polity. In: Bulmer S, Lequesne C (eds) The member States of the European Union. Oxford University Press, Oxford, pp 119–141

Anderson J (2003) Europeanization in context: concept and theory. In: Dyson K, Goetz KH (eds) Germany, Europe and the politics of constraint. Oxford University Press, New York, NY, pp 37–53

Anderson K, Hassel A (2013) Pathways of change in CMEs. Training regimes in Germany and the Netherlands. In: Wren A (ed) The political economy of the service transition. Oxford University Press, Oxford, pp 171–194

Anderson K, Oude Nijhuis D (2011) The comparative political economy of collective skill formation. In: Busemeyer M, Trampusch C (eds) The comparative political economy of collective skill systems. Oxford University Press, Oxford, pp 101–125

Angelova M, Dannwolf T, König T (2012) How robust are compliance findings? A research synthesis. J Eur Publ Policy 19(8):1269–1291

Ante C (2008) The German vocational education and training system in a European perspective: addressing challenges with a higher proportion of school-based learning? Master thesis, Hertie School of Governance

Ante C (2009) Von den Nachbarn lernen und die Berufsausbildung in Deutschland modernisieren. Friedrich-Ebert-Stiftung, Bonn

Ante C (2010) Auswirkungen des Strukturwandels und der demografischen Entwicklung auf die Berufsausbildung in Mecklenburg-Vorpommern und abzuleitende Handlungsspielräume für die Landespolitik. Friedrich-Ebert-Stiftung, Schwerin

Arbeitsgruppen zur Einbeziehung nicht-formal und informell erworbener Kompetenzen in den DQR (2011) Empfehlungen der Arbeitsgruppen zur Einbeziehung nicht-formal und informell erworbener Kompetenzen in den DQR – abgestimmt zwischen den beiden Vorsitzenden, 22.11.2011. http://www.deutscherqualifikationsrahmen.de/de?t=/documentManager/sfdoc. file.supply&fileID=1348521739557. Retrieved 29 Dec 2009

Ata M (2011) Abitur soll mehr wert sein als Ausbildung. http://www.sueddeutsche.de/karriere/streit-um-abschluesse-abitur-soll-mehr-wert-sein-als-ausbildung-1.1166149. Retrieved 10 Oct 2012

Autorengruppe Bildungsberichterstattung (2008) Bildung in Deutschland 2008. Ein indikatorengestützter Bericht mit einer Analyse zu Übergängen im Anschluss an den Sekundarbereich I. W. Bertelsmann, Bielefeld

Autorengruppe Bildungsberichterstattung (2010) Bildung in Deutschland 2010. Ein indikatorengestützter Bericht mit einer Analyse zu Perspektiven des Bildungswesens im demografischen Wandel. W. Bertelsmann, Bielefeld

Baethge M (2006) Das deutsche Bildungs-Schisma: Welche Probleme ein vorindustrielles Bildungssystem in einer nachindustriellen Gesellschaft hat. SOFI-Miteilungen 34:13–27

Baethge M, Achtenhagen F, Arends L (2008) How to compare the performance of VET systems in skill formation. In: Mayer K, Solga H (eds) Skill formation. Interdisciplinary and cross-national perspectives. Cambridge University Press, Cambridge, pp 230–254

Baethge M, Solga H, Wieck M (2007) Berufsbildung im Umbruch. Signale eines überfälligen Aufbruchs. Friedrich-Ebert-Foundation, Berlin

Banse P (2012) Abi und Gesellenprüfung - gleichwertig? http://www.dradio.de/dlf/sendungen/campus/1665686/. Retrieved 10 Oct 2012

Baron S (2007) Das duale System der Berufsausbildung unter dem Einfluss der europäischen Berufsbildungspolitik. Entwicklungsprozesse und Herausforderungen. http://duepublico.uni-duisburg-essen.de/servlets/DocumentServlet?id=17021. Retrieved 17 Oct 2013

BDA (Bundesvereinigung der Arbeitgeber) (2007) Neue Strukturen in der dualen Ausbildung: Beschluss des BDA-Ausschusses Bildung/Berufliche Bildung und des BDA-Arbeitskreises Berufliche Bildung. Bundesvereinigung der Deutschen Arbeitgeberverbände, Berlin

Becker G (1964) Human capital. A theoretical and empirical analysis, with special reference to education. Columbia University Press, New York, NY

Becker M, Spöttl G (2006) Transfer von Ausbildungsleistungen in Europa. ECVET-Modelle und Lösungsansätze aus dem Leonardo-Projekt VQTS. In: Loebe H, Severing E (eds) Europäisierung der Ausbildung. Ergebnisse einer Fachtagung des Forschungsinstituts Betriebliche Bildung und des Zentrums für Ausbildungsmanagement Bayern. Bertelsmann, Bielefeld, pp 117–132

Becker M, Luomi-Messerer K, Markowitsch J, Spöttl G (2007) Berufliche Kompetenzen sichtbar machen. Arbeitsprozessbezogene Beschreibung von Kompetenzentwicklungen als Betirag zur ECVET-Problematik. BWP 3:17–21

Beicht U, Walden G (2004) Kosten-Nutzen-Relationen in der betrieblichen Berufsausbildung. In: Krekel E, Walden G (eds) Zukunft der Berufsausbildung in Deutschland: Empirische Untersuchungen und Schlussfolgerungen. Ergebnisse der BIBB-Fachtagung am 4./5. November 2003 in Bonn. Bundesinstitut für Berufsbildung, Bonn, pp 34–52

Berger K (2004) Öffentliche und betriebliche Aufwendungen zur Finanzierung beruflicher Ausbildung im Zeitraum 1980–2002. Datenlage, Analyse und Schlussfolgerungen. Bundesinstitut für Berufsbildung, Bonn

Berger K, Walden G (2002) Außerbetrieblich und doch "betriebsnah" – Zwischenbilanz und Perspektiven der Bund-Länder-Ausbildungsplatzprogramme Ost. BWP 4:17–21

BIBB (Bundesinstitut für Berufsbildung) (2009) Datenreport zum Berufsbildungsbericht 2011. Informationen und Analysen zur Entwicklung der beruflichen Bildung. BIBB, Bonn

BIBB (Bundesinstitut für Berufsbildung) (2011a) Empfehlung des Hauptausschusses des Bundesinstituts für Berufsbildung (BIBB) zum weiteren Vorgehen bei der Erarbeitung des Deutschen Qualifikationsrahmens (DQR). BIBB, Bonn, 16 Feb 2011

BIBB (Bundesinstitut für Berufsbildung) (2011b) FuE-Projekte des Bundesinstituts für Berufsbildung im Bereich ECVET - DECVET. Information für die Mitglieder der Hauptausschuss-AG DQR/DECVET. BIBB, Bonn, 11 Mar 2011

BIBB (Bundesinstitut für Berufsbildung) (2012a) Datenreport zum Berufsbildungsbericht 2012. Informationen und Analysen zur Entwicklung der beruflichen Bildung. BIBB, Bonn

BIBB (Bundesinstitut für Berufsbildung) (2012b) Ausbildungsbetriebsquote. http://www.bibb.de/dokumente/pdf/ausbildungsbetriebsquote_d_1999-2010.pdf. Retrieved 20 Sept 2012

BIBB (Bundesinstitut für Berufsbildung) (2012c) Erste Erfahrungen mit ECVET, dem Europäischen Kreditpunktesystem in der beruflichen Bildung. http://www.good-practice.de/strukturen_beitrag4654.php. Retrieved 27 Mar 2012

BIBB (Bundesinstitut für Berufsbildung) (2012d) Stellungnahme. Öffentliches Fachgespräch zum Thema „Grenzüberschreitende Kooperation im Bereich der Berufsbildung". A-Drs. 17(18) 304a. 17 Oct 2012. Deutscher Bundestag, Ausschuss für Bildung, Forschung und Technikfolgenabschätzung, Berlin

BIBB-Hauptausschuss (2007) Ausbildung für Altbewerber über Ausbildungsbausteine – Gemeinsame Position der Beauftragten der Arbeitgeber, Arbeitnehmer und der Länder des Hauptausschusses des Bundesinstituts für Berufsbildung zur Pilotinitiative des Bundesministeriums für Bildung und Forschung (BMBF). 13 June 2007

Bieber T (2010) Europe à la Carte? Swiss convergence towards European policy models in higher education and vocational education and training. Swiss Polit Sci Rev 16(4):773–800

Biemans H, Nieuwenhuis L, Poell R, Mulder M, Wesselink R (2004) Competence-based VET in the Netherlands: background and pitfalls. Bwp@ Berufs- und Wirtschaftspädagogik – online, Ausgabe 7, 1–14

BIS (Department for Business Innovation and Skills) (2010) Skills for sustainable growth. Strategy document. http://www.bis.gov.uk/assets/BISCore/further-education-skills/docs/S/10-1274-skills-for-sustainable-growth-strategy.pdf. Retrieved 7 Mar 2013

BITKOM, Gesamtmetall, VDMA and ZVEI (2007) Die Anforderungen des Beschäftigungssystems: Ein Beitrag zur Gestaltung des Deutschen Qualifikationsrahmens. BITKOM, Gesamtmetall, VDMA, ZVEI, Berlin

Bjornavold J, Coles M (2007) Governing education and training: the case of qualifications frameworks. Eur J Vocat Training 42/43:203–235

Blavoukos S, Oikonomou G (2012) Is 'Europeanization' still in academic fashion? Empirical trends in the period 2002–2011. Comparing and contrasting "Europeanization": concepts and experiences, Athens, 14–16 May 2012

BLK (Bund-Länder-Kommission für Bildungsplanung und Forschungsförderung) (2004) Strategie für Lebenslanges Lernen in der Bundesrepublik Deutschland. BLK, Bonn

Blyth M (2009) An approach to comparative analysis or a subfield within a subfield? Political economy. In: Lichbach M, Zuckerman A (eds) Comparative politics. Rationality, culture and structure. Cambridge University Press, Cambridge, pp 193–219

BMBF (Bundesministerium für Bildung und Forschung) (1999) Berufsbildungsbericht 1999. BMBF, Bonn

BMBF (Bundesministerium für Bildung und Forschung) (2007) Berufsbildungsbericht 2007. BMBF, Bonn

BMBF (Bundesministerium für Bildung und Forschung) (2010) Berufsbildungsbericht 2010. BMBF, Bonn

BMBF (Bundesministerium für Bildung und Forschung) (2011) Berufsbildungsbericht 2011. BMBF, Bonn

BMBF (Bundesministerium für Bildung und Forschung) (2012a) Berufsbildungsbericht 2012. BMBF, Bonn

BMBF (Bundesministerium für Bildung und Forschung) (2012b) Internationale Berufsbildungskooperation: Erfolgreicher Export von Bildungsangeboten. http://www.bmbf.de/de/17127.php. Retrieved 12 July 2012

BMBF (Bundesministerium für Bildung und Forschung) (2012c) Forum 2: Lernergebnisorientierung der Ordnungsmittel. Dritte Fachtagung „Der Deutsche Qualifikationsrahmen für lebenslanges Lernen", Berlin, 11 Sept 2012

BMBF (Bundesministerium für Bildung und Forschung) (2013) Berufsbildungsbericht 2013. BMBF, Bonn
BMBF (Bundesministerium für Bildung und Forschung), KMK (Kultusministerkonferenz) (2007) Deutsche Stellungnahme zu einem Europäischen Leistungspunktesystem für die berufliche Bildung (ECVET). http://ec.europa.eu/education/ecvet/results_en.html. Retrieved 5 Oct 2012
BMBF (Bundesministerium für Bildung und Forschung), KMK (Kultusministerkonferenz) (2009) Gemeinsamer Bericht des BMBF und der KMK. Beitrag zur Zwischenberichterstattung 2010 im Rahmen des Arbeitsprogramms der EU-Bildungsminister „Allgemeine und berufliche Bildung 2010", 5 June 2009
BMBF (Bundesministerium für Bildung und Forschung), KMK (Kultusministerkonferenz) (2012) Sachstandsbericht. Erarbeitung eines Deutschen Qualifkationsrahmens (DQR), June 2012
Böhm M (2012) Kultusminister finden Abi wertvoller als Lehre. Retrieved 10 Oct 2012, from http://www.spiegel.de/schulspiegel/abi/bildungsabschluessekultusminister-finden-abi-wertvoller-als-lehre-a-793288.html
Born V (2012) Outcome-orientierte Gestaltung der Ordnungsmittel: Das Beispiel der beruflichen Bildung. Dritte Fachtagung „Der Deutsche Qualifikationsrahmen für lebenslanges Lernen", Berlin, 11 Sept 2012
Börzel T (2005) How the European Union interacts with its member states. In: Bulmer S, Lequesne C (eds) The member states of the European Union. Oxford University Press, Oxford, pp 45–69
Börzel T, Risse T (2011) From Europeanisation to diffusion: introduction. West Eur Politics 35(1):1–19
Brandsma J (2006) Gestaltung dynamischer Berufsbildungs-Curricula. Der Fall Niederlande. In: Grollmann P, Kruse W, Rauner F (eds) Europäisierung Beruflicher Bildung. Eine Gestaltungsaufgabe. LIT Verlag, Münster, pp 95–114
British Chambers of Commerce (2012) Exporting is good for Britain and exporters need. http://www.britishchambers.org.uk/assets/downloads/policy_reports_2012/12-04-05%20FACTSHEET%20-Trade%20SKILLS%20%28KM%29.PDF. Retrieved 14 Mar 2013
Brockmann M, Clarke L, Méhaut P, Winch C (2008) Competence-based vocational education and training (VET): the cases of England and France in a European perspective. Vocat Learn 1(3):227–244
Brockmann M, Clarke L, Winch C (eds) (2010) Bricklaying is more than Flemish bond. Bricklaying qualifications in Europe. European Institute for Construction Labour Research, Brussels
Brunner S, Esser H, Kloas P-W, Witt D (2005) Berufliche Bildung für Europa: Modell für einen europäischen und nationalen Qualifikationsrahmen. BWP 3:45–48
Bundesministerium für Bildung und Forschung (BMBF) (2014) Die Pilotinitiative DECVET. Retrieved 5 Oct 2014, from http://www.bmbf.de/de/15504.php
Büchs M (2007) New governance in European social policy. The open method of coordination. Palgrave Macmillan, Houndmills, Basingstoke
Büchs M (2008) The open method of coordination as a 'two-level game'. Policy Politics 36(1):21–37
Bulmer S (2007) Theorizing Europeanization. In: Graziano P, Vink M (eds) Europeanization: new research agendas. Palgrave Macmillan, Houndmills, Basingstoke, pp 46–58
Bulmer S, Lequesne C (2005) The EU and its member states: an overview. In: Bulmer S, Lequesne C (eds) The member states of the European Union. Oxford University Press, Oxford, pp 1–20
Busemeyer M (2009a) Asset specificity, institutional complementarities and the variety of skill regimes in coordinated market economies. Socio-Econ Rev 7(3):375–406
Busemeyer M (2009b) Die Europäisierung der deutschen Berufsbildungspolitik. Sachzwang oder Interessenpolitik? Friedrich-Ebert-Stiftung, Bonn
Busemeyer M (2012) Reformperspektiven der berufichen Bildung. Erkenntnisse aus dem internationalen Vergleich. Friedrich Ebert Stiftung, Bonn
Busemeyer M, Thelen K (2011) Institutional change in German vocational training: from collectivism towards segmentalism. In: Busemeyer M, Trampusch C (eds) The comparative political economy of collective skill formation. Oxford University Press, Oxford, pp 68–100

Busemeyer M, Trampusch C (2011a) Review article: Comparative political science and the study of education. Br J Polit Sci 41(2):413–443

Busemeyer M, Trampusch C (2011b) The comparative political economy of collective skill formation. In: Busemeyer M, Trampusch C (eds) The comparative political economy of collective skill systems. Oxford University Press, Oxford, pp 3–38

BWP (2007) „Bildung verbindet". Interview mit der Bundesministerin für Bildung und Forschung, Dr. Annette Schavan, MdB. BWP 3:5–6

Cabinet Office (N.N.) Public bodies 2009. http://www.civilservice.gov.uk/wp-content/uploads/2011/09/PublicBodies2009_tcm6-35808.pdf. Retrieved 16 Mar 2013

Campbell J, Pedersen O (2007) The varieties of capitalism and hybrid success: Denmark in the global economy. Comp Polit Stud 40(3):307–332

CBI (Confederation of British Industry) (2011a) Action for jobs. How to get the UK working. CBI, London

CBI (Confederation of British Industry) (2011b) Building for growth: business priorities for education and skills. Education and skills survey 2011. CBI, London

Cedefop (2009) European guidelines for validating non-formal and informal learning. Publications Office of the European Union, Luxembourg

Cedefop (2010a) A bridge to the future. European policy for vocational education and training 2002–2010. Publications Office of the Europen Union, Luxembourg

Cedefop (2010b) The development of national qualifications frameworks in Europe. Publications Office of the European Union, Luxembourg

Cedefop Refernet (ed) (2011) United Kingdom. Country report. http://libserver.cedefop.europa.eu/vetelib/2011/2011_CR_UK.pdf. Retrieved 6 Mar 2013

Chalmers D, Lodge M (2003) The open method of co-ordination and the European welfare state. Discussion Paper No. 11. ESRC Centre for Analysis of Risk and Regulation, London School of Economics and Political Science, London, June 2003

Coles M (2006) A review of international and national developments in the use of qualifications frameworks. ETF. http://www.etf.europa.eu/pubmgmt.nsf/%28getAttachment%29/4B4A9080175821D1C12571540054B4AF/$File/SCAO6NYL38.pdf. Retrieved 14 July 2011

Coles M (2007) Qualifications frameworks in Europe: platforms for collaboration, integration and reform. Making the European Learning Area a Reality, Munich, 3–5 June 2007

Colo (2008) Prepared for the future. Dutch qualifications for the labour market. Colo, Zoetermeer

Colo (2011) Workplacement companies NL. Colo, Zoetermeer

Council of the European Communities (1976) Resolution of the Council and of the Ministers of Education, meeting within the Council of 9 February 1976, comprising an action programme in the field of education. OJ C 038, 9 Feb 1976

Council of the European Communities (1977) Council Directive 77/452/EEC of 27 June 1977 concerning the mutual recognition of diplomas, certificates and other evidence of the formal qualifications of nurses responsible for general care, including measures to facilitate the effective exercise of this right of establishment and freedom to provide services. 77/452/EEC

Council of the European Communities (1980) Council Directive 80/154/EEC of 21 January 1980 concerning the mutual recognition of diplomas, certificates and other evidence of formal qualifications in midwifery and including measures to facilitate the effective exercise of the right of establishment and freedom to provide services. 80/154/EEC

Council of the European Communities (1985a) Council Decision of 16 July 1985 on the comparability of vocational training qualifications between the Member States of the European Community. 85/368/EEC

Council of the European Communities (1985b) Consolidated version of Council Directive 85/433/ECC of 16 September 1985 concerning the mutual recognition of diplomas, certificates and other evidence of formal qualifications in pharmacy, including measures to facilitate the effective exercise of the right of establishment relating to certain activities in the field of pharmacy. 85/433/ECC

Council of the European Communities (1989) Council Directive 89/48/EEC of 21 December 1988 on a general system for the recognition of higher education diplomas awarded on completion of professional education and training of at least three years' duration. 89/48/EEC

Council of the European Communities (1992) Council Directive 92/51/EEC of 18 June 1992 on a second general system for the recognition of professional education and training to supplement Directive 89/48. 92/51/EEC

Council of the European Economic Communities (1963) Council Decision of 2 April 1963 laying down general principles for implementing a common vocational training policy. 63/266/EC

Council of the European Union (2002a) Council Resolution of 19 December 2002 on the promotion of enhanced European cooperation in vocational education and training. 2003/C 13/02

Council of the European Union (2002b) Detailed work programme on the follow-up of the objectives of education and training systems in Europe.

Council of the European Union (2004a) Draft Council Conclusions on quality assurance in vocational education and training. 9599/04, 18 May 2004

Council of the European Union (2004b). Draft Conclusions of the Council and of the representatives of the Governments of the Member States meeting within the Council on Common European Principles for the identification and validation of non-formal and informal learning. 9600/04 EDUC 118 SOC 253, 18 May 2004

Council of the European Union and European Commission (2004) Education & Training 2010. The success of the Lisbon strategy hinges on urgent reforms. Joint interim report of the Council and the Commission on the implementation of the detailed work programme on the follow-up of the objectives of education and training systems in Europe. 2004/C 104/01, 30 Apr 2004

Crouch C (2005) Capitalist diversity and change. Recombinant governance and institutional entrepreneurs. Oxford University Press, Oxford

Crouch C, Finegold D et al (1999) Are skills the answer? The political economy of skill creation in advanced industrial countries. Oxford University Press, Oxford

Cuddy N, Ward C (2010) A bridge to the future. European policy for vocational education and training 2002–10. National policy report – United Kingdom. http://libserver.cedefop.europa.eu/vetelib/2010/vetpolicy/2010_NPR_UK.pdf. Retrieved 21 Mar 2013

Culpepper P (1999a) Introduction: Still a model for the industrialized countries? In: Culpepper P, Finegold D (eds) The German skills machine: sustaining comparative advantage in a global economy. Berghahn Books, Oxford, pp 1–34

Culpepper P (1999b) The future of the high-skill equilibrium in Germany. Oxf Rev Econ Policy 15 (1):43–59

Culpepper P (2003) Creating cooperation. How states develop human capital in Europe. Cornell University Press, Ithaca, NY

Culpepper P (2007) Small states and skill specificity. Austria, Switzerland, and interemployer cleavages in coordinated capitalism. Comp Polit Stud 40(6):611–637

Culpepper P, Thelen K (2008) Institutions and collective actors in the provision of training: historical and cross-national comparisons. In: Mayer K, Solga H (eds) Skill formation: interdisciplinary and cross-national perspectives. Cambridge University Press, New York, NY, pp 21–49

De la Porte C, Pochet P (2002) Building social Europe through the open method of coordination. Peter Lang, Brussels

Dehnbostel P, Neß H, Overwien B (2009) Der Deutsche Qualifikationsrahmen (DQR) – Positionen, Reflexionen und Optionen. Gutachten im Auftrag der Max-Traeger-Stiftung. Gewerkschaft Erziehung und Wissenschaft, Frankfurt

Deissinger T, Heine R, Ott M (2011) The dominance of apprenticeships in the German VET system and its implications for Europeanisation: a comparative view in the context of the EQF and the European LLL strategy. J Vocat Educ Training 63(3):397–416

DEQA-VET (2010) Deutsche Referenzstelle für Qualitätssicherung in der beruflichen Bildung. DEQA-VET Flyer

Detmar B, de Vries I (2009) Beroepspraktijkvorming in het MBO. Ervaringen van leerbedrijven. Dijk 12, Amsterdam

Deutscher Bundestag (2006) Antrag CDU Fraktion, SPD Fraktion. Weiterentwicklung der europäischen Berufsbildungspolitik. Drucksache 16/2996

Deutscher Bundestag (2007) Beschlussempfehlung und Bericht des Ausschusses für Bildung, Forschung und Technikfolgenabschätzung (18. Ausschuss). Drucksache 16/5760

Deutscher Bundestag (2008) Antwort der Bundesregierung auf die Kleine Anfrage der Abgeordneten Cornelia Hirsch, Dr. Lothar Bisky, Volker Schneider (Saarbrücken), Dr. Petra Sitte und der Fraktion DIE LINKE. – Drucksache 16/9232. Drucksache 16/9514

Deutscher Bundestag (2009) Antrag CDU Fraktion, SPD Fraktion. Gestaltung des Deutschen Qualifikationsrahmens. Drucksache 16/13615

Deutscher Bundestag (2010a) Wortprotokoll 19. Sitzung. Öffentliche Anhörung zum Thema „Europäischer Qualifikationsrahmen/Deutscher Qualifikationsrahmen". Protokoll 17/19. Deutscher Bundestag, Ausschuss für Bildung, Forschung und Technikfolgenabschätzung, Berlin

Deutscher Bundestag (2010b) Stärkung der Qualität und Zukunftsfähigkeit der dualen Berufsausbildung. Antwort der Bundesregierung. Drucksache 17/3563. Deutscher Bundestag, Ausschuss für Bildung, Forschung und Technikfolgenabschätzung, Berlin

Deutscher Bundestag (2011) Antrag SPD Fraktion. Gleichwertigkeit von Berufsbildung und Abitur sichern. Drucksache 17/7957

Deutscher Bundestag (2012) Stenografischer Bericht. 155. Sitzung. Plenarprotokoll 17/155

Deutscher Bundesverband für Logopädie (2012) Pressemitteilung: Deutscher Qualifikationsrahmen (DQR): Deutscher Bundesverband für Logopädie mahnt angemessene Einstufung der Logopäden an. Deutscher Bundesverband für Logopädie. http://www.dbl-ev.de/index.php?id=1507&tx_ttnews[tt_news]=2559&cHash=1e51f81e41. Retrieved 10 Oct 2012

Deutscher Hochschulverband (2010) Zur Einführung eines Deutschen Qualifikationsrahmens für lebenslanges Lernen. http://www.hochschulverband.de/cms1/778.html. Retrieved 11 Apr 2014

Dewe B, Weber P (2007) Wissensgesellschaft und Lebenslanges Lernen. Eine Einführung in bildungspolitische Konzeptionen der EU. Julius Klinkhardt, Bad Heilbrunn

DGB (Deutscher Gewerkschaftsbund) (2005) Stellungnahme des Deutschen Gewerkschaftsbundes (DGB) zum Konsultationsdokument „Der Europäische Qualifikationsrahmen – Ein Transparenz-Instrument zur Förderung von Mobilität und Durchlässigkeit". DGB, Berlin, 6 Dec 2005

DGB (Deutscher Gewerkschaftsbund) (2007) Stellungnahme des Deutschen Gewerkschaftsbundes (DGB) zum Arbeitsdokument der Kommissionsdienststellen „Das europäische Leistungspunktesystem für die Berufsbildung (ECVET) – Ein europäisches System für die Übertragung, Akkumulierung und Anerkennung von Lernleistungen im Bereich der Berufsbildung". DGB, Berlin, 26 Feb 2007

DGB (Deutscher Gewerkschaftsbund) (2008) Deutscher Qualifikationsrahmen. Vorschlag des Deutschen Gewerkschaftsbundes. DGB, Berlin, 21 Apr 2008

DGB (Deutscher Gewerkschaftsbund) (2010) Stellungnahme. Öffentliche Anhörung „Europäischer Qualifikationsrahmen/Deutscher Qualifikationsrahmen (EQR/DQR)". A-Drs. 17(18)83g. 7/7/10. Deutscher Bundestag, Berlin

DGB (Deutscher Gewerkschaftsbund) (2011) Der Deutsche Qualifikationsrahmen (DQR). Chancen und Risiken aus gewerkschaftlicher Sicht. DGB, Berlin, Feb 2011

DGB (Deutscher Gewerkschaftsbund) (2012) Ausbildungsreport 2012. DGB, Berlin, Sept 2012

DIHK (Deutscher Industrie- und Handelskammertag) (2007) „Dual mit Wahl": Ein Modell der IHK-Organisation zur Reform der betrieblichen Ausbildung. DIHK, Berlin

DIHK (Deutscher Industrie- und Handeslkammertag) (2010) Ausbildung 2010. Ergebnisse einer DIHK- Unternehmensbefragung. http://www.dihk.de/inhalt/download/ausbildungsumfrage_10.pdf. Retrieved 5 June 2010

Dilger B, Sloane P (2012) Kompetenzorientierung in der Berufsschule. Handlungskompetenz in den Versionen der Handreichungen der KMK zur Entwicklung lernfeldorientierter Lehrpläne. BWP 4:32–35

Drexel I (2005) Das Duale System und Europa. Ein Gutachten im Auftrag von Ver.di und IG Metall. ver.di/IG Metall, Berlin/Frankfurt

Dustmann C, Schoenberg U (2008) Why does the German apprenticeship system work? In: Mayer K, Solga H (eds) Skill formation. Interdisciplinary and cross-national perspectives. Cambridge University Press, Cambridge, pp 85–108

Duvekot R (2010) European inventory on validation of non-formal and informal learning 2010. Country report: Netherlands. http://libserver.cedefop.europa.eu/vetelib/2011/77473.pdf. Retrieved 25 Jan 2013

EACEA (Education Audiovisual & Culture Executive Agency) (2009) Organisation of the education system in the Netherlands 2008/2009. http://eacea.ec.europa.eu/education/eurydice/documents/eurybase/eurybase_full_reports/nl_en.pdf. Retrieved 25 Jan 2013

Ebner C, Nikolai R (2010) Duale oder schulische Berufsausbildung? Entwicklungen und Weichenstellungen in Deutschland, Österreich und der Schweiz. Swiss Polit Sci Rev 16 (4):617–648

ENQA-VET (European Network for Quality Assurance in Vocational Education and Training) (2008) Report of the peer learning activity on the role of social partners in quality procedures in VET. Berlin, 7–9 Oct 2008

Erhel C, Mandin L, Palier B (2005) The leverage effect. The open method of co-ordination in France. In: Zeitlin J, Pochet P, Magnusson L (eds) The open method of coordination in action: the European employment and social inclusion strategies. Peter Lang, Brussels, pp 217–224

Ertl H (2002) The role of EU programmes and approaches to modularisation in vocational education: fragmentation or integration? Herbert Utz Verlag, München

Ertl H (2006) European Union policies in education and training: the Lisbon agenda as a turning point? Comp Educ 42(1):5–27

Esser F (2012) Die Umsetzung des Deutschen Qualifikationsrahmens. Hintergrund, Sachstand und anstehende Aufgaben. BWP 3:47–51

Esser F, Kloas P-W, Witt D (2005) Überlegungen für die Konstruktion eines integrierten NQF-ECVET-Modells. Papier der Abteilung Berufliche Bildung des Zentralverbands des Deutschen Handwerks

Estevez-Abe M, Iversen T, Soskice D (2001) Social protection and the formation of skills: a reinterpretation of the welfare state. In: Hall P, Soskice D (eds) Varieties of capitalism. The institutional foundations of comparative advantage. Oxford University Press, Oxford, pp 145–183

Euler D (1998) Modernisierung des dualen Systems. Problembereiche, Reformvorschläge, Konsens- und Dissenslinien. Bund-Länder-Kommission für Bildungsplanung und Forschungsförderung, Bonn

Euler D (2006) Qualitätsentwicklung in der Berufsausbildung. In: Zöller A (ed) Vollzeitschulische Berufsausbildung – eine gleichwertige Partnerin des dualen Systems? W. Bertelsmann Verlag, Bielefeld, pp 48–75

Euler D, Severing E (2006) Flexible Ausbildungswege in der Berufsbildung. Ziele, Modelle, Maßnahmen. Bertelsmann, Bielefeld

European Commission (1989) Education and training in the European Community. Guidelines for the medium term: 1989–1992. Communication from the Commission to the Council. COM (89)236 final, 2 June 1989

European Commission (1991) Commission memorandum on vocational training in the European Community in the 1990s. COM(91) 397 final

European Commission (1993a) Green paper on the European dimension of education. COM (93) 457 final

European Commission (1993b) White paper on growth, competitiveness and employment. The challenges and ways forward into the 21st century. COM(93) 700

European Commission (1995) Teaching and learning. Towards the learning society. White paper on education and training. COM(95) 590 final
European Commission (2000) A memorandum on lifelong learning. Commission Staff Working Paper. SEC(2000) 1832
European Commission (2001a) Report from the Commission. The concrete future objectives of Education Systems. COM(2001) 59
European Commission (2001b) Making a European area of lifelong learning a reality. Communication from the Commission. COM(2001) 678 final
European Commission (2002) Education and training in Europe: diverse systems, shared goals for 2010. The work programme on the future objectives of education and training systems. Office for the Publications of the European Communities, Luxembourg
European Commission (2004) The new generation of Community education and training programmes after 2006. Communication from the Commission. COM(2004) 156 final
European Commission (2006a) European Credit System for Vocational Education and Training (ECVET). A system for the transfer, accumulation and recognition of learning outcomes in Europe. Commission staff working document. SEC(2006) 1431
European Commission (2006b) Progress towards the Lisbon objectives in education and training. Report based on indicators and benchmarks. Report 2006. Commission staff working document. COM(2006) 639. 16 May 2006
European Commission (2010) Communication from the Commission to the European Parliament, the Council, the European Economic and Social Committee and the Committee of the Regions. A new impetus for European cooperation in Vocational Education and Training to support the Europe 2020 strategy. COM(2010) 296 final
European Commission (2012) Proposal for a Council Recommendation on the validation of non-formal and informal learning. COM(2012) 485 final
European Council (2000) Presidency conclusions. Lisbon European Council, 23 and 24 March
European Council (2002) Presidency conclusions. Barcelona European Council, 15 and 16 March 2002
European Ministers for Vocational Education and Training, European Social Partners and European Commission (2010) The Bruges Communiqué on enhanced European Cooperation in Vocational Education and Training for the period 2011–2020
European Parliament and the Council (2004) Decision on a single Community framework for the transparency of qualifications and competences (Europass). 2241/2004/EC
European Parliament and the Council (2005) Directive 2005/36/EC of the European Parliament and of the Council of 7 September 2005 on the recognition of professional qualifications. 2005/36/EC
European Parliament and the Council (2008) Recommendation of the European Parliament and of the Council of 23 April 2008 on the establishment of the European Qualifications Framework for lifelong learning. 2008/C 111/01
European Parliament and the Council (2009a) Recommendation of the European Parliament and of the Council of 18 June 2009 on the establishment of a European Quality Assurance Reference Framework for Vocational Education and Training. 2009/C 155/01
European Parliament and the Council (2009b) Recommendation of the European Parliament and of the Council of 18 June 2009 on the establishment of a European Credit System for Vocational Education and Training (ECVET). 2009/C 155/02
Fahle K, Thiele P (2003) Der Brügge-Kopenhagen-Prozess – Beginn der Umsetzung der Ziele von Lissabon in der beruflichen Bildung. BWP 4:9–12
Falkner G (2007) Social policy. In: Graziano P, Vink M (eds) Europeanization: new research agendas. Palgrave Macmillan, Houndmills, Basingstoke, pp 253–265
Falkner G, Hartlapp M, Treib O (2007) Worlds of compliance: why leading approaches to European implementation are only "sometimes-true theories". Eur J Polit Res 64(3):395–476
Falkner G, Treib O (2008) Three worlds of compliance or four? The EU-15 compared to new member states. JCMS 46(2):293–313

Falkner G, Treib O, Hartlapp M, Leiber S (2005) Complying with Europe. EU harmonisation and soft law in the member states. Cambridge University Press, Cambridge

Feller G (1999) Ausbildung an Berufsfachschulen – Ein differenziertes und flexibles Qualifiakationssystem. In: Kaiser F-J (ed) Berufliche Bildung in Deutschland für das 21. Jahrhundert. Beiträge zur Berufsbildungsforschung der AG BFN Nr 4. Bundesanstalt für Arbeit, Nürnberg, pp 439–450

Finegold D (1999) The future of the German skill-creation system. Conclusions and policy options. In: Culpepper P, Finegold D (eds) The German skills machine: sustaining comparative advantage in a global economy. Berghahn Books, New York, NY, pp 403–430

Finegold D, Soskice D (1988) The failure of training in Britain: analysis and perscription. Oxf Rev Econ Policy 4(3):21–53

Fioretos O (2001) The domestic sources of multilateral preferences: varieties of capitalism in the European community. In: Hall P, Soskice D (eds) Varieties of capitalism: the institutional foundations of comparative advantage. Oxford University Press, Oxford, pp 213–244

Frank I (2012a) Lernergebnisorientierung in Ordnungsmitteln – Stand und Herausforderungen. Dritte Fachtagung „Der Deutsche Qualifikationsrahmen für lebenslanges Lernen", Berlin, 11 Sept 2012

Frank I (2012b) Start frei für die kompetenzorientierte Gestaltung der Ordnungsmittel? Konsequenzen des DQR für die Ordnungsarbeit. BWP 4:49–52

Frank I, Gutschow K, Münchhausen G (2003) Vom Meistern des Lebens – Dokumentation und Anerkennung informell erworbener Kompetenzen. Grundsätzliche Überlegungen und internationale Beispiele. BWP 4:16–20

Frank I, Hensge K (2007) Ausbildungsbausteine – ein Königsweg für Strukturreformen in der Berufsbildung? BWP 2:40–44

Franz W, Soskice D (1995) The German apprenticeship system. In: Butler F, Franz W, Schettkat R, Soskice D (eds) Institutional frameworks and labor market performance. Comparative views on the U.S. and German economies. Routledge, London, pp 208–334

Freitag W (2012) Creditsysteme, Qualifikationsrahmen und Anrechnung. Reflexion auf Basis der wissenschaftlichen Begleitung der BMBF-Initiative „Anrechnung beruflicher Kompetenzen auf Hochschulstudiengänge" (ANKOM). Dritte Fachtagung „Der Deutsche Qualifikationsrahmen für lebenslanges Lernen", Berlin, 11 Sept 2012

Früh M (2010) Qualitätssicherung in der beruflichen Bildung. Master thesis, Helmut Schmidt Universität

Gans S (2013) Revised: Associate-degree programme attracts mainly MBO graduates. CBS. http://www.cbs.nl/en-GB/menu/themas/onderwijs/publicaties/artikelen/archief/2013/2013-3763-her.htm. Retrieved 30 Jan 2013

Gehmlich V (2009) Die Einführung eines Nationalen Qualifikationsrahmens in Deutschland (DQR) – Untersuchung der Möglichkeiten für den Bereich des formalen Lernens. W. Bertelsmann, Bielefeld

Gehmlich V (2012) Forum 3: Leistungspunktesysteme und andere transparenz- und mobilitätsfördernde Instrumente. Fragestellungen. Dritte Fachtagung „Der Deutsche Qualifikationsrahmen für lebenslanges Lernen", Berlin, 11 Sept 2012

Geldermann B, Seidel S, Severing E (2009) Rahmenbedingungen zur Anerkennung informell erworbener Kompetenzen. W. Bertelsmann, Bielefeld

George A, Bennett A (2005) Case studies and theory development in the social sciences. MIT Press, Cambridge, MA

Gericke N, Krupp T, Troltsch K (2009) Unbesetzte Ausbildungsplätze – warum Betriebe erfolglos bleiben. Ergebnisse des BIBB-Ausbildungsmonitors. BIBB Report Nr. 10/2009

Glocke J (2006) Der europäische Qualifikationsrahmen – Positionen und Perspektiven. In: Loebe H, Severing E (eds) Europäisierung der Ausbildung. Ergebnisse einer Fachtagung des Forschungsinstituts Betriebliche Bildung und des Zentrums für Ausbildungsmanagement Bayern. Bertelsmann, Bielefeld, pp 103–116

Gonon P (2004) Allgmeinbildung und Berufsbildung zwischen curricularer und systematischer Differenzierung und Integration – das Beispiel der schweizerischen Berufsmatur. In: Lechner E, Pöggeler F (eds) Allgemeinbildung und Berufsbildung. Konkurrenz und Kongruenz der Konzepte im Europa des 20. Jahrhunderts. Peter Lang, Frankfurt a.M., pp 79–100

Gordon J (1999) Approaches to transparency of vocational qualifications in the EU. Eur J Educ 34 (2):203–217

Government of the United Kingdom (2007) UK response to a proposed European Credit System for Vocational Education and Training. http://ec.europa.eu/education/ecvt/results/uk_en.pdf. Retrieved 23 Mar 2013

Graf L (2009) Applying the varieties of capitalism approach to higher education: comparing the internationalisation of German and British universities. Eur J Educ 44(4):569–585

Graf L (2013) The hybridization of vocational training and higher education in Austria, Germany, and Switzerland. Budrich UniPress, Olpaden

Greinert W-D (2000) Organisationsmodelle und Lernkonzepte in der beruflichen Bildung. Nomos Verlagsgesellschaft, Baden-Baden

Greinert W-D (2004) European vocational training 'systems' – some thoughts on the theoretical context of their historical development. Vocat Training 2:18–25

Grollmann P, Spöttl G, Rauner F (eds) (2006) Europäisierung Beruflicher Bildung – eine Gestaltungsaufgabe. LIT Verlag, Hamburg

Gutschow K, Seidel S (2010) Kann der Deutsche Qualifikationsrahmen zur Anerkennung nicht formalen und informellen Lernens beitragen? BWP 5:45–48

Hall P (1993) Policy paradigms, social learning, and the state: the case of economic policymaking in Britain. Comp Politics 23:275–29

Hall P (2008) Systematic process analysis: when and how to use it. Eur Polit Sci 7(3):304–317

Hall P, Soskice D (2001) Introduction. In: Hall P, Soskice D (eds) Varieties of capitalism: the institutional foundations of comparative advantage. Oxford University Press, Oxford, pp 1–68

Hall P, Soskice D (2003) Varieties of capitalism and institutional change: a response to three critics. Comp Eur Politics 1(2):241–250

Hall P, Thelen K (2005) Institutional change in varieties of capitalism. International Sociological Association, Research Committee, 19 Annual Conference, Chicago, IL

Hall P, Thelen K (2009) Institutional change in varieties of capitalism. Socio-Econ Rev 7(1):7–34

Hancké B, Rhodes M (2005) EMU and labor market institutions in Europe. The rise and fall of national social pacts. Work Occup 32(2):196–228

Hancké B, Rhodes M, Thatcher M (eds) (2007) Introduction: Beyond varieties of capitalism. Oxford University Press, Oxford

Hanf G (2012) Connecting lines between the DQR and the Recognition Act. http://www.bibb.de/en/62718.htm. Retrieved 12 Dec 2012

Hanf G, Rein V (2006a) Towards a national qualifications framework for Germany. Reflections from a VET research standpoint. http://www.bibb.de/en/25722.htm. Retrieved 14 July 2011

Hanf G, Rein V (2006b) Nationaler Qualifikationsrahmen – eine Quadratur des Kreises? Herausforderungen und Fragestellungen im Spannungsfeld von Politik, Berufsbildung und Wissenschaft. Bwp@ Berufs- und Wirtschaftspädagogik – online, Ausgabe 11

Hanf G, Rein V (2007) Europäischer und Deutscher Qualifikationsrahmen – eine Herausforderung für Berufsbildung und Bildungspolitik. BWP 3:7–12

Hantrais L (2007) Social policy in the European Union. Palgrave Macmillan, Houndmills, Basingstoke

Hartung S, Leber U (2004) Betriebliche Ausbildung und wirtschaftliche Lage – Empirische Ergebnisse es IAB-Betriebspanels. In: Krekel E, Walden G (eds) Zukunft der Berufsausbildung in Deutschland: Empirische Untersuchungen und Schlussfolgerungen. Ergebnisse der BIBB-Fachtagung am 4./5. November 2003 in Bonn. Bundesinstitut für Berufsbildung, Bonn, pp 111–129

Hassel A (2007) What does business want? Labour market reforms in CMEs and its problems. In: Hancké B, Rhodes M, Thatcher M (eds) Beyond varieties of capitalism. Conflict, contradictions, and complementarities in the European economy. Oxford University Press, Oxford, pp 253–277

Haverland M (2006) Does the EU *cause* domestic developments? Improving case selection in Europeanisation research. West Eur Politics 29(1):124–146

Haverland M (2007) Methodology. In: Graziano P, Vink M (eds) Europeanization. New research agendas. Palgrave Macmillan, Houndsmills, Basingstoke, pp 59–70

Hay C (2005) Two can play at that game...or can they? Varieties of capitalism, varieties of institutionalism. In: Coates D (ed) Varieties of capitalism, varieties of approaches. Palgrave Macmillan, London, pp 106–121

Heinze T (2013) A tale of many stories. Explaining policy diffusion between European higher education systems. Free University of Berlin. http://www.diss.fu-berlin.de/diss/receive/FUDISS_thesis_000000094761. Retrieved 4 June 2014

Held D, McGrew A, Goldblatt D, Perraton J (1999) Global transformations: politics, economics and culture. Stanford University Press, Standford, CA

Her Majesty's Treasury (2006) The Leitch review of skills: Prosperity for all in the global economy-world class skills. HMSO, Norwich

Herdegen M (2009) Der Europäische Qualifikationsrahmen für lebenslanges Lernen – Rechtswirkungen der Empfehlung und Umsetzung im deutschen Recht. Rechtsgutachten im Auftrag des Bundesministeriums für Bildung und Forschung

Héritier A (1996) The accommodation of diversity in European policy-making and its outcomes: regulatory policy as a patchwork. J Eur Publ Policy 3(2):149–176

Hillmert S (2002) Stabilität und Wandel des „deutschen Modells": Lebensverläufe im Übergang zwischen Schule und Beruf. In: Wingers M, Sackmann R (eds) Bildung und Beruf. Ausbildung und berufsstruktureller Wandel in der Wissensgeselltschaft. Juventa Verlag, Weinheit, pp 65–82

Hillmert S (2008) When traditions change and virtues become obstacles. In: Mayer K, Solga H (eds) Skill formation. Interdisciplinary and cross-national perspectives. Cambridge University Press, New York, NY, pp 50–81

Hinz T (1999) Vocational training and job mobility in comparative perspective. In: Finegold D, Culpepper P (eds) The German skills machine: sustaining comparative advantage in a global economy. Berghahn Books, New York, NY, pp 159–188

Holm U (2004) Gesellschaftliche Partizipation und Kompetenzerwerb: Erwachsenenbildung im Großbritannien des 20. Jahrhunderts. In: Lechner E, Pöggeler F (eds) Allgemeinbildung und Berufsbildung. Konkurrenz und Kongruenz der Konzepte im Europa des 20. Jahrhunderts. Peter Lang, Frankfurt am Main

Höpner M, Schäfer A (2008a) Grundzüge einer politökonomischen Perspektive auf die europäische Integration. In: Höpner M, Schäfer A (eds) Die Politische Ökonomie der europäischen Integration. Campus, Frankfurt, pp 11–45

Höpner M, Schäfer A (2008b) Eine neue Phase der europäischen Integration: Legitimitätsdefizite europäischer Liberalisierungspolitik. In: Höpner M, Schäfer A (eds) Die Politische Ökonomie der Europäischen Integration. Campus, Frankfurt, pp 129–156

Hoppe M (2005) Merkmale und Besonderheiten vollzeitschulischer Berufsausbildung in den Niederlanden, Österreich und Dänemark. BWP 4:51–54

Houwing H, Vandaele K (2011) Liberal convergence, growing outcome divergence? Institutional continuity and changing trajectories in the 'low countries'. In: Becker U (ed) The changing political economies of small west European countries. Amsterdam University Press, Amsterdam, pp 125–148

Hövels B, Roelofs M (2007) Vollzeitschulische Berufsausbildung in ausgewählten Europäischen Ländern mit dualen Berufsbildungsangeboten. Die Niederlande. Endbericht. Kenniscentrum Beroepsonderwijs Arbeidsmarkt, Nijmegen

Howell C (2003) Review: Varieties of capitalism: and then there was one? Comp Politics 36 (1):103–124
IG Metall (2007) Frankfurter Erklärung: Lernen und Arbeiten in europäischen Kernberufen. IG Metall-Vorstand, Frankfurt am Main
IKEI (2012) Apprenticeship supply in the Member States of the European Union. Final report. Publications Office of the European Union, Luxembourg
Innovationskreis berufliche Bildung (2007) 10 Leitlinien zur Modernisierung und Strukturverbesserung der beruflichen Bildung: Empfehlungen und Umsetzungsvorschläge. BMBF, Berlin, 16 July 2007
Jakobi A (2009) International organizations and lifelong learning. Palgrave Macmillan, Houndmills, Basingstoke
Jakobi A, Martens K, Wolf K (eds) (2010) Education in political science. Routledge, Milton Park
Katzenstein P (1978) Conclusion: Domestic structures and strategies of foreign economic policy. In: Katzenstein P (ed) Between power and plenty. Foreign economic policies of advanced industrial states. The University of Wisconsin Press, Madison, WI, pp 295–336
Keep E (2007) The multiple paradoxes of state power in the English education and training system. In: Clarke L, Winch C (eds) Vocational education. International approaches, developments and systems. Routledge, London, pp 161–175
Keune M (2008) Die Grenzen der europäischen Arbeitsmarktintegration: Koalitionen, Interessensvielfalt und institutionelle Hindernisse. In: Höpner M, Schäfer A (eds) Die Politische Ökonomie der Europäischen Integration. Campus, Frankfurt, pp 279–309
King L (2007) Central European capitalism in comparative perspective. In: Hancké B, Rhodes M, Thatcher M (eds) Beyond varieties of capitalism. Oxford University Press, Oxford, pp 309–327
King G, Keohane R, Verba S (1994) Designing social inquiry: scientific inference in qualitative research. Princeton University Press, Princeton, NJ
Kleibrink A (2011) The EU as a norm entrepreneur: the case of lifelong learning. Eur J Educ 46 (1):70–84
KMK (Secretariat of the Standing Conference of the Ministers of Education and Cultural Affairs of the Länder in the Federal Republic of Germany) (2009) Hochschulzugang für beruflich qualifizierte Bewerber ohne schulische Hochschulzugangsberechtigung. Beschluss der Kultusministerkonferenz vom 06.03.2009
KMK (Secretariat of the Standing Conference of the Ministers of Education and Cultural Affairs of the Länder in the Federal Republic of Germany) (2011) Ergebnisse der 335. Plenarsitzung der Kultusministerkonferenz am 20./21. Oktober 2011 in Berlin. KMK. http://www.kmk.org/no_cache/presse-und-aktuelles/meldung/ergebnisse-der-335-plenarsitzung-der-kultusministerkonferenz-am-2021-oktober-2011-in-berlin.html?cHash=d9078f5f2de31abaf00f5524f4c8d56a&sword_list[0]=europ%C3%A4ischer&sword_list[1]=qualifikationsrahmen. Retrieved 20 Oct 2012
Knill C (2001) The Europeanisation of national administrations: patterns of institutional change and persistence. Cambridge University Press, Cambridge
Knodt M, Corcaci A (2012) Europäische Integration. Anleitung zur theoriegeleiteten Analyse. UVK, Konstanz
Kohlrausch B (2009) A ticket to work? Policies for the young unemployed in Britain and Germany. Campus Verlag, Frankfurt
Kremer M (2007) Die europäische Berufsbildungspolitik aus Sicht des Bundesinstituts für Berufsbildung. In: Kaune P, Rützel J, Spöttl G (eds) Berufliche Bildung – Innovation – Soziale Integration. Bertelsmann Verlag, Bielefeld, pp 32–42
Kuda E, Strauß J (2006) Der Europäische Qualifikationsrahmen – Chancen oder Risiken für Arbeitnehmer und ihre berufliche Bildung in Deutschland? WSI Mitteilungen 11:630–637
Kühne A (2012) Das deutsche Abitur fällt aus dem Rahmen. http://www.tagesspiegel.de/wissen/bildung-und-beruf-das-deutsche-abitur-faellt-aus-dem-rahmen/6133840.html. Retrieved 19 Oct 2012

Küßner K (2009) Europäischer Bezugsrahmen für Qualitätssicherung in der beruflichen Aus- und Weiterbildung – Umsetzung in Deutschland. BWP 5:5–8
Küßner K (2012) Kriterien für die Implementierung von ECVET. Dritte Fachtagung „Der Deutsche Qualifikationsrahmen für lebenslanges Lernen", Berlin, 11 Sept 2012
KWB (Kuratorium der deutschen Wirtschaft für Berufsbildung) (2005) Vocational training for Europe. European Qualifications Framework (EQF) and European Credit Transfer System for Vocational Education and Training (ECVET). KWB, Bonn
KWB (Kuratorium der Deutschen Wirtschaft für Berufsbildung) (2007) Position of leading German business organisations on Commission staff working document European Credit system for Vocational Education and Training (ECVET). KWB, Bonn, March 2007
KWB (Kuratorium der Deutschen Wirtschaft für Berufsbildung) (2008a) Deutscher Qualifikationsrahmen (DQR). KWB, Bonn, 28 Mar 2008
KWB (Kuratorium der Deutschen Wirtschaft für Berufsbildung) (2008b) Creation of a European Quality Assurance Reference Framework for vocational education and training (EQARF). Position on the European Commission's proposal for a recommendation of the European Parliament and of the Council. KWB, Bonn
KWB (Kuratorium der Deutschen Wirtschaft für Berufsbildung) (2010) Creation of a European Quality Assurance Reference Framework for vocational education and training (EQARF). Position on the European Commission's proposal for a recommendation of the European Parliament and of the Council. KWB, Bonn
KWB (Kuratorium der Deutschen Wirtschaft für Berufsbildung) (2012) Stellungnahme zum Europäischen Leistungspunktesystem für die Berufsbildung (ECVET). KWB, Bonn, 20 Apr 2012
Lambertz G (2012) Thesen. Dritte Fachtagung „Der Deutsche Qualifikationsrahmen für lebenslanges Lernen", Berlin, 11 Sept 2012
Lanning T (2012) The real story behind the rise in apprenticeships under the coalition. http://careers.guardian.co.uk/careers-blog/rise-in-apprenticeships-under-coalition. Retrieved 26 Mar 2013
Le Deist F, Winterton J (2011) Synthesis report on comparative analysis of the development of apprenticeship in Germany, France, the Netherlands and the UK. ESC, Toulouse
Le Mouillour I, Gelibert D (2007) Wenn ECVT umgesetzt werden soll, ...Zwei europäische Studien entwickeln erste Vorschläge. BWP 4:37–41
Lehmann A (2012) Geselle vs. Abiturient? Wer kann mehr? http://www.taz.de/!83305/. Retrieved 10 Oct 2012
Leibfried S (2005) Social policy. Left to the judges and the markets? In: Wallace H, Wallace W, Pollack M (eds) Policy-making in the European Union. Oxford University Press, Oxford, pp 243–278
Leney T (2010) Vocational education and training (VET) system & qualifications: UK. VET Conference, Barcelona, Nov 2010
Maes M (2004) Vocational education and training in the Netherlands. Office for Official Publications of the European Communities, Luxembourg
Mahoney J (2004) Comparative-historical methodology. Annu Rev Sociol 30:81–101
Martinaitis Ž (2010) The political economy of skills formation: explaining differences in Central and Eastern Europe. http://vddb.laba.lt/fedora/get/LT-eLABa-0001:E.02~2010~D_20101102_153847-42081/DS.005.1.01.ETD
Menz G (2003) Re-regulating the single market: national varieties of capitalism and their responses to Europeanization. J Eur Publ Policy 10(4):532–555
Menz G (2005) Varieties of capitalism and Europeanization. National responses to the single European market. Oxford University Press, Oxford
Milner S (1998) Training policy. Steering between divergent national logics. In: Hine D, Kassim H (eds) Beyond the market. The EU and national social policy. Routledge, London, pp 156–177

MOCW (Ministry of Education Culture and Science) (2007) 2008 Joint Interim Report of the Council and the Commission. Contribution of the Netherlands. Ministry of Education, Culture and Science, The Hague, April 2007; amended version September 2007

MOCW (Ministry of Education Culture and Science) (2009) 2010 Joint Report on the Implementation of the Education and Training 2010 Work Programme. The Netherlands' Report. Ministry of Education, Culture and Science, The Hague, April 2009

MOCW (Ministry of Education Culture and Science) (2012) Key figures 2007–2011. Ministry of Education, Culture and Science, The Hague

Molina Ó, Rhodes M (2007) The political economy of adjustment in mixed market economies: a study of Spain and Italy. In: Hancké B, Rhodes M, Thatcher M (eds) Beyond varieties of capitalism. Oxford University Press, Oxford, pp 223–252

Mucke K (2004) Förderung der Durchlässigkeit zwischen beruflicher und hochschulischer Bildung. BWP 6:11–16

Naurin D, Wallace H (2008) Introduction: From rags to riches. In: Naurin D, Wallace H (eds) Unveiling the Council of the European Union. Games Governments Play in Brussels. Palgrave Macmillan, Houndmills, Basingstoke, pp 1–22

Nehls H (2012) Thesen zur Validierung non-formal und informell erworbener Kompetenzen. Dritte Fachtagung „Der Deutsche Qualifikationsrahmen für lebenslanges Lernen", Berlin, 11 Sept 2012

Nickel S, Duong S (2012) Studieren ohne Abitur: Monitoring der Entwicklungen in Bund, Ländern und Hochschulen. Arbeitspapier Nr. 157. July 2012. Gütersloh, CHE Gemeinnütziges Centrum für Hochschulentwicklung

Nickolaus R (2009) Qualität in der beruflichen Bildung. In: Münk H, Weiß R (eds) Qualität in der beruflichen Bildung. Forschungsergebnisse und Desiderata. W. Bertelsmann, Bielefeld, pp 13–34

NLQF Nationaal Coördinatiepunt (2012) Final report. Conference: Lessons learned and to be learned, Utrecht, 18–19 June 2012

OECD (2008) Jobs for youth. Netherlands. OECD, Paris

Ofqual (2012) Annual Qualifications Market Report 2012. Ofqual/12/5164

Ofqual et al. (2011) Implementation of the European Qualifications Framework in the UK: 2010–2011. http://www2.ofqual.gov.uk/files/2011-implementation-of-eqf-in-uk.pdf?Itemid=185. Retrieved 21 Mar 2013

Olsen J (2002) The many faces of Europeanization. EJCMS 40(5):921–952

Onderwijsraad (1999) A portrayal of School quality. Proposals for the responsible publication of data on the quality of schools. Summary. Onderwijsraad, The Hague

Onderwijsraad (2005) Higher education for half of the Dutch population. http://www.onderwijsraad.nl/upload/english/publications/engelse_ samenvatting_de_helft_van_nederland_hoogopgeleid_copy.pdf. Retrieved 23 Jan 2013

Ostheim T, Zohlnhöfer R (2004) Europäisierung der deutschen Arbeitsmarkt- und Beschäftigungspolitik? Der Einfluss des Luxemburg-Prozesses auf die deutsche Arbeitsmarktpolitik. In: Lütz S, Czada R (eds) Wohlfahrtsstaat – Transformation und Perspektiven. VS Verlag für Sozialwissenschaften/GWV Fachverlage, Wiesbaden, pp 373–401

Pfeifer H, Wenzelmann F (2009) Kosten und Nutzen der betrieblichen Berufsausbildung in Deutschland – Ergebnisse der BIBB-Betriebsbefragung. Die Ausbildungsentscheidung von Betrieben. Ökonomische Forschungsansätze und Analysen, Bonn, 23 and 24 Sept 2009, BIBB

Plug E, Groot W (1998) Apprenticeship versus vocational education: exemplified by the Dutch situation. http://www.economists.nl/files/20050824-p04.pdf. Retrieved 21 Jan 2013

Powell J (2009) Von schulischer Exklusion zur Inklusion? Eine neo-institutionalistische Analyse sonderpädagogischer Fördersysteme in Deutschland und den USA. In: Koch S, Schemmann M (eds) Neo-Institutionalismus in der Erziehungswissenschaft. VS Verlag für Sozialwissenschaften, Wiesbaden, pp 213–232

Powell J, Solga H (2008) Internationalization of vocational and higher education systems – a comparative-institutional approach. Wissenschaftszentrum Berlin für Sozialforschung, Berlin

Powell J, Trampusch C (2011) Europeanization and the varying responses in collective skill systems. In: Busemeyer M, Trampusch C (eds) The comparative political economy of collective skill formation. Oxford University Press, Oxford, pp 284–313

Przeworski A, Teune H (1970) The logic of comparative social inquiry. Krieger, Mallabar

Purz S (2011) Duale Studiengänge als Instrument der Nachwuchssicherung Hochqualifizierter. Peter Lang, Frankfurt am Main

Putnam R (1988) Diplomacy and domestic politics. The logic of two-level games. Int Organ 42(2):427–460

QAA (Quality Assurance Agency for Higher Education), SCQF (Scottish Credit and Qualifications Framework) Partnership, CCEA (Council for the Curriculum, Examinations and Assessment CCEA), Ofqual, Welsh Government, QQI (Quality and Qualifications Ireland) (2011) Qualifications can cross boundaries. A rough guide to comparing qualifications in the UK and Ireland. http://www.qaa.ac.uk/en/publications/documents/qualifications-can-cross-boundaries.pdf. Retrieved 20 Mar 2013

QCDA (Qualifications and Curriculum Development Authority), CCEA (Council for the Curriculum Examinations and Assessment), SCQF (Scottish Credit and Qualifications Framework) Partnership, Welsh Government (2009) Report referencing the qualifications frameworks of the United Kingdom to the European qualifications framework. http://ec.europa.eu/education/lifelong-learning-policy/doc/eqf/ukreport_en.pdf. Retrieved 19 Mar 2013

Radaelli C (2003) The Europeanization of public policy. In: Featherstone K, Radaelli C (eds) The politics of Europeanization. Oxford University Press, Oxford, pp 27–56

Raffe D, Gallacher J, Toman N (2008) Das schottische Rahmensystem für Anrechnungseinheiten und Qualifikationen (SCQF): Ein Beispiel für den Europäischen Qualifikationsrahmen. Europäische Zeitschrift für Berufsbildung 42/43(3/1):68–80

Rauner F (2005) Rettet den Facharbeiter! Die Zeit, 1 Dec 2005

Rauner F (2006) Europäische Berufsbildung – eine Voraussetzung für die im EU-Recht verbriefte Freizügigkeit der Beschäftigten. In: Grollmann P, Spöttl G, Rauner F (eds) Europäisierung Beruflicher Bildung – eine Gestaltungsaufgabe. LIT Verlag, Hamburg, pp 35–52

Rauner F, Grollmann P (2006) Berufliche Kompetenz als Maßgabe für einen europäischen Berufsbildungsraum – Anmerkungen zu einem europäischen Qualifikationsrahmen. In: Grollmann P, Spöttl G, Rauner F (eds) Europäisierung Beruflicher Bildung – eine Gestaltungsaufgabe. LIT Verlag, Hamburg, pp 115–126

Reuling J (2000) Integration von vollzeitschulischer und dualer Berufsausbildung – Niederländische Konzepte und Erfahrungen. In: Zimmer G (ed) Zukunft der Berufsausbildung. Zweite Modernisierung unter Beteiligung der beruflichen Vollzeitschulen. W. Bertelsmann, Bielefeld, pp 131–139

Richard D (2012) The Richard review of apprenticeships. http://www.schoolforstartups.co.uk/richard-review/richard-review-full.pdf. Retrieved 14 Mar 2013

Risse T, Green Cowles M, Caporaso J (2001) Europeanization and domestic change: introduction. In: Green Cowles M, Caporaso J, Risse T (eds) Transforming Europe: Europeanization and domestic change. Cornell University Press, Ithaca, NY, pp 1–20

Roberts K (2004) School-to-work transitions: why the United Kingdom's educational ladders always fail to connect. Int Stud Sociol Educ 14(3):203–214

Schäfer A (2005) Die neue Unverbindlichkeit. Wirtschaftspolitische Koordinierung in Europa. Campus, Frankfurt

Schäfer A (2006) Aufstieg und Grenzen der Offenen Methode der Koordinierung. WSI Mitteilungen 10:540–545

Scharpf F (1999) Governing in Europe: effective and democratic? Oxford University Press, Oxford

Scharpf F (2002) The European social model: coping with the challenges of diversity. JCMS 40(4):645–670

Scharpf F (2006) The joint-decision trap revisited. J Common Market Stud 44(4):845–864
Scharpf F (2008a) Negative und Positive Integration. In: Höpner M, Schäfer A (eds) Die Politische Ökonomie der europäischen Integration. Campus, Frankfurt, pp 49–87
Scharpf F (2008b) Individualrechte gegen nationale Solidarität. In: Höpner M, Schäfer A (eds) Die Politische Ökonomie der europäischen Integration. Campus, Frankfurt, pp 89–99
Schavan A (2010) Der Deutsche Qualifikationsrahmen für lebenslanges Lernen. Rede der Bundesministerin für Bildung und Forschung, Prof. Dr. Annette Schavan, MdB, anlässlich der Eröffnung der 2. Fachtagung zum Deutschen Qualifikationsrahmen, Berlin, 19 Oct 2010
Schmidt V (2002) Europeanization and the mechanics of economic policy adjustment. J Eur Publ Policy 9(6):894–912
Schmidt V (2011) Small countries, big countries under conditions of Europeanisation and globalisation. In: Becker U (ed) The changing political economies of small west European countries. Amsterdam University Press, Amsterdam, pp 149–172
Schneider M, Paunescu M (2012) Changing varieties of capitalism and revealed comparative advantages from 1990 to 2005: a test of the Hall and Soskice claims. Socio-Econ Rev 10(4):731–753
Schönfeld G, Wenzelmann F, Dionisius R, Pfeifer H, Walden G (2010) Kosten und Nutzen der dualen Ausbildung aus Sicht der Betriebe. Ergebnisse der vierten BIBB-Kosten-Nutzen-Erhebung. W. Bertelsmann, Bielefeld
Smits W (2005) The quality of apprenticeship training. Conflicting interests of firms and apprentices. ROA, Maastricht
Soskice D (1993) Social skills from mass higher education: rethinking the company-based initial training paradigm. Oxf Rev Econ Policy 9(3):101–113
Soskice D (1994) Reconciling markets and institutions: the German apprenticeship system. In: Lynch L (ed) Training and the private sector: international comparisons. University of Chicago Press, Chicago, IL, pp 25–60
Steedman H (2001) Benchmarking apprenticeship: UK and Continental Europe compared. Centre for Economic Performance, London School of Economics and Political Science. http://eprints.lse.ac.uk/20098/1/Benchmarking_Apprenticeship_ UK_and_ Continental_Europe_Compared.pdf. Retrieved 11 Mar 2013
Steedman H (2010) The state of apprenticeship in 2010. London School of Economics and Political Science, London
Steedman H (2011) Apprenticeship policy in England: increasing skills versus boosting young people's job prospects. Centre for Economic Performance, London School of Economics and Political Science. http://cep.lse.ac.uk/pubs/download/pa013.pdf. Retrieved 11 Mar 2013
Streeck W (1991) On the institutional conditions of diversified quality production. In: Matzner E, Streeck W (eds) Beyond keynesianism. Edward Elgar, Aldershot, pp 21–61
Streeck W (1997) German capitalism: does it exist? Can it survive? In: Crouch C, Streeck W (eds) Political economy of modern capitalism. Mapping convergence and diversity. SAGE, London, pp 33–54
Streeck W (2009) Re-forming capitalism. Institutional change in the German political economy. Oxford University Press, Oxford
Streeck W (2011) Skills and politics: general and specific. In: Busemeyer MR, Trampusch C (eds) The comparative political economy of collective skill formation. Oxford University Press, Oxford, pp 317–352
Streeck W (2013) Gekaufte Zeit. Die vertagte Krise des demokratischen Kapitalismus. Suhrkamp, Berlin
Streeck W, Thelen K (2005) Introduction: Institutional change in advanced political economies. In: Streeck W, Thelen K (eds) Beyond continuity. Institutional change in advanced political economies. Oxford University Press, Oxford, pp 1–39
StvdA (Stichting van de Arbeid) (2005) Contribution of the Dutch social partners to the 2005–2008 National Reform Programme in the context of the Lisbon strategy. http://www.

stvda.nl/en/publication/~/media/Files/Stvda/Talen/Engels/2005/nota_20050900_engels.ashx. Retrieved 23 Jan 2013

StvdA (Stichting van de Arbeid) (2006) Contribution of the Dutch social partners to the National Reform Programme in the context of the Lisbon strategy. Update 2005/2006. http://www.stvda.nl/en/publication/~/media/Files/Stvda/Talen/Engels/2006/nota_20061000_engels.ashx. Retrieved 23 Jan 2013

StvdA (Stichting van de Arbeid) (2007) Contribution of the Dutch social partners to the National Reform Programme in the context of the Lisbon strategy. Update 2006/2007. http://www.stvda.nl/en/publication/~/media/Files/Stvda/Talen/Engels/2007/en_20071008.ashx. Retrieved 23 Jan 2013

StvdA (Stichting van de Arbeid) (2008) Contribution of the Dutch social partners to the National Reform Programme in the context of the Lisbon strategy. Update 2007/2008. http://www.stvda.nl/en/publication/~/media/Files/Stvda/Talen/Engels/2008/en_20081010.ashx. Retrieved 23 Jan 2013

StvdA (Stichting van de Arbeid) (2011) Contribution of the Dutch social partners to the National Reform Programme within the context of the EU 2020 Strategy. http://www.stvda.nl/en/publication/~/media/Files/Stvda/Talen/Engels/2011/20110400_EN.ashx. Retrieved 23 Jan 2013

StvdA (Stichting van de Arbeid) (2012) Contribution of the Dutch social partners to the National Reform Programme within the context of the EU 2020 Strategy. http://www.stvda.nl/en/publication/~/media/Files/Stvda/Talen/Engels/2012/20120418_EN.ashx. Retrieved 23 Jan 2013

Thelen K (2004) How institutions evolve: the political economy of skills in Germany, Britain, the United States, and Japan. Cambridge University Press, Cambridge

Thelen K (2007) Contemporary challenges to the German vocational training system. Regul Governance 1:247–260

Thelen K, Busemeyer M (2008) From collectivism towards segmentalism: institutional change in German vocational training. Dicussion Paper 08/13. Max Planck Institute for the Study of Societies, Cologne

Trampusch C (2008) Jenseits von Anpassungsdruck und Lernen: die Europäisierung der deutschen Berufsbildung. Zeitschrift für Staats- und Europawissenschaften 6(4):577–605

Trampusch C (2009) Europeanization and institutional change in vocational education and training in Austria and Germany. Governance 22(3):369–395

Trampusch C (2010a) The politics of institutional change. Transformative and self-preserving change in the vocational education and training system in Switzerland. Comp Politics 42 (2):187–206

Trampusch C (2010b) Employers, the state, and the politics of institutional change: vocational education and training in Austria, Germany, and Switzerland. Eur J Polit Res 49(4):545–573

Trampusch C, Eichenberger P, de Roo M, Bartlett Rissi R, Bieri I, Schmid L, Steinlin S (eds) (2010) Continuing vocational training in the Netherlands. REBECA (Research on Social Benefits in Colletive Agreements). Database, Part 2 'Social Benefits in Collective Agreements'. Institute of Political Science, University of Berne

Transeqframe (Trans-European Qualications Framework Development) (2005) Country report WP 3: The Netherlands. http://www.transeqframe.net/Report_and_outcomes/Policy/National%20reports/policy_nr_nl.pdf. Retrieved 4 Feb 2013

Troltsch K, Gerhards C, Mohr S (2012) Vom Regen in die Traufe? Unbesetzte Ausbildungsstellen als künftige Herausforderung des Ausbildungsstellenmarktes. BIBB Report 19/12. BIBB, Bonn

Trubek D, Trubek L (2005) The open method of co-ordination and the debate over ‚Hard' and ‚Soft' law. In: Zeitlin J, Pochet P, Magnusson L (eds) The open method of coordination in action: the European employment and social inclusion strategies. Peter Lang, Brussels, pp 83–103

Tweede Kamer der Staten-Generaal (2011a) Leven Lang Leren. Brief van de Minister van Onderwijs, Cultuur en Wetenschap. Vergaderjaar 2010–2011, 30 012, nr. 34

Tweede Kamer der Staten-Generaal (2011b) Leven Lang Leren. Verslag van een schriftelijk overleg. vergaderjaar 2011–2012, 30 012, nr. 35

Uhly A, Kroll S, Krekel E (2011) Strukturen und Entwicklungen der zweijährigen Ausbildungsberufe des dualen Systems. Ergebnisse aus der Berufsbildungsstatistik der statistischen Ämter des Bundes und der Länder (Erhebung zum 31.12) sowie der BIBB-Erhebung über neu abgeschlossene Ausbildungsverträge zum 30.9. Bonn

Uhly A, Troltsch K (2009) Duale Berufsausbildung in der Dienstleistungs- und Wissensökonomie. Zeitschrift für Berufs- und Wirtschaftspädagogik 105(1):15–32

UK National Coordination Points (2010) Referencing the UK frameworks to the European qualifications framework for lifelong learning. Report of the UK EQF Launch Conference, Edinburgh, 26–27 April 2010. http://www2.ofqual.gov.uk/files/2010-uk-eqf-launch-conference-report.pdf?itemid=185. Retrieved 19 Mar 2013

Unwin L (2006) Creating knowledge and skills: the troubled relationship between company, college and apprentices in UK apprenticeships. In: Eckert M, Zöller A (eds) Der europäische Berufsbildungsraum – Beiträge der Berufsbildungsforschung. W. Bertelsmann, Bielefeld, pp 113–124

Van Bijsterveldt-Vliegenthart M (2007) European credit system for VET. Letter to Ján Figel', Member of the European Commission. The Hague, MOCW

Van Bruggen M (2011) ECVET en het mbo. Hoe zit het nu in Nederland? Colo, Zoetermeer

Van den Boom T (2011) Quality assurance in VET NL. System of quality assurance and improving in VET. PowerPoint Presentation, 26 Sept 2011

Van der Sanden K, Smit W, Dashorst M (2012) The referencing document of the Dutch National Qualifications Framework to the European Qualifications Framework

Van Evera S (1997) Guide to methods for students of political science. Cornell University Press, Ithaca, NY

Van Gent B (2004) The irresistible rise of vocational training and professional education – The Dutch case. In: Lechner E, Pöggeler F (eds) Allgemeinbildung und Berufsbildung. Konkurrenz und Kongruenz der Konzepte im Europa des 20. Jahrhunderts. Peter Lang, Frankfurt am Main, pp 251–263

Van IJsselmuiden P (2009) MBO internationalisation agenda. Ministry of Education, Culture and Science, The Hague

Van Klaveren M, Salverda W, Tijdens K (2009) Retail jobs in the Netherlands: low pay in a context of long-term wage moderation. Int Lab Rev 148(4):413–438

Van Lieshout H (2007) Different hands. Markets for intermediate skills in Germany, the U.S. and the Netherlands. Doctoral thesis. http://igitur-archive.library.uu.nl/dissertations/2008-0402-200621/lieshout.pdf. Retrieved 28 Jan 2013

Visser J (2005) The OMC as selective amplifier for national strategies of reform. What the Netherlands want to learn from Europe. In: Zeitlin J, Pochet P, Magnusson L (eds) The open method of coordination in action: the European employment and social inclusion strategies. Peter Lang, Brussels, pp 173–215

Visser K (2010a) Netherlands. VET in Europe – country report. ecbo, Utrecht/'s-Hertogenbosch, Sept 2010

Visser K (2010b) A bridge to the future: European VET policy 2002 – 2010. National policy report – the Netherlands. ecbo, Utrecht, Summer 2010

Visser K, Westerhuis A, Hövels B (2009) The position of upper secondary vocational education outside the Netherlands. Retrieved 21 Jan 2013, from http://www.ecbo.nl/ECBO/RefNet/docs/09-1020_59799ne%28Bewerkt%20syntheserapport%29.pdf

Vitzthum T (2012) Schavan will es beim Abitur wie Frankreich machen. Die Welt, 24 Jan 2012

Völpel E (2012) Das Abitur bleibt erst einmal außen vor. *TAZ*, 31 Jan 2012

Walden G (2006) Wenn sich der Ausbildungsmarkt verändert.... In: Zöller A (ed) Vollzeitschulische Berufsausbildung – eine gleichwertige Partnerin des dualen Systems? W. Bertelsmann, Bielefeld, pp 36–47

Walden G (2009) Ausbildung und Qualifikationsentwicklung im Dienstleistungsbereich. Perspektiven der Erwerbsarbeit –Facharbeit in Deutschland, Presentation, Gesprächskreis Arbeit und Qualifizierung der Friedrich-Ebert-Stiftung, Berlin, 12 Oct 2009

Walkenhorst H (2005) The changing role of EU education policy a critical assessment. EUSA ninth biennial international conference, Austin, TX

Wallace H (2000) Europeanisation and globalisation. New Polit Econ 5(3):369–382

Werner G, Rothe G (2011a) Reformbedarf für die berufliche Aus- und Weiterbildung in Deutschland. Wirtschaft und Erziehung 1–2:3–8

Werner G, Rothe G (2011b) Reformbedarf für die berufliche Aus- und Weiterbildung in Deutschland – Teil 2. Wirtschaft und Erziehung 3:55–63

Wesselink R, Biemans H, Mulder M, Van den Elsen ER (2007) Kompetenzbasierte Berufsbildung aus der Sicht der niederländischen Wissenschaftler. Europäische Zeitschrift für Berufsbildung 1:41–56

Westerhuis A (2009) EQF-Ref. Wp3: EQF referencing process – exchange of experience. Case study The Netherlands. ecbo, Utrecht, July/Oct 2009

Wolf A (2011) Review of vocational education – the Wolf report. DfA, London

Wood S (2001) Business, government, and patterns of labor market policy in Britain and the Federal Republic of Germany. In: Hall P, Soskice D (eds) Varieties of capitalism. The institutional foundations of comparative advantage. Oxford University Press, Oxford, pp 247–274

Zeitlin J (2005) Conclusion: The open method of coordination in action: theoretical promise, empirical realities, reform strategy. In: Zeitlin J, Pochet P, Magnusson L (eds) The open method of coordination in action: the European employment and social inclusion strategies. Peter Lang, Brussels, pp 447–503

Zeitlin J (2009) The Open Method of Coordination and reform of national social and employment policies. Influences, mechanisms, effects. In: Zeitlin J, Heidenreich M (eds) Changing European employment and welfare regimes. The influence of the open method of coordination on national reforms. Routledge, London

CPSIA information can be obtained
at www.ICGtesting.com
Printed in the USA
LVOW04*1938111016
508325LV00019B/171/P